Emerging Spatial Information Systems and Applications

Brian N. Hilton
Claremont Graduate University, USA

IDEA GROUP PUBLISHING
Hershey • London • Melbourne • Singapore

Acquisition Editor:	Michelle Potter
Senior Managing Editor:	Jennifer Neidig
Managing Editor:	Sara Reed
Development Editor:	Kristin Roth
Copy Editor:	Susanna Svidunovich
Typesetter:	Marko Primorac
Cover Design:	Lisa Tosheff
Printed at:	Integrated Book Technology

Published in the United States of America by
Idea Group Publishing (an imprint of Idea Group Inc.)
701 E. Chocolate Avenue
Hershey PA 17033
Tel: 717-533-8845
Fax: 717-533-8661
E-mail: cust@idea-group.com
Web site: http://www.idea-group.com

and in the United Kingdom by
Idea Group Publishing (an imprint of Idea Group Inc.)
3 Henrietta Street
Covent Garden
London WC2E 8LU
Tel: 44 20 7240 0856
Fax: 44 20 7379 3313
Web site: http://www.eurospan.co.uk

Library of Congress Cataloging-in-Publication Data

Emerging spatial information systems and applications / Brian N. Hilton, editor.
p. cm.
Summary: "This book presents innovative spatial information systems developed for a specific problem or decision-making situation. It also discusses key concepts and theories underlying current spatial information systems and technology trends and emerging concepts that may impact spatial information system development and applications in the future"--Provided by publisher.
Includes bibliographical references and index.
ISBN 1-59904-075-1 (hardcover) -- ISBN 1-59904-076-X (softcover) -- ISBN 1-59904-077-8 (ebook)
1. Geographic information systems. 2. Spatial analysis (Statistics) I. Hilton, Brian N., 1959-
G70.212.E44 2007
910.285--dc22

2006027711

British Cataloguing in Publication Data
A Cataloguing in Publication record for this book is available from the British Library.

All work contributed to this book is new, previously-unpublished material. The views expressed in this book are those of the authors, but not necessarily of the publisher.

Dedication

To my wife, June, whose support,
patience, and love made this book possible.

Emerging Spatial Information Systems and Applications

Table of Contents

Foreword viii

Preface xii

Section I:
Introduction

Chapter I
Geospatial Web Services 1
Peisheng Zhao, George Mason University, USA
Genong Yu, George Mason University, USA
Liping Di, George Mason University, USA

Chapter II
Spatial Information System Development: The Role of Information System Design Theory and Ontologies 36
Brian N. Hilton, Claremont Graduate University, USA
Richard J. Burkhard, San Jose State University, USA
Tarun Abhichandani, Claremont Graduate University, USA

Section II:
Challenges for Spatial Information Systems

Section III:
Decision-Making Environments

Foreword

Spatial information systems were created manually for many years. For example, historically, the source of cholera in London in 1854 was found by John Snow, by mapping where victims of the disease lived. The graph clearly showed them to be close to the Broad Street Pump,[1] one of the city's water wells. Another example is Zipf's Law,[2] which predicted that a number of sociological phenomena. His regression model followed a straight line on log-log paper. For example, Zipf's law describes the rank of metropolitan statistical areas (SMSAs) in the census of cities over 2,500 plotted against their population, or, for that matter, the number of copies of a St. Louis newspaper bought in suburbs out to 150 miles.

What is new in our computer age is that storage capacity, computing speed, and technology all grew to the point where large volumes of geographic and spatial information can be used for understanding business and other phenomena.

Spatial information covers all sorts of data (e.g., demographics, customer locations, real estate locations and values, and asset location). Sears, for example, uses spatial information to find the optimal routing for its 1,000 delivery trucks that cover 70% of the U.S. population. To use the system, they hand-coded millions of customers' addresses, put them in their data base, and then use the results to determine routes each day.

A spatial information system is more complex than a conventional back-office database system. In many respects, it is like a CAD/CAM system where data is kept on each of many layers, and the layers can be superimposed on one another as the user chooses. The spatial information system accesses spatial and attribute information, analyzes it, and produces outputs with mapping and visual displays. It needs to keep data on spatial boundaries and on attributes of the data. It includes tools and models to manipulate the data and boundary information. Furthermore, rather than just adding up columns of numbers, it requires understanding and using numerical algorithms, statistics, and operations research optimization and simulation techniques. In addition, spatial tools act on boundary layers, including union, overlay, buffering, nearest neighbor, and spatial attraction. You need much more expertise and capability to deal with spatial information systems data than with ordinary databases.

Despite the complexity, or perhaps because of its complexity, spatial information systems provide capabilities that offer competitive advantage. Of course, determining the extent of that advantage is a difficult task. Pick[3] points out that the up-front data costs tend to be much higher (more data needs to be acquired) and some costs, such as training needed for users with no experience, are difficult to estimate accurately. Furthermore, many more of the benefits are intangibles compared to conventional systems. For example, spatial information system applications tend to move up the value chain of a firm as they are used for planning or decision support (see Section III of this book). The value of the visualization aspects of spatial information systems is hard to quantify because we know little about how visual models improve decision-making.

An important recent example of a spatial information system is the global positioning systems (GPS) in your car. I have one, and it changes the way that I find my destination. Other new technologies associated with current spatial information systems include RFID, mobile wireless, and server software that deliver spatial information systems over the Internet. Enterprise applications, such as ORACLE, now provided GIS add-ons.

The book presents a sampling of what is going on in spatial information systems from a conceptual and application viewpoint. The book is divided into four sections:

I. Introduction

II. Challenges for Spatial Information Systems

III. Decision-Making Environments

IV. Future Trends and Technologies

Each of the sixteen chapters focus on a different application. Several themes do recur. One is the use of Web services for geospatial applications. In the past, all portions of a spatial information system resided in a single location. To undertake a new project often required adding software at that location. The new idea, which is gaining wide currency, is that the needed calculations can be subdivided into pieces,[4] each of which can be done by specialized programs, and that those programs may reside at a number of locations. Thus, data is sent to a vendor who provides the needed portion of the program, runs the calculation, and returns the computed values as inputs to the next subroutine or module.

The book brings together work by a large number of researchers looking at applying methods and techniques, including some that were developed for other purposes. You will find discussions of ontologies, directories, semantic Webs, agent theory, and robotics among others. In supporting decision-making, there are chapters on snow removal operations, determining suitable habitats for endangered species, and planning confined animal feeding operations. There are other intriguing applications such as:

- Using spatial information systems in teaching children content at the K-12 level by using a browser, without needing to teach them about the underlying system
- Identifying community-based resources, to provide a database of existing services, design the needed communications, identify missing resources, and other societal implications
- Visualizing the distribution of rare plants and other endangered species by using sensor networks that bring together DBMS, spatial information systems, and Web development technology

In short, the book leads you to start thinking about using spatial information systems in ways that almost none of us even conceived of only a few years ago. That is progress.

Paul Gray
Professor Emeritus and Founding Chair
School of Information Systems and Technology
Claremont Graduate University
Claremont, CA 91711 USA

Endnotes

1. Tufte, E. (1983). *The visual display of quantitative information* (Chap. 2). Cheshire, CT: Graphics Press.
2. Goode, H. H., & Machol, R. E. (1957). *Systems engineering.* New York: McGraw-Hill.
3. Pick, J. B. (Ed.). (2005). *Geographic information systems in business* (p. 384). Hershey, PA: Idea Group Publishing.
4. Sub-routines or modules in the old language of computing.

Paul Gray is professor emeritus and founding chair of the School of Information Systems and Technology at Claremont Graduate University, USA. Before coming to Claremont in 1983, he was a professor at Stanford University, Georgia Tech, USC, and Southern Methodist. Prior to that, he worked for 18 years in research and development organizations, including 9 years at SRI International. He is the author of three "first papers": in crime in transportation, in telecommuting, and in group decision support systems. He is the author of over 130 journal articles and 13 books, including *Manager's Guide to Making Decisions in Information Systems* (Wiley, 2006). His honors include the LEO award for lifetime achievement from AIS, a Fellow of both AIS and INFORMS, a winner of the NATO Systems Science Prize, and Outstanding Information Systems Educator of 2000. He was president of TIMS in 1992-1993. He is the founding editor of *Communications of AIS*, serving from 1999 to 2005.

Preface

When a thing is new, people say: 'It is not true.' Later, when its truth becomes obvious, they say: 'It is not important.' Finally, when its importance cannot be denied, they say: 'Anyway, it is not new.

~ William James, 1896

Several emerging phenomena and technologies, such as the increasing availability of mature open source software and the continuing evolution of distributed computing, are introducing a new dynamic into information system development. Specifically, these phenomena and technologies are enabling the development of a variety of innovative spatial information systems. This book contains several chapters that present innovative spatial information systems that have been developed for a specific problem or decision-making situation. Also included are several chapters that discuss key concepts and theories underlying current spatial information systems as well as technology trends and emerging concepts that may impact spatial information system development and applications in the future. Chapters are typically presented as case studies, are grounded in information science research, and have a specific practical application.

Spatial Informatics and Emerging Technologies

Spatial informatics can be described as the sciences concerned with the collection, manipulation, classification, analysis, storage, and retrieval of recorded spatial data, information, and knowledge. These sciences are utilized in the development, management, and use of spatial information systems. Of particular interest to researchers and practitioners alike, is the impact that emerging technologies may have on these systems. Open source software and distributed computing (a brief overview of each is presented below) are two of the many emerging phenomena and technologies that are impacting the development of spatial information systems.

Open Source Software

Free and open source software is software that gives users the right to run, copy, distribute, study, change, and improve it as they see fit, without the need to receive permission from or make additional payments to any external group or person (Bollinger, 2003). Perhaps two of the most well-known examples of open source software are the operating system Linux and the Apache Web server. Linux is the second most commonly-used operating system (Windows is number one) (Netcraft, 2001; The Economist, 2001) while Apache is the principal Web server in use today (72% vs. Windows 22%) (Security Space, 2006).

Mature open source software solutions have expanded the number of acquisition choices available to the organization beyond traditional closed source (commercial or proprietary) software solutions. As a result, there now exists the possibility of mixing open source and closed source solutions to best meet the information system needs of the organization. There are four strategies (Bollinger, 2003) for mixing open source and closed source software:

1. **Distribution mixing:** Open source and closed source software can be stored and transmitted together.
2. **Execution mixing:** Open source and closed source software can run at the same time on the same computer or network.
3. **Application mixing:** Open source can rely on closed source software to provide it with services and visa versa.
4. **Service mixing:** Open source can provide generic services to closed source software and visa versa.

Table 1. Comparison of open, mixed, and closed source software

	Open Source Software	Mixed Source Software	Closed Source Software
Operating System	Linux	Windows	Windows
Web Server	Apache	IIS	IIS
Database	MySQL	MySQL	MSSQL
Scripting Language	PHP	PHP	ASP

Table 1 illustrates the concept of open source/closed source software mixing in relation to the typical Internet-based information system.

As illustrated in Table 1, this specific collection of open source software represents the technologies that represent the open source Internet platform: LAMP = Linux + Apache + MySQL + (PHP | Perl | Python). The mixed source solution consists of an operating system and Web server supplied by Microsoft, Inc.; the database and scripting language are open source. The closed source solution is completely proprietary and is based on additional products from Microsoft – MS SQL database server and the Active Server Page scripting language. This is one example that illustrates the impact of open source software on information system development; in the chapters that follow, several more are presented.

Distributed Computing

A distributed computing system consists of multiple software components on multiple computers running as a single system (International Business Machines Corporation, 2004). Furthermore, the computers in a distributed system can be physically close together and connected by a local network, or they can be geographically distant and connected by a wide area network. A distributed system can comprise any number of possible configurations: mainframes, personal computers, workstations, minicomputers, and so forth. The goal of distributed computing is to construct a system such that it appears and acts as a single computer. Numerous emerging technologies are supporting the development of distributed computing and applications. These include:

- **Web services** have emerged as a popular standards-based framework for accessing network applications. Web services consist of a set of messaging protocols, programming standards, and network registration and discovery facilities that expose business functions to authorized parties over the Internet from any Web-connected device (Oracle Corporation, 2001). Basically, Web services allow specific application logic to be exposed and used between independent applications with a minimum knowledge of the Web service and/or underlying application. The advent of Web services promises to let organizations connect their applications to any number of other organizations relatively inexpensively and easily (Hagel, 2002).

- **Grid computing** has emerged as an important new field, distinguished from conventional distributed computing by its focus on large-scale resource sharing, innovative applications, and, in some cases, high-performance orientation (Foster, Kesselman et al., 2001). Grid computing seeks to address many of the problems associated with the continuing evolution of distributed computing, in particular, controlled and coordinated resource sharing and use for problem-solving in dynamic, scalable, multi-institutional virtual organizations (a set of individuals and/or institutions linked through resource sharing rules). In this instance, resource sharing is not primarily file exchange, but direct access to computers, software, data, and other resources, that is, those resources required by the range of collaborative, problem-solving, and resource brokering strategies that are emerging in industry, science, and engineering. Resource sharing in this situation is highly controlled and coordinated, with resource providers and consumers clearly defining the rules regarding what is shared, who is allowed to share it, and the conditions under which sharing occurs.
- **The portable Internet** is a platform for high-speed data access using Internet protocol (IP) and includes advanced short-range wireless technologies (within 30 meters) such as Bluetooth, medium-range wireless technologies (at least 150 meters) such as WiFi, and long-range wireless technologies (up to 50 kilometers) such as WiMAX as well as several advanced techniques that make more efficient use of the available spectrum, including spread spectrum, smart antennae, agile radios, and mesh networks. A wireless IP platform can be used to carry not only high-speed services, such as video entertainment and data transfer, but also medium-speed services, such as Web-browsing, and low-speed services such as voice or e-mail. As such, it is potentially substitutable over a wide-range of existing networks and services, and could impact a large number of current business models (International Telecommunications Union, 2004).

The emerging spatial information systems and applications that appear in the following chapters, encompass, in some manner, aspects of the open source software and distributed computing technologies described above.

Book Organization

Section I: Introduction

This section presents information regarding key concepts and theories underlying current spatial information systems. For instance, **Chapter I**, by Zhao, Yu, and Di, introduces all aspects of geospatial Web services from service-oriented architecture to service implementation. It covers the life cycle of geospatial Web services in terms of geospatial interoperable standards, including publish, discovery, invocation, and orchestration. Semantic issues regarding geospatial data and services are discussed, and the applications of standard-compliant geospatial Web services are reviewed.

Chapter II, by Hilton, Burkhard, and Abhichandani, presents an approach to an ontology-based information system design theory for spatial information system development. This approach addresses the dynamic nature of information system development at the beginning of the 21st century and addresses the question of how to establish relationships between the various design components of a spatial information system. An example of this approach is presented, along with examples of the various ontologies utilized in the design of this particular spatial information system.

Section II: Challenges for Spatial Information Systems

This section presents those innovative spatial information systems that have been developed for a specific problem. As seen in **Chapter III**, Judith Woodhall discusses how the need for geospatially-enabled data messaging among emergency response agencies can be enabled with the emergency provider access directory (EPAD). She describes the directory, how it enables message routing, and its fit into a boarder E-Safety network. She also discusses the architectural components of the EPAD, specifically the geographic information system module, and how Web services and open source products were used in the design to enhance the EPAD service offering.

Chapter IV, by Gunjan Kalra, discusses the process of providing information in its most accurate, complete form to its users, and the difficulties faced by the users of the current information systems. She describes the impact of prevalent technologies such as the multi-agent systems and the Semantic Web in the area of information supply via an example implementation and a model use case. She also offers a potentially more efficient and robust approach to information integration and supply process.

Ku and Zimmermann, in **Chapter V**, present an information architecture using Web services for exchanging and utilizing geotechnical information, which is of critical interest to a large number of municipal, state, and federal agencies as well as private enterprises involved with civil infrastructures. They propose an infrastructure of Web services, which handles geotechnical data via an XML format, report on its design, and share some initial experiences.

Chapter VI, by June K. Hilton and David E. Drew, discusses ScienceMaps, an online resource portal for standards-based science instruction using GIS technology. ScienceMaps is unique in that it concentrates on using GIS to teach, not on teaching GIS. Using an Internet-based GIS, ScienceMaps provides access to GIS technology and data to anyone, anywhere, with access to an Internet browser.

Section III: Decision-Making Environments

This section examines those spatial information systems that have been developed for a specific decision-making situation or environment. Gao and Sundaram, in **Chapter VII**, draw from several relevant disciplines to overcome the problems identified in various areas of spatial decision support and propose a generic spatial decision-making process and a domain-independent spatial decision support system (SDSS) framework and architecture to support this process. They develop a flexible SDSS to demonstrate an environment in which decision-makers can utilize various tools and explore different scenarios to derive a decision.

As seen in **Chapter VIII**, Sugumaran, Ilavajhala, and Sugumaran discuss the development of an intelligent Web-based spatial decision support system and demonstrate it with a case study for planning snow removal operations. They illustrate how traditional decision support system (DSS) and Web-based spatial DSS can be further improved by integrating expert knowledge and utilizing intelligent software components (such as expert systems and intelligent agents) to emulate the human intelligence and decision-making.

In **Chapter IX**, Todd G. Olson and Brian N. Hilton discuss Conservation Studio, a spatial information system that automates the entire process of conservation modeling, simulation, and planning. Conservation Studio consists of four software modules: Data Acquisition Interface, Habitat Suitability Analyst, Conservation Criteria Developer, and Implementation Modeler, the latter of which models the outcome of using tradable conservation credits to conserve habitat resources in a specified geographical plan area.

Chapter X, by Sugumaran and Bakker, discusses the need for the development of a decision support system to assist in the selection of an appropriate location for the development of future confined animal feeding operations (CAFO) structures. Furthermore, it presents the development of a decision support tool to aid CAFO managers and producers in selecting appropriate locations for animal confinements using geographic information system technology and CAFO regulations in Iowa.

Section IV: Future Trends and Technologies

This section highlights technology trends and emerging concepts and considers how they may impact spatial information system development and/or applications in the future. In **Chapter XI**, Lars Brodersen and Anders Nielsen, present the relationships and impacts between the various components of the spatial data infrastructure (SDI) and geo-communication. They also discuss a model for the organization of the passive components of the infrastructure, that is, legislation, collaboration, standards, models, specifications, Web services, and information.

Fengxian Fan, in **Chapter XII**, explores an implementation to process and interpret the data gathered by wireless sensor networks deployed to monitor rare plants and other endangered species. The system she presents in this chapter combines database management technology, geographic information system, and Web development technology to visualize the data gathered by these wireless sensor networks.

Chapter XIII, by Ibach, Malek, and Tamm, reviews the enabling technologies that drive system development and also discusses market factors, security and privacy concerns, and standardization processes that need to be taken into account concerning the "global real-time enterprise". The SEMALON (SEMAntic LOcation Network) approach is proposed as a basic infrastructure for discovery and composition of location-based services. A case study implementation for NOMADS Campus, a distributed spatial information system on the campus at Humboldt University Berlin, is presented.

Tolone, Xiang, Raja, Wilson, Tang, McWilliams, and McNally, in **Chapter IV**, propose a knowledge-driven methodology that facilitates the extraction of critical infrastructure (CI) information from public domain, that is, open source, municipal data sets. The proposed methodology was tested successfully on a municipality in the Southeastern United States and is considered to be a viable choice for CIP professionals in their efforts to gather CI information for scenario composition and vulnerability assessment.

In **Chapter XV**, Lyn Kathlene describes and analyzes the effectiveness of two methodological techniques, cognitive mapping and geographical information systems (GIS), for identifying social service resources. She also examines the processes used to integrate hand-drawn map information into geo-coded data points and provides recommendations for improving efficiency and precision.

In the final chapter, **Chapter XVI**, by Bruemmer, Few, and Nielsen, research to study and improve an operator's ability to navigate or tele-operate a robot that is distant from the operator through the use of a robot intelligence architecture and a virtual 3D interface is presented. Their results suggest that performance is improved when the robot assumes some of the navigational responsibilities or the interface presents spatial information as it relates to the pose of the robot in the remote environment.

References

Bollinger, T. (2003). *Use of Free and Open Source Software (FOSS) in the U.S. Department of Defense.* The MITRE Corporation.

Foster, I., Kesselman, C., et al. (2001). The anatomy of the grid: Enabling scalable virtual organizations. *International Journal of Supercomputer Applications, 15*(3).

Hagel, J. (2002). *The strategic value of Web services.* New York: McKinsey and Company.

International Business Machines Corporation. (2004). *TXSeries™ for MultiplatformsConcepts and Planning Version 5.1.* Armonk, NY: International Business Machines Corporation.

International Telecommunications Union. (2004). *ITU Internet reports: The portable Internet.* Geneva, Switzerland: International Telecommunications Union.

Netcraft (2001). Netcraft Web Server Survey — June 2001.

Oracle Corporation (2001). *Oracle 9i Application Server: Web Services Technical White Paper.* Redwood Shores, CA: Oracle Corporation.

Security Space. (2006, January 1). Web Server Survey.

The Economist (2001). *Survey of software: Out in the open.* The Economist.

Acknowledgments

I would like to thank the chapter authors for their hard work and fine contributions. I would also like to thank those who participated in the review process, both contributors as well as outside reviewers.

I would also like to acknowledge the faculty and staff in the School of Information Systems and Technology at Claremont Graduate University. I appreciated your support and assistance throughout this endeavor.

Section I

Introduction

Chapter I

Geospatial Web Services

Peisheng Zhao, George Mason University, USA
Genong Yu, George Mason University, USA
Liping Di, George Mason University, USA

Abstract

As Web service technologies mature in recent years, a growing number of geospatial Web services designed to interoperate spatial information over the network have emerged. Geospatial Web services are changing the way in which spatial information systems and applications are designed, developed, and deployed. This chapter introduces all aspects of geospatial Web services from service-oriented architecture to service implementation. It covers the life cycle of geospatial Web services in terms of geospatial interoperable standards, including publish, discovery, invocation, and orchestration. To make geospatial Web services more intelligent, semantic issues about geospatial data and services are discussed here. Furthermore, the applications of standard-compliant geospatial Web services are also reviewed.

Introduction

Web service technology promises standard-based information interoperability. There are many different definitions for Web services (Andersson, Greenspun, & Grumet, 2003; Booth et al., 2004; Hirsch & Just, 2003; Mateos, Zunino, & Campo, 2005; Skonnard, 2002; Vaughan-Nichols, 2002). In essence, a Web service is a modular, self-describing, and self-contained software application which is discoverable and accessible through standard interfaces over the network (Tsalgatidou & Pilioura, 2002).

The core technology associated with Web service is the standardization of data/message exchange between applications or systems during every stage of their life cycle, including transporting, invoking, and discovering (Akinci, 2004; Di, 2004a; Hecht, 2002). XML (eXtensible Markup Language) is used as the primary language to encode data/message in Web services since it hides the details of underlying transport protocols and provides a platform-independent structured information format. Structured information can be exchanged using standard protocols, such as simple object access protocol (SOAP), or XML-RPC (Gudgin, Hadley, Mendelsohn, Moreau, & Nielsen, 2003; Winer, 1999). The public interface (functionality and input/output parameters) of a Web service is described following a machine-processable format, such as Web Service Description Language (WSDL) (Booth & Liu, 2005; Chinnici, Haas, et al., 2005; Chinnici, Moreau, Ryman, & Weerawarana, 2005; Christensen, Curbera, Meredith, & Weerawarana, 2001; Vedamuthu, 2005). A standard registry or catalog is often used to publish and discover these Web services, such as UDDI (Universal Description, Discovery and Integration) (Booth et al., 2004; Clement, Hately, Riegen, & Rogers, 2004). These characters distinguish a Web service from traditional proprietary distributed systems, such as distributed common object model (DCOM) by Microsoft, java remote method invocation API (RMI) by Sun, and common object request broker architecture (CORBA) by Object Management Group (OMG).

The major benefit of Web services is the interoperability enabled by those standards; in other words, Web services are capable of collaborating process control and sharing data and information across applications over different platforms (Di, 2005; Di, Zhao, Yang, Yu, & Yue, 2005; Kralidis, 2005). A Web service hides all the details of implementation under a well-defined interface, and thus other applications or services can invoke such a Web service through the standard interface. Such type of interoperation is not just limited within one organization, but also can be conducted across organizations. From the technical point of view, the advantages of using Web services can be summarized as: (1) enabling the sharing of computational resources (hardware, software, and data/information holdings) across the organization boundary; (2) easy to maintain and wrap legacy system since the modularity of Web service allows the partial updating and change to existing systems; (3) independent from platforms and operating systems since Web services interact with clients or other Web services through standard messages; and (4) independent from programming languages and implementations as long as the claimed interfaces are obeyed (Akinci, 2004; Di, 2004a; Kralidis, 2005; Zhao et al., 2004). Other advantages are: real-time data access, on-demand/customized information delivery, value-added composition, easy integration, and extended collaboration (Kralidis, 2005). These benefits are achieved at the slightest cost of performance compared to proprietary distributed computing approaches. Overall, Web services are more suitable for handling huge-amount, distributed, and diverse geospatial data/information as compared to the conventional approach of geospatial data dissemination.

Traditionally, geospatial information is delivered to end users through media such as magnetic tapes (e.g., 8mm storage tape, computer compatible tape), optical disks (e.g., CD-ROM, DVD), and electronic transfer (e.g., file transfer protocol, hypertext transfer protocol, simple mail transfer protocol). Often a catalog is provided for searching the data in granules or some pre-determined units, and a matched list of geographic information is given for downloading or mailing. The problems with such approaches to deliver geospatial information are numerous (Di & McDonald, 2005; Di, Yang, Deng, Deng, & McDonald, 2002; Kralidis, 2005). Firstly, the geospatial information is delivered in file-based format and is not customizable. Geospatial information may be packaged in a provider-defined size, which potentially lead to overload of network (with larger dataset than user desires) or to under-sized data (with many small datasets to meet user's requirement that leave a lot of work on converting and merging these datasets). Geospatial information may not be updated timely with the most current status as the data change at the provider's site. Delay of obtaining data may not be desirable when the study is very time-sensitive. Secondly, the process to obtain geographic information is labor-intensive. With the traditional approach, a user may spend a lot of time in many steps: (1) identifying data source and its catalog, (2) interactively searching the dataset with multiple attempts to narrow down the desired dataset, (3) downloading the data or waiting for the data media to be delivered, (4) converting and importing the data into the system the user uses, and (5) processing the data and presenting the results. All of these processes cannot be automated or prescribed with batch-processing plans. Thirdly, geospatial information is not interoperable. The information may be stored in vendor's proprietary formats, and a specific processing has to be taken care of before it can be used in user's system. The messages communicated between different vendors' systems always cannot be directly processed by other machines or systems. Finally, it is very difficult to share the value-added geospatial information. A user may be in need of a processing function that the provided software package does not possess and then be pushed to purchase a suite of software to get the specific information. All these issues with the traditional geospatial information dissemination and processing are what Web services promise to solve, by leveraging Web service capabilities: (1) modularity for the sharing of specific function, (2) standard interfaces for the interoperability of applications, (3) on-demand capability for the customized, real-time value-added geospatial information delivery, and (4) self-contained functionality for the loosely-coupled operation on dataset. The marriage of Web service with geospatial information leads to geospatial Web services.

Generally, a geospatial Web service can be viewed as a modular Web application that provides services on geospatial data, information, or knowledge (Di, Zhao, Yang, Yu, & Yue, 2005). It refers to the use of Web services technologies to manage, analyze, and distribute spatial information. Furthermore, a geospatial Web service can be sorted and searched through its geospatial characteristics, such as location, area, neighborhood, and other spatial features. As a Web service, a geospatial Web service involves three actors: user entity (consumer), provider entity (provider), and register entity (broker) (Booth et al., 2004). Basic operations during the life cycle of a geospatial Web service include publication, discovery, binding, invoking, and execution. The interfaces of some geospatial Web services have been standardized. The most important players for such standardization efforts are ISO/TC211 and Open Geospatial Consortium (OGC). Because of the influential specifications from OGC, geospatial Web services have an add-on unique geospatial flavor on the message-communicating other than those popular W3C Web services standards such as WSDL, SOAP and UDDI. Geospatial Web services focus on standard interface directly through HTTP protocol, which is now recognized as more related to representation state transfer (REST) (Booth et al., 2004; Fielding, 2000). Further details about the OGC standards will be discussed in "Standards for Geospatial Web Services." Geospatial Web services are changing the way in which spatial information systems and applications are designed, developed, and deployed. The added characters give a flexible extension of functionality required to enable the interoperable operation of geospatial data and their processing.

In this chapter, following the lead of standards and the ultimate goal of interoperability, we will cover all aspects of geospatial Web services from conceptual level to technology level. In "Standards for Geospatial Web Services," the interoperability standards, especially those from ISO and OGC, will be introduced. In "Geospatial Web Service Implementation," examples will be given to illustrate the life cycle of Geospatial Web services and guide readers how to design, create, deploy, and execute Geospatial Web services. "Geospatial Web Service Discovery" discusses the discovery of geospatial Web service with three approaches — registry, index, and peer-to-peer. Registry, or service catalog, will be the main focus. "Geospatial Web Service Orchestration" presents the composition of Web services or assembling individual services into a more useful process flow. The section "Geospatial Web Service Solutions" introduces some Geospatial Web service solutions that are widespread in use. "Semantic Issues on Geospatial Web Service" touches the most advanced aspects of Geospatial Web services, semantics. Finally, a short summary and future direction are given.

Standards for Geospatial Web Services

Geospatial interoperability is achieved through the use of standards by different standard-setting organizations, including government organizations (e.g., FGDC), international standard bodies (e.g., ISO), and industry associations (e.g., OGC) (Groot & McLaughlin, 2000; Kralidis, 2005). Major bodies for standards of geospatial Web services are ISO/TC211, OGC, FGDC/NSDI (EOP, 2003; Evans & Bambacus, 2005; ISO/TC211, 2005; OGC, 2005a). The general Web service standard stacks can be partitioned into three parts: data (message encoding), interface (transport protocol), and metadata (ontology), which cover all the aspects of interoperations (Alameh, 2001; Nebert, 2005). These are similar in geospatial Web services. At the data level, the standards specify the message encoding and data formatting that are used for communicating between Web services and applications. At the interface level, the standards define common interfaces for both applications/Web services and human users. At the metadata level, a set of consensus data types and descriptions are associated with each Web service or data.

One should notice that OGC geospatial Web services are different from Web services in the e-business world. OGC geospatial Web services have been developed in parallel with the evolution of W3C and OASIS Web services. Standards from W3C and OASIS, such as WSDL, SOAP, and UDDI, are the standards for Web services in the e-business world. The OGC geospatial Web services do not comply with these Web service standards. Recently, OGC started to explore the possibilities in bridging the gaps and implementing OGC Web services using W3C/OASIS Web services (Duschene & Sonnet, 2005a, 2005b; Lieberman, Reich, & Vretanos, 2003; Sonnet, 2004; Sonnet & Savage, 2003). Another move in standardization of geospatial Web services is the exploration of the semantic Web. OGC initiated the geospatial semantic Web interoperability experiment in April, 2005 (Bacharach, 2005).

Web Service Standard Stacks

Web services are an emerging technology for which standards are currently in great need. Many organizations are participating in the standardization of data, interfaces, and metadata, such as World Wide Web Consortium (W3C), Organization for the Advancement of Structured Information Standards (OASIS), and Internet Engineering Task Force (IETF) (Alameh, 2001; IETF, 2005; Kralidis, 2005; Nebert, 2005; OASIS, 2005; W3C, 2005b; Wilkes, 2005). Figure 1 shows the protocols for Web services that are either widely-adopted or in development. The bold-faced protocols formed the *de facto* core standards for Web services. XML is the underlying language used to encode messages, metadata, schema, and interfaces. XSD (XML schema) replaces document type definition (DTD) to define information structure (W3C, 2005a). SOAP is a commonly-used message encoding protocol (Gudgin,

Figure 1. Web service protocol stack (Source: Tsalgatidou & Pilioura, 2002; Wilkes, 2005)

Security: WS-Security, WS-SecurityPolicy, WS-Trust, XKMS, WS-SecureConservation, WS-Federation, SAML, XACML

Process	Orchestration: BPEL4WS, WS-CDL, WSCI Transaction: WS-Transactions, WS-Coordination, WS-CAF Asynchronous service: ASAP
Metadata	Service description: **WSDL***, OWL-S Cataloguing: **UDDI**, WSIL Policy: WS-Policy, WS_PolicyAssertations Other: WS-MetadataExchange
Messaging	Events: WS-Eventing, WS-Notification Sessions: WS-Enumeration, WS-Transfer Routing: WS-Addressing, WS-MessageDelivery Reliability:WS-ReliableMessaging, WS-Reliability Message: **SOAP**, MTOM
Type	Schema: **XSD, DTD**, OWL
Data	Vector: SVG Data: **XML**

Managment: WSDM, WS-Manageability, WS-Provisioning

*Bold face protocols or standards are most popularly adopted in industry.

Hadley, Mendelsohn, Moreau, & Nielsen, 2003). WSDL is used for describing each Web service, including input/output, operations, and underlying transport protocols (Christensen, Curbera, Meredith, & Weerawarana, 2001). UDDI is a protocol for building a directory of Web services (Clement, Hately, Riegen, & Rogers, 2004). Other protocols are mostly in the stage of early adoption, experimentation, or specification proposal (Wilkes, 2005).

Geospatial Web Service Standard Stacks

OGC and ISO/TC211 are the major players in standardizing geospatial Web services. OGC specifications focus on developing implementation standards while ISO/TC 211 is concentrating on developing theoretical/abstract standards. ISO/TC 211 standards specify methods, tools, and services for acquiring, processing, analyzing, accessing, presenting, and transferring spatial information between different users, systems, and locations. OGC specifications support the full integration of "geo-enabled" Web services into mainstream computing to make complex spatial information and services accessible and useful with all kinds of applications. Through the cooperation between ISO TC 211 and OGC, most of approved OGC implementation standards are either already ISO standards or in the process to become the ISO standards (Di, 2003).

Figure 2. Geospatial Web service standard stack (Source: ISO/TC211, 2005; Nebert, 2005; OGC, 2005a)

Process	Query: ISO 19125-1 Integrative: WPS
Metadata	Service description: WSDL, ISO 19119, ISO19109 Data description: ISO19115:2003, ISO TS19139 Cataloguing: CAT, ISO19110:2005
Messaging	Application interfaces: WCS, WFS, WMS, WICS, WCTS, CQL User interface: WMC Message: HTTP PUT/GET
Type	Schema: XSD, DTD, OWL
Data	Vector: GML Data file: SDTS, VPF, DIGEST, HDFEOS Data: XML

Since 1999, OGC has finished phase 1, 2, and 3 of Open Web Services (OWS) initiatives in 2002, 2004, and 2005 that addresses geospatial interoperability requirements and standards to enhance the discovery, retrieval, and use of geospatial information and geoprocessing services. Under these OGC initiatives, a series of geospatial Web services specifications have been published, such as Web coverage service (WCS) (Evans, 2003), Web feature service (WFS) (Vretanos, 2005), Web map service (WMS) (de La Beaujardiere, 2004), Web image classification

Figure 3. Overall architecture of OGC geospatial Web services (Source: Nebert, 2005)

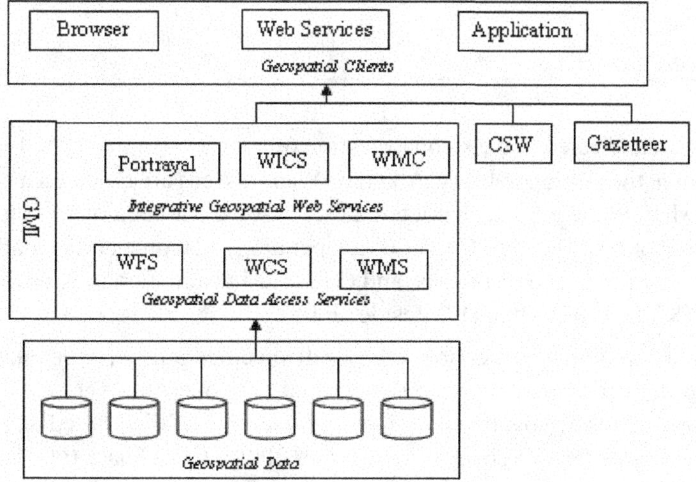

service (WICS) (Yang & Whiteside, 2005), Web coordinate transformation service (WCTS) (Whiteside, Müller, Fellah, & Warmerdam, 2005). Those specifications are the foundation for geospatial interoperability (Di, 2005b). Figure 2 shows most standards and specifications for geospatial Web services.

Similar to the standards for general Web services, these standards and specifications can also be grouped into three groups: data, interface, and metadata. They play different roles in the overall architecture of OGC geospatial Web service. The data standards specify the storage file format of geospatial data. The interface specifications enable the interactions between geospatial Web services. The metadata are used to describe geospatial data and geospatial Web services. Figure 3 shows the overall architecture of OGC geospatial Web services.

Data Standards

The standardization for geospatial data formats sets a good basis for geospatial Web services to communicate with each other in an understandable format. These efforts have resulted in many specifications and standards for data storage and exchange, such as digital line graph (DLG), digital raster graph (DRG), spatial data transfer standard (SDTS), and hierarchical data format for Earth observation system (HDFEOS) (Alameh, 2001; GSFC, 2005). In compliance with ISO 19118 for the transport and storage of geospatial information, the OGC Geography Markup Language (GML) provides an open, portable, and vendor-neural framework to define geographic features and datasets (Cox, Daisey, Lake, Portele, & Whiteside, 2004). GML uses XML text to encode geometry and properties of geographic feature, spatial reference system, and feature collections. The GML also absorbs great graphic quality of scalable vector graphics (SVG). These data formats are commonly used for the delivery of geospatial data with geospatial Web services.

Interface Standards

OGC has been dedicated to the standardization of interfaces of geospatial Web services to enable the interoperability. All OGC Web services are based on a common model and share some unified characteristics: (1) some common operation request and response contents (e.g., *getCapabilities* operation), (2) some unified parameters for operation requests and responses, and (3) exclusive adoption of XML and key-value-pair (KVP) in encoding (Whiteside, 2005).

Under such a common specification, a series of specifications were developed and adopted for delivering and analyzing geospatial data over the Web. CAT defines a catalog service for discovery, browsing, and querying of distributed and heterogeneous catalog servers (Nebert & Whiteside, 2004). Coordinate transformation service (CT) specifies interfaces for positioning, coordinate systems, and their transformation (Daly, 2001). WCS defines common interfaces for grid analysis and processing (Burry, 2001; Di, 2005b). WFS uses GML to encode geographic features and defines common interfaces to handle geographic vector information (Vretanos, 2005). WMS enables the display of registered and superimposed map-like views of geographic information in some image formats (e.g., JPEG) (de La Beaujardiere, 2004). Web map context (WMC) supports the creation and manipulation of a context map that consists of several WMS maps (Sonnet, 2005). Location service (OpenLS) describes an open platform for location-based application servers and outlines related activities (Mabrouk, 2005).

Metadata Standards

To enable human interpretation and machine processing of geospatial data and geospatial Web services, another important standardization endeavor is the definition of a common metadata (description about data or services). For geographic information, ISO19115 provides abstract guidelines for geographic information metadata and ISO19119 for geospatial services metadata (ISO/TC211, 2002b, 2003a). ISO 19139 defines the XML schema for ISO19115 (ISO/TC211, 2003b).

ISO 19115 defines metadata for geospatial data product in fourteen parts: (1) metadata entity set (*MD_Metadata*) is the mandatory part that includes identification, constraints, data quality, maintenance, spatial representation, reference system, content, portrayal catalog, distribution, metadata extension, and application schema; (2) identification (*MD_Identification*) uniquely identifies the data by defining format, graphic overview, specific uses, constraints, keywords, maintenance and aggregate information; (3) constraint (*MD_Constraints*) defines the restrictions placed on the data; (4) data quality (*DQ_DataQuality*) contains quality of the dataset and information about the sources and production processes; (5) maintenance (*MD_MaintenanceInformation*) describes the scope and frequency of updating; (6) spatial representation (*MD_SpatialRepresentation*) points out the mechanism to represent spatial information; (7) reference system (*MD_ReferenceSystem*) describes spatial and temporal reference system; (8) content (*MD_ContentInformation*) identifies the feature catalog; (9) portrayal catalog (*MD_PortrayalCatalogReference*) gives the type for displaying data; (10) distribution (*MD_Distribution*) describes the distributor of the data; (11) metadata extension (*MD_MetadataExtentionInformaiton*) is for user-specified extensions; (12) application schema (*MD_ApplicationSchemaInformation*) is for the schema used to build a dataset; (13) extent (*EX_Extent*) describes the spatial and temporal extent; and (14) citation and responsible party (*CI_Citation and CI_ResponsibleParty*) provides citation information.

ISO 19119 presents taxonomy of geospatial services and gives a list of example geospatial services in each service category. Major geographic services are: (1) geographic human interaction, for example, catalog viewer, geographic feature editor, (2) geographic model/information management, for example, feature access, map access, catalog service, (3) geographic workflow/task management, for example, chain definition service, workflow enactment service, (4) geographic processing (spatial, thematic, temporal, and metadata), for example, coordinate conversion service, thematic classification service, temporal reference system transformation service, statistical calculation service, (5) geographic communication, for example, encoding service, transfer service, and (6) geographic system management.

Geospatial Web Service Implementation

There are many tools available for the implementation and deployment of Web services. Theoretically, any programming languages can be used in developing Web services.

Web Service Implementation

Web service, technically and typically, uses WSDL to describe interfaces, encodes communicate messages using SOAP, and publishes itself in a UDDI registry. A typical process to create a Web service from scratch: (1) starts with the WSDL design using Unified Modeling Language (UML) or other visual design tools, (2) decides the message styles (either RPC encoded/literal or document encoded/literal), (3) develops the program, and (4) ends with the publication and testing of the Web services in a SOAP container (Peltz, 2003).

Another approach is to adapt the existing programs and expose some of their functions as Web services (Peltz, 2003). The task to deploy such Web services mainly involves the creation of adapters that make the legacy system compatible with the Web services. For example, a developer may create an HTTP adapter to convert the input and output between SOAP and HTTP messages, or may develop a Java adapter to call the C/C++ component through Java native interface (JNI) if the published Web service container is a Java server page container (e.g., Axis for Java). Other design patterns may be considered to efficiently re-use the Web services and balance the loading of network traffic, such as MVC (model-view-controller), and asynchronous messaging (Peltz, 2003).

Geospatial Web Service Implementation

In the implementation of geospatial Web services, similar approaches can be applied. In a narrower sense, geospatial Web services are limited to those following geospatial standards, such as OGC WFS, WCS, and WICS. In a broader sense, geospatial Web services embrace Web services that handle geospatial data and provide services to processing geospatial data. Examples are the Web services adapted from geographic resource analysis support system (GRASS) at LAITS (GRASS, 2005; LAITS, 2005).

Implement Standard Geospatial Web Services

A typical implementation practice for OGC geospatial Web services may start with the analysis of the geospatial data to be served and determine the proper interfaces to be implemented, especially those optional operations and parameters. Secondly, all the internal functions should be coded and tested modularly. Thirdly, these required interfaces (operations) and their parameters should be exposed by abiding the relevant specifications. Finally, test and debugging should be carried out. A series of quality assurance and performance evaluation should be conducted (Di, 2004b; Kolodziej, 2004; Zhao et al., 2004).

It is essential to implement the specific interfaces for developing OGC Web services. Some of the interfaces are mandatory. Others are optional. For example, the operations of *GetCapabilities*, and *GetMap* in WMS are mandatory, and its GetFeatureInfo operation is optional (de La Beaujardiere, 2004; Kolodziej, 2004). Furthermore, the parameters for each operation are partly required and partly optional. For example, the *GetMap* operation of a WMS require parameters of "VERSION=1.3.0", "REQUEST=GetMap", "LAYER=?", "STYLES=?", "CRS=?", "BBOX=?,?,?,?", "WIDTH=?", "HEIGHT=?", and "FORMAT=?". Other KVP (key value pairs) are optional, such as "TRANSPARENT=TRUE|FALSE", "BGCOLOR=?", and "EXCEPTIONS=?".

Currently, OGC Web service supports only HTTP GET and/or HTTP PUT binding at the transport level by default. This is one aspect that differs from the W3C/OASIS Web services. OGC is trying to bridge this gap by making some experiments on SOAP binding. OGC Web services can be published through common gateway interface (CGI) (a standard to interact with external applications through an information servers, such as HTTP or Web servers), servlets (a Java-enabled server), active server pages (ASP) (a Microsoft-based approach), Java server pages (JSP) (a Java-enabled approach), and ASP.NET (a Web page service upon a Microsoft .NET framework).

When there are existing routines or Web services, the adaptation of these geoprocessing services or functional modules to comply with OGC specifications may be required. There are three possible cases: (1) to adapt a Web service, an OGC-compliant translator (using XSL/XSLT) may be sufficient since the encoding is already XML-based, (2) to adapt a server program, extra operations may be required to meet the specifications, and (3) to adapt a client, corresponding operations may be implemented to access the OGC-compliant Web services (Kolodziej, 2004; Zhao et al., 2004; Zhao, Nusser, & Miller, 2002).

Implement Customized Geospatial Web Services

In most cases, we may still be required to deploy some specific geospatial Web services that complete certain geospatial operations. If so, the developers may need some thinking on determining which operations are to be published, how to manage the intermediary and temporary file spaces, how to achieve the best performance in a distributed environment, and how to secure the system at large. This is especially true for these legacy geographic information systems. Their rich functions may be demanded in a service-oriented environment. Here we use one case that we adapted the GRASS functions and publish most of the operations as geospatial Web services at LAITS. These services are required for the effective demonstration on the intelligent chaining of Web services using a large repository of geospatial Web services.

GRASS has a huge number of operations. It is a comprehensive system of more than 350 programs for raster/vector geographic data manipulation, image processing, and map production. The functions range over spatial analysis, map generation (on paper and monitor), data visualization (2-dimensions, 2.5-dimentions, and 3-dimensions), data modeling, database management, and data manipulation (GRASS, 2005). In order to make GRASS functions as Web services, the first issue is to transfer these functions from a desktop environment to a networked environment. As a stand-alone system, the GRASS starts with a series of global variable initialization and keeps several states over the execution of programs. These need to be adapted to handle multiple routines running simultaneously. This can be solved by wrapping the initialization with each function to be explored, or every function would start with a set of own initialization. The second issue is what functions are proper to be deployed as Web services, and what is the basic level of operations to be exposed, command level or combined script. The command level is an individual program in GRASS to complete a small operation, such as Fast Fourier Transform, statistical summation, and optimum-index-factor table calculation. The combined script may complete a series of operations by editing and executing a script file of multiple steps of commands. The solutions are: (1) The Web service should be mainly based on the command level as this is the lowest level of function units. At this level, the creation of Web services from each command is straightforward, so as to ease the maintenance when new functions are added into GRASS. Combined operation can be easily achieved by combining several Web services through workflow manager, such as BPEL engines; and (2) Some commands are not exposed as Web services, especially those purely dealing with disk storage and monitor display. Finally, the use of customized geospatial Web services by an OGC-compliant Web service or an OGC-compliant client is a big issue. The input and output geospatial data are not exposed through an OGC-compliant data services. They are merely a universal resource identification (URI). This can be resolved by providing a series of wrap services to enable the feeding of geospatial data from an OGC-compliant data- providing service and the delivering of geospatial data to an OGC-compliant data server. By doing so, the intermediate processes are invisible to OGC-compliant geospatial services, but they can be easily handled by following Web service standards.

Geospatial Web Service Discovery

One of the first steps in consuming geospatial Web services is to find the desired geospatial Web services. Web service discovery is to locate a machine-processable description of a Web service that meets desired functional criteria. There are mainly three types of approach: Registry, Index, and Peer-to-Peer (Booth et al., 2004). Similarly, geospatial Web services can be searched through these three approaches.

Search by Registry

A registry is a catalog or a directory that is authoritative on the description of each registered Web service or metadata. The "catalog" plays a "directory" role: Providers advertise the availability of their resources through metadata, and users can then query the metadata to discover interesting resources and determine how to access those resources at run time (Nebert & Whiteside, 2004; Zhao et al., 2004). The success of a registry search highly depends upon what metadata is recorded for each geospatial Web service and how they are managed. If limited metadata information is registered, a search may give an explosive number of returns because of the broad matching. Heavy requirements on the metadata information would be a burden for the provider to submit all the details. There are many efforts in building the core metadata that are necessary for describing a geospatial Web services. Leading standards are ISO19115 for data and ISO19119 for service (ISO/TC211, 2002a, 2002b, 2003a).

Internally, a registry can be organized into a database, either a relational database system or an XML-based database. Once all the metadata information is entered into the registry, users or applications can query the registry with certain constraints clauses or criteria and retrieve matched service descriptions. Figure 4 illustrates major actors who interact with the registry and main operations which the actors perform on the registry.

Figure 4. Geospatial Web Registry Server

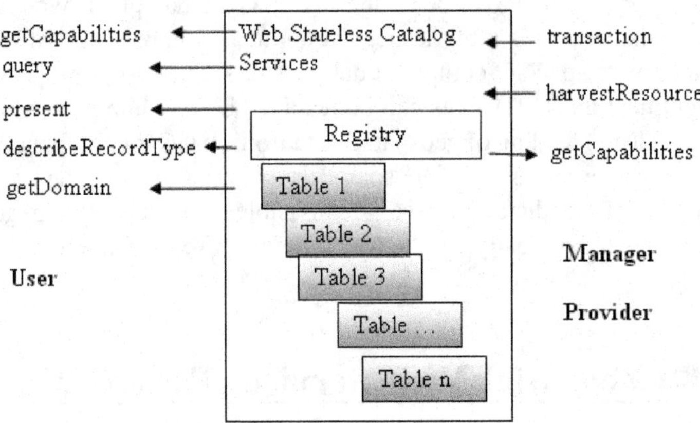

In a distributed infrastructure, the registry is presented as a Web service which targets at interoperation with client applications or other Web services (Alameh, 2001). In such a case, certain interoperable interfaces should be followed for the design of the registry service. UDDI is a standard registry to manage Web services with simple object access protocol (SOAP) as messaging protocol and Web Service

Figure 5. A simplified illustration of ebXML information model (Source: OASIS/ebXML, 2003)

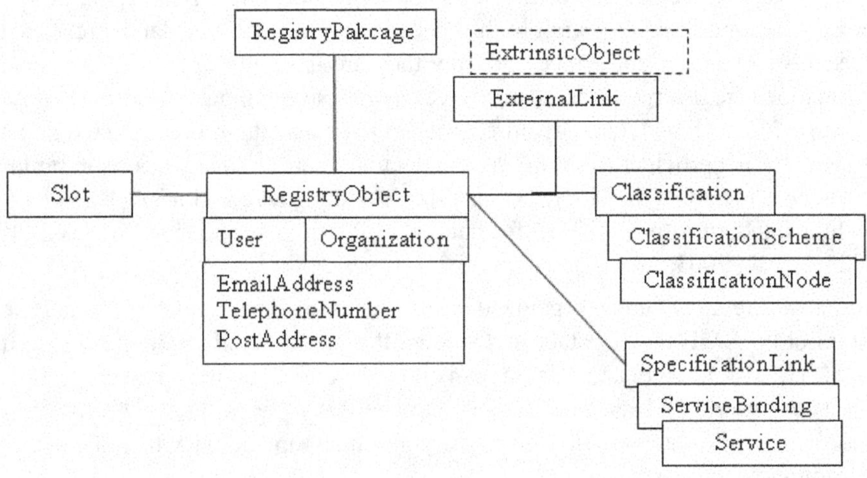

Description Language (WSDL) as Web service description language. And the OGC Catalog Service for Web (CSW) is a standard specification specifically designed for cataloging geospatial Web services (Martell, 2004; Voges & Zenkler, 2005; Wei et al., 2005; Zhao et al., 2004).

The information model of CSW is based on ebXML information model (ebRIM) (see Figure 5) (OASIS/ebXML, 2003). Table 1 lists classes used in this information model. The ebRIM is designed to be extensible through several mechanisms, either creating an ExtrinsicObject or adding a Slot. Therefore, CSW can easily be extended to describe different objects, such as organization, data, and services. For geospatial data and geospatial Web services, it is logical to extend the internal description capability of an CSW registry server with metadata described by ISO 19115 and ISO 19119 (Wei et al., 2005).

Table 1. Classes in an ebRIM

Class	Description
RegistryObject	The base object for the registry
RepositoryItem	Any object in a repository for storage and safekeeping
Slot	Arbitrary attributes to the RegistryObject
Association	Define the many-to-many relationship between objects in the information model
ExternalIdentifier	Additional identifier information to a RegistryObject
ExternalLink	An URI to external RegistryObject
ClassificationScheme	A scheme to classify RegisttryObject instances
ClassificationNode	A child node to a ClassificationScheme
Classification	A taxonomy value in a classification scheme
RegistryPackage	A group of Registry
AuditableEvent	An audit trail for RegistryObject instances
User	A registered user
PostalAddress	A postal address
E-mailAddress	An e-mail address
Organization	For example, submitting organization
Service	Service information
ServiceBinding	Technical information on a specific way to access a specific interface of a Service
SpecificationLink	A link referring to the technical specification that describes how to use the service

Table 2. CSW interfaces and their operations (Source: Nebert & Whiteside, 2004)

Interface	Operation	Description
OGC_Service	getCapabilities()	To retrieve metadata describing what the Catalog Service can provide
Discovery	query()	To execute a query that searches the cataloged metadata and returns results satisfying the search criteria
	present()	To retrieve selected metatdata for specific records
	describeRecordType()	To retrieve type definitions used for that dataset
	getDomain()	To retrieve the domain (allowed values) of a metadata property or request parameter
Manager	transaction()	To request a specific set of "insert", "update", and "delete" action
	harvestResource()	To retrieve a resource from a specified location and to optionally create one or more entries for that resource
Session	Not discussed. Possible operations are: cancel(), close(), initialize(), and status().	
BrokedAccess	No discussed. Possible operation is order().	

The CSW interfaces are well-defined that unify the operations for the registration of new geospatial data/Web services and the query and retrieval of item description. Table 2 lists the interfaces and operations defined by CSW. This specification is still in evolving.

Search by Index

A search for geospatial Web services can be done more actively by using an index approach. The index approach harvests the Web services by crawling through all Web sites and servers and collects their metadata information into an indexer. This approach is a bottom-up search in which several dedicated crawlers keep on scrubbing through all Web sites to find geographical data and geospatial Web services. Figure 6 shows a proposed architecture for such an index search engine. The OGC Registry can be used to manage these collected metadata, and the query interfaces can follow the OGC Registry standard as well. The difference is that such an approach relies upon a passive publication of geospatial Web service and geospatial data; the crawlers of the search engine scrub through the Web to find this data instead of providers' submission.

The most challenge in this approach is how to determine if a link or Web service is geospatial or non-geospatial. The accuracy of identifying geospatial data and geospatial Web service depends upon the metadata associated with each data or Web service. For standard geospatial data (e.g., HDF-EOS file), an extraction of internal

Figure 6. Crawler-based geospatial Web service discovery

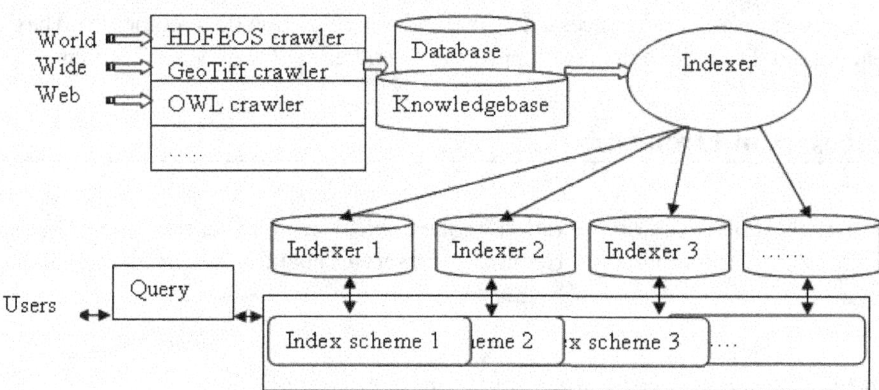

geospatial information will gather its geographic extent, time, and coordinate systems. For standard-compliant geospatial Web services (such as OGC WFS, WCS), further contents can be extracted by calling its standard interface, for example, getCapabilities for OGC-compliant geospatial Web services. For semantically-described geospatial Web service or data (such as associated taxonomy information in Ontology Language for Web [OWL]), a reasoner can be embedded to extract geospatial knowledge, such as class hierarchy of the data.

Search by Peer-to-Peer

Peer-to-peer (P2P) computing treats each computer as equally as another computer in the network. It is a different view from client/server architecture. Grid computing is considered as a P2P. The P2P search architecture does not need a centralized registry or a collected indexer. Each node in the P2P responds to the queries it receives (Booth et al., 2004). Once a user submits a query, the query is passed on to each individual node in the P2P network and returns the matched results through relaying. Such a search system may suffer performance inefficiencies, for example, lag time in propagation of queries and relaying of matches, and incomplete routing through the network.

Geospatial Web Services Orchestration

Assembling individual geospatial Web services into a service chain for representing a more complicated geospatial model and process flow proves to be essential for complex geospatial applications and knowledge discovery (Di, 2004a; Di, 2004c; Di, 2005; Di, 2005a). Such a process is called geospatial Web service orchestration. Service orchestration introduces a new method of application development and has great potential to reduce the development time and effort for new applications.

Processes of Orchestration

Geospatial Web service orchestration, in the context of this chapter, is nearly exchangeable with choreography, to embrace any service chaining activities, including

Figure 7. Typical composite processes for service chaining

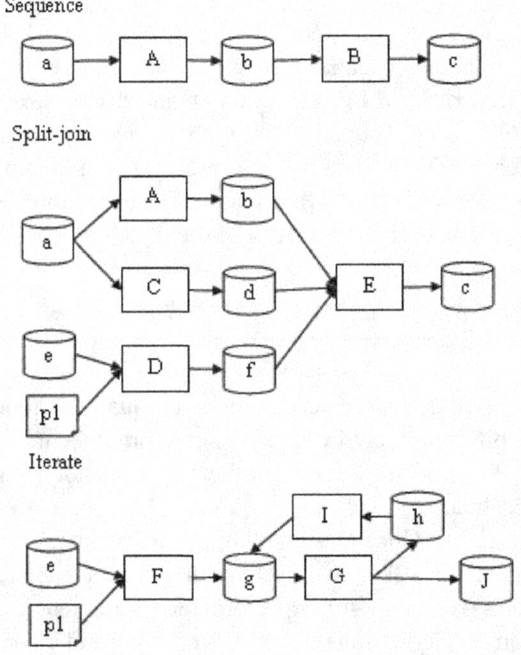

a – DEM data; A – Slope gradient calculation service; b – slope gradient data; B – landslide susceptibility model (based on slope only); c – landslide susceptibility; C – Slope aspect calculation service; d – slope aspect data; e – Landsat image; p1 – training sample pair; D – maximum likelihood classifier; f – land cover map; E – landslide susceptibility model (weighted evaluation); F – Neural network weight-initializing and data-preparing service; g – dataset with weight (including Landsat image, training samples, neuron weights); G – forward neural network classifier and validation; h – dataset with weight; I – backpropagation weight adjustment service; J – land cover classification both top-down (orchestration) and bottom-up (choreography) service composition. Typical processes in service chain include *Sequence, Split, Split + Join, Choice, Any-Order, Condition, If-Then-Else, Iterate, Repeat-While, and Repeat-Until.* Figure 7 illustrates some typical composite processes by aggregating Web services or orchestrating (conducting) heterogeneous Web services.

Orchestration Approaches

Geospatial Web service orchestration can be completed in three approaches: transparent, translucent, and opaque (Alameh, 2001; Di, 2004b; ISO/TC211, 2002b).

Transparent Geospatial Web Services Orchestration

\With transparent geospatial Web service orchestration, the user plays a central role in finding all the required geospatial Web services and geospatial data. Once the user identifies all the required services or data, a composite process can be achieved by two ways: The user invokes the services one by one in a user-controlled sequence (see Figure 8(a)), or the user creates a composite process in Business Process Execution Language (BPEL) or OWL-based Web service ontology (OWL-S) and execute the composite process using a proper engine (see Figure 8(b) for a composite sequence) (Andrews et al., 2003; Arkin et al., 2005; Martin et al., 2004). For the former, the user takes care of the sequence of requests as well as the transfer of information between geospatial Web services. For the latter, the user pre-composes the sequence and the information or message is directly relayed between geospatial Web services.

Translucent Geospatial Web Service Orchestration

A workflow management service or a composition service is used in such a case to coordinate all the invocation and scheduling of component Web services. The user or expert only needs to prepare an abstract composite service and store it in a composite service repository. The user later on can view and adjust the component Web service using a composite service editor/viewer.

Opaque Geospatial Services Orchestration

From the user viewpoint, an opaque geospatial Web service chain acts exactly the same as a simple Web service — the user sets all the required parameters, submits the request, and gets back the results without knowing what are the component Web services. From the system viewpoint, the opaque Web service chain can be a

Figure 8. Transparent geospatial Web service chaining (Source: Alameh, 2001)

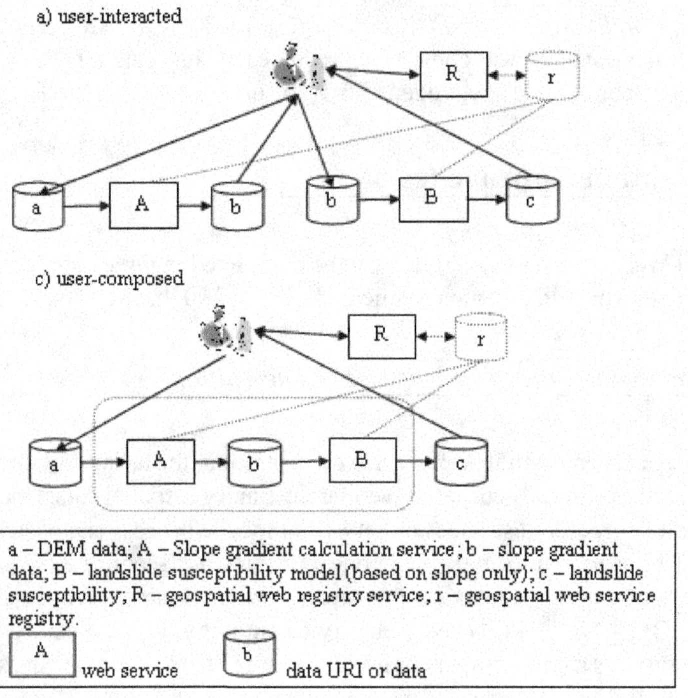

Figure 9. Translucent geospatial Web service chaining (Source: Alameh, 2001)

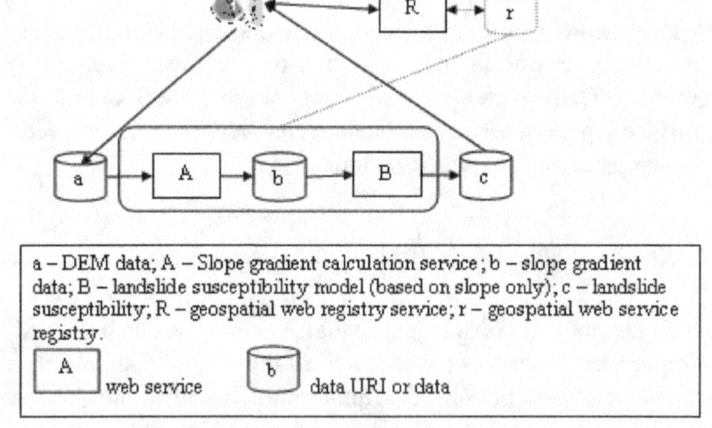

Figure 10. Opaque geospatial Web service chaining (Source: Alameh, 2001)

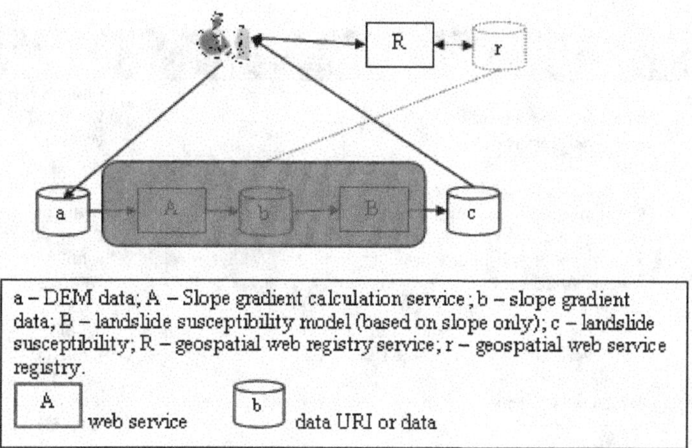

pre-defined composite Web service or a dynamically-chained Web service. For the former, the component Web services are fixed for the service chain even though the user does not know what they are. These can be pre-defined by experts. For the latter, the component Web services can only be fixed when the specific request is fixed. Some intelligent reasoning is used to complete the chaining instantly. This is especially useful in serving earth-science data when the data needs some intermittent process to meet customized requirements of users (Di et al., 2005).

Geospatial Web Service Solutions

The emerging standards enable the sharing of spatial data (data service) and processing functions (Web services) over the Web. Envisioning the prospect of avoiding the headache of formatting, geo-referencing, and integrating spatial data with existing data, all sectors (governments, industries, educational institutes, and individuals) are getting involved in publishing their geospatial Web services following these standards (Sayar, Pierce, & Fox, 2005). More than 260 products have claimed to be complaint with or implementing OGC specifications or interfaces (OGC, 2005b). Figure 11 shows part of the summary report for the compliant or implementing OGC specifications and services. Web map service (WMS), Web feature service (WFS), and Geography Markup Language (GML) are among the most popular specifications. By further analyzing the products claimed to be compliant with OGC

Figure 11. Part of the statistical summary of OGC specification or interface implementations (Source: OGC, 2005b)

Total (Compliant)	Specification / Version	Abrv / Version
107 (16)	Web Map Service (1.1.1)	WMS 1.1.1
105 (0)	Web Map Service (1.0)	WMS 1.0
103 (0)	Web Map Service (1.1)	WMS 1.1
67 (7)	Web Feature Service (1.0)	WFS 1.0
31 (0)	Geography Markup Language (2.1.1)	GML 2.1.1
28 (0)	Geography Markup Language (2.0)	GML 2.0
27 (0)	Filter Encoding (1.0)	Filter 1.0
21 (0)	Web Map Context Documents (1.0)	WMC 1.0
20 (7)	Simple Features - SQL - Normalized Geometry (1.1)	SFS(NG) 1.1
19 (0)	Styled Layer Descriptor (1.0)	SLD 1.0
19 (0)	Web Feature Service (Transactional) (1.0)	WFS(T) 1.0
17 (0)	Geography Markup Language (3.0)	GML 3.0
14 (1)	Catalog Interface (1.0)	CAT 1.0
14 (10)	Simple Features - SQL - Types and Functions (1.1)	SFS(TF) 1.1
12 (0)	Simple Features - SQL (1.1)	SFS 1.1
12 (0)	Gazetteer (0.8)	Gaz 0.8
12 (0)	Geography Markup Language (2.1.2)	GML 2.1.2
12 (0)	Web Terrain Server (0.3.2)	WTS 0.3.2
11 (5)	Simple Features - SQL - Binary Geometry (1.1)	SFS(BG) 1.1
10 (0)	Catalog Interface (1.1.1)	CAT 1.1.1
9 (0)	WMS Part 2: XML for Requests using HTTP Post (0.0.3)	WMS POST 0.0.3
8 (0)	Web Registry Server (0.0.2)	WRS 0.0.2

specifications, this section gives users a head-start guide to know about commercial and open-source programs.

Server-Side Solutions

More and more geospatial software products have been published using standards-compliant specifications, for example, GeoMedia WebMap (Intergraph), and ArcWeb services (ESRI). Table 3 lists some of the server-side products that support OGC specifications, including WMS, WFS, catalog service specification (CAT), GML, simple feature — SQL (SFS), and WCS. To achieve more interoperability, several data services from governments start to implement these specifications. Geospatial-one-stop (geodata.gov) is one of them which support a wide suite of OGC specifications.

Client-Side Solutions

On the client side, more and more client software have claimed that they support the access of geospatial data and services through open geospatial standards, for

Table 3. List of standard-compliant geospatial web-services (server side) (Source: OGC, 2005b)

Specification	Product
WMS 1.0, 1.1, 1.1.1	MapServer 3.5, 4.2; CarbonTools 2; Drill Down Server Web services; TakukGIS Developer Kernel; POLYGIS MAPSERVER 9.1; SuperGIS 1.2; SuperWebGIS 1.2; e-NeXt server 6.2; GIS Broker 3.3; TerraVision WMS Server 1.1; PostGIS / PostgreSQL 0.8.0; rasdaman 5.1; XIS (Extensible information Systems) 1.1; WebPix WMS Web service 1.0; Geomatica - WebServer Suite 10.0; shp2gml GeoBroker 1.1; Oracle Application Server MapViewer, 10g Release 2 (10.1.2); COP-WDS 1.1; SpatialFX 4.0; Navici; GIS/LINE WMS 1.0; DMAP GIDB Portal OGC Web services WMS 1.1.1, 1.1.0; MIT Ortho Server ; MiraMon Map Server 5.0; MapXtreme 2004 6.1, Java Edition 4.7;WEGA-MARS 3.1, 4.1; LuciadMap 4.2, 5; deegree owsProxy 0.5, deegree Web Map Service 1.1.2;Gothic Integrator: Java Edition (GI:JE) WMS, Gothic WebMapper v4-1a-12a-2; JGisBr - JGisCatalogo V2; WMSControl.Net 1.0b; RedSpider Catalog 2.0, Web 3.0, 3.1, 3.3;International Interfaces AWMS Server and Cookbook 1; GeoMedia; XtraWMS 0.38; JCarnacGIS 2.0; FasterMap 1.0; Geologica Map Server 1.1; GeoServer 1.2; GeoSecurity 2.0; GIS Portal 2.0; Global Aerial and Satellite Image Service 3.0g-business integrator 2.0; Exposure Image Server 1, Spatial Server 1; SclMapProxy 1; SclMapServer 2.30; GenaWare 8; sisIMS 2004.0301; GE Smallworld Internet Application Server; PlanAccess WMS 1.5; FreeStyle Suite 1.15; NAVImap 1; ArcIMS 3.0, 4.0, 4.0.1, 9.0; GIS Portal Tool Kit 2.0; iSMART 4.3; Demis Map Server 2.0, 3.0, 4.0; XMap Web 3.0; CubeServ – Web Map Server 2.10.7, Cascading Web Map Server 4.0.2; sdi.suite terraCatalog 2.0, terrainServer 1.0; ArcIMS to OGC Connector 1.2; Map Manager 3.2; Service manager 3.0; Web Enterprise Suite 3.1; Web Feature Portrayal Service 1.2; SpatialAce Web Map Server 2.0; CARIS Chartserver 2.0, Spatial Fusion 2.5.1, 3.0, 3.2, Cascading Web Map Server 3.2; HPDWeb 1.1; Cadcorp GeognoSIS.NET V6.1, SIS Feature Server 6, Map Server 5.2, 6, 6.1; GeoMapServer 1.0; Autodesk WMS Extention 6.3; SICAD/open – IMS 6.0, SICAD/Raster – IMS 6.0, SICAD/SD – IMS 6.0; GeoServer 4.1
WFS 1.0	MapServer 4.2; CarbonTools 2; TakukGIS Developer Kernel 8.x; SuperWebGIS 1.2; Geomatica-WebServer Suite 10.0; GEOINTEGRATION 2.0; GIS/LINE WFS 1.0; LuciadMap 5; deegree Web Feature Service 1.2.1; Gothic WebMapper v4-1a-12a-2; RedSpider Catalog 2.0, Web 3.0, 3.3; GeoMedia; JCarnacGIS 2.0; GeoServer 1.2; g.business integrator 2.0, organizer 2.0; FreeStyle Suite 1.15; Cartalinea Geographic Data Server (GDS) 1.4; ArcIMS 4.0, 4.0.1, 9.0, 9.1; GIS Toolk Kit 2.0; CubeServ – Web Feature Server 2.10.7; sdi.suite terraCatalog 2.0; Meta Manager – WFS 5.0; Service Manager 3.0; CARIS Spatial Fusion 3.2; Cadcorp GeognoSIS.NET V6.1; LIDS Application Server 6.5.3
GML 1.0, 2.0, 2.1.1, 2.1.2, 3.0, 3.1	MapServer 4.2; CarbonTools 2; TatukGIS Developer Kernel 8.x;SuperWebGIS 1.2; WFS Server 1.0; PCI Web Prototypes 0.1; shp2gml GeoBroker 1.1; Envinsa 3.5; MapInfo Routing J Server 3.2; MapMaker J Server 3.0; MapXtreme 2004 6.1, Java Edition 4.7; LuciadMap 5; degree Web Feature Service 1.2.1; Gothic WebMapper v4-1a-12a-2; RedSpider Web 3.3; GeoMedia; JCarnacGIS 2.0; FasterMap 1-0; g.buisiness integrator 2.0; SclFeatureServer 1.3; Cartalinea Geographic Data Server (GDS) 1.4; ArcIMS; iSMART 4.3; CubeServ – Web Map Server; Map manager 3.2; XchainJ 1.1; LIDS Application Server 6.5.3
SFS	TatukGIS Developer Kernel 8.x; PostGIS / PostgreSQL 0.8.0; Oracle Application Server Map Viewer, 10g, Oracle8i Spatial 8.1.x; MapInfo SpatialWare 4.5-4.8; JGisBr-JGisCatalogo v2; GeoMedia Data Server for Oracle Object Model Server 05.01; IBM DB2 Spatial Extender 7.1, 8.1; GeoTask Server on IBM DB2, on Oracle 9i; sisNET 2004; ArcSDE; TOPOBASE Geodataserver; AEDIDB (option AEDIDB-SimpleFeature) 3.5
CAT 1.0, 2.0	deegree Web Catalog Service; JGisBr- JGisCatalogo V2; RedSpdier Catalog 2.0; SMMS GeoConnect 5.x; ogcatsrv 1.2; ArcIMS Metadata Server; GIS Portal Tool Kit 2.0□con terra Catalog Server 1; Meta Miner 3.1
WCS 0.7, 1.0	Geomatica –WebServer Suite 10.0; MiraMon Map Server 5.0; LuciadMap 5; deegree Web Coverage Service 1.1.5; RedSpider Catalog 2.0, Web 3.1, 3.3; ArcGIS Server 9.0; GIS Portal Tool Kit 2.0

Table 4. List of standard-compliant geospatial web-services (client-side only) (Source: OGC, 2005b)

Specification	Product
WMS 1.0, 1.1, 1.1.1	Gaia 2; J2ME WMS Client 1.0.1; Skylab GPS Simulator 1.1; WebMap Composer 2.03; Arc3WMS 1.0; XIS View Point 1.1; NACMAP 4.0; Internet Mapping Framework 1.0.0; Java based wmsClient 1; deegree iGeoPortal 0.3; deeJUMP 1.0; RedSpider Studio 3.0; GeoMedia Viewer; XtraZWMSClient 0.27; Community Mapbuilder mapbuilder-lib; g.business navigator 2.0; Mapplets 5.0; sclMapJSClient; WebWraptor 1.0; sisVIEW 1.0; ArcExplorer Web; Chameleon 1.x; CubeXPLOR 2.10.7; sdi.suite mapClient 1.0; Mapbender 1.4, 2.0; CARIS WMS Client 1.0; Cadcorp apSIS 6; SICAD-IS D-HTML Client 6.0, HTML Client 6.0, Java Client 6.0
WFS 1.0	Gaia 2; WebMap Composer 2.03; deegree iGeoPortal 0.3; deeJUMP 1.0; RedSpider Studio 3.0; GeoMedia Viewer; g.business organizer 2.0; SclMapJSClient; ArcGIS Data Interoperability Extension 9.0; Chameleon 1.x
GML 1.0, 2.0, 2.1.1, 2.1.2, 3.0, 3.1	Gaia 2; GO Loader 0.3; deegree iGeoPortal 0.3; RedSpider Studio 3.0; GeoMedia Viewer; sisVIEW 1.0; ArcGIS Data Interoperability Extension 9.0;CubeXPLOR 2.10.7;
SFS	Munsys Cadasrral/Drainage/Electricity/Roads/Sewer/Water; MapInfo Professional 8.0; JGisBr-JGisEditor V2; HiRDB Spatial Search Plug-in 01-01; Spatial Database Engine for DB2 Datajoiner (Infomix or Oracle) 3.0.2; Cadcorp SIS 5.2
CAT 1.0, 2.0	JGisBr-JGisEditor V2; ogcatclt 1.2; Catalog Server for Informix 1; terraCatalog 1.2

example, ArcExplorer Web (ESRI), Interoperability Add-on for ArcGIS (ESRI), MapInfo Professional (MapInfo), and GeoMedia (Intergraph). Most server-side vendors have their own clients to access their standards-compliant servers with similar names. Table 4 gives some extra client applications that implement the OGC specifications.

Open-Source Solutions

One noticeable aspect is that open source software products are emerging as a key force in developing standard-compliant geospatial Web services and clients. For the server side, examples of geospatial Web services are LAITS OGC WCS, WICS, and WMS from George Mason University (http://laits.gmu.edu), MapServer (University of Minnesota), and GeoTools Web Map Server (http://www.geotools.org). For the client side, examples of standards-supported clients include the LAITS client (George Mason University) and the MapServer client (University of Minnesota), and so forth. These offer researchers the opportunity to explore the mechanisms in designing, developing, implementing, and testing of geospatial Web services.

Semantic Issues on Geospatial Web Service

With ever-growing geospatial Web services and geospatial data, it is very important to find the proper data and service matching specific requirements. Metadata is always used in describing and discovering geospatial Web services. However, mismatching may arise due to semantic ambiguity, or the same term used in different domains may lead to a different meaning (Sivashanmugam et al., 2003). This section reviews the semantic issues and their possible solutions for geospatial Web services.

Semantic Issues

Metadata for geospatial Web services can be classified into three levels: syntactic, structural, and semantic (Sheth, 1999, 2003; Sivashanmugam et al., 2003). Syntactic metadata describes basic sources and simple authorship information about geospatial Web services, such as data file format, creation date, sources, file size, and authors. Structural metadata describes the structure of geospatial data and the functions of the geospatial Web services, such as XML schema, data organization types (vector or raster), and functional types (data conversion, manipulation). Semantic metadata defines the context or domain of the geospatial data and geospatial services, such as thematic type for data (e.g., landslide in geoscience, population distribution in economic geography) and functional domain types (e.g., vegetation index computation in remote sensing, land surface temperature estimation in climate).

Figure 12. Data and their semantic hierarchy (Source: Sheth, 1999, 2003; Sivashanmugam et al., 2003)

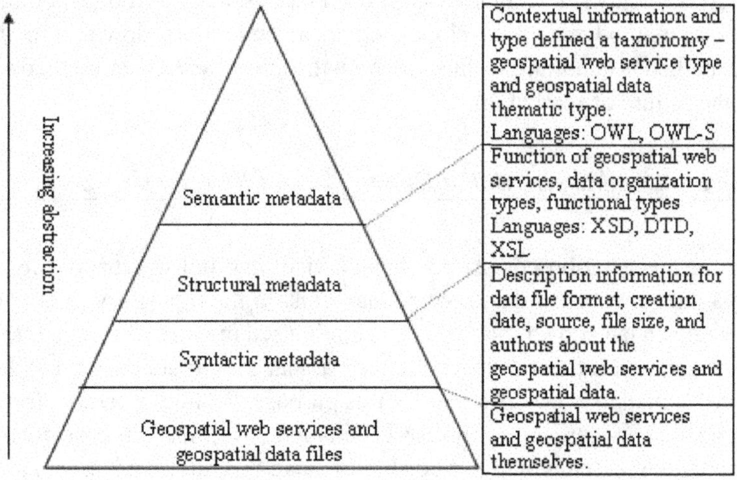

Semantic issues for interoperability have been recognized in many distributed multiple data systems (Kashyap & Sheth, 1996; Sheth, 1991; Sivashanmugam et al., 2003). Similar semantic issues rise for geospatial Web service chaining. For example, a geospatial service chain is required to compute a landslide susceptibility map, given a large repository of geospatial Web services. A landslide susceptibility model (as a Web service) may take seven input datasets: surface slope, surface aspect, base rock slope, base rock aspect, depth to base rock, soil moisture, and vegetation. All these input data types may not be directly available at data repositories, but they can be derived from some other Web services. Therefore, the first task is to find the Web services with output matching the required data type. The following problems may occur if semantics is not considered.

Semantic Issue 1: Ambiguous Match Due to Lack of Semantics

Each output of the services may be represented by a URI (universal resource identification) string, or other basic data types (e.g., integer, double, or single). If the match criteria are only defined as the match on data types (e.g., the only search criterion being that the output of a service is a URI string), the returned results may be overwhelming, containing numerous improper matches. This is because a URI string may carry different meaning.

Semantic Issue 2: Ambiguous Match Due to Incomplete Semantics

If the search criteria is based upon the service structure (e.g., a service with one input of DEM and one output of slope), the returned results may not satisfy the exact requirement; an improper computation algorithm may have been used to derive the slope. There are many algorithms for slope calculations: neighborhood method, quadratic surface method, maximum slope method, and maximum downhill method. If a desired method is quadratic surface method, the match with other methods would result in the failure of searching.

Semantic Issue 3: Missed Match Due to Lack of Relationship Semantics

A search for a vegetation cover map data service may fail to retrieve any match although a land cover map data service may exist in the repository. It is common knowledge that a land cover map can be actually used in place of a vegetation map since the vegetation categories (forest land, grass land, cultivated land) available in the land cover map may be sufficient for this purpose. Without a clear definition of the relationship between vegetation cover and land cover maps in the semantics of the metadata, the search would not be able to make this intelligent association.

Semantic Solutions

One solution to the above problems is to add semantic information to each geospatial data and geospatial Web services using a proper common ontology. An ontology is a specific set of vocabulary and relationships that have explicit assumptions about the intended meanings and relationships of the vocabulary in the set (Sivashanmugam et al., 2003). It is a technology that enables the computer-understandable description of Web services. Emerging standards for ontology are OWL, OWL-S, and Semantic Web services Language (SWRL) (Dean & Schreiber, 2004; Horrocks, Patel-Schneider, Boley, Tabet, Grosof, & Dean, 2003; Martin et al., 2004). These standards evolve the description of Web services from a syntactical description to a semantic description, mainly based on description logic. These can be used to describe the taxonomy of geospatial data and geospatial Web services and define their relationships with one another. Then, a reasoner can be used to validate the logic and induce the relationship underlying every term. A match can be made using this knowledge by matching both data semantics for input and output and functional semantics for the Web services (Di, 2004c; Di, 2005a; Di et al., 2005; Sivashanmugam et al., 2003; Zhao et al., 2004).

Conclusion

Web services give promising prospects in interoperability across applications and organizational boundary, independence from languages, and ease of maintenance. Geospatial data and service dissemination can take advantage of Web services to achieve higher usability and efficiencies. This chapter covers all aspects of the life cycle for geospatial Web services, including standards, implementation, discovery, and orchestration. It also reviews example solutions and applications leveraging the standards for geospatial Web services. Semantic issues and possible solutions are discussed.

Web service is an emerging technology. Standards, specifications, and practices for Web service are evolving. The same is also true to geospatial Web services. Many issues in the geospatial Web services still need to be explored. The following lists a few:

1. **A Web service is originally designed to be stateless:** However, transaction is required in many cases because geospatial modeling is a complicated process requiring multiple interactions. How to evolve the geospatial Web service to deal with transactions should be further studied.

2. **Web service uses plain XML as the base to communicate between applications:** Compared to other distributed computing approaches, Web service is relatively poor in performance and lack of security. These issues should be researched for geospatial Web services as well.
3. **Semantics for geospatial Web services is in development:** Many research issues need to be solved before an operational geospatial semantic Web can be established.

Acknowledgments

The authors of this chapter, as well as some of the example systems and services discussed in the chapter, were supported fully or partially with grants from the NASA Earth Science Data and Information System Project (ESDISP) (NCC5-645, PI: Dr. Liping Di), NASA Earth Science Technology Office (ESTO) (NAG-13409, PI: Dr. Liping Di), NASA REASoN program (NNG04GE61A, PI: Dr. Liping Di), and National Geospatial-intelligence Agency (NGA) University Research Initiative (NURI) (HM1582-04-1-2021, PI: Dr. Liping Di). We also sincerely thank to our colleagues at Laboratory for Advanced Information Technology and Standards, George Mason University. Numerous discussions with our colleagues at LAITS have brought forth much inspiration and enlightenment and shaped the chapter.

References

Akinci, H. (2004, 12-23 July). *Geospatial Web services for e-municipality.* Paper presented at the XXth ISPRS Congress, Istanbul, Turkey.

Alameh, N. S. (2001). *Scalable and extensible infrastructures for distributing interoperable geographic information services on the Internet.* Cambridge, MA: Massachusetts Institute of Technology..

Andersson, E., Greenspun, P., & Grumet, A. (2006). *Software engineering for internet applications.* Cambridge, MA: The MIT Press.

Andrews, T., Curbera, F., Dholakia, H., Goland, Y., Klein, J., Leymann, F., et al. (2003). *Business Process Execution Language for Web services (Version 1.1).* Retrieved from http://dev2dev.bea.com/webservices/BPEL4WS.html

Arkin, A., Askary, S., Bloch, B., Curbera, F., Goland, Y., Kartha, N., et al. (2005, July 13). *Web Services Business Process Execution Language Version 2.0*

(Working Draft). Retrieved from http://www.oasis-open.org/apps/org/workgroup/wsbpel/

Bacharach, S. (2005). *OGC to begin geospatial semantic Web interoperability experiment.* Retrieved August 20, 2005, from http://www.opengeospatial.org/press?page=pressrelease&year=0&prid=220

Booth, D., Haas, H., McCabe, F., Newcomer, E., Champion, M., Ferris, C., et al. (2004, February 11). *Web services architecture* (W3C Working Group Note). Retrieved August 8, 2005, from http://www.w3.org/TR/2004/NOTE-wsdl20-primer-20050803/

Booth, D., & Liu, C. K. (2005, August 3). *Web Services Description Language (WSDL) Version 2.0 Part 0: Primer* (W3C Working Draft). Retrieved from http://www.w3.org/TR/2005/WD-wsdl20-primer-20050803/

Burry, L. (2001). *OpenGIS implementation specification: Coordinate tansformation services, revision 1.00.* Retrieved August 20, 2005, from http://portal.opengeospatial.org/files/?artifact_id=6628

Chinnici, R., Haas, H., Lewis, A., Moreau, J. -J., Orchard, D., & Weerawarana, S. (2005, August 3). *Web Services Description Language (WSDL) Version 2.0 Part 2: Adjuncts* (W3C Working Draft). Retrieved from http://www.w3.org/TR/2005/WD-wsdl20-adjuncts-20050803/

Chinnici, R., Moreau, J.-J., Ryman, A., & Weerawarana, S. (2005, August 3). *Web Services Description Language (WSDL) Version 2.0 Part 1: Core Language* (W3C Working Draft). Retrieved from http://www.w3.org/TR/2005/WD-wsdl20-20050803/

Christensen, E., Curbera, F., Meredith, G., & Weerawarana, S. (2001, March 15). *Web Services Description Language (WSDL) 1.1* (W3C Note). Retrieved from http://www.w3.org/TR/2001/NOTE-wsdl-20010315

Clement, L., Hately, A., Riegen, C. Y., & Rogers, T. (2004, October 19). *UDDI Version 3.0.2* (UDDI Spec Technical Committee Draft). Retrieved from http://uddi.org/pubs/uddi-v3.0.2-20041019.htm

Cox, S., Daisey, P., Lake, R., Portele, C., & Whiteside, A. (2004). *OpenGIS Geography Markup Language (GML) implementation specification.* Retrieved August 20, 2005, from http://schemas.opengis.net/gml/3.1.0/base/

Daly, M. (2001). *OpenGIS implementation specification: Coordinate transformation services, revision 1.00.* Retrieved August 20, 2005, from http://portal.opengeospatial.org/files/?artifact_id=999

Dean, M., & Schreiber, G. (2004). *OWL Web Ontology Language reference.* Retrieved from http://www.w3.org/TR/2004/REC-owl-ref-20040210/

de La Beaujardiere, J. (2004). *OpenGIS Web map service, Version 1.3.* Retrieved August 20, 2005, from http://portal.opengeospatial.org/files?artifact_id=5316

Di, L. (2003, July 21-25). The development of remote-sensing related standards at FGDC, OGC, and ISO TC 211. In *Proceedings of 2003 IEEE International Geoscience and Remote Sensing Symposium (IGARSS 2003)*, Toulouse, France.

Di, L. (2004a). Distributed geospatial information services-architectures, standards, and research issues. In *The International Archives of Photogrammetry, Remote Sensing, and Spatial Information Sciences* (Vol. XXXV, Part 2, Commission II).

Di, L. (2004b). GeoBrain — A Web services based geospatial knowledge building system. In *Proceedings of the Fourth annual NASA Earth Science Technology Conference*, Palo Alto, CA.

Di, L. (2004c, September 20-24). A framework for intelligent geospatial knowledge discovery at Web service environment. In *Proceedings of 2004 IEEE International Geoscience and Remote Sensing Symposium (IGARSS 2004)*, Anchorage , AK.

Di, L. (2005, July 25-29). Customizable virtual geospatial products at Web/grid service environment. In *Proceedings of 2005 IEEE International Geoscience and Remote Sensing Symposium (IGARSS 2005)*, Seoul, Korea.

Di, L. (2005). A framework for construction of Web-service based intelligent geospatial knowledge systems. *Journal of Geographic Information Science, 11*(1), 24-28.

Di, L. (in press). The open GIS Web service specifications for interoperable access and services of NASA EOS Data. In J. Qu., et al. (Eds.), *Earth science satellite remote sensing*. Springer-Verlag.

Di, L., & McDonald, K. (2005). The NASA HDF-EOS Web GIS software suite (NWGISS). In J. Qu., et al. (Eds.), *Earth science satellite remote sensing*. Springer-Verlag.

Di, L., Yang, W., Deng, M., Deng, D., & McDonald, K. (2002). Interoperable access of remote sensing data through NWGISS. In *Proceedings of 2002 IEEE International Geoscience and Remote Sensing Symposium (IGARSS 2002)*, Toronto, Canada (pp. 255-257).

Di, L., Zhao, P., Yang, W., Yu, G., & Yue, P. (2005, July 25-29). Intelligent geospatial Web services. In *Proceedings of 2005 IEEE International Geoscience and Remote Sensing Symposium (IGARSS 2005)*, Seoul, Korea.

Duschene, P., & Sonnet, J. (2005a). *OGC WCS change request: Support for WSDL & SOAP, Version 0.1.0*. Retrieved August 20, 2005, from http://portal.opengeospatial.org/files/?artifact_id=9540

Duschene, P., & Sonnet, J. (2005b). *OGC WMS change request: Support for WSDL & SOAP*. Retrieved August 20, 2005, from http://portal.opengeospatial.org/files/?artifact_id=9541

EOP (2003). Coordinate geographic data acquisition and acess; the national spatial data infrastructure, *Federal Register, 68*, 10619-10633.

Evans, J. D. (2003). *OpenGIS Web coverage service (WCS) Version 1.0.0*. Retrieved August 20, 2005, from https://portal.opengeospatial.org/files/?artifact_id=3837

Evans, J. D., & Bambacus, M. J. (2005, 25-29 July). *NASA's earth-sun system gateway: An open standards-based portal to geospatial data and services*. Paper presented at the IEEE 25th Anniversary International Geoscience and Remote Sensing Symposium, Seoul, Korea.

Fielding, R. T. (2000). *Architectural styles and the design of network-based software architectures*. Irvine, CA: University of California, Irvine.

GRASS (2005). *Geographic resource analysis support system*. Retrieved August 10, 2005, from http://grass.itc.it/

Groot, R., & McLaughlin, J. D. (2000). *Geospatial data infrastructure: Concepts, cases, and good practice*. Oxford, England; New York: Oxford University Press.

GSFC (2005). *HDF-EOS*. Retrieved August 20, 2005, from http://hdfeos.feos.gsfc.nasa.gov/

Gudgin, M., Hadley, M., Mendelsohn, N., Moreau, J. -J., & Nielsen, H. F. (2003, June 24). *SOAP Version 1.2 Part 1: Messaging framework (W3C Recommendation)*. Retrieved from http://www.w3.org/TR/soap12/

Hecht, L., Jr. (2002). *Web services are the future of geoprocessing*. Retrieved August 14, 2006, from http://www.geoplane.com/gw/2002/02/06/206apng.asp

Hirsch, F., & Just, M. (2003, May 5). *XML key management (XKMS 2.0) Requirements* (W3C Note). Retrieved from http://www.w3.org/TR/2003/NOTE-xkms2-20030505

Horrocks, I., Patel-Schneider, P. F., Boley, H., Tabet, S., Grosof, B., & Dean, M. (2003). *SWRL: A Semantic Web Rule Language combining OWL and RuleML*. Retrieved from http://www.daml.org/2003/11/swrl/

IETF. (2005). *The Internet Engineering Task Force*. Retrieved August 20, 2005, from http://www.ietf.org/

ISO/TC211. (2002a). *Draft new work item proposal: Geographic information — metadata: Part 2 - Metadata for imagery and gridded data*. Retrieved from http://www.isotc211.org/protdoc/211n1337/211n1337.pdf

ISO/TC211. (2002b). *Geographic information services*. Retrieved from http://www.ncits.org/ref-docs/DIS19119.PDF

ISO/TC211. (2003a). *Geographic information — metadata*. Retrieved from http://www.ncits.org/ref-docs/FIDIS_19115.pdf

ISO/TC211. (2003b). *ISO 19139 dataset implementation model and schema, Version 0.7*. Retrieved August 20, 2005, from http://metadata.dgiwg.org/ISO19115/ISO19115_v0_7detail.htm

ISO/TC211. (2005). *ISO/TC211 Geographic information/geomatics*. Retrieved August 20, 2005, from http://www.isotc211.org/

Kashyap, V., & Sheth, A. P. (1996). Semantic and schematic similarities between database objects: A context-based approach. *VLDB Journal, 5*(4), 276-304.

Kolodziej, K. (2004). *OpenGIS Web map server cookbook, Version 1.0.2*. Retrieved August 20, 2005, from http://portal.opengeospatial.org/files/?artifact_id=7769

Kralidis, A. (2005). *Geospatial Web services: An evolution of geospatial data infrastructure*. Ottawa, Ontario, Canada: Carleton University.

LAITS (2005). *Mobilization of NASA EOS data and information through Web services and knowledge management technologies for higher-education teaching and research*. Retrieved August 20, 2005, from http://geobrain.laits.gmu.edu

Lieberman, J., Reich, L., & Vretanos, P. (2003). *OWS 1.2 UDDI experiment, Version 0.5*. Retrieved August 20, 2005, from http://portal.opengeospatial.org/files/?artifact_id=1317

Mabrouk, M. (2005). *OpenGIS® location service (OpenLS) implementation specification: Core services, Version 1.1*. Retrieved August 20, 2005, from http://portal.opengeospatial.org/files/?artifact_id=8836

Martell, R. (2004). *OGC™ catalogue services — ebRIM (ISO/TS 15000-3) profile of CSW*. Retrieved from https://portal.opengeospatial.org/files/index.php?artifact_id=6495

Martin, D., Burstein, M., Hobbs, J., Lassila, O., McDermott, D., McIlraith, S., et al. (2004, November 22). *OWL-S: Semantic markup for Web services (W3C Member Submission)*. Retrieved from http://www.w3.org/Submission/2004/SUBM-OWL-S-20041122/

Mateos, C., Zunino, A., & Campo, M. (2005). Integrating intelligent mobile agents with Web services. *International Journal of Web Services Research, 2*(2), 85-103.

Nebert, D. (2005). *Current standards, specifications, and practices of relevance to SDI development*. Retrieved August 20, 2005, from http://www.anzlic.org.au/pubinfo/2413322725

Nebert, D., & Whiteside, A. (2004). *OpenGIS catalogue services specification*. Retrieved from http://portal.opengeospatial.org/org/files/?artifact_id=5929&version=1

OASIS. (2005). *Organization for the Advancement of Structured Information Standards*. Retrieved August 20, 2005, from http://www.oasis-open.org/home/index.php

OASIS/ebXML. (2003). *OASIS/ebXML registry informaiton model V2.5*. Retrieved from http://www.oasis-open.org/committees/regrep/documents/2.5/specs/ebrim-2.5.pdf

OGC. (2004). *Critical infrastructure protection initiative, Phase 2 (CIPI2)*. Retrieved August 20, 2005, from http://www.opengeospatial.org/initiatives/?iid=66

OGC. (2005a). *OpenGIS specifications*. Retrieved August 20, 2005, from http://www.opengeospatial.org/specs/download.php?view=IS&keyword=&excel=1

OGC. (2005b). *Resources — registered products*. Retrieved from http://www.opengeospatial.org/resources/?page=products

Peltz, C. (2003). *Best practices for Web services development*. Retrieved August 20, 2005, from http://devresource.hp.com/drc/resources/WSBestPractices/index.jsp

Peltz, C., & Rogers, C. (2003). *Leveraging open source for Web servies development*. Retrieved August 20, 2005, from http://devresource.hp.com/drc/technical_white_papers/wsopenrc.pdf

Sayar, A., Pierce, M., & Fox, G. (2005). *OGC compatible geographical information services*. Bloomington, IN: Indiana University.

Sheth, A. P. (1991). Semantic issues in multidatabase systems. *SIGMOD Record, 20*(4), 5-9.

Sheth, A. P. (1999). Changing focus on interoperability in information systems: From system, syntax, structure to semantics. In M. F. Goodchild, M. J. Egenhofer, R. Fegeas, & C. A. Kottman (Eds.), *Interoperating geographic information systems* (pp. 5-30). Boston: Kluwer Academic Pub.

Sheth, A. P. (2003). Semantic meta data for enterprise information integration. *DM Review, 13,* 52-54.

Sivashanmugam, K., Sheth, A., Miller, J., Verma, K., Aggarwal, R., & Rajasekaran, P. (2003). Metadata and semantics for Web services and processes. In W. Benn, P. Dadam, S. Kirn & R. Unland (Eds.), *Datenbanken und Informationssysteme: Festschrift zum 60. Geburtstag von Gunter Schlageter* (pp. 245-271). Hagen, Germany: Fachbereich Informatik.

Skonnard, A. (2002). *The XML files: The birth of Web services.* Retrieved August 14, 2006, from http://msdn.microsoft.com/msdnmag/issues/02/10/xmlfiles/

Sonnet, J. (2004). *OWS 2 common architecture: WSDL SOAP UDDI, Version 1.0.0.* Retrieved August 20, 2005, from https://portal.opengeospatial.org/files/?artifact_id=8348

Sonnet, J. (2005). *OpenGIS Web map context implementation specification, Version 1.1.* Retrieved August 20, 2005, from https://portal.opengeospatial.org/files/?artifact_id=8618

Sonnet, J., & Savage, C. (2003). *OWS 1.2 SOAP experiment report.* Retrieved August 20, 2005, from http://portal.opengeospatial.org/files/?artifact_id=1337

Tsalgatidou, A., & Pilioura, T. (2002). An overview of standards and related technology in Web services. *Distributed and Parallel Databases, 12*, 135-162.

Vaughan-Nichols, S. J. (2002). Web services: Beyond the hype. *Computer, 35*(2), 18-21.

Vedamuthu, A. S. (2006). *Web Services Description Language (WSDL) Version 2.0 SOAP 1.1 binding* (W3C Working Draft). Retrieved August 14, 2006, from http://www.w3org/TR/wsdl20-soap11-binding/

Voges, U., & Zenkler, K. (2005). *OpenGIS catalog services specification 2.0 — ISO19115/ISO19119 application profile for CSW 2.0, Version 0.9.3.* Retrieved from https://portal.opengeospatial.org/files/?artifact_id=8305

Vretanos, P. A. (2005). *OpenGIS Web feature service implementation specification, Version 1.1.0.* Retrieved August 20, 2005, from https://portal.opengeospatial.org/files/?artifact_id=8339

W3C. (2005a). *W3C XML schema.* Retrieved August 20, 2005, from http://www.w3.org/XML/Schema

W3C. (2005b). *World Wide Web Consortium.* Retrieved August 20, 2005, from http://www.w3.org/

Wei, Y., Di, L., Zhao, B., Liao, G., Chen, A., Bai, Y., et al. (2005, 25-29 July). *The design and implementation of a grid-enabled catalogue service.* Paper presented at the IEEE 25th Anniversary International Geoscience and Remote Sensing Symposium, Seoul, Korea.

Whiteside, A. (2005). *OGC Web services common specification.* Retrieved August 20, 2005, from https://portal.opengeospatial.org/files/?artifact_id=8798

Whiteside, A., Müller, M. U., Fellah, S., & Warmerdam, F. (2005). *OGC Web coordinate transformation service (WCTS) draft implementation specification, Version 0.3.0.* Retrieved August 20, 2005, from https://portal.opengeospatial.org/files/?artifact_id=8847

Wilkes, L. (2005). *The Web services protocol stack.* Retrieved August 20, 2005, from http://roadmap.cpdiforum.com/reports/protocols/index.php

Winer, D. (1999). *XML-RPC specification.* Retrieved from http://www.xmlrpc.com/spec

Yang, W., & Whiteside, A. (2005). *OGC Web image classification service (WICS) impementation specification, Version 0.3.3.* Retrieved August 20, 2005, from http://portal.opengeospatial.org/files/?artifact_id=8981

Zhao, P., Chen, A., Liu, Y., Di, L., Yang, W., & Li, P. (2004, 12-13 November). *Grid metadata catalog service-based OGC Web registry service.* Paper presented at the 12th ACM International Workshop on Geographic Information Systems (ACM-GIS 2004), Washington DC.

Zhao, P., Nusser, S., & Miller, L. (2002). *Design of field wrappers for mobile field data collection.* Paper presented at the Proceedings of the Tenth ACM International Symposium on Advances in Geographic Information Systems (ACM-GIS 2002), McLean, VA.

Chapter II

Spatial Information System Development: The Role of Information System Design Theory and Ontologies

Brian N. Hilton, Claremont Graduate University, USA
Richard J. Burkhard, San Jose State University, USA
Tarun Abhichandani, Claremont Graduate University, USA

Abstract

An approach to an ontology-based information system design theory for spatial information system development is presented. This approach addresses the dynamic nature of information system development at the beginning of the 21st century and addresses the question of how to establish relationships between the various design components of a spatial information system. It should also help to automate and guide the design process while at the same time improve the quality of the process along with its outputs. An example of this approach is presented, along with examples of the various ontologies utilized in the design of this particular spatial information system. Finally, a method to mitigate the issues regarding the organization and management of a growing library of ontologies is discussed.

Introduction

Spatial informatics, as a field of study within the information sciences, is concerned with the development of spatial information systems for a specific problem or decision-making environment. Moreover, the development of these spatial information systems is being influenced by many factors: the increasing breadth and depth of various emerging technologies, the nearly exponential increase in the quantity of spatial data, and the growing awareness in many domains of the impact these systems can have within these domains. As a result, there is a need for an approach to spatial information system development that addresses these, and other, influences.

Action research and improvement research are two approaches for conducting research in the information sciences that employ methods in which the explicitly-expected outcomes include the solving of a problem or the building of a system (Truex, 2001). These research approaches differ from explanatory or descriptive research, which focus on explaining phenomena rather than solving problems. Furthermore, "whereas explanation of research methods and traditions are based in natural science and are well established, improvement research methods and traditions are relatively new and are closer to engineering or computer science modes of research" (Truex, 2001, p. 7). Information system design theory (ISDT) is one example of these approaches that has at its core three key elements: a set of user requirements, a set of system features, and a set of principles for guiding the process of development. Specifically, an ISDT can be thought of as a complete package of guidance for designers and practitioners facing particular sets of circumstances that are based in theory (Markus, Majchrzak, & Gasser, 2002).

An ontology is a hierarchical structuring of knowledge, similar to a dictionary or glossary, but with greater detail and structure. An ontology consists of a set of concepts, axioms, and relations, and provides a number of potential benefits in processing knowledge, including the externalization of domain knowledge from operational knowledge, sharing of common understanding of subjects among human and also among computer programs, and the reuse of domain knowledge (Lee et al., 2004). The impact of ontologies in the information sciences can be seen, on the methodological side, through the adoption of a highly interdisciplinary approach to ontology development, while on the architectural side, in the role that an ontology can play in an information system, leading to the perspective of ontology-driven information systems (Guarino, 1998).

Increasing international competitiveness and technological advances have prompted the need for organizations to (Green, Kennedy, & McGown, 2002):

- Exploit emerging technologies more rapidly
- Reduce design time-scales

- Provide "right first time" design
- Innovate more frequently and produce more innovative products
- Improve the reliability of products and systems

Consequently, industry and academia have been directing research towards developing methods to automate and guide the design process while at the same time improving the quality of the process along with its outputs (Green et al., 2002). This chapter follows in this vein.

Information System Design Theory

Design Research

The challenge of design for spatial information systems reflects many of the design issues that are seen in the information systems discipline as a whole, as well as the related disciplines of engineering and computer science. A key influence on design in information systems is the work of Herbert Simon, whose concepts influence the development of many aspects of design science theory and the disciplines that contribute to spatial informatics. Simon argued that design sciences for artificial, or created, systems would find their substance in the generation of artifacts (Simon, 1996) that are attempts to meet the purposes of the designers. These artifacts, such as information system software elements, are synthesized from various contributing areas and typically emulate natural systems in some way. In spatial information systems such as geographic information systems (GIS), an example of a natural system is found in the high-level view of a terrain as obtained from an aircraft or satellite. This emulation can be supplemented with multiple dimensions of quantitative data from other sources such as geometric projection systems, which are combined into the artifact of the GIS software element. In this model, the GIS exemplifies computer systems that are designed to emulate human activities, particularly thought processes (Freeman & Hart, 2004).

The view that such artifacts should be a central focus of effort, both in theory and in practice, in information systems research has gained considerable attention (Orlikowski & Iacono, 2001). The design science approach to information systems research "seeks to extend the boundaries of human and organizational capabilities by creating new and innovative artifacts" such as information systems applications implemented in computer software (Hevner, March, Park, & Ram, 2004). In information system design research, increased understanding of the problem area is expected to result from the activities of building the artifact itself (Vaishnavi & Kuechler, 2004)

Simon and others maintain that the development of such artifact-based systems will be most efficient if the developers follow a pattern of several general classes of activity. The first of these activities is creating design alternatives and representing these alternatives by means of appropriate representational models. The spatial systems specialty within the field of information systems has developed a variety of such models, many of which are discussed in the following chapters. Next, a series of solution approaches are generated followed by assessment of usability and human factors such as interface design. Finally, the actual artifacts are developed, usually in the form of a series of prototypes, which in turn are evaluated. Many variants of this iterative process are familiar within design-based disciplines (NSF, 2004).

The task of designing spatial systems presents special opportunities to emulate natural systems by allowing visual and cognitive ordering of information to enhance its communication power. Such information visualization tools allow the user to examine the "terrain" of information (Bederson, 2001; Shneiderman, Card, Norman, Tremaine, & Waldrop, 2001). The analytical potential of information visualization methods is important in any context where a large body of data forms the basis for decision-making. In particular, visualization tools have special relevance in situations in which the decision maker faces information overload and hidden or ambiguous patterns in the decision-basis information, such as what one might face in the following situations.

For example, spatial information system artifacts can enable pattern discovery through visual inspection that can be superior to other, non-spatial information system methods (Gershon, Eick, & Card, 1998). Pattern discovery through interactive techniques as provided in spatial information systems can augment the information search process in unexpected ways (Kreuseler & Schumann, 1999). In addition, the visualization of spatial information can allow users to intelligently develop specific questions to be asked via more traditional mechanisms, such as search engines (Shneiderman, 1999).

The unique opportunity for a spatial information system to emulate and extend natural human processes places it in a special position to develop as an important specialty within the information systems field, as well as to contribute to the body of work in information system design theory.

Information System Design Theory

As presented by Walls, Widmeyer, and El Sawy, 1992), the concern of researchers in the Information Systems discipline is the design of systems and the development of system design theories that address the question of how to establish relationships between components of a system to achieve a specific result. An information system design theory (ISDT), then, refers to an integrated prescription consisting of a particular class of user requirements, a type of system solution (with distinctive features), and a set of effective development practices (Markus et al., 2002). Here, Walls et al. refer to meta-requirements (user requirements), which describe the specific goals that are applicable to any system of the type to which the theory relates. Meta-design (system solution) describes the specific artifacts that are applicable to the meta-requirements, while the design method (effective development practices) describes the procedures to be utilized in building a system of the type to which the theory relates. Underlying these three features (meta-requirements, meta-design, design method) of an ISDT are kernel theories (an academic theory and/or a practitioner theory-in-use) that enable the formulation of empirically-testable hypotheses relating the design theory to expected outcomes. The ISDT addresses both the product of the design effort, which is typically an artifact or instantiation, and the process of design. In this way, the method of design can be adapted to the meta-requirements of the product. These design theory characteristics help to establish why the application of one particular ISDT to a specific situation yields better results than the application of a different ISDT. For example, "it should be possible to establish empirically that the application of Decision Support System design theory to a particular set of requirements produces better results than applying Transaction Processing System design theory to the same requirements" (Markus et

Figure 1. Components of an information system design theory

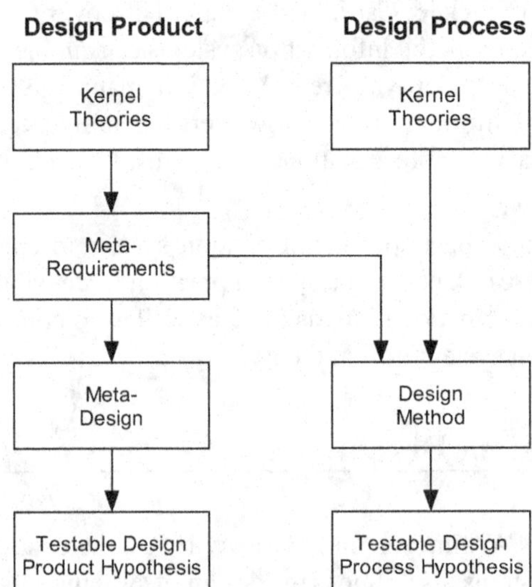

al., 2002, p. 181). Figure 1 illustrates the relationships between the components of an ISDT where the meta-requirements and meta-design form the core of the design product, while the design method forms the core of the design process.

Ontologies

Ontology Fundamentals

Ontology development is a descriptive activity that seeks to provide taxonomies and definitive descriptions of the kinds and structures of objects, properties, events, processes, and relations in every area of reality (Smith, 2003). The main purpose of developing ontologies is to provide machine-processable semantics of information sources that can be communicated between different agents (software and humans) (Fensel, 2003). Ontologies can serve as a common foundation for building and assessing systems in particular domains (Embley, 2004; Sugumaran & Storey, 2002). They offer specifications of various kinds and general interrelationships (Geroimenko, 2003) that can be utilized in designing cohesive systems. Appropriately, an ontology is defined as a formal, explicit specification of a shared conceptualization (Gruber, 1993). It is important to note that these conceptualizations can be shared between agents (software and human) and that they serve a specific context in a particular domain.

Protégé Ontology Editor and Knowledge Acquisition System

Protégé is an integrated software tool used by system developers and domain experts to develop knowledge-based systems (Stanford Medical Informatics, 2003). Such systems are enhanced by ontology-derived common vocabularies that allow researchers to share information in a domain, and the best examples of such ontology-based systems include machine-interpretable definitions of basic concepts in the domain and relations among them (Noy & McGuinness, 2003). As such, applications developed with Protégé are used in problem solving and decision-making in a particular domain. Noy and McGuinness (2003) identified five major reasons for developing an ontology. They are:

- Sharing common understanding of the structure of information among people or software agents

- Enabling reuse of domain knowledge
- Making explicit domain assumptions
- Separating the domain knowledge from the operational knowledge
- Analyzing domain knowledge

Noy and McGuinness further state that problem-solving methods, domain-independent applications, and software agents use ontologies and knowledge bases built from ontologies as data. Figure 2 is a basic example of an ontology developed using Protégé that describes a newspaper that defines classes, the class hierarchy, slots and slot-value restrictions, relationships between classes, and properties of these relationships.

An ontology includes a formal explicit description of concepts (classes) in a particular domain or field. Attributes (slots) describe various features of each concept. These slot-values may have restrictions (constraints). An ontology, together with a set of individual instances, comprises a knowledge base. Since instances may be the best description of unique classes, there is often little distinction between the ontology-defined class and the instances of the larger knowledge base.

Figure 2. Protégé ontology editor and knowledge acquisition system — newspaper example

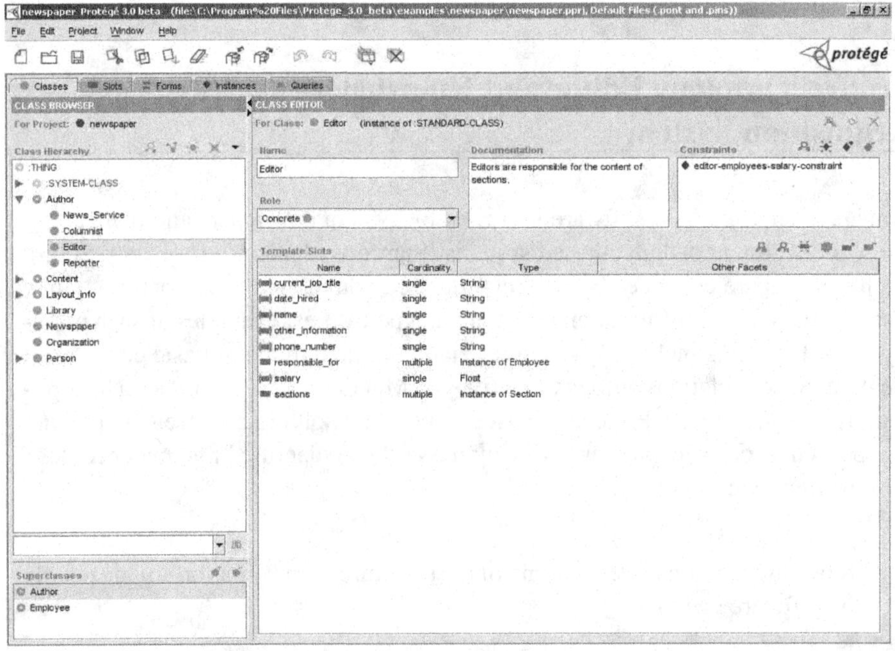

Application of Information System Design Theory and Ontologies for Spatial Information System Development

The approach to spatial information system development presented here builds on the foundation of design research, specifically, ISDT and the use of ontologies to address the question of how to establish relationships between the various design components of a spatial information system. The example presented below is that of a particular spatial information system, a proximate commuting system.

Proximate Commuting

Transportation demand management (TDM) is a general term for strategies that result in the efficient use of transportation resources. One TDM strategy is commute trip reduction (CTR), a program that gives commuters resources and incentives to reduce their automobile trips (Victoria Transport Policy Institute, 2005). These programs, such as rideshare matching, alternative scheduling, and tele-work, may be encouraged or required by local, regional, state, or federal policies.

One CTR program, proximate commuting, allows employees to shift to work sites that are closest to their homes. Here, spatial analysis is performed that identifies the commutes of employees of multi-location organizations that could be reduced by working at a closer location. Proximate commuting is a potential employer-based travel-demand management program under which large, decentralized employers reassign each voluntary participant to a job location (with the same employer) closer to the participant's residence to reduce commuting distances (Rodriguez, 2001). A

Table 1. Design product — proximate commuting system

Feature	Definition	Realization in a Spatial Information System
Kernel theories	Core theories that support and guide the design	Multi-criteria decision-making [1] Spatial decision support systems [1] Spatial cognition [1]
Meta-requirements	Meta-requirements describe the specific goals that are applicable to any system of the type to which the theory relates.	Geographic human interaction services [2] Geographic model/information management services [2] Geographic workflow/task management services [2] Geographic processing services [2] Geographic communication services [2] Goal: Clarity [3] Goal: Efficiency [3]

Table 1. continued

Meta-design	Meta-design describes the specific artifacts that are applicable to the meta-requirements.	Geographic viewer [2] Feature access service [2] Coverage access service [2] Coverage access service — sensor [2] Route determination service [2] Proximity analysis service [2] Geographic annotation service [2] Transfer service [2] Messaging service [2] Remote file and execution management [2] Feature: Maps [3] Feature: Place directories [3] Feature: Page form and performance [3]
Testable hypothesis	Hypotheses that are open to empirical testing	It is possible to develop a proximate commuting system using the ISDT for SDSS. A proximate commuting system built using the ISDT for SDSS will be more open, useful, and innovative.

Note: [1] *concepts and theories ontology;* [2] *geographic services ontology;* [3] *advanced traveler information systems ontology*

spatial information system, a group of procedures that provide data input, storage and retrieval, mapping, and spatial analysis for both spatial and attribute data to support the decision-making activities of the organization (Grimshaw, 2000), is particularly suited to perform the spatial analysis required for proximate commuting. Tables 1 and 2 present an instance of an ontology-based ISDT, for a proximate commuting system prototype that was developed by the lead author (Hilton, 2003).

Table 2. Design process — proximate commuting system

Feature	Definition	Realization in a Spatial Information System
Kernel theories	Core theories that support and guide the design process	Human-centered design [1] Quality in use [1] Prototyping [1]
Design method	Design method describes the procedures to be utilized in building a system of the type to which the theory relates.	Understand and specify the context of use [1] Specify the user and organizational requirements [1] Produce design solutions [1] Evaluate designs against requirements [1] User evaluation of functionality, reliability, usability, and efficiency [1] Iterative development process [1] Utilize service organizer folder [2]
Testable hypothesis	Hypotheses that are open to empirical testing	Systems built using the ISDT for SDSS will better meet the needs of both the user and organization. The level of adoption for a system built using the ISDT for SDSS will be higher than other approaches.

Note: [1] *concepts and theories ontology;* [2] *geographic services ontology*

Ontologies for Spatial Information System Development

Following the guidelines for building spatial information system ontologies (Linkova, Nedbal, & Rimnac, 2005), several ontologies were developed and used in the creation of the ISDT for proximate commuting outlined above. These ontologies are accessible through a Web-based portal for spatial information system development. This portal contains the following ontologies, as well as, those developed by other researchers related to spatial information system development (Drexel University, 2005; Jet Propulsion Laboratory — NASA, 2005; Umweltbundesamt — Austria, 2005; University of Muenster, 2005).

Spatial Information System Ontology

The use of ontologies in information systems (Guarino, 1998) and in spatial information systems has been discussed in Fonseca, Egenhofer, Agouris, and Câmara

Figure 3. Spatial information system ontology — proximate commuting system instance

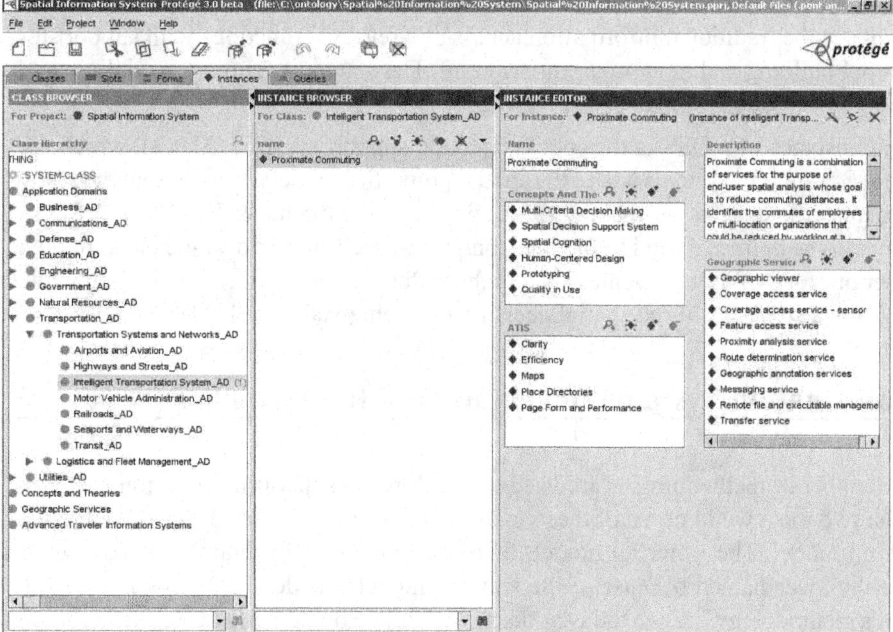

(2002), Fonseca, Egenhofer, Davis, and Câmara (2002), Lin and Ludäscher (2003), and Weissenberg, Voisard, and Gartmann (2004). The following example builds on the ideas and concepts of these researchers and presents a methodology for spatial information system development. This methodology assists developers in determining how best to organize and incorporate the various ontologies into a coherent, useful, ontology-based ISDT for spatial information systems. Figure 3 is an illustration of this ontology as developed in Protégé.

In the above example, various ontologies related to spatial information system development have been merged into an instance of a spatial information system ontology using the application domain ontology as the organizing framework. These ontologies, detailed below, include concepts and theories, geographic services, and advanced traveler information systems. As seen in this example, an instance of an Intelligent transportation system, a proximate commuting system, has been designed using these ontologies.

Concepts and Theories Ontology

Spatial Decision Support Systems

Decision support systems (DSS) are "interactive, computer-based systems that aid users in judgment and choice activities. They provide data storage and retrieval but enhance the traditional information access and retrieval functions with support for model building and model-based reasoning. They support framing, modeling, and problem solving" (Druzdzel & Flynn, 2000, p. 794).

One instance of a DSS is the spatial decision support systems (SDSS), which are decision support systems where the spatial properties of the data to be analyzed play a major role in decision-making (Seffino, Medeiros, Rocha, & Yi, 1999). A SDSS can also be defined as an interactive, computer-based system designed to support a user or group of users in achieving a higher effectiveness of decision making while solving a semi-structured spatial decision problem (Malczewski, 1997).

Information Systems Development Methodologies

A number of methodologies are used to develop and support information systems. The two most well known of these methodologies are the waterfall model and the spiral model. The waterfall model, first developed by Royce and popularized by Boehm, was named because of the way the model was depicted (Abrams, 1998). This methodology, known today as the systems development life cycle, is a common method for systems development in many organizations, featuring several phases that mark the progress of the systems analysis and design effort (Hoffer, George, & Valacich, 1998). The spiral model depicts the systems development life cycle as a series of cycles in which the development team cycles through each of the phases at varying levels of detail (Hoffer et al., 1998).

To some observers, the waterfall model appears to focus on a linear-bounded process, while the spiral model emphasizes cyclic recurring activities. Others have observed that the waterfall can be rolled up or the spiral can be unrolled, thereby mapping one model to the other (Abrams, 1998). The cyclic or iterative nature of these approaches is especially characteristic of rapid application development methods such as prototyping (Hoffer et al., 1998).

The prototyping development methodology has been described as a revolutionary rather than an evolutionary change in the system development process (Naumann & Jenkins, 1982). Prototyping is a four-step interactive process between the user and the builder. Here, an initial version is defined, constructed, and used quickly; as problems and misfits are discovered, revisions and enhancements are made to the working system in its user's environment (Naumann & Jenkins, 1982).

Human-Centered Design

One instance of an information systems development methodology is human-centered design. As defined by the International Standards Organization, human-centered design is an approach to interactive system development that focuses specifically on making systems useable (International Organization for Standardization, 1997). Human-centered design integrates a number of disciplines including information science and the behavioral sciences. Human-centered design has the following characteristics:

- Active involvement of users and a clear understanding of user task requirements
- Appropriate allocation of function between users and technology
- Iteration of design solutions
- Multi-disciplinary design

The International Organization for Standardization has outlined a methodology (International Organization for Standardization, 1997), which includes specific steps to take during system development to address the above characteristics. These human-centered design activities include:

- Understanding and specifying the context of use
- Specifying the user and organizational requirements
- Producing design solutions
- Evaluating designs against requirements

This human-centered design process iterates through these activities until the system meets specified functional, user, and organizational requirements.

Quality in Use

Quality in use is defined as the extent to which an entity satisfies stated and implied needs when used under stated conditions (International Organization for Standardization, 1997). Put another way, quality in use is the combined effect of the software quality characteristics for the user (Bevan, 1999). As such, quality in use is the user's view of the quality of a system containing software measured in terms of the result of using the software rather than properties of the software itself. In addition, the relationship of quality in use to the other software quality characteristics depends on the type of user, for instance:

- For the end user, quality in use is mainly a result of functionality, reliability, usability, and efficiency.
- For the person maintaining the software, quality in use is a result of maintainability.
- For the person porting the software, quality in use is a result of portability.

Quality in use should be the major design objective for an interactive product so that the product can be used for its intended purpose. Increased quality in use brings significant benefits including the following:

- Increased efficiency
- Improved productivity
- Reduced errors
- Reduced training
- Improved acceptance

Figure 4 is an illustration of this ontology as developed in Protégé.

Figure 4. Concepts and theories ontology

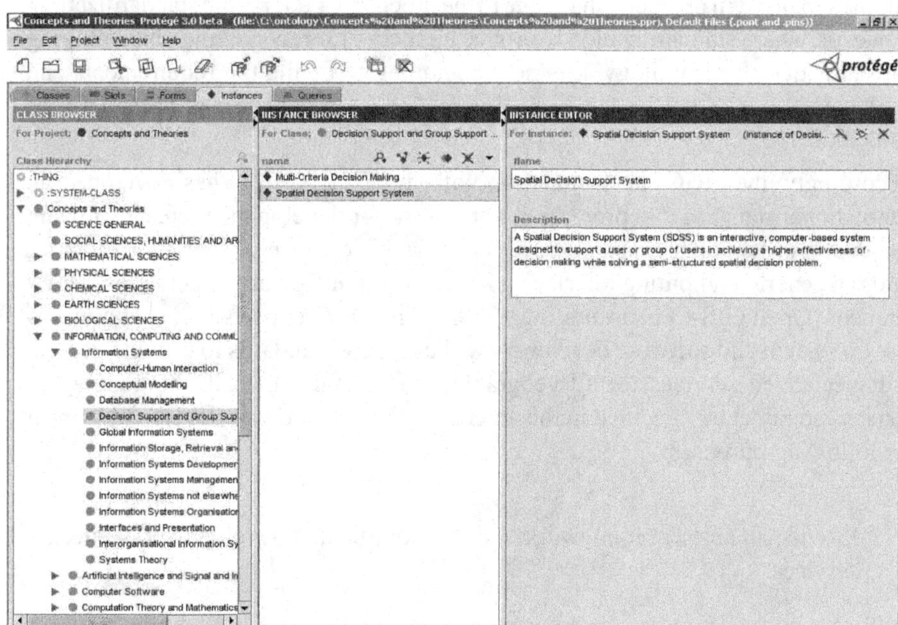

Geographic Services Ontology

The International Organization for Standardization has established a structured set of standards for information concerning objects or phenomena that are directly or indirectly associated with a location relative to the Earth (International Organization for Standardization, 2000). The mandate for the International Organization for Standardization Technical Committee (ISO/TC) 211 is to develop an integrated set of standards for geographic information that:

- Increases the understanding and usage of geographic information
- Increases the availability, access, integration, and sharing of geographic information
- Promotes the efficient, effective, and economic use of digital geographic information and associated hardware and software systems
- Contributes to a unified approach to addressing global ecological and humanitarian problems

The ISO/TC 211 expects that innovative, new, and unknown technologies and application domains will present a challenge to the process of geographic standardization. However, where standardization was once a process for recognizing and codifying the status quo of technology, it is now beginning to define the requirements and implementations of new technology (International Organization for Standardization, 2000).

Accordingly, the OGC, in conjunction with the ISO/TC 211, has developed an international standard that provides a framework for developers to create software that enables users to access and process geographic data from a variety of sources across a generic computing interface within an open information technology environment (Open GIS Consortium Inc., 2002). The OGC expects that spatial information system and software developers will use these standards to provide general and specialized services for all geographic information. In fact, the geographic services architecture specified in this international standard was developed to meet the following purposes:

- Provide an abstract framework to allow coordinated development of specific services

Figure 5. Geographic services ontology

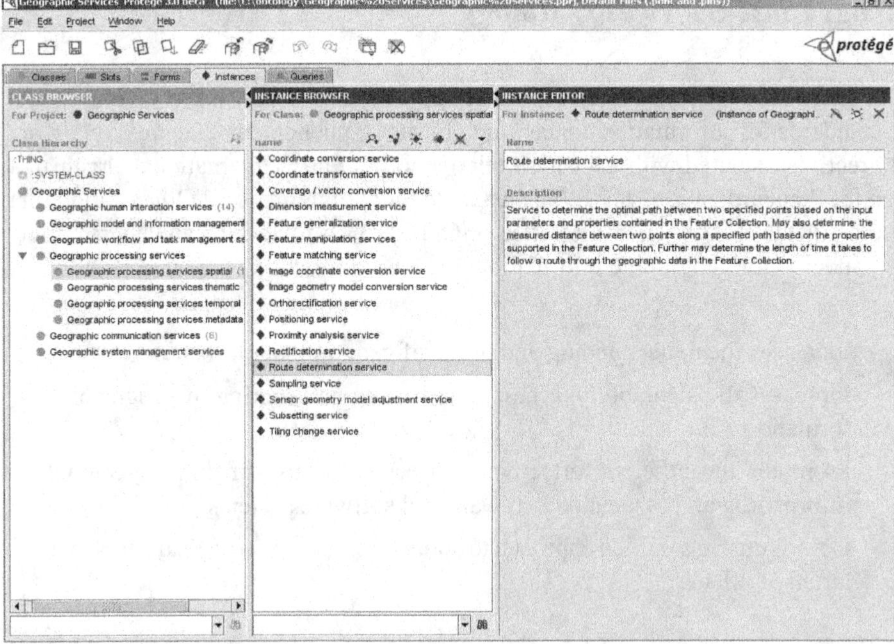

- Enable interoperable data services through interface standardization
- Support development of a service catalog through the definition of service metadata
- Allow separation of data instances and service instances
- Enable use of one provider's service on another provider's data
- Define an abstract framework, which can be implemented in multiple ways

The geographic services architecture specified in this international standard contains six classes of geospatial technology services. Contained within each of these classes are many geospatial design elements (instances); the complete list of geographic services as outlined by the OGC can be found in Open GIS Consortium Inc. (2002). Figure 5 is an illustration of this ontology as developed in Protégé.

Advanced Traveler Information Systems Ontology

Intelligent transportation systems (ITS) encompass a broad range of wireless and wireline communications-based information, control, and electronics technologies. When integrated into the transportation system infrastructure, and in vehicles themselves, these technologies help monitor and manage traffic flow, reduce congestion, provide alternate routes to travelers, enhance productivity, and save lives, time, and money (Intelligent Transportation Society of America, 2005). Examples of ITS include:

- Advanced traveler information systems deliver data directly to travelers, enabling them to make choices about alternate routes or modes of transportation.
- Advanced traffic management systems employ a variety of detectors, cameras, and communication systems to monitor traffic, optimize signal timings on major arterials, and control the flow of traffic.
- Incident management systems provide traffic operators with the tools to respond to accidents, hazardous spills, and other emergencies.

The advanced traveler information systems (ATIS) ontology is a compilation of several ATIS customer demand factors (traveler characteristics, trip types, and modes of transportation) and Transitweb design resources, both outlined as follows.

ATIS Customer Demand Factors

ATIS can be defined in two ways: (1) real-time network information, whether traffic or transit; and (2) traveler information, such as route guidance or destination information, provided on advanced technologies, such as mobile phones enabled by wireless application protocol, personal digital assistants, the Internet, and in-vehicle computers. Consequently, traveler demand for ATIS traffic services can be based on four factors:

1. Regional traffic context
2. Quality of ATIS services
3. Individual trip characteristics
4. Characteristics of the traveler

The regional traffic context includes attributes of the region, such as highway-roadway network and capacity, levels of traffic congestion, and future highway-roadway expansion plans. Information quality determines whether, how frequently, and with what level of confidence travelers consult traveler information. The trip purpose, the time and length of the trip, and the particular route or route choices available to the individual traveler all significantly affect whether individuals consult traffic information. The fourth factor includes user values and attitude characteristics, which are important determinants of use patterns, behavioral responses, and valuation of ATIS (Lappin, 2000).

Traveler Characteristics

A recent study (Pucher & Renne, 2003) found that the private car continues to dominate urban travel among every segment of the American population, including the poor, minorities, and the elderly. This study, drawing on the 2001 National Household Travel Survey, confirms most of the same travel trends and variations among socioeconomic groups documented by previous surveys. While the private car continues to dominate travel, there are important variations in auto ownership and travel behavior by household income, race/ethnicity, gender, and age. Overall, the poor, racial, and ethnic minorities, and the elderly have much lower mobility rates than the general population. Moreover, the poor, Blacks, and Hispanics are far more likely to use public transit than other groups (minorities and low-income households account for 63% of public transit riders). Different socioeconomic groups also have different rates of carpooling, taxi use, bicycling, and walking as well as travel different distances at different times of day.

Trip Types and Modes of Transportation

The Nationwide Personal Transportation Survey (Research Triangle Institute, 1997) is an inventory of daily personal travel and is an authoritative resource for national data on daily trips including:

- Purpose of the trip (work, shopping, etc.)
- Means of transportation used (car, bus, subway, walk, etc.)
- How long the trip took, that is, travel time
- Time of day the trip took place
- Day of week the trip took place, and, if a private vehicle trip
- Number of people in the vehicle, that is, vehicle occupancy
- Driver characteristics (age, sex, worker status, education level, etc.)
- Vehicle attributes (make, model, model year, amount of miles driven in a year)

As such, this resource is used to examine travel behavior at the individual and household level including: characteristics of travel (use of the various modes, amount and purpose of travel by time of day and day of week, and vehicle occupancy), the relationship between demographics and travel (changes in personal mobility among women, older Americans, and low-income households), and the public's perceptions of the transportation system.

TransitWeb Design Resources

TransitWeb, a service of the United States Department of Transportation, is an online portal designed to bring together a variety of resources to help transit agencies better communicate with their customers through Web sites and ITS-related technologies (United States Department of Transportation, 2005a). One of these resources, The Usability Guidelines for Transit Web Sites (United States Department of Transportation, 2005b), outlines five basic principles for achieving usable transit Web sites. These principles are:

- **Efficiency:** Minimize user time and effort to reach information
- **Clarity:** Make the available content and options as clear as possible to the user
- **Proportionality:** Keep design elements proportional to their functionality

- **Consistency:** Use consistent design elements on all pages
- **Organization:** Put related things together

There are many features that transit Web sites should provide to support these principles and TransitWeb has identified several of these design features:

- **Content organization:** Organizing, distributing, and linking content throughout the site
- **Navigation:** Design of the menu and other aids to site navigation common to all pages
- **Home page:** Design of the home page of the Web site
- **Maps:** Design of system and route maps
- **Itinerary maker:** Design of an interactive itinerary planner
- **Schedules:** Design of pages for accessing and displaying route schedules
- **Place directories:** Design of directories of streets, points of interest, towns, or other geographic features intended to provide users with a means to select an acceptable route when planning a trip

Figure 6. Advanced traveler information systems ontology

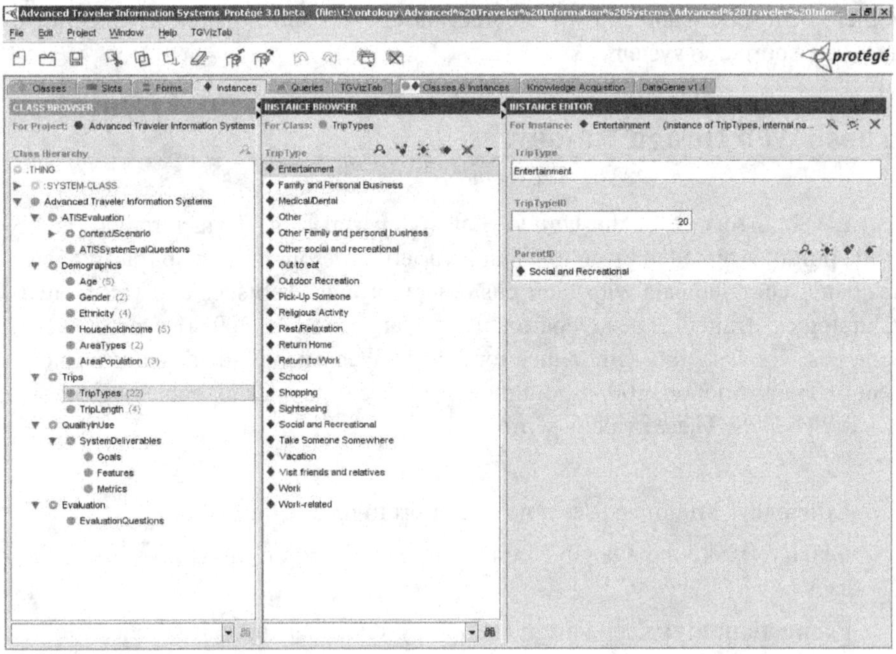

- **Page form and performance:** Design and characteristics of site pages in general
- **Content:** Form, format, and appearance of site content in general
- **Links:** Presence, position, and appearance of links in general

In addition, TransitWeb provides specific details regarding the qualities of these features. These qualities were transformed into the form of questions to guide the design process. Figure 6 is an illustration of this ontology as developed in Protégé.

Application Domains Ontology

The application domains ontology, a high-level classification schema, represents a large number of subject areas and encompasses a wide-range of disciplines specific to spatial information systems and applications. For example, the metadata++ model and system was developed as a domain-specific digital library for use in natural resource management in conjunction with the USDA Forest Service, the USDI Bureau of Land Management, and the USDI Fish and Wildlife Service (Delcambre et al., 2005). Similar application domain ontologies have been developed in this

Figure 7. Application domains ontology

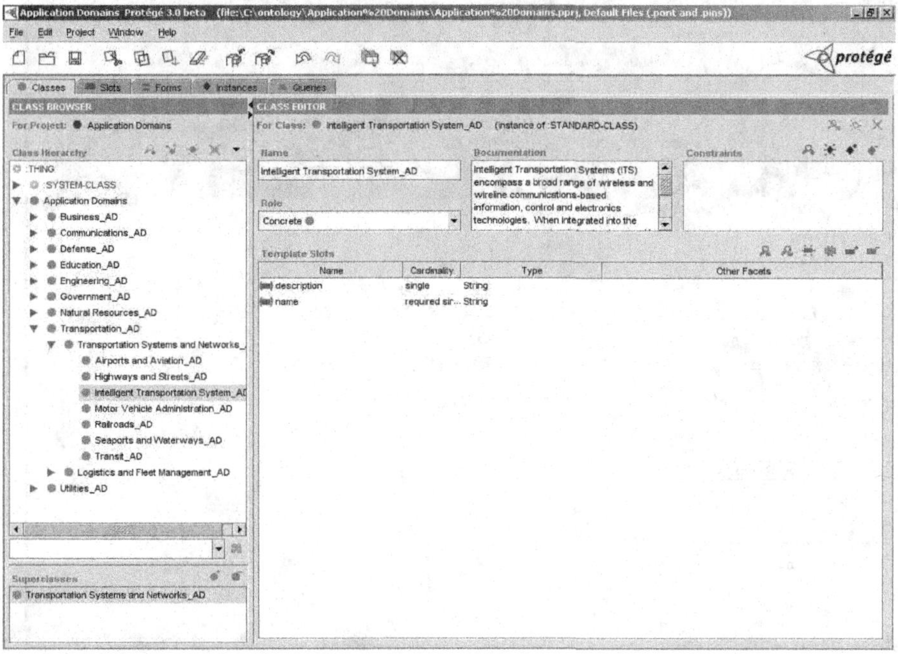

manner (Fonseca, Egenhofer, Agouris, & Câmara, 2002; Fonseca, Egenhofer, Davis, & Câmara, 2002; Lin & Ludäscher, 2003; Stoimenov, Stanimirovic, & Djordjevic-Kajan, 2005; Weissenberg et al., 2004). Figure 7 is an illustration of this ontology as developed in Protégé.

Conclusion and Future Research

The example presented above regarding the use and application of ontologies was relatively straightforward to organize and manage. However, as the number of ontologies grows, these issues (organization and management) will become of greater concern. Below is a discussion of one method to address these concerns.

Management of Ontology Libraries

An ontology library system is a library system that offers various functions for managing, adapting, and standardizing groups of ontologies and fulfills the needs

Figure 8. Spatial information system ontology library

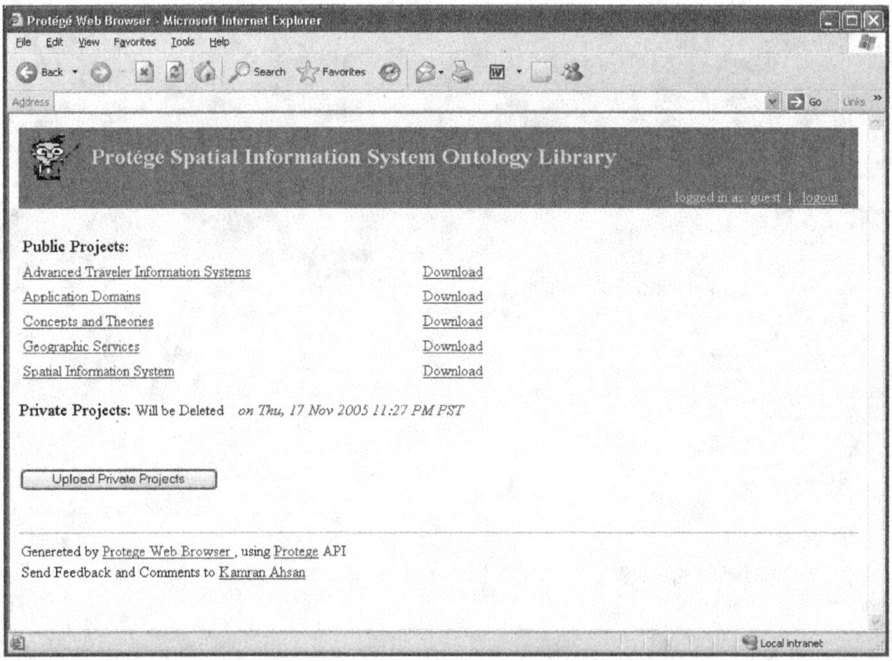

for re-use of ontologies (Ding & Fensel, 2001). The primary objective of ontology management systems is to provide holistic control over management activities for ontological information by externalizing them from application programs (Lee et al., 2004). The mapping of ontologies to conceptual schemas is made using three different levels of abstractions: formal, domain, and application levels (Fonseca, Davis, & Câmara, 2003). At the formal level, highly abstract concepts are used to express the schema and the ontologies. At the domain level, the schema is regarded as an instance of a generic model. At the application level, the focus is on the particular case of spatial application. Figure 8 illustrates an instance of a spatial information system ontology library with respect to the spatial information system described in the preceding sections.

The Protégé Web browser, seen in Figure 8, allows users to browse, share, and edit their protégé ontologies over the Internet. It also provides the functionality to perform a text-based search of the knowledge base.

The spatial information system presented above is one example of the use of ISDT and ontologies for the design and development of systems of this type. As the use of these systems grows, it is hoped that this method of system design and development will prove valuable.

References

Abrams, M. D. (1998). *Security engineering in an evolutionary acquisition environment.* Paper presented at the New Security Paradigms Workshop, Charlottsville, VA.

Bederson, B. B. (2001). *Making visualization work.* (Presentation): CS/HCI Depts, University of Maryland.

Bevan, N. (1999). Quality in use: Meeting user needs for quality. *The Journal of Systems and Software, 49*, 89-96.

Delcambre, L., Nielsen, M., Tolle, T., Weaver, M., Maier, D., & Price, S. (2005). *NSF project: Harvesting information to sustain our forests.* Paper presented at the National Digital Government Conference 2005, Atlanta, GA.

Ding, Y., & Fensel, D. (2001). *Ontology library systems: The key to successful ontology re-use.* Paper presented at the Infrastructure and Applications for the Semantic Web, International Semantic Web Working Symposium, Stanford, CA.

Drexel University (2005). *List of ontologies for geographic information standards provided by ISO.* Retrieved from http://loki.cae.drexel.edu%7Ewbs/ontology/list.htm

Druzdzel, M. J., & Flynn, R. R. (2000). *Decision support systems: Encyclopedia of library and information science*. New York: Marcel Dekker, Inc.

Embley, D. W. (2004). *Toward semantic understanding — an approach based on information extraction ontolgies.* Paper presented at the Proceedings of the Fifteenth Conference on Australasian Database, Dunedin, New Zealand.

Fensel, D. (2003). *Ontologies: A silver bullet for knowledge management and electronic commerce*. Berlin, DE: Springer-Verlag.

Fonseca, F., Davis, C., & Câmara, G. (2003). Bridging ontologies and conceptual schemas in geographic information integration. *GeoInformatica, 7*(4), 355-378.

Fonseca, F., Egenhofer, M., Agouris, P., & Câmara, G. (2002). Using ontologies for integrated geographic information systems. *Transactions in GIS, 6*(3), 231-257.

Fonseca, F., Egenhofer, M., Davis, C., & Câmara, G. (2002). Semantic granularity in ontology-driven geographic information systems. *Annals of Mathematics and Artificial Intelligence, 36*(1-2), 121-151.

Freeman, D., & Hart, D. (2004). A science of design for software-intensive systems. *Communications of the ACM, 47*(8), 19-21.

Geroimenko, V. (2003). *Dictionary of XML technologies and the semantic Web.* Berlin, DE: Springer Verlag.

Gershon, N., Eick, S., & Card, S. K. (1998, March-April). Information visualization. *Interactions, 5*(2), 9-15.

Green, G., Kennedy, P., & McGown, A. (2002). Management of multi-method engineering design research: A case study. *Journal of Engineering Technology Management, 19*, 131-140.

Grimshaw, D. (2000). *Bringing geographical information systems into business.* New York: John Wiley and Sons, Inc.

Gruber, T. R. (1993). A translation approach to portable ontology specification. *Knowledge Acquisition, 5*, 199-220.

Guarino, N. (1998). *Formal ontology and information systems.* Paper presented at the 1st International Conference on Formal Ontology in Information Systems (FOIS '98), Trento, IT.

Hevner, A., March, S., Park, J. A, & Ram, S. (March, 2004). Design science in information systems research. *MIS Quarterly, 28*(1), 75-105.

Hilton, B. (2003). *The impact of open source software and Web services on information system development: An investigation of proximate computing.* Claremont, CA: School of Information Science, Claremont Graduate University.

Hoffer, J. A., George, J. F., & Valacich, J. S. (1998). *Modern systems analysis and design*. Reading, MA: Addison-Wesley.

Intelligent Transportation Society of America. (2005). *What is ITS?* Retrieved from http://www.itsa.org/subject.nsf/vLookupAboutITSA/What+is+ITS!OpenDocument

International Organization for Standardization. (1997). *Human-centered design processes for interactive systems* (ISO 13407). Geneva.

International Organization for Standardization. (2000). *Draft Business Plan of ISO/TC 211 — geographic information/geomatics*. Geneva.

Jet Propulsion Laboratory — NASA (2005). *Semantic Web for Earth and Environmental Terminology Ontologies*. Retrieved from http://sweet.jpl.nasa.gov/ontology/

Kreuseler, M., & Schumann, H. (1999). Information visualization using a new focus + context technique in combination with dynamic clustering of information space. In *Proceedings of ACM PNPIVM 1999,* Kansas City, MO (pp. 1-5). New York: ACM Press.

Lappin, J. (2000). What have we learned about intelligent transportation systems and customer satisfaction? In J. E. Lappin (Ed.), *What have we learned about intelligent transportation systems? For the ITS Joint Program Office, Federal Highway Administration* (JPO Doc. No. 13390). Washington, DC: United States Department of Transportation, Federal Highway Administration.

Lee, J., Goodwin, R., Akkiraju, R., Ranganathan, A., Verma, K., & Goh, S. W. (2004). *Towards enterprise-scale ontology management*. Hawthorne, NY: IBM T. J. Watson Research Center.

Lin, K., & Ludäscher, B. (2003). *A system for semantic integration of geologic maps via ontologies*. Paper presented at the Semantic Web Technologies for Searching and Retrieving Scientific Data, Sanibel Island, FL.

Linkova, Z., Nedbal, R., & Rimnac, M. (2005). *Building ontologies for GIS* (No. 932). Prague, CZ: Institute of Computer Science, Academy of Sciences of the Czech Republic.

Malczewski, J. (1997, October 6, 1998). *Spatial decision support systems, NCGIA core curriculum in GIScience*. Retrieved from http://www.ncgia.ucsb.edu/giscc/units/u127/u127.html

Markus, L., Majchrzak, A., & Gasser, L. (2002). A design theory for systems that support emergent knowledge processes. *MIS Quarterly, 26*(3), 179-212.

Naumann, J. D., & Jenkins, A. M. (1982). Prototyping: The new paradigm for systems development. *MIS Quarterly, 6*(3), 29-44.

Noy, N. F., & McGuinness, D. L. (2003). *Ontology development 101: A guide to creating your first ontology*. Retrieved from http://protege.stanford.edu/

NSF. (2004). Science of design for information systems: Report of the NSF workshop, Seattle, 2003. *ACM SIGMOD Record, 33*(1), 133-137.

Open GIS Consortium Inc. (2002). *The OpenGIS Abstract Specification, Topic 12: OpenGIS Service Architecture, Version 4.3*. Wayland, MA: Open GIS Consortium, Inc.

Orlikowski, W., & Iacono, C. (2001). Desperately seeking the "IT" in IT research — a call to theorizing the IT artifact. *Information Systems Research, 12*(2), 121-134.

Pucher, J., & Renne, J. (2003). Socioeconomics of urban travel: Evidence from the 2001 NHTS. *Transportation Quarterly, 57*(3), (49–77).

Research Triangle Institute. (1997). *Nationwide personal transportation survey* (No. FHWA-PL-98-002). Research Triangle Park, NC: Research Triangle Institute.

Rodriguez, D. A. (2001). *Proximate commuting: Hype or potential? An evaluation* (No. Transportation Research Record 1675). Washington, DC: Transportation Research Board, National Research Council.

Seffino, L. A., Medeiros, C. B., Rocha, J. V., & Yi, B. (1999). WOODSS — a spatial decision support system based on workflows. *Decision Support Systems, 27*, 105-123.

Shneiderman, B. (1999). *Crossing the information visualization chasm*. Retrieved March 15, 2004, from http://www.cs.umd.edu/hcil/pubs/presentations/info-viz-chasmslides/

Shneiderman, B., Card, S. K., Norman, D. A., Tremaine, M., & Waldrop, M. M. (2001). CHI@20: Fighting our way from marginality to power. In *ACM CHI 2002 Conference on Human Factors in Computing Systems* (pp. 688-691). Minneapolis, MN: ACM Press.

Simon, H. (1996). *The sciences of the artificial* (3rd ed.). Cambridge, MA: MIT Press.

Smith, B. (2003). Ontology. In L. Floridi (Ed.), *Blackwell guide to the philosophy of computing and information* (pp. 155-166). Oxford, UK: Blackwell.

Stanford Medical Informatics. (2003). *Protégé-2000 user's guide*. Retrieved from http://protege.stanford.edu/

Stoimenov, L., Stanimirovic, A., & Djordjevic-Kajan, S. (2005). *Development of GIS interoperability infrastructure in local community environment.* Paper presented at the FIG Working Week 2005, and the 8th International Conference for Global Spatial Data Infrastructure (GSDI-8), Cairo, EG.

Sugumaran, V., & Storey, V. C. (2002). Ontologies for conceptual modeling: Their creation, use, and management. *Data Knowledge and Engineering, 42*(3), 251-271.

Truex, D. (2001). Three issues concerning relevance in IS research: Epistemology, audience, and method. *Communications of AIS, 6*(24), 1-10.

Umweltbundesamt—Austria. (2005). *Umweltbundesamt: CEDEXProtege.* Retrieved from http://www.unweltbundesamt.at/umweeltdaten/schnittsellen/cedex/cedex_protege/?&tempL=1

United States Department of Transportation. (2005a). *TransitWeb: A Website design and traveler information resource for transit agencies.* Retrieved from http://www.transitweb.its.dot.gov/Introduction.asp

United States Department of Transportation (2005b). *Website Usability Guidelines —an online handbook for making public transit Web sites easy to use.* Retrieved from http://www.transitweb.its.dot.gov/guidelines/complete_guidelines.asp

University of Muenster. (2005). *Ontologies developed in ACE-GIS.* Retrieved from http://musil.uni-muenster.de/onto/ACE/

Vaishnavi, V., & Kuechler, W. (2004, January 20). *Design research in information systems.* Retrieved from http://www.isworld.org/Researchdesign/drisISworld.htm

Victoria Transport Policy Institute. (2005). *Online transportation demand management encyclopedia.* Retrieved from http://www.vtpi.org/tdm/index.php

Walls, J. G., Widmeyer, G. R., & El Sawy, O. A. (1992). Building an information system design theory for vigilant EIS. *Information Systems Research, 3*(1), 36-59.

Weissenberg, N., Voisard, A., & Gartmann, R. (2004). *Using ontologies in personalized mobile applications.* Paper presented at the 12th Annual ACM International Workshop on Geographic Information Systems, Washington, DC.

Section II

Challenges for Spatial Information Systems

Chapter III

Geospatially Enabled Directory for Emergency Response Interoperability

Judith Woodhall, COMCARE, USA

Abstract

This chapter discusses how the need for geospatially-enabled data messaging among emergency response agencies can be enabled with the Emergency Provider Access Directory (EPAD). It describes the directory, how it enables message routing, and its fit into a broader E-Safety Network. It also discusses the architectural components of the EPAD, specifically the geographic information system (GIS) module, and how Web services and open source products were used in the design to enhance the EPAD service offering, an offering that has the potential to bring emergency agencies one step closer to realizing interagency interoperability for advanced response to emergency events.

Introduction

In an era when technology can bring news, current events, and entertainment to the farthest reaches of the world, many emergency response agencies cannot share data with one another, even if they are in the same jurisdiction. Yet, emergencies demand real-time data. Most of today's efforts to improve interoperability have been focused on wireless voice communications. Led by state and local public safety experts and supported by the Department of Homeland Security (DHS), SAFECOM program, and significant federal funding, wireless first responder interoperability is moving forward. While voice or radio interoperability is a critical need for responders at the scene, voice represents only one side of the interoperability equation.

COMCARE is a national non-profit alliance dedicated to advancing emergency response by promoting modern, interoperable emergency communications systems, and the development of new procedures, training, and tools to maximize value for emergency responders. COMCARE encourages cooperation across professional, jurisdictional, and geographic lines, and works to integrate the emergency response professions, government, private industry, and the public. Its vision is to create an environment of borderless, geographically-targeted information sharing to achieve the most advanced response to emergencies. To that end, it has created the E-Safety Network, a framework for establishing a unified emergency Web services information architecture that ties together the various data systems used by all emergency response organizations.[1]

Background

Even after September 11, 2001, Columbine, the Northeast blackout, the California wildfires, and the recent hurricane seasons, there is still no national comprehensive emergency infrastructure that allows agencies to communicate data with one another across professions and across jurisdictions. Time and time again, important information about an emergency event does not reach the right people at the right time, resulting in unnecessary loss of life and property. During the 2003 SARS (severe acute respiratory syndrome) outbreak in Toronto, first responders and emergency medical personnel learned of the outbreak through the media, not from public health officials, hospitals, or other medical organizations (SARS Commission, 2004).

During the Oklahoma City bombing incident, responders lacked important information needed to understand damage from the blast and where victims might be found. According to the former assistant chief of the Oklahoma City Fire Department, it would have been useful to have blueprints, personnel lists, and data estimating blast effects and impacts to the buildings early in the response process. Other communications problems also hindered response efforts. Because of overload and chaos, voice communications were unreliable. In addition, the 9-1-1 center did not have a direct line to the Emergency Medical Services (EMS) agency, and hospitals were not even in the communications loop. According to the Police Department Final Report, this situation highlighted the need for electronic data links between emergency agencies and the need to extend data access into the field (Manzi, Powers, & Zetterman, 2002).

On January 6, 2005, at 2:40 AM, two freight trains collided in Graniteville, South Carolina, releasing an estimated 11,500 gallons of chlorine gas (CDC, 2005). Two hours later, the public information director was asked to issue a federal Emergency Alert System (EAS) warning (Lipowicz, 2005). The director used the telephone to issue the warning to local radio and TV stations, but he could not be certain it actually reached anyone. Because of the early hour, many radio stations were not staffed, and there was no guarantee that residents were listening to the radio or watching TV. The Federal Communications Commission (FCC) mandates that all TV and radio stations are required to carry any presidential warning message. However, when operated regionally, it relies on voluntary participation from radio and broadcast television stations (FCC, 2004). And its reach is limited. The system does not include all the other communications devices that consumers have (from cable TV to personal computers with Internet access to telephones, cell phones, and beepers). Most residents did not know about the spill until they woke up and had limited time to react. Unfortunately for them, chlorine gas is so deadly that it was used as a chemical weapon in World War I. The gas is heavier than air and sinks to the ground. Unknowingly, some Graniteville residents dropped down to the ground to get air as they might in a smoky fire (Hajek, Shapiro, Cooper, & Lewis, 2005). This mistake cost them their lives. A better, more targeted, and comprehensive public warning system could have helped (Lipowicz, 2005).

In all these events, emergency agencies and responders lacked vital information about who should be contacted and how. In some instances, voice communications did not work; in others, voice was inadequate. Data communications facilitated by a routing service could have helped to deliver the right information to those who needed it.

Of course, many agencies do exchange data electronically. Unfortunately, they either do so within their own professional silos (law enforcement to law enforcement, fire to fire, etc.) or they use the same software products. If agencies want to share data but do not want to procure the same software, they must absorb the costs of customizing an interface and developing their own routing directories so that they know to whom, to where, and how information should flow. As many agencies have learned, this customization scenario only leads to software incompatibility and obsolescence when one or both agencies buy new software or install upgrades. In addition, the cost of keeping a routing directory up-to-date can sky rocket.

It is impractical to expect all of the 100,000+ emergency agencies in the United States to use the same software or to spend limited funds developing customized interfaces and proprietary data routing utilities. However, many agencies have done just that. The result has been multiple specialized directories of varying levels of completeness and accuracy; all failing to provide a practical and reliable basis for routing emergency information immediately to all of the right agencies, particularly when multiple professions or jurisdictions are involved.

Another facet of the problem is that few, if any, of the existing directories can be queried in geospatial terms. Moreover, these directories generally function in a "top-down" sense, operating through telephone trees and "blast-fax" systems, or at best, mass e-mail alerts, and are often effectively useless for intercommunication between parties at "ground level" or for timely relay of information back to decision-makers at the top.

The lack of a shared, comprehensive routing directory is not only a problem during major emergencies and disasters; it is also increasingly evident that it would have significant value in day-to-day emergency operations. For example, the consumer and commercial telematics providers, such as OnStar[2] and Qualcomm,[3] need to deliver vehicle incident data, immediately after a theft or accident, to a number of agencies such as law enforcement, fire, emergency medical services, hospitals, and transportation, but either do not know who those agencies are, or their computer addresses, or, usually, both. In another incident, an urgent alert or public warning may need to be delivered to recipients in a geographic area, which may or may not correspond to any predetermined jurisdictional or physical boundary. In addition, in a large-scale disaster there is an immediate and massive requirement to marshal state and local first responder resources. Each of these scenarios requires a directory to route information based on the geography of the emergency event. COMCARE's E-Safety Network enabled by the Emergency Provider Access Directory[4] (EPAD) can provide one solution.

Architecture Overview

Architectures can be broken down into macro and micro levels. At the macro level, enterprise architectures provide a big picture view and encourage holistic understanding of various parts that make up the architecture. They manage the complexity of the enterprise and align business strategies with implementations. At the micro level, system architectures define the form and function of a system by defining discrete, non-overlapping parts or components. The E-Safety Network provides the enterprise architecture for interoperable emergency data communications that includes the EPAD system.

Figure 1. E-Safety Network: Five architectural layers

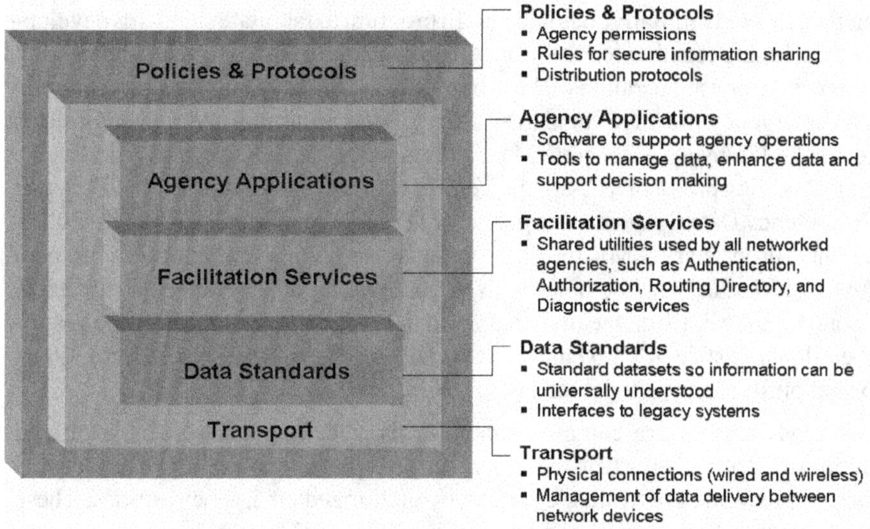

E-Safety Network

The E-Safety Network is a unified emergency Web services information architecture that ties together the various application systems used by law enforcement, fire, emergency medical, public health, transportation, emergency management, and homeland security agencies, among others (COMCARE, October, 2004). It treats the entire emergency response community as one extended enterprise, providing a framework within which each entity can operate. It is open, platform-neutral, and standards-based to enable flexible interoperability across organizations, technology platforms, and implementation methods.

There are five architectural layers (Figure 1) that must be in place to achieve effective data interoperability. These layers include data *transport*, *data standards*, shared *facilitation services*, individual *agency applications*, and the *policies and protocols* that govern the use of the system when data interoperability is achieved.

The *transport* layer represents the networks used for communications. This layer manages the end-to-end delivery of messages and determines how data are transferred between network devices. It manages user sessions and dialogues and controls the establishment and termination of logic links between users. The E-Safety Network requires reliable and secure broadband data connections using Internet protocols.

Data standards create a common language that enables data sharing among individual agency application systems. The Department of Homeland Security Disaster Management eGov Initiative has launched a program to facilitate standards development by bringing together leaders from all professions needing to share data during emergency response operations. These practitioners develop and field test common sets of emergency message standards. Over the last year, this and related projects have resulted in many eXtensible Markup Language (XML) standards such as the common alerting protocol[5] (CAP), the Vehicular Emergency Data Set[6] (VEDS), and the Emergency Data Exchange Language[7] (EDXL) suite of standards (XML, 2005). These non-proprietary XML message formats use simple object access protocol (SOAP) "packaging" for both specialized and general emergency data exchange. For content, they draw on the dictionary and data model work of other efforts such as the Global Justice XML Data Model (OJP, 2005) and the new DHS National Information Exchange Model (NIEM) (NIEM, 2005).

Facilitation services are common shared tools, services, and resources offered through a collective effort of the emergency response community. They enable interoperability and are available for use by authorized emergency entities. These services include, but are not limited to, security, diagnostics, routing directory, identity management, access control, digital rights management, and authentication. By using these shared facilitation services, agencies do not have to spend their limited funds creating and maintaining these functions on their own. EPAD as a routing directory is one of these services.

The fourth layer represents the wide array of *agency applications* used for emergency preparedness, response, and recovery. These systems include complex computer-aided dispatch systems (CAD), Web-based emergency management tools, local and statewide geographic information systems (GIS), hospital capacity reporting systems, and other innovative applications for data collection, analysis, and presentation. Agencies are encouraged to purchase systems that best meet their needs. However, in order to operate within the E-Safety Network, these applications must be able to send and receive XML messages to and from other applications in standardized formats. It should not matter to a 9-1-1 CAD system that it is receiving data from an emergency management tool about a flood, a telematics message from OnStar, a bio-terrorism alert from the Center for Disease Control (CDC), or data from a wireless or Voice over Internet protocol (VoIP) call. The same standardized data interface should be used.

Lastly, the E-Safety Network is not complete without the *policies and protocols* that determine rules for operating within it. Does a hospital have the same privileges as the county Department of Transportation (DOT), the 9-1-1 center, the police, or the towing company? Who has access to what data and who is allowed to send what messages? Some of these policies are already in place today. For instance, a 9-1-1 center is required to alert certain agencies when there is a hazardous materials (HAZMAT). A fire chief becomes the incident commander if there is an explosion, and then sets up an Incident Command System (ICS) with required sections and reports. Emergency Medical Services (EMS) may only administer certain kinds of treatment to patients in ambulances. Only the secretary of DHS or his designee can change the alert level, or communicate it. Only the president or his designee can activate the Emergency Alerting System. These are only a few examples of the types of policies and protocols needed for data interoperability. Many more still need to be developed before this type of architecture is deployed.

Emergency Provider Access Directory

The Emergency Provider Access Directory is a facilitation service as described above. As a routing directory, it is the cornerstone of the E-Safety Network because without it, the routing of geographically-targeted emergency messages could not occur. The idea is simple: Create a directory that allows authorized emergency response organizations (not individuals) to register so they can receive information about emergency events for which they have a need or interest. Registration enables agencies to receive the right information when they need it; it prevents the receipt of unwanted or irrelevant information. This simple act of EPAD registration supports the automatic routing of vital information about a mass emergency or a single event quickly and securely.

During registration, agencies and other organizations involved in emergency response efforts choose what information (emergency event types[8]) they want to receive for which geographic areas. They indicate when and how they want to receive it, and they classify their information so that only those with the proper authority can access it. Once entities are registered, messaging systems (or application systems with messaging capabilities) can query EPAD to determine to which agencies they need to send information. EPAD returns a list of agencies along with their computer addresses and prioritized contact information so that messages can be automatically routed to responsible agencies based on their geographic areas of responsibility and their incident information preferences.

EPAD System Architecture

The EPAD system follows an N-tier architectural design (Figure 2) that separates software into different functional areas: presentation layer, business logic layer, common business layer, infrastructure service layer, and data access layer. The Web services integration layer within the EPAD system allows for a standardized interface to be exposed and provides data for applications that require information from

Figure 2. EPAD N-tier system architecture

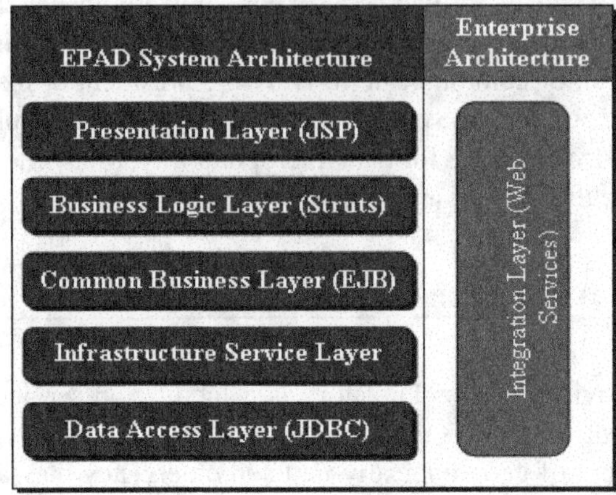

Figure 3. EPAD system view

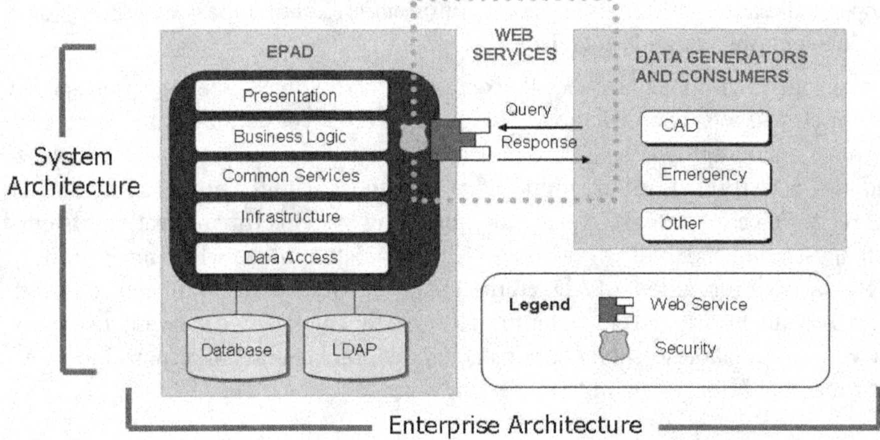

the EPAD. The components that make up the N-tiered system, including the data sources, will not expose any remote interface to external applications. All external applications will communicate to the EPAD through the Web services interface (Figure 3) (COMCARE, June, 2005).

The functional architecture of the EPAD identifies six distinct Web service components as well as three standard XML interfaces that interact with the EPAD system. The EPAD Web service components include:

- **Administration services:** for agency and user set-up
- **Directory services:** for housing agency information
- **Geographic information system (GIS) services:** for establishing jurisdictional or interest area boundaries
- **Identity rights management services:** for authentication and authorization
- **Import services:** for the automatic uploading of agency and GIS information into the EPAD when agencies already have this information electronically from other in-house systems
- **Directory management services:** for ensuring data integrity and reporting on directory activity

The three standard XML interfaces include:

- **Incident sending and routing query:** where the EPAD is queried to determine if the agency is authorized to send an incident message and who within a given area should receive the message
- **Authentication/authorization query:** to determine the authenticity of and privileges granted to a given agency/user
- **GIS query:** to establish, view, and name specific geographic areas

While all of these components are needed, the geographic information system (GIS) services module is the most critical for the agency notification capability enabled by the EPAD. It allows agencies to specify jurisdictions and geographic areas of interest pertinent to their responsibility. Using the GIS services module, agencies attribute these areas of interest with event type(s), responsibility type (primary, support, advisory, or informational), and the timeframes in which their interests are active. For example, a fire department may need to respond to fire emergencies for multiple counties, but only has EMS responsibility within one county. It may also provide backup services for a third county during certain timeframes. All of these conditions must be identified during the registration process so that the system can accurately identify who needs to be notified when.

EPAD Technology Components

COMCARE's goal is to design EPAD using open source technology whenever possible. The use of open source technologies was driven by COMCARE to achieve interoperability with other systems, scalability in terms of performance and cost, reusability, and minimal vendor lock-in to a particular platform. Table 1 lists the

Table 1. EPAD solution set; open source solutions are in italics

Logical Component	Product	Version
Operating System	*Red Hat Linux Enterprise AS*	Enterprise AS 4.0
Web Server	*Apache Web Server*	Apache 1.3 & 2.x
Web Container	*Tomcat*	Tomcat 4.x & 5.x
Application Server	*JBoss Application Server*	JBoss AS 4.x
Database	*PostgreSQL (including Spatial PostgreSQL)*	PostgreSQL 8.x
LDAP Server	Sun ONE Directory Server*	Sun ONE DS 5.2+
Access Manager and Identity Manager	Oracle/Oblix COREid, SHAREid, and COREsv	COREid: 7.0.3+, SHAREid: 2.5+, COREsv 4.+
GIS Components	*PostGIS*	PostGIS 1.0
	MapServer	MapServer 4.4.2
	GeoServer	GeoServer 1.2.4
	Moxi Media IMF	IMF Enterprise Edition (for OpenGIS)
	TopoZone Web Mapping Service	GeoZone OGC WMS

*Note: * Sun Directory Server was used instead of Open LDAP because the solution selected for access control and identity management did not support Open LDAP.*

open and proprietary products used in the EPAD system. These products reside on different servers and are used to support all EPAD functions. Figure 4 shows the interactions among the components and the systems on which they reside.

Tomcat is an open source product that is commonly referred to as a "Web" or "servlet" container and has the ability to run on the chosen Linux operating system. It implements the servlet and the Java Server Pages (JSP) specifications from Sun Microsystems. Since Tomcat does not fully support the Java 2 Enterprise Edition (J2EE) and is unable to execute Enterprise Java Beans (EJBs), the JBoss application server is used as the EJB container.

PostgreSQL is one of the recommended open source database solutions for Linux. It is an object-relational database management system (ORDBMS) based on POSTGRES, Version 4.2, developed at the University of California at Berkeley Computer Science Department. It is highly scalable and is optimized to store and process geospatial data.

Public, free spatial data is being used to define agency boundaries nationwide. The data, known as topologically integrated geographic encoding and referencing (TIGER) data, is provided by the United States Census Bureau and can be used to derive layers for state, county, local government, and tribal jurisdictions. TIGER boundary data for the EPAD are extracted and loaded using open source PostGIS[9] which spatially enables the PostgreSQL object relational database.

Figure 4. EPAD system layout

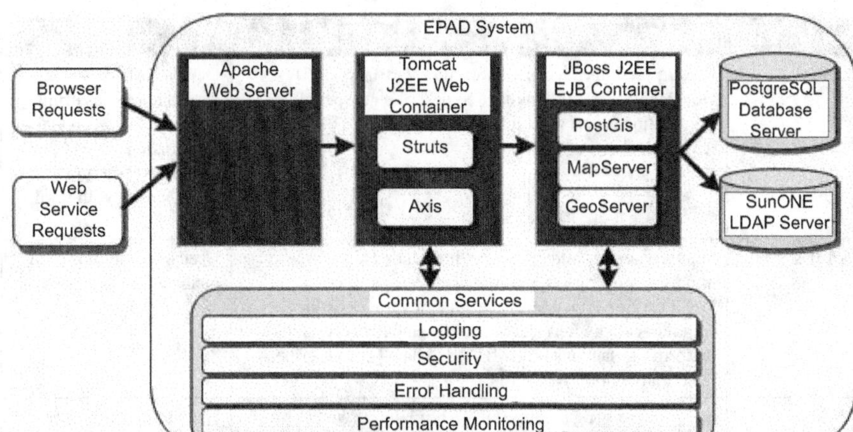

MapServer, an open source map generation component, is used to create maps for interactive EPAD applications. MapServer is accessed using the Open Geospatial Consortium (OGC) Web Map Service (WMS) protocol (2004). Moxi Media™ is an OGC compliant, non-open source rapid development environment written primarily in JSP. Moxi Media™ is used in the EPAD to support the interactive mapping portion of the EPAD and to generate map views and map thumbnails.

Base mapping is being provided via a remote WMS service provided by TopoZone. When an agency map thumbnail is created in the EPAD for an interest area, separate WMS calls are made, one local to display the jurisdiction boundaries, one remote to TopoZone to generate a basemap. Then the two images are overlaid to create the map thumbnail in the EPAD. In the interactive mapping portion of the EPAD application, the boundary and base map images are retrieved and overlaid as transparent graphic image files to create the map view.

Table 2 summarizes the national geospatial standards used in the EPAD GIS module (COMCARE, June, 2005).

EPAD GIS Services Module

There are two main components in the EPAD GIS services module: an administration interface to support visual interaction with geospatial information, and a query interface to support the Web services queries to the GIS database.

Table 2. National geospatial standards used in EPAD

National Geospatial Standards		
GML 3.1.1	https://portal.opengeospatial.org/files/?artifact_id=7174 Geography Markup Language to describe geospatial information (v2.x) with enhanced features (v3.0 – 3D, temporal, etc)	OGC's XML-based language used as primary definition of geospatial information stored in PostGIS server and interchanged with third parties
WFS 1.0 & 1.1	http://geoserver.sourceforge.net/html/index.php http://www.opengeospatial.org/specs/?page=specs Web Feature Service interface specification to define communication interface with WFS-enabled servers to perform transactions on GML-based data (get, describe, lock, transaction) over HTTP	Used as communication media with GeoServer
WMS 1.3	http://mapserver.gis.umn.edu/doc.html, http://www.opengeospatial.org/specs/?page=specs OGC's web map service interface specification to define requests for mapping information retrieved over HTTP. Capable of retrieving multiple map layers.	Used as communication media with MapServer to retrieve map layer information or map snapshots based on geo point definitions (lat/long, projection, output type — JPEG, GIF, etc)
SFS 1.1	http://www.postgis.org/ Simple features specification for SQL is OGC's specification to represent data model for storing of geospatial information using SQL92 with geometry types.	Used for storing of geospatial information in PostGIS Server

The administration interface presents a series of pull-down menus that allow an agency to select jurisdictional polygons and associate them with information about the agency and its emergency response capabilities. The combination of these polygons with information about an agency's capabilities forms the spatial EPAD database. The second component is the query support for the Web service interface. The EPAD Web service allows organizations that have defined an incident location to pass location information and event type information to EPAD, causing EPAD to spatially query the EPAD database and develop lists of agencies for alert purposes. The message sent to EPAD from these agencies contains spatial object(s) in OGC well known text (WKT) format (see Figure 5 for examples) representing the locations of incidents as geographic primitives (points, lines, and polygons). WKT is then used in the OGC simple feature specification for SQL format (1999) that is used to query the database.

When an emergency event occurs and a system needs to send an incident message, that system sends a Web service query (Figure 6) to the EPAD and its respective

Figure 5. WKT examples

POINT(10 10)
- A Point.

LINESTRING(10 10, 20 20, 30 40)
- A LineString with three points.

POLYGON((10 10, 10 20, 20 20, 20 15, 10 10))
- A Polygon with one exterior ring and zero interior rings.

MULTIPOINT(10 10, 20 20)
- A MultiPoint with two Points.

MULTILINESTRING((10 10, 20 20), (15 15, 30 15))
- A MultiLineString with two LineStrings.

MULTIPOLYGON(((10 10, 10 20, 20 20, 20 15, 10 10)), ((60 60, 70 7, 80 60, 60 60)))
- A MultiPolygon with two Polygons.

GEOMETRYCOLLECTION(POINT(10 10), POINT(30 30), LINESTRING(15 15, 20 20))
- A GeometryCollection consisting of two Points and one LineString.

Figure 6. Incident routing query

The GetAgenciesForMultipleEverything method provides the most options for performing an incident routing query. The following code example shows how to call the GetAgenciesForMultipleEverything method:

```
EPADWebServicesClient WebServicesClient = new
EPADWebServicesClient();
private void GetAgencies_EPAD(string gisCoordinates, string
levelCodes, string incidentCodes, string agencyCodes)
{
  try
  {
// ---- call the webservice and return recipients
Session["User.MessageRecipients"] =
WebServicesClient.GetAgenciesForMultipleEverything_EPAD(
        (string)Session["User.Username"],
(string)Session["User.password"],
gisCoordinates,levelCodes,incidentCodes,agencyCodes);
  }
  // -- Authentication failed
  catch(SoapHeaderException eSoap)
  {
        lblError.Visible = true;
        lblError.Text = eSoap.Message.ToString();
  }
}
```

GIS services module giving the event type, the time of the event, and the location of the event. This module matches the location information in the request to agencies registered in the corresponding area to determine which agencies should be receiving this information. When matching requests to registrants, the GIS module must accurately translate and transform the location information of the request to locations on file. Since many agencies use different GIS systems, the EPAD GIS services module must be able to accurately "translate" the location information it receives so that the proper agencies are notified.

Figure 7 shows how a Web services query is satisfied using the EPAD architecture. A first responder sends a message containing a location in Well Known Text to the EPAD. The EPAD parses the message and generates a spatial SQL query to send to the database. The EPAD system adds a buffer to the query to handle horizontal error in the TIGER boundary data as well as error (in as far as it can be determined) in the incoming message. The query is then run against all data layers simultaneously, and returns matching agencies that desire notification. This list is passed to a messaging system[10] that sends out alerts according to the agencies' instructions received from the EPAD (COMCARE, October, 2004).

Accuracy of GIS Data

TIGER data is developed by the United States Census Bureau to support the mapping and related geographic activities required by the decennial census. The census requires a high level of relative accuracy, but does not place a premium on absolute

Figure 7. Translating a Web service query

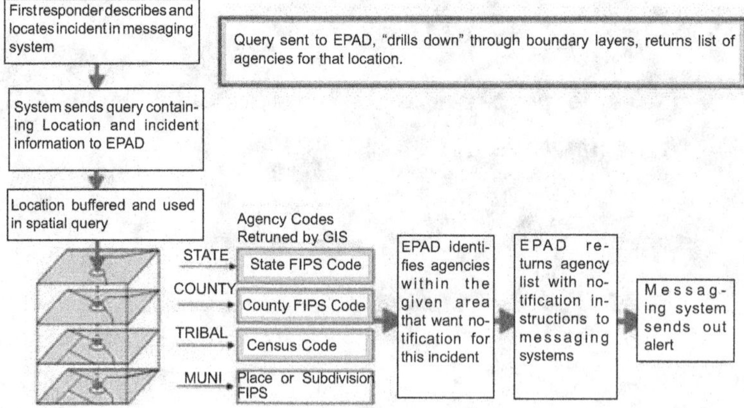

horizontal accuracy.[11] When messages containing spatial coordinates are passed to the EPAD's Web services interface, the coordinates are used in a spatial query against the EPAD database. Because of known horizontal error in the TIGER data and because of much less predictable error in the incoming coordinate data, there is a chance that all of the desired agencies will not be returned by the EPAD system without the addition of an error factor. This factor makes the spatial object of the incoming message larger before passing it to the EPAD.

The key question is how much larger to make the spatial query to achieve the desired result of returning all appropriate agencies all of the time. The GIS term for making the spatial object larger is "buffering." If the buffer added to the object is too small, the system risks not returning an agency that should have been returned and subsequently notified. Obviously, depending on the type of event, a missed agency notification could have serious consequences. If the buffer is too large, a large number of agencies nowhere near the incident are returned. For the EPAD, it is probably more important to capture all agencies registered for notification in a larger area and take a chance that extra agencies are notified rather than miss an agency.

Nevertheless, a reasonable estimate of the maximum horizontal error for both the TIGER and incoming coordinates must be developed. The National Map Accuracy Standard (NMAS) developed by the United States Geological Survey may be used as a starting point to define horizontal error for the two sources (TIGER and the location information in the request). NMAS defines maximum acceptable horizontal error for datasets at various scales such that 90% of well-defined points fall within the acceptable error level for data of a given accuracy level. The challenge is to arrive at a buffer value that delivers the correct set of agencies (from a spatial query perspective) close to 100% of the time.

According to the U.S. Census Bureau, TIGER, which was developed by hand digitizing 1:100,000 scale paper survey sheets, generally meets national map accuracy standards for 1:100,000 scale data. This means that 90% of well-defined points should fall within 166.7 feet of the feature they are describing. If one were to use 166.7 feet as a buffer, 10% of the time one could expect a spatial query to miss one or more agencies. In a study that compared global positioning system (GPS) gathered point locations corresponding to features in TIGER such as road intersections, the displacement between the original map and the GPS-enhanced road positions was often as large as 210 feet (Liadis, 2000). Clearly the buffer distance for TIGER will need to be greater than 166.7 feet.

More problematic is the coordinate information that comes to the EPAD as part of Web service queries. By requiring additional information in the Web service message, it may be possible to develop a rule-based approach to improving accuracy. For example, information in the message for "technique used to derive coordinates" could be used to estimate the size of the buffer to be applied. If data describing the accuracy of the coordinate being sent can be included in the Web services message, it would be possible to develop custom buffers on-the-fly based on the accuracy defined in the message.

Assuming the NMAS standard represents one standard deviation, it is also possible to calculate buffers to fit any desired confidence level. If the accuracy of the incoming coordinates is unknown, this approach can be applied to incoming coordinate values. The two error levels expressed in feet may then be added together to obtain a total buffer distance to apply. This would result in a one-size-fits-all approach for handling the total expected horizontal error. Both buffer calculation techniques are planned for the EPAD.

Another type of error inherent in TIGER data is attribute error. Attribute error results when a polygon does not have the correct descriptive database information linked to it. In the case of this project, key attribute fields are federal information processing standards (FIPS) codes and name information. For the EPAD, attribute error is estimated using a sampling approach, which randomly selects records, then compares the results to some known source for boundary information.

EPAD Next Generation

While the system design and components identified here are adequate for current EPAD processing, changes will need to be made as the EPAD is extended for information sharing during international emergency events. Immediate consideration needs to be given for the inclusion of boundary data for Mexico and Canada so that incidents traversing borders can be handled in the same manner as any other incidents. Boundary data sources for both countries need to be identified. While census organizations exist in Mexico and Canada, it is not known exactly how the data provided by those organizations compare to the U.S. Census TIGER dataset. Some questions that need to be considered when incorporating data from Mexico and Canada include the spatial accuracy of each country's census data, their use of FIPS or equivalent codes, the data formats used, licensing restrictions, and each country's update cycles.

Political boundary data for both Canada and Mexico are currently available in some form, and data samples appear to match the United States fairly closely in terms of jurisdiction hierarchy. While the spatial fit appears close when viewing all of North America, there are gaps and overlaps between country datasets. A brief examination of the border data match up between the U.S. and Mexico found gaps as large as 5 kilometers between country border lines, as well as large areas of overlap. An examination of the match between the U.S. and Canada found significant gaps and overlaps, although not quite as large as those found between the U.S. and Mexico.

In most cases, it will not be possible to determine which country's boundary is correct for a given location along a boundary line. A relatively simple rectification process would involve choosing one boundary and correcting the other boundary to match the first. In order to determine the best approach for addressing border error between the U.S., Mexico, and Canada, careful consideration will be given to the ways in which the EPAD will be used for border-related events and the consequences of incorrect results being returned by queries. This consideration will include an assessment of the legal consequences of incorrect queries. (Of course, an understanding of the legal repercussions relating to incorrect query results is important to consider in relation to all areas of the EPAD system.)

Another consideration for the project will be deciding the best way to provide a basemap service. The first option, currently in use, is to purchase an existing basemap service such as TopoZone. The second option is to build a basemap service in-house. The two approaches have their advantages and disadvantages in different areas.

A commercial solution provides access to commercially-provided databases that are more complete than TIGER in terms of road coverage for fast developing areas of the country. However, TopoZone, the product offering selected for the EPAD, does not provide basemapping services for Mexico or Canada. In addition, a remote service such as TopoZone is accessed across the Internet and therefore could affect system performance as Internet traffic patterns vary.

By building an in-house basemap service, a reasonably consistent basemap across the U.S., Mexico, and Canada can be created by using a combination of data sources. Also, an in-house service will, assuming loads are well balanced, provide much faster response times than an Internet-based service. It will also give more control when it comes to system stability and scalability issues. Unless another commercial product offering can provide the same benefits, it is likely that a custom-developed basemap service will be deployed.

Open Source Advantage

COMCARE's goal in requesting the use of open source technologies for the EPAD was the result of two major factors. First and foremost, it was to reduce its dependence on particular software vendors and their respective upgrade schedules. COMCARE, along with EPAD users, wanted the freedom to do what it wanted to do when it wanted to do it. Secondly, while open source software is not "free", it does lower the total cost of ownership (TCO) particularly when the EPAD has to scale quickly during national and international roll-outs. As a nonprofit wishing to operate the EPAD as a common utility, a lower TCO is important. COMCARE knows it has to pay for application system administration and support costs, the fact that it did not have the initial software license costs and will not have the annual maintenance fees weighed heavily in the decision. Of course, only mature and established open source offerings were chosen with hopes that the value of the decision will be preserved long term.

When COMCARE first suggested the open source option in early 2004, many felt this approach might be difficult to achieve. That was then. In the May, 2005, issue of Government Technology, open source offerings are becoming mainstream even in the public sector. Mississippi is using open source software for a new mobile data infrastructure called the Mississippi Automated System Project (MASP). Chicago is using it for a vehicle registration system that will issue over 1 million vehicle stickers per year (Peterson, 2005). Only time will tell if these open source decisions were good ones.

Conclusion

While the EPAD is not a production system as yet, many scenario-based demonstrations of the E-Safety Network and EPAD have been conducted. The results are always the same. Data messaging is an important and necessary component of emergency response efforts. If an EPAD-enabled E-Safety Network was available during the events sited in this chapter, many of the communications problems experienced in Toronto, Oklahoma City, and Graniteville, SC, may have been solved.

During the SARS outbreak, public health officials could have easily routed messages to the right agency destinations, without needing to know their electronic addresses. Medical and emergency professionals throughout the region, if they were registered in EPAD, would have had the information they needed to recognize SARS and understand treatment protocols so they could have provided faster and better response (COMCARE, December, 2004).

In Oklahoma City, requests for blueprints, personnel listings, and bomb effects could have been issued as soon as dispatch was notified of the bombing. Responders would have had the information they needed when they arrived at the scene, the 9-1-1 center could have communicated with EMS, and the hospitals would have been kept informed about injuries, casualties, and requests for resources (COMCARE, November, 2004).

The South Carolina Emergency Management Division, after running a plume model based on wind direction for the chlorine gas spill, could have easily targeted and routed messages to the appropriate emergency personnel, radio and television stations, and other disparate public alerting mechanisms without making telephone calls. The public would have had the information they needed in time to take appropriate action (COMCARE, March, 2005).

When it comes to emergency response, location does matter. By using the data-sharing framework of the E-Safety Network and registering in the EPAD, agencies can be assured that the right information will reach the right people at the right time. The technical complexities of the EPAD were discussed in this chapter. Agencies that register in the directory probably do not realize what it takes to make this happen. Luckily, they do not need to know.

References

Center for Disease Control (CDC). (2005, January). Public health consequences from hazardous substances acutely released during rail transit — South Carolina, 2005; Selected states, 1999-2004. *Morbidity and Mortality Weekly Report, 54*(03), 64-67.

COMCARE. (2004, October). *The E-Safety Network and EPAD architecture: Data system interoperability for homeland security and emergency response.* Washington, DC: COMCARE.

COMCARE. (2004, November). EPAD in action — emergency management (Oklahoma City Bombing). *EPAD Case Study 2.0.* Washington, DC: COMCARE.

COMCARE. (2004, December). EPAD in action — public health (SARS). *EPAD Case Study 3.0.* Washington, DC: COMCARE.

COMCARE. (2005, March). EPAD in action — public warning (SC Train Derailment). *EPAD Case Study 4.0.* Washington, DC: COMCARE.

COMCARE. (2005, June). *EmergencyProvider Access Directory (EPAD): Define and design phase technical design document, Version 1.1.* Washington, DC: COMCARE.

Cooper, J. M., Lewis, J. C., Hajek, F. P. & Shapiro, R. N., (2005, Winter). South Carolina chlorine gas disaster shows risks to public. *Back on Track*, Virginia Beach, VA: Hajek, Shapiro, Cooper, & Lewis.

Federal Communications Commission (FCC). (2004, August). *Review of the Emergency Alert System, notice of proposed rulemaking* (EB Docket No. 04-296, FCC 04-189, para. 12).

Lipowicz, A. (2005, January). South Carolina chlorine accident showed officials a better Emergency Alert System is needed. *CQ homeland security local response.* Retrieved February 11, 2005, from http://www.cq.com

Liadis, J. S. (2000). GPS TIGER accuracy analysis tools (GTAAT) evaluation and test results. *TIGER operation branch, geography division in the U.S. Census Bureau.* Retrieved from http://www.census.gov/geo/www/tiger/gtaat2000.pdf

Manzi, C., Powers, M. J., & Zetterland, K. (2002). *Critical information flows in the Alfred P. Murrah building bombing: A case study* (Special Report 3). Washington, DC: Chemical and Biological Arms Control Institute.

National Information Exchange Model (NIEM). (2005). *National information exchange model.* Retrieved from http://niem.gov

O'Connor, J. (2005, January). Graniteville toll rises to 9. *The State,* Columbia, SC, A1.

Office of Justice Programs (OJP). (2005). *Information technology initiatives: Global Justice XML Data Model.* Retrieved from http://www.it.ojp.gov/topic.jsp?topic_id.43

Open Geospatial Consortium (OGC), Inc. (2004, August). *Web map service, Version 1.3* (Project Document OGC 04-024). Wayland, MA: OGC

Open Geospatial Consortium (OGC), Inc. (1999, May). *OpenGIS simple feature specification for SQL, Revision 1.1* (Project Document 99-049). Wayland, MA: OGC.

Peterson, S. (2005, May). Proving its mettle. *Government Technology, 18*(5), 18-24, 64.

SARS Commission. (2004, April). SARS and public health in Ontario. *The SARS Commission Interim Report.* Toronto, Canada: SARS Commission.

XML Cover Pages. (2005, December). *XML and emergency management.* Retrieved from http://XML.coverpages.org/emergencyManagement.html

Endnotes

1 COMCARE's definition of "emergency agency" is broader than the traditional first responder community. For the E-Safety Network and EPAD, the term includes any government, private or non-governmental organization that participates in emergency preparedness and/or response activities. This includes fire, law enforcement and emergency medical services, as well as utilities, other private infrastructure companies, schools, and tow truck drivers. The total universe described by this term can exceed 250,000.

2 OnStar uses automatic crash notification (ACN) technology, bringing together emergency service providers, wireless telephone, and satellite technologies, to help protect owners and their automobiles.

3 Qualcomm supplies a product called OmniTRACS to trucking and construction equipment fleets. OmniTRACS includes tamper-alert systems, panic alarms,

and satellite-tracking capabilities to help minimize vehicle tampering and theft and to help facilitate quick emergency response when an accident occurs.

4 A prototype of the EPAD (www.epad.us) was developed by DICE Corporation in 2003. This prototype enabled COMCARE to demonstrate the data interoperability concept. However, the design of the EPAD described in this document was funded by a grant from the Department of Justice. As COMCARE contractors, Proxicom, Inc., of Reston, VA, and Advanced Technology Solutions, Inc., of Lancaster, PA, developed the technical design.

5 The common alerting protocol (CAP) standard is an open, non-proprietary Organization for the Advancement of Structured Information Standards (OASIS) standard for the exchange of emergency alerts and public warnings over data networks and computer-controlled warning systems.

6 The Vehicular Emergency Data Set (VEDS) is an XML standard for the transmission of telematics data to emergency agencies. Initially designed to transmit ACN crash data to an emergency agency, VEDS also serves as a data receptacle, collecting important bits of information as the response effort unfolds. The data set can contain data transmitted directly from the vehicle like vehicle speed, airbag deployment, direction of force and rollover, as well as information from the telematics provider about the vehicle and its owner. Questions asked by a 9-1-1 operator about the age and gender of the occupants and data from responders and witnesses at the scene can also be added.

7 The Emergency Data Exchange Language (EDXL) represents a suite of emergency messaging standards. The first EDXL standard developed is the “Distribution Element” or DE. While different from the other EDXL messages sets, this standard acts as a container that facilitates the routing of message sets (any properly formatted XML emergency message) to recipients. The DE carries and routes “payload” message sets by specifying key routing information such as event type and affected geography as well as basic information about an emergency incident. In June, 2006, the OASIS international standards consortium announced the approval of the Emergency Data Exchange Language Distribution Element (EDXL-DE) version 1.0 as an OASIS Standard.

8 Event types represent a variety of emergency incidents. Values for this data element are specified as part of the EDXL DE standard. Currently, there are over 100 event types specified for use.

9 PostGIS has been developed by Refractions Research as a research project in open source spatial database technology. PostGIS is released under the GNU General Public License.

10 A messaging system or message broker accepts signals from an application system that wishes to send an emergency message and routes the message to the

appropriate parties based on information received from the EPAD. It functions as a signal clearinghouse and notification service, using the incoming signal as the driver and the EPAD database as the source data from which routing is performed. It can be an independent service used by many application systems or the functionality can be embedded into individual applications systems.

11 Absolute horizontal accuracy represents the difference between the represented coordinates and their true position. It is expressed as a circular error at 90 percent probability.

Chapter IV

The Weather Tool: An Agent-Based Approach to Information Integration

Gunjan Kalra, Quantum Leap Innovations, USA

Abstract

This chapter discusses the process of providing information in its most accurate, complete form to its users and the difficulties faced by the users of the current information systems. The chapter describes the impact of prevalent technologies such as the multi-agent systems and the Semantic Web in the area of information supply via an example implementation and a model use case. The chapter offers a potentially more efficient and robust approach to information integration and supply process. The chapter intends to highlight the complexities inherent in the process of information supply and the role of emerging information technologies in solving these challenges.

Introduction

The progress in distributed computing has played a significant role in facilitating replacement of large, monolithic databases with smaller and conceptually self-contained databases. This has resulted in efficient yet "ever-expanding" clusters of heterogeneous sources of data (*data sources*) such as the traditional databases, Web sites, e-mails, and operational applications. The need to view and analyze data from various data sources unified under one application context has become more prevalent and has gained prominence among data analysts, both in the information technology industry and academia. For example, large-scale enterprises have a growing demand for enterprise integration products, while data mining researchers need a unified view of data from different sources to select and test their algorithms. The task of providing integrated data management within one umbrella is particularly challenging. In this chapter, we describe the need and evolution of the Weather Tool system, a weather data provisioning and integration system accessible via a standard application programming interface (API). The chapter begins with an introduction to the evolution of sources of data and to the problem of weather data integration. Some of the previous and existing data integration technologies and products are then summarized. The chapter will also address some of the new technologies that the data/information integration systems benefit greatly from, including the agent technology and the Semantic Web. We then provide an overview of the Weather Tool architecture (and an example application) that enables integration of several data sources to provide a unified data environment. The architecture discussion describes how *data processing services* are provisioned in a dynamically-changing environment. The advantages and pitfalls of such a system are elaborated, followed by a discussion of potential improvements in the architecture. The chapter briefly discusses the core ideas of Quantum Leap Innovation, Inc. (QLI) intelligent data management (IDM) framework, the generalized, enhanced version of the Weather Tool effort. This framework is aimed at performing beyond the Weather Tool's single repository approach to data integration by incorporating several strategies for on-demand, data access and analysis remotely, thereby avoiding creation of redundant intermediary repositories. Finally, the chapter highlights the need, evolution, and importance of data/information integration efforts.

Evolution from Large Databases to Large Data Environment

Historically, due to high set-up and maintenance costs for databases, extremely large volumes of data were stored in one database; this strategy was considered efficient and had the advantage of easy access to all data. In reaction to the scale and complexity of such large databases, data analysts have often created and exploited selective views of subsets of the large databases. Since the advent of cheaper, flexible, and more efficient data-storage solutions, the large databases have made way for individual databases that store smaller sets of relevant data. These databases have varying data access mechanisms and protocols that are usually dependent upon non-standard, product specific technology. Some examples of commonly-used relational databases are MySQL, Oracle, Postgres, and DB2.

Data-access mechanisms for the databases vary in complexity of implementation and user-friendliness. The most common, structurally straightforward but tricky to use data-access mechanism is Structured Query Language (SQL) that allows formation of data queries via a set of special commands and keywords. Relatively more expressive and easy-to-use approaches involve the graphical user interface (GUI) applications developed using technologies such as Visual Basic, Java, and so forth. However, these involve long implementation times. More recent tools that have been developed for easier implementation, use, and data access are the Web sites that enable access to remote databases via Web pages. The Web sites/portals that are easily customized to create data-access forms have become an important source of information in today's world. There are examples of Web sites functioning not only as data-access mechanisms but also as sources of intermediate transient data that can become crucial input to relevant applications. Examples include unprocessed weather data, hourly stock market data, and event announcements. Transient data inherently do not require elaborate storage but often becomes invaluable for certain categories of consumers. For instance, unprocessed weather data can help in assessing weather conditions and road conditions in the absence of validated weather data. Event announcements, though not useful once the event is over, can be of great use in estimating population densities and movements in cities and can also help in highlighting the factors that affect the cities' economies.

The popular adoption of Web sites as front-ends to relational databases has resulted in the emergence of many heterogeneous data sources, a large data environment with easy accessibility via the Internet. Other than the inherent efficiency and easy maintainability aspects of having relatively small, self contained data sources, the industry has recognized the advantages of dynamically composing new data structures from the data in these data sources. There is high potential that analyzing previously unknown combinations of data will result in useful data that can even be life-saving in certain situations. These combinations are not known in advance and the data sources have complex and often unique access mechanisms, as they were not designed to be used in conjunction with each other. This makes it inefficient to use traditional IT development mechanisms to integrate such sources statically, especially in view of the computational costs and the configuration overhead involved in run-time addition of new data sources. In the following subsection, we describe one such data integration problem in the weather domain, where all components of weather data are not available at one data source.

The Weather Problem

The data retrieval process assumes knowledge of at least the structure of the data and at times of other constraints pertinent to the data source. The retrieval process entails the basic data processing steps starting with data extraction, followed by data validation, completion, and optional transformation and storage. In case of storage, one must also worry about storage and consolidation of the corresponding meta-data with the existing data. Increasing the number of data sources only escalates the complexity in providing these data processing services. Adding to the complexity of data retrieval, there are types of data, such as news reports, demographic data, and weather data that change over time and impose extra processing to account for the constant updates. Furthermore, the data may need to be extracted from more than one relevant source, each with their own formats. Data from different sources vary not just by data quality and content, but also by data format and update frequencies

Figure 1. National Climatic Data Center's (NCDC) text-based validated historical data

http://www.ncdc.noaa.gov/servlets/ULCD?stnid=ILG&randomnum=20865118011475&VARVALUE=ILG200406&wh - Microsof...
File » Address http://www.ncdc.noaa.gov/servlets/ULCD?stnid=ILG&randomnum=20865118011475&VARVALUE=ILG200406&which=ASCII+Download+

```
Month:, 06/2004
Station Name:, "NEW CASTLE COUNTY AIRPORT" Call Sign:, ILG
Day,Time,StationType,Maint Indic,SkyConditions,Visibility,Weather Type,Dry Bulb Faren,Dry Bulb Cel,Wet Bul
01,0012,AO2 ,-,BKN008 BKN080 OVC100                            ,3SM    ,-,-,-,-,-,-,-,     , 4   ,310,-,0  ,
01,0051,AO2 ,-,OVC008                                          ,3SM    ,-,59   ,  15.0,58   ,  14.7,58   ,  1
01,0151,AO2 ,-,OVC008                                          ,3SM    ,-,59   ,  15.0,58   ,  14.7,58   ,  1
01,0237,AO2 ,-,OVC010                                          ,3SM    ,-,-,-,-,-,-,-,     , 4   ,320,-,0  ,
01,0244,AO2 ,-,FEW005 OVC010                                   ,3SM    ,-,-,-,-,-,-,-,     , 4   ,330,-,0  ,
01,0251,AO2 ,-,FEW005 OVC012                                   ,3SM    ,-,59   ,  15.0,58   ,  14.7,58   ,  1
01,0351,AO2 ,-,FEW005 OVC012                                   ,3SM    ,-,59   ,  15.0,58   ,  14.7,58   ,  1
01,0442,AO2 ,-,OVC008                                          ,3SM    ,-,-,-,-,-,-,-,     , 4   ,050,-,0  ,
01,0451,AO2 ,-,OVC008                                          ,3SM    ,-,59   ,  15.0,58   ,  14.7,58   ,  1
01,0551,AO2 ,-,OVC008                                          ,7SM    ,-,60   ,  15.6,59   ,  14.9,58   ,  1
01,0651,AO2 ,-,SCT008 OVC016                                   ,6SM    ,BR                  ,61   ,  16.1,60
01,0751,AO2 ,-,FEW006 OVC018                                   ,5SM    ,BR                  ,63   ,  17.2,61
01,0827,AO2 ,-,BKN014 OVC019                                   ,10SM   ,-,-,-,-,-,-,-,     , 5   ,300,-,0  ,
01,0838,AO2 ,-,OVC016                                          ,10SM   ,-,-,-,-,-,-,-,     , 6   ,310,-,0  ,
01,0851,AO2 ,-,FEW013 OVC018                                   ,10SM   ,-,64   ,  17.8,61   ,  16.1,59   ,  1
01,0951,AO2 ,-,BKN018                                          ,9SM    ,-,67   ,  19.4,63   ,  17.4,61   ,  1
01,1051,AO2 ,-,SCT024                                          ,10SM   ,-,70   ,  21.1,64   ,  18.0,61   ,  1
01,1130,AO2 ,-,SCT022 SCT030 BKN036                            ,7SM    ,TSRA                ,-,-,-,-,-,-,
01,1135,AO2 ,-,SCT019 BKN031 BKN070                            ,6SM    ,RA                  ,-,-,-,-,-,-,
01,1137,AO2 ,-,SCT019 BKN031 BKN035                            ,6SM    ,-TSRA               ,-,-,-,-,-,-,
01,1151,AO2 ,-,FEW021 BKN037 OVC050                            ,5SM    ,-RA BR              ,67   ,  19.4,65
01,1251,AO2 ,-,FEW048                                          ,10SM   ,-,70   ,  21.1,65   ,  18.4,62   ,  1
01,1351,AO2 ,-,FEW100                                          ,10SM   ,-,73   ,  22.8,67   ,  19.3,63   ,  1
01,1403,AO2 ,-,FEW060                                          ,10SM   ,VCTS                ,-,-,-,-,-,-,
01,1423,AO2 ,-,BKN029 BKN060                                   ,7SM    ,RA                  ,-,-,-,-,-,-,
01,1431,AO2 ,-,BKN031 BKN049 OVC060                            ,8SM    ,RA                  ,-,-,-,-,-,-,
01,1451,AO2 ,-,BKN027                                          ,10SM   ,-RA                 ,65   ,  18.3,60
01,1501,AO2 ,-,SCT025                                          ,10SM   ,-,-,-,-,-,-,-,     , 6   ,250,-,0  ,
01,1551,AO2 ,-,SCT045 SCT070 OVC090                            ,10SM   ,-RA                 ,61   ,  16.1,58
01,1605,AO2 ,-,BKN028 BKN070 BKN090                            ,8SM    ,-RA                 ,-,-,-,-,-,-,
01,1615,AO2 ,-,SCT028                                          ,10SM   ,-,-,-,-,-,-,-,     , 7   ,220,-,0  ,
01,1651,AO2 ,-,CLR                                             ,10SM   ,-,64   ,  17.8,61   ,  16.1,59   ,  1
01,1751,AO2 ,-,CLR                                             ,10SM   ,-,66   ,  18.9,62   ,  16.6,59   ,  1
```

Done Internet

Figure 2. National Oceanic and Atmospheric Administration's (NOAA) textual forecast data

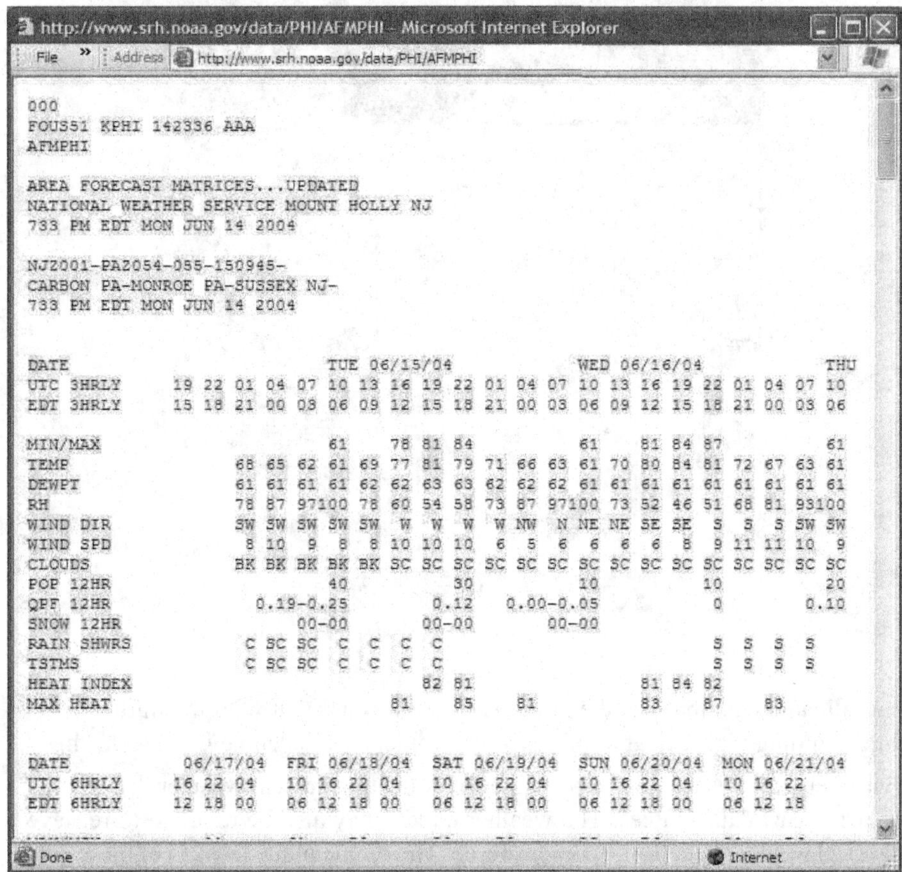

http://www.srh.noaa.gov/data/PHI/AFMPHI - Microsoft Internet Explorer

File » Address http://www.srh.noaa.gov/data/PHI/AFMPHI

```
000
FOUS51 KPHI 142336 AAA
AFMPHI

AREA FORECAST MATRICES...UPDATED
NATIONAL WEATHER SERVICE MOUNT HOLLY NJ
733 PM EDT MON JUN 14 2004

NJZ001-PAZ054-055-150945-
CARBON PA-MONROE PA-SUSSEX NJ-
733 PM EDT MON JUN 14 2004

DATE                         TUE 06/15/04            WED 06/16/04                THU
UTC 3HRLY         19 22 01 04 07 10 13 16 19 22 01 04 07 10 13 16 19 22 01 04 07 10
EDT 3HRLY         15 18 21 00 03 06 09 12 15 18 21 00 03 06 09 12 15 18 21 00 03 06

MIN/MAX                          61    78 81 84          61    81 84 87          61
TEMP                    68 65 62 61 69 77 81 79 71 66 63 61 70 80 84 81 72 67 63 61
DEWPT                   61 61 61 61 62 62 63 63 62 62 62 61 61 61 61 61 61 61 61 61
RH                      78 87 97100 78 60 54 58 73 87 97100 73 52 46 51 68 81 93100
WIND DIR                SW SW SW SW SW  W  W  W  W NW  N NE NE SE SE  S  S  S SW SW
WIND SPD                 8 10  9  8  8 10 10 10  6  5  6  6  6  6  8  9 11 11 10  9
CLOUDS                  BK BK BK BK BK SC SC SC SC SC SC SC SC SC SC SC SC SC SC SC
POP 12HR                         40          30          10          10          20
QPF 12HR                  0.19-0.25        0.12   0.00-0.05           0        0.10
SNOW 12HR                     00-00       00-00       00-00
RAIN SHWRS               C SC SC  C  C  C  C                          S  S  S  S
TSTMS                    C SC SC  C  C  C  C                          S  S  S  S
HEAT INDEX                                82 81                81 84 82
MAX HEAT                               81    85    81          83    87    83


DATE               06/17/04  FRI 06/18/04  SAT 06/19/04  SUN 06/20/04  MON 06/21/04
UTC 6HRLY         16 22 04   10 16 22 04   10 16 22 04   10 16 22 04    10 16 22
EDT 6HRLY         12 18 00   06 12 18 00   06 12 18 00   06 12 18 00    06 12 18
```

Done Internet

(how often data is made available). For example, news articles differ in content and quality over a period of time, across different newspapers and Web sites. Moreover, several news providers may write articles on different aspects of the same incident. News is validated typically anywhere from a few hours to days.

Weather data is a good example of time-varying data. The National Climatic Data Center's (NCDC) Web site allows its users to view validated historical data in textual form (Figure 1); the National Oceanic and Atmospheric Administration's (NOAA) Web site (Figure 2) shows forecast data for the next ten days in textual form, and National Weather Service's (NWS) web-site has non-validated forecast data in graphical form (Figure 3). These sources are all showing different aspects of weather, potentially for the same geographical location, and two of them have

Figure 3. National Weather Service HTML-based forecast data

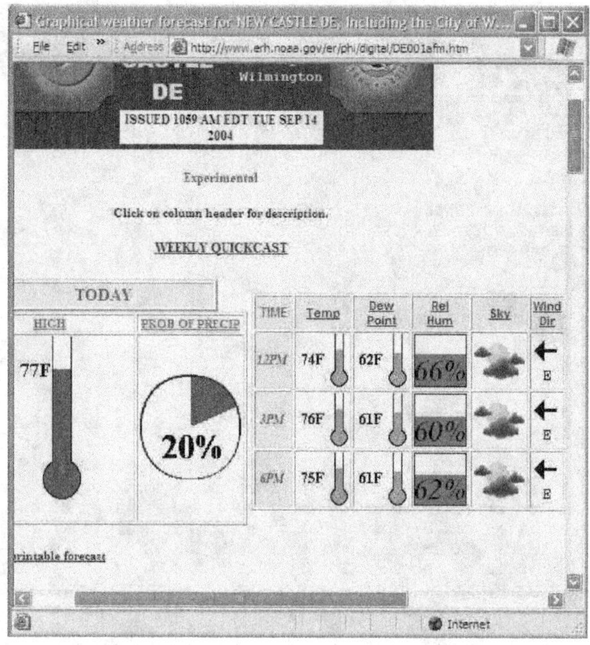

non-validated data that has the potential to be inconsistent with the third source, while claiming higher quality in terms of completeness, accuracy, and so forth.

A weather expert is usually responsible for collecting current weather data from a set of forecast data sources. The weather expert may also be required to retrieve historical weather data from another source. The often unique formats of these data require the expert to go through specific data extraction procedures for all the required locations. The locations that can be designated by zip codes can quickly rise in number, with 99 being the number for the state of Delaware, one of the smaller states in the U.S. Following the collection of data, the expert may be required to validate and convert this data into standard format. Sources with transient data entail provisioning of efficient storage in the form of caches or extra data repositories. This also helps to avoid duplicating efforts for future access by applications that require weather data.

Furthermore, as forecast weather data is validated (typically within two or three days), the expert must update the repository accordingly. The expert is also responsible for providing weather data to the relevant applications in the required formats. If the applications require advanced meteorological data such as radiosonde (upper air) data, the expert must integrate weather data from the different sources per location and date.

Static and consistent data can be directly retrieved from the data sources. However, in the case of weather, where tools and applications (consumers) require time-variant data, extra care must be taken while automating the retrieval process to account for a series of data processing steps needed to make the data useful for analysis. Consumers must maintain their own enormous databases in cases where the providers only store the data temporarily. Hence there is a need for a Weather Tool that enables a logical value chain with individual system components for carrying out the various services required for handling time-sensitive information. Although the industry is still looking for better solutions for realizing dynamic, distributed, real-time clusters of data sources, a lot of foundational work has already been explored by the research community and identified by the industry.

Information Integration

In this section we discuss some of the data integration technologies and solutions that have been prevalent in the past. The essence of the prior approaches can also be seen in the newer technologies. In addition to touching on the progress of data and information integration in academia, we discuss the direction that industry has been taking to handle the data integration problem.

Research Efforts

The two main aspects of databases that have formed the basis for new information integration technologies and products are the storage mechanism and the structure and semantics of data. Relational databases and its derivatives, including federated databases (Sheth & Larson, 1991) have been the most commonly-used test bed for such technologies. Relatively recent and widely-adopted information integration systems are the data warehouses that facilitate data acquisition, storage, and distribution. However, these systems are used primarily for historical, non-operational data via a central repository to aid the management's decision-making process. Data warehouses also deal with data consolidation issues even though the consolidation structure and rules for preset collections of databases are determined initially at the system set-up time and are difficult to change. In addition, adding a new source not only requires bringing down the system temporarily, but also necessitates incorporating consolidation and verification rules for the new source. Widom (1995) outlines the various research issues related to the design and implementation of data warehouses. Pure data warehouse technology has further been combined with materialized WHIPS (Labio et al., 1997) and virtual (Zhou, Hull, King, & Franchitti, 1995) views for defining and maintaining data warehouses. There have also been mediator-based architectures (Wiederhold, 1992) where the users and the applications have been layered with custom software to enable integration via standard APIs. This is an "on-demand" approach since a data source is integrated into the system only when there is a query for information that it provides. In the database realm, there are always two main disadvantages associated with channeling data into the central repository structure: static, diverse, and domain-specific (non standard) data structure, and a predetermined set of data sources.

Two assumptions made by the above database approaches for integrating heterogeneous data sources are that all the information sources to be integrated are known a priori and that there is a uniform notion of semantics across the sources. There is a separate community of researchers in source integration that focuses on the uniform semantics aspect. Many wrapper-mediator style systems adopt either a predefined global schema (Cohen, 1998; Genesereth, Keller, & Duschka, 1997) or construct one based upon the source schemas (Bergamaschi, Castano, & Vincini, 1999), for describing the information and their sources. Wrappers interpret and maintain local information about their information sources in terms of the global schema. A mediator handles the user queries, sends them to the appropriate wrapper, and consolidates the individual results. Several methodologies applied in such architectures include a common thesaurus in the MOMIS (Bergamaschi, Castano, & Vincini, 1999) project, description logic in the Information Manifold (Levy, 1998), knowledge representation techniques in the InfoMaster (Genesereth, Keller, & Duschka, 1997) efforts, AI planning techniques in the OCCAM (Kwok & Weld, 1996) project, and highly structured relational models in the WHIRL (Labio et al., 1997) effort. For Web information sources in particular, learning by induction has been applied to create wrappers, including the work by Kushmerick (Kushmerick, Weld, & Doorenbos, 1997) and Muslea (Stalker) (Muslea, Minton, & Knoblock, 1999). These wrapper induction systems apply machine learning algorithms to learn Web resource extractors by using manually-labeled training data sets. In our system, we focus more on the overall optimized efficiency of the system rather than on that of the individual agent.

As we progress towards distributed, mobile, and unstable yet flexible systems, where new providers of information come in and go out of existence unpredictably, we need to take dynamism and adaptability features into account as these information providers make significant contributions to the data in demand. To address the second assumption of fixed sources, we draw upon the concept of intelligent software agents (Etzioni & Weld, 1995; Wooldridge & Jennings, 1995). Researchers have implemented several architectures for data and information integration by using the agent paradigm. Decker, Sycara, and Williamson (1997) "agentify" the wrapper-style architecture as "middle agents" that provide the service of mediating between information producers and consumers. Decker et al. describe nine categories of middle agents based upon the knowledge of consumers' preferences and providers' capabilities. Of particular interest with regard to unstable data environments is the category of "broker-agents," where the consumers and the providers do not know each other's capabilities and preferences, and the brokers are responsible for solving the connection problem between them. However, the condition where a consumer's preferences are not met completely by one producer and the broker must arrange for a combination of producer services is not adequately addressed. For example, if the only available information producer does not provide the data in the desired format, the consumer may end up looking for an appropriate translation service as a separate transaction. The consumer has to specify the relevant preference to be able to find the translation service required for the desired format. Furthermore, in case the producers have partial information, the consumer has to either know or learn information-specific rules for merging the components or look for an information consolidation service.

RETSINA (Sycara, Decker, Pannu, Williamson, & Zeng, 1996), MIKS (Bergamaschi et al., 2001), KRAFT (Preece, Gray, & Hui, 1999) and InfoSleuth (Bayardo et al., 1997) are representative examples of agent-based information integration efforts. There are architectural similarities between InfoSleuth and the Weather Tool, specifically in terms of the type and roles of the agents. They do not mention incorporation of actively changing Web sources (in content and layout). In addition, they do not provide for caching frequently-queried information; this may result in unnecessary communication and overloading of their resource agents. In the Weather Tool, the weather data repository reduces most response times to a single lookup in the repository. IDM goes further to incorporate data caching at the various system components. InfoSleuth describes a few fixed, yet complicated, interaction protocols for communication of data across the various agents. Our system is able to dynamically adopt more efficient protocols, according to where the data is actually stored. Finally, InfoSleuth provides a Web interface for human users, whereas our system provides an agent-based API that can be easily used by other software applications.

Although the agent paradigm is not very evident in the commercial data integration technologies in the industry, there is presence and proven successful use of enterprise integration products at two levels of enterprise assets, namely the data and the application. The following subsection provides an overview of such technologies.

Technologies in the Industry — ETL, EAI and EII

The business community has adopted products geared towards solving the various integration issues within an enterprise. Efforts have focused on integration at the data and application level. Enterprises typically deal with data, software tools that analyze this data, and the information that is generated by these tools. Integration at the data and tools level is an important element in providing a global view of an enterprise's asset (customers, products, sales, etc), market status (stock prices, sales), and growth profile (predictive analysis). Data integration facilitates easy, uniform access to operational data existing in applications and databases and to archival databases for efficient statistical and predictive analysis. Data integration is also a step towards achieving a standard notion of semantics for the enterprise in terms of enterprise metadata. Application integration enables data exchange and change propagation among a set of applications, thus providing the ability to influence an application's analysis with external information.

Besides being a solution to data integration, well-adopted complex data architectures, including data warehouses, operational data stores, data marts, and multidimensional analytical databases, provide efficient information services to the enterprise applications. Such architectures provide metadata standards for fixed applications, which have traditionally been scoped to individual departments. Integrating new enterprise systems into these architectures and enabling data exchange across departments has proven to be expensive, both cost- and effort-wise.

The extract, transform, and load technology (ETL) has dealt with the challenges involved in accessing data across applications. Although the ETL tools are popular, they function in batch mode, extracting, transforming, and loading batches of data, typically once in 24 hours to one month (depending upon the type of data). In the present highly competitive markets, an enterprise's survival and success is highly dependent upon real-time information.

Newer generations of enterprise applications have been geared towards enabling real-time distributed computing. As these applications have become more efficient, they behave more specifically in terms of their metadata and repositories, data translation tools, and interaction protocols, thus locking critical information in proprietary systems. This has led to severe impediments to the flexibility, integrity, accessibility, and maintainability of overall enterprise information and metadata. Enterprise application integration (EAI) technology has focused on methods and tools for real-time integration and coordination of data exchange and information communication between legacy applications and databases, and systems based on new technologies. EAI solutions consist of a messaging system, a middleware for message routing and data transformation, and a collection of application specific adapters. Separation of brokering functionality into a middleware has proven to be flexible, but EAI solutions still involve static configurations. In other words, integrating new systems have still required bringing down the system temporarily for modifications to the middle layer's interface and to the standard data model being used.

EAI is crucial to enterprises for maintaining integrity in enterprise data, keeping widespread heterogeneous systems in synch, but EAI solutions are specific to a given set of applications. It would be a great advantage if new system components (applications or databases) and/or new data types could be dynamically linked to the set of existing components without having to deal with any static configurations or even having to reboot the system. Intelligent data management (IDM) intends to provide such a dynamic and extensible framework for the creation, extension, and efficient utilization of an enterprise's data stores and data.

The characteristic functionalities and goals of the enterprise information integration (EII) technology are very similar to those of intelligent data management. EII stemmed out of the persistent need to seamlessly access data and information residing in systems across the enterprise as one unit instead of having to deal with the intricacies of the individual systems. EII converges on real-time integration of (components of) data from several data sources primarily by labeling data with a unified, consistent, and semantically-rich metadata. EII is well suited for data sources that are not stable and whose content gets updated often. Some of the common tasks within EII and IDM are data extraction, cleansing, standardizing, validating, and optionally labeling and formatting. Some of the current technologies in the research community have high potential of enabling flexible, robust, and efficient EII solutions. The following section delves into the details of two such technologies.

The Prevailing Technologies

Realizing the data environment, as discussed in the previous sections, will rely on sophisticated frameworks supporting distributed computing with certain "intelligence" features. The word "intelligence" here signifies special features of a technology that distinguishes it from other technologies in terms of performance and operability. Examples of such features include the ability of systems components to interact with their environment, and the ability of system components to understand (process) system data. As the research community continues to build innovative intelligence technologies, the task of putting together these technologies for realizing vital market solutions becomes even more interesting and viable. In the following sub-sections, we discuss some of the technologies that have the potential and inherent robustness for supporting near real-time information integration efforts and how Quantum Leap Innovations, Inc. (QLI) is using them to provide one such solution. In particular, we will discuss the Semantic Web and agent technology that have already impacted a host of industries such as the Web economies, the mobile industry, and the IT industry.

The Semantic Web

The Semantic Web technology constitutes a new way of representing Web content that makes it processable by software tools with the capability of processing and otherwise supporting the semantic Web content. The Semantic Web is an effort of the World Wide Web Consortium (W3C) to enhance and standardize the content being displayed on Web sites by marking it with meaningful tags, making it easy for the reasoner software to manipulate it. The Semantic Web boasts of ubiquity as it is accessible via standard network protocols by any application or software. The Semantic Web languages are based on the XML technology that originally gave arbitrary, user-defined, structure to the Web content. The representation scheme is based on a special syntax, resource description framework (RDF), that uses unique resource identifiers (URI) (strings starting with "http:" or "ftp :") to represent data. The RDF is a syntax language that allows data to be represented in the form of triples, binding three data items in a "subject — object — predicate" relationship. A collection of RDF triples defines resources and relations among them, thus mapping the data to a model that is inherently decentralized and universally accessible. This syntax is used to create languages/schemas/metadata for representing data. These schemas in the Semantic Web terminology are referred to as ontologies. Since these ontologies are easily accessibly via the Internet, applications can efficiently share and access this metadata to understand the data being represented by them. The basic schema created using the RDF syntax is the RDF Schema that gives types/categories to data and thus imparts a hierarchy structure to data. RDFS allows tags to define classes and properties and add properties to classes of data.

Higher levels of Semantic Web languages impart more logic and reasonability features to data by adding further vocabulary to the existing semantics. One of the most important of these languages in this context is the Web Ontology Language (OWL) that has been formally described by the W3C in terms of a set of documents (OWL). The OWL vocabulary allows the users to impart more structure to their data by adding more features to the properties and classes. These features range from special relations among classes such as union and disjoint-ness, to creating hierarchy of properties and assigning of attributes to properties, quantification, and equality of classes. The Semantic Web languages tend to get very verbose and should be dealt with preferably via special editors such as SWOOP and Protégé for generating and editing ontologies. There are other tools for supporting these languages such as Jena and Pellet ontology reasoners and Schemagen and Kazuki that provide Java support in terms of creating Java classes for OWL, DAML, or RDFS vocabularies.

In the Weather Tool, we demonstrate how data schema can be used to create a very flexible yet stable network of data sources. The section on IDM further describes the use of ontologies in the IDM framework.

Multi-Agent Systems (MAS)

The agent paradigm involves realizing the functional components in a system as software agents (Etzioni & Weld, 1995; Wooldridge & Jennings, 1995) and having them interoperate in an agent-based environment. A software agent is a software program that can control its execution in terms of carrying out specific tasks, perceiving, and interacting with its execution environment and other software agents. An agent is also a piece of software with rules for achieving its functionality and for finding and responding to the input that it receives from other agents and its environment with minimal (run time) participation of the human user. Agents exhibit goal-directed behavior and can cooperate in teams, usually via asynchronous message passing. Agent communication is typically realized via messages. Agents can be made "more intelligent" by augmenting them with the capabilities of learning from their past executions and of adapting to perform better in similar situations. A multi-agent system (MAS) consists of an execution environment, agents that are executed in the environment, and resources that are shared and consumed by the agents. A multi-agent system has decentralized and asynchronous information, communication, and control architecture and provides industry standard mechanisms for agent discovery, monitoring, communication, and cooperation between agents. The agent systems provide directory services where agents register the services that they provide to allow other agents to find them. They also provide means for appropriate communication to invoke the registered services. Certain implementations of agent systems also provide for agents to migrate between machines by virtue of being complete units of execution that allow them to make their own decisions.

Agents perform tasks in the form of executing services. In an agent-based approach to data integration, the data sources are represented as data provisioning services with specifications for how to discover and invoke these services in industry standard formats. Other required functionalities are also realized by service provisioning. This service-oriented architecture enables a dynamic environment where service providing agents can enter and leave the system without disrupting any functionality of the operational system. When new data sources to be integrated into the system are identified, representative service providing agents can be implemented and added to the system seamlessly. The relevant data services for the new data source can be easily built into representative agents. The agents can then advertise the new data source and the relevant data processing services, enabling the data from the new source to be integrated into the system.

Weather Tool

Weather Tool is an agent-based system for provisioning weather data from a dynamic collection of data sources via one standard interface. Weather Tool makes use of the above mentioned state of the art AI technologies to enable an agent-based, service-oriented framework for bringing many data sources together in a virtually integrated environment. The goals that the weather tool has achieved are the ability to access data from a given data source and to integrate a new data source into the system. Data access involves setting up a standard data querying mechanism. The

Semantic Web technology is not fully utilized in the Weather Tool, but the system clearly highlights its advantages. All the functionalities in the Weather Tool are realized as services. The following subsection elaborates on these services. The services are provided by software agents.

Weather Tool Data Services

The Weather Tool system components are implemented as services in an agent system. Details of the agent system that we use are mentioned in the next subsection. In the context of data retrieval from weather Web sites and databases, the data must go through a series of processing steps before it can be efficiently utilized by the concerned applications. The data (pre) processing techniques that we include in the Weather Tool are described below along with other agent services that make up the Weather Tool:

- **Data provisioning (retrieval) service:** Providers of this service are responsible for allowing access to a data source. The service provider connects to the data source and captures the data as it exists at the source including the source-specific formatting. For example, this service would post a query at the Weather Channel's (WC) Web site and return the resultant Web page with HTML formatting. In the Weather Tool the data provisioning service providers are implemented as wrapper-style agents that have a thin logic component dealing mainly with the process of retrieving data from the source as requested by the user.
- **Standardizing and completion services:** The standardizing service involves extracting the essential parts of data by removing the source formatting from the originally-retrieved data and converting it to a standard storage-efficient format for potential data requirements. For example, this service would parse the weather data fields' values into java objects that are easily updated and maintained. Typically, standardization also includes completion service that is responsible for filling in any missing values in the data.
- **Validation service:** Data validation involves applying domain specific rules to ensure data correctness. As per Lab Compliance's Glossary (LabCompliance), data validation is "A process used to determine if data are inaccurate, incomplete, or unreasonable. The process may include format checks, completeness, checks, check key tests, reasonableness checks, and limit checks." Some examples of this service are checking if -1000 degrees Fahrenheit is a valid value for temperature, updating today's weather (available from the forecast service) with historical data when it is available and replacing any missing value in the temperature field by the standard value (-273 degrees Fahrenheit).

- **Updating service:** The data updating service comes in handy where data is pushed from data source to data consumers. In this case, the consumers can subscribe to a set amount of data and then the data source (or the data provisioning service) can initiate a data updating service to ensure that data is sent to the consumers periodically.
- **Consolidation service:** The data consolidation service is responsible for appropriately merging data from many sources into one repository. This service is highly dependant on domain specific rules to carry out its functionality. It is essential for the designer/implementer of this service to encode the domain rules for correct fusion of data. As per British Columbia Government's Information Resource Management's glossary (BCG), data integration is the process of "blending data items from various distinct sources to create a larger and more comprehensive body of knowledge." For example, historical and forecast weather data as retrieved from their sources is stored in one repository.
- **Storage service:** As evident from the name, the data storage service is responsible for providing efficient storage mechanisms for data.
- **Formatting and translation services:** This service includes converting data into application-specific formats, for example, geographical information systems (GIS) applications may require data in the form of GIS layers, whereas traffic monitoring tools may require the same data in the text form.

These services can be combined in numerous ways resulting in different architectures that can be utilized as per the system's requirements.

System Architecture

Our agent-based data integration system consists of software agents providing combinations of data processing services in a heterogeneous, distributed environment, as best suited for the problem of weather data provisioning (Figure 4). In Figure 4, we depict agents as special three-part images that are explained in our previous paper (Kalra & Steiner, 2005). The Weather Tool's agent system is implemented and deployed using our in-house agent development and deployment framework, multi-agent development environment (MADE). MADE provides essential enhancements to JADE (Java agent development environment) (Bellifemine, Poggi, & Rimassi, 1999) with simplified interfaces for agent development and capabilities such as subscription services. JADE is a Java-based middle-layer software framework for agent development and deployment supporting the FIPA standards (FIPA). JADE provides the Agent Communication Language (ACL) message performatives and protocols for agent communication. At this point, we use a pre-determined metadata for describing the services in the absence of Semantic Web technology. Agents register

Figure 4. System architecture for the weather tool

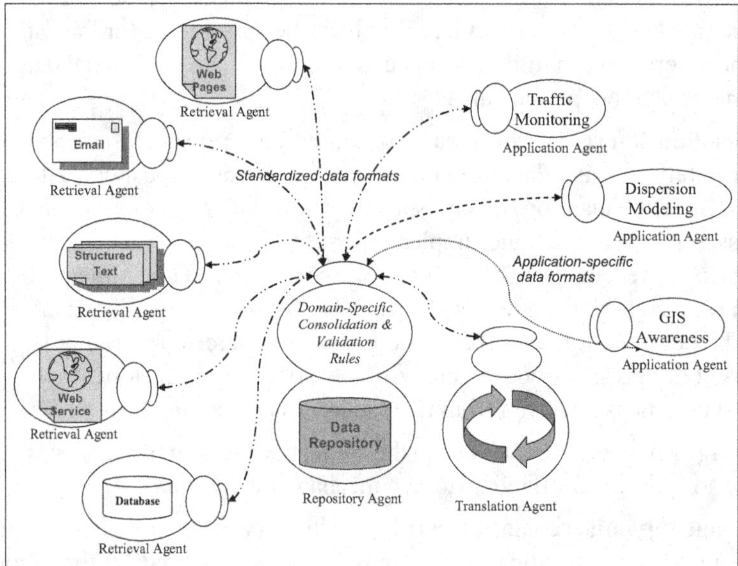

and advertise their services, namely the "retrieval," "repository," and "translation" services (as described as follows) using the JADE directory facilitator (DF).

We use service descriptions to describe the type and content of the data provided by a source for the agents to publish their services. These services descriptions can then be discovered by other agents in the system. The system has four types of agents: retrieval agents, repository agents, translation agents and application agents. Once registered, the retrieval agents either start retrieving data from their sources or wait for a request for data. The repository agent, after registering its repository service with DF, looks up the retrieval services and subscribes to them. The repository agent periodically checks for and subscribes to new retrieval agents that join the system. The application agents look up the weather repository service and subscribe to them for their data requirements. The repository agent looks up and invokes translation services when data is requested in formats other than its standard, data storage format.

- **Retrieval agents:** The Weather Tool retrieval agents provide the data extraction, parsing, and standardizing services. These lightweight, wrapper-style agents extract data as it exists at the data sources, use custom weather data format ("QLI Format") to parse the data into, and pass the weather data to their subscribers. The retrieval agents are implemented specific to the data source they are responsible for retrieving data from and are hence lightweight in terms of process logic and concentrate only on the process of retrieval. These agents do not maintain any repositories of the data they collect.

- **Repository agents:** The repository agents provide the data completion, consolidation, storage, and updating services. Repository agents either subscribe to or send individual requests to the available retrieval agents as per the user input. In our current implementation, the repository agent maintains a repository of weather data in QLI format using the MySQL database. The repository agent also uses the discovery and the integration of agent services to segregate the original data request into individual service-specific requests.
- **Translation agents:** The translation agents provide format conversion services between the QLI Format and other source-specific formats. The translation agents apply information-specific conversion rules and are very specialized in particular format conversions. The translation agents publish the formats of their input and output data. For example, GIS Data Converters translate data from weather repository specific "QLI format" to GIS application specific format. For example, agents that wrap any GIS applications extract a set of weather data attributes from the repository storage format.
- **Application agents:** Application agents are wrapper-style representatives of various applications in the Weather Tool and act as information consumers. Application agents look up and either request for or subscribe to repository agents that provide services for the type of data that they require.

The Weather Tool Test Case

Beyond the need to directly inform human users, weather data is often an input for many software applications including emergency response tools that support scenario planning and building foresight for emergency planners. The applications require different components of weather data as input, for example, viewing daily-summarized weather data on a map of a geographical area helps provide a situational view of the world. In our test case, maps/GIS are one of the weather data consumers.

The other application in the test case is a traffic monitoring and forecasting service. Besides analyzing, predicting, and planning for the current traffic purely based upon the time of the day and the road conditions, a traffic monitoring system should take into account current and forecast weather conditions. Warnings such as snow, ice, and high winds can help traffic experts to anticipate traffic problems, slowdowns, and accidents, due to poor road conditions. For such applications, the weather requirements can range from historical to forecast weather data.

Weather data comprises of readings on weather elements such as temperature, pressure, wind speed, wind direction, dew point, precipitation, humidity, and so forth. The weather experts collect data by using sensors and other advanced equipment, for example, the surface weather data (weather at sea-level) for a given time and location is measured and can be accessed at the National Weather Service (NWS) Web site. Weather data is validated within two to three days and can be accessed at the National Climatic Data Center (NCDC) Web site (NCDC) for a few pre-determined weather stations only. National Oceanic and Atmospheric Administration (NOAA) has non-validated current forecast data. The Forecasts Systems Laboratory's (FSL) Web site allows requests for weather data at several altitudes in the atmosphere, the radiosonde data (A radiosonde is an instrument for sending sensors up in the layers of the atmosphere for measuring weather data). In the test case, there is one retrieval agent each for the NCDC and the NOAA Web site. The NOAA-agent retrieves data every hour as the NOAA Web site has transient data. The NCDC and FSL agents retrieve data on demand as the corresponding sites maintain their own repositories and provide URL-based query support. In the test case, we have the following agents:

- The retrieval agents:
  - **NOAA forecast agent:** Retrieves forecast weather data from the NOAA Web site
  - **NOAA historical agent:** Extracts validated historical weather data from the NCDC Web site
- The application agents:
  - **Map agent:** Represents a map component that displays the map of Delaware with various layers of geographical data including location of schools, fire departments, police stations, and hospitals
  - **Traffic agent:** Represents a traffic monitoring and analysis application
- The repository agents:
  - **Weather repository agent:** Stores data and provides complete weather data for a given date and location to application agents
- The translation agents:
  - **Map translation agent:** Provides QLI Format to GIS layer format conversion
  - **Traffic translation agent:** Provides QLI Format to traffic specific format conversions.
  - **NOAA forecast agent:** Retrieves and parses data from the NOAA forecast service Web site into standard JAVA objects. The NOAA Web site is shown in Figure 2. Detailed forecast data is available for the next 60 hours and summarized data exists for the next ten days. NOAA Historical Agent retrieves and parses data from the NCDC Web site on demand.

Historical data is available for every hour in the format shown in Figure 1. Historical data for a day only becomes available after two to three days. Historical data is validated by the experts and is more detailed than the forecast data in terms of available weather attributes.

The map agent represents a GIS application that allows users to view data from the geographical perspective, based upon data such as latitude and longitude. Weather data for such applications is typically measured for an area or a point. GIS applications can provide the geographical perspective for weather data by showing their coverage area on the map of a region. The traffic agent represents a traffic monitoring and analysis application that utilizes the wind speed and other daily warnings fields such as heavy rain, snow, sleet, icy road conditions, and so forth, of the weather data. As weather data exists in the repository for a region and a time, the traffic agent requests and subscribes to current weather data for the geographical regions to which the various roadways belong.

The map translation agent extracts certain features from the standard weather data, thereby reducing the set of attributes to those required by the map agent. The traffic translation agent extracts wind speed and other warnings from the standard format weather data. The weather repository agent stores forecast and historical data into one weather repository as and when it gets updates and new data from the scrapers. The weather repository agent also performs validation, completion, and consolidation of data. It successfully updates the previously-existing forecast data when the corresponding historical validated data becomes available.

The NOAA forecast agent and the NOAA historical agent register with the JADE directory facilitator service as "weather retrieval" service providers. These agents retrieve data and send update messages with the current results either to their subscribers or to the requesting agent. The weather repository agent registers its "weather repository" service and performs a DF look-up of weather retrieval service providers. The weather repository agent subscribes to all the resultant agents using the subscribe messages. The map agent and the traffic agent, as per their requirements, perform look-up for weather repository services and either subscribe to or send queries to the resultant agent(s) using the ACL subscribe or query messages. The map translation agent and the traffic translation agent register their "map conversion" and "traffic conversion" services with the DF, respectively. The weather repository agent checks its repository for requested weather data and accordingly sends requests to appropriate retrieval agents. The weather data requests are channeled to appropriate translator agents in case of a specific format request. The results received from the translation agents are sent to the requesting application agents in appropriate ACL inform or query reply messages.

Example Enhancement

The Weather Tool test case worked well, with agents registering, finding, and invoking the various data services. At this point, we identified a need to introduce a new application to the Weather Tool. This application is an air quality modeling system that models the transport of pollutants in the air following an accidental or intentional release of a biological or chemical substance. The specific application is CALPUFF (CALPUFF) that is the default choice of the U.S. Environmental Protection Agency (EPA) for modeling long-range transport of the pollutants. CALPUFF computes an approximate plume of the pollutant over a period of time based upon the weather data for that time period. The assessment of the pollutants is done based upon the weather data in a geographical area. The details of CALPUFF and the weather data used by CALPUFF can be found in our previous paper (Kalra & Steiner, 2005).

To integrate the air quality modeling system, we needed a translation agent for converting standard data to the formats that CALPUFF required, the "CALPUFF translation" agent. We also built the logic for merging the radiosonde observations with the existing surface weather data into a service providing agent — the "radiosonde consolidation" agent. As and when the radiosonde data for a time and location becomes available, it is added to the existing surface data for the same time and location. We also implemented a new retrieval agent; the "radiosonde agent" that periodically retrieved and parsed data from the FSL Web site and passes on the results to its subscribers. The weather repository agent employed the CALPUFF translation agent to combine the radiosonde data for a particular time and region with the existing weather record for that time and region.

Once the required agents were implemented, there was no need to bring down the system to incorporate this new weather data source. Rather, upon launching, the new retrieval, translation, and the consolidation agents dynamically joined the system by registering their retrieval, translation, and consolidation services respectively with the DF. During its periodic check for new weather retrieval service providers, the weather repository agent subscribed to the new retrieval agent and started receiving the new weather data. Finally, to get the newly available data from the weather repository agent to CALPUFF programmatically, we wrapped the CALPUFF modeling system with an application agent, the plume agent.

Conclusion

"The Goods." The example enhancement mentioned in the previous section demonstrates how flexible agent architectures can be used for solving a variety of problems associated with collecting data from a number of disparate, independently-managed information sources, where the quality, format, and sources of the data may change over time. It allows for dynamically integrating new agents corresponding to new

sources and data formats without hampering the operational system. It also enables the sharing of data in different formats and different subscription models over a wide range of applications.

The Weather Tool's agent-based approach proves to have many advantages over the current approaches. The Weather Tool seamlessly handles new data sources as opposed to the statically-configured data warehouses. The Weather Tool architecture has middle layer repository agents acting as data provisioning, data consolidation, and validation service providers. The other approaches handle mostly validated data, as adding a validation logic layer to the system components can slow down information flow considerably.

"The Bads." Our current architecture strictly associates one data source with each retrieval agent. This can be extended to have one retrieval agent scrape data from many sources. This allows the retrieval agents to continue to scrape data from other sources when it fails to scrape data from a particular source due to changes such as format change. The data retrieval agents can be enhanced to include a thin verification and consolidation layer to support the above functionality. Another important direction for improvement is to have discovery-style retrieval agents that go out and search for the relevant sources given concise information descriptions. This will also take care of the source failure case, which is not addressed in the current system.

The Weather Tool stores all its standardized, integrated, and validated data in a single central repository, thus giving rise to a single point of failure. The best solution for this would be to implement a federated network of replicated and/or distributed repositories as an extension to this architecture.

The Weather Tool in its current form assumes that the data sources (new and existing) and the external applications understand and share a common metadata that is used for representing the services and the service descriptions. These restrictions make the Weather Tool rely upon certain constants that are not industry standards by any measure. The obvious solution to this problem is to use Semantic Web technology. Another problem is associated with the absence of a required service, where a similar service exists in the system but remains invisible to the system. The extensions of the semantic technology, specifically the concept of metadata/schema/ontology mapping is key to solving this problem. The ontology mapping tools derive mappings between two data schemas using concepts such as word processing, information flow, and so forth. In the next section, we talk about the next generation of the Weather Tool that takes advantage of the Semantic Web technology for enhanced performance and flexibility.

From the overall architecture point of view, the vision is to have a completely-autonomous adaptive network that adapts to the data traffic and determines when and where data should be cached or stored while at the same time optimizing the request-response time. Such a vision is also planned for in the next generation of the Weather Tool.

Intelligent Data Management: The Second Generation

The Weather Tool has performed very well within the context of the weather-related applications. The agent-based, service-oriented architecture of the Weather Tool has brought known and unknown data sources within one data environment, where their data is accessible at a central repository. The idea of intelligent data management (IDM) has evolved to overcome the universal schema and the central repository aspects. The IDM framework enables connectivity to a set of disparate data sources (including applications) QLI's IDM framework provides dynamic integration and (re-) configuration of several diverse, geographically-apart data sources, thereby offering a virtual data environment. No data is collected centrally but the data sources are polled for data on demand. IDM draws upon the service oriented architecture (SOA), Semantic Web (SW), and multi-agent system (MAS) technologies for representing, deploying, combining, and invoking various data-processing services (such as data gathering, validation, completion, translation, and formatting). These services are provided by agents supported by MAS mechanisms for agent discovery, communication, cooperation, and easy system configuration for service deployment and usage. The agents perform semantic similarity matching between the data requests and available data provisioning services and invoke them to fulfill the requests. The IDM architecture also provides for a simple, machine-processable, highly-structured query-based data access interface to its users. The query interface allows for formulation, decomposition, and solving of queries based upon representative keywords. The keyword queries range from keywords-based search for unstructured plain text data to highly-structured schema templates across a large number of heterogeneous data sources. Scalability in terms of functionality and types of queries as well as the number of data sources has been one of the guiding factors of the architecture of the query interface.

Conclusion

Effective operation within any enterprise relies heavily upon persistent, ad hoc, and intelligent collection of data from geographically-distributed heterogeneous sources. The advantage of information as derived from efficient and effective data retrieval is crucial to effective enterprise management. As the number of relevant data sources increases, the complexity of integrating them into the existing system renders the current information technology systems incapable of providing information to the analysts. The demand for innovative technology supporting dynamic data integration in a highly distributed environment is unprecedented, both in the industry and academia. We discuss our efforts on the Weather Tool, a service-oriented agent-based approach to data integration that facilitates data collection by means of data provisioning and processing services. We further describe our ongoing work on the intelligent data management framework that is an enhanced, domain-independent version of the Weather Tool.

References

AccuWeather, Inc. (n.d.). *World weather — local weather forecast.* Retrieved from http://www.accuweather.com

AFEI, The Association for Enterprise Integration (AFEI). (n.d.). Retrieved from http://www.afei.org

Bayardo, R. J., Bohrer, W., Brice, R., Cichoki, A., Fowler, J., Helal, A., et al. (1997). Infosleuth: Agent-based semantic integration of information in open and dynamic environments. *ACM SIGMOD*, 195-206.

Bellifemine, F., Poggi, A., & Rimassi, G. (1999). Jade: A fipa-compliant agent framework. *Practical Applications of Intelligent Agents and Multi-Agents,* 97-108.

Bergamaschi, S., Cabri, G., Guerra, F., Leonardi, L., Vincini, M., & Zambonelli, F. (2001). Supporting information integration with autonomous agents. In *Proceedings of the Fifth International Workshop CIA-2001 on Cooperative Information Agents*, Modena, Italy.

Bergamaschi, S., Castano, S., & Vincini, M. (1999). Semantic integration of semistructured and structured data sources. *SIGMOD Record Special Issue on Semantic Interoperability in Global Information*, *28*(1).

CALPUFF, The Atmospheric Studies Group. (n.d.). *ASG at Earth Tech: Official CALPUFF.* Retrieved from http://www.src.com/calpuff/calpuff1.htm

Cohen, W. W. (1998). The WHIRL approach to data integration. *IEEE Intelligent Systems*, *13*, 20-24.

Decker, K., Sycara, K., & Williamson, M. (1997). Middle-agents for the Internet. In *Proceedings of the 15th International Joint Conference on Artificial Intelligence*, Nagoya, Japan.

Etzioni, O., & Weld, D. S. (1995). Intelligent agents on the Internet: Fact, fiction, and forecast. *IEEE Expert*, *10*(4), 44-49.

FIPA. (n.d.). *Welcome to the foundation for intelligent physical agents.* Retrieved from http://www.fipa.org/

FSL, Forecasts Systems Laboratory. (n.d.). *FSL radiosonde database information page*. Retrieved from http://raob.fsl.noaa.gov/Raob_Software.html

Genesereth, M. R., Keller, A. M., & Duschka, O. M. (1997). Infomaster: An information integration system. *SIGMOD Record (ACM Special Interest Group on Management of Data), 26*(2).

Government of British Columbia. (n.d.). *Information resource management glossary*. Retrieved from http://www.cio.gov.bc.ca/other/daf/IRM_Glossary.htm

Kalra, G., & Steiner, D. (2005). Weather data warehouse: An agent-based data warehousing system. In *Proceedings of the Hawaii International Conference on System Sciences-38*.

Kushmerick, N., Weld D., & Doorenbos, R. (1997). Wrapper induction for information extraction. In *Proceedings of the 15th International Joint Conference on Artificial Intelligence (IJCAI)*, Japan (pp. 729-737).

Kwok, C. T., & Weld, D. S. (1996). *Planning to gather information* (Tech. Rep. No. UW-CSE-96-01-04). University of Washington.

LabCompliance. (n.d.). Glossary related to compliance for analytical laboratories: c-d. *LabCompliance Glossary*. Retrieved from http://www.labcompliance.com/glossary/c-d-glossary.htm

Labio, W., Zhuge, Y., Wiener, J. L., Gupta, H., Garcia-Molina, H., & Widom, J. (1997). The WHIPS prototype for data warehouse creation and maintenance. In *Proceedings of the 1997 ACM SIGMOD International Conference on Management of Data*, Tucson, AZ.

Levy, A. (1998). The information manifold approach to data integration. *IEEE Intelligent Systems*, 1312-1316.

Muslea, I., Minton, S., & Knoblock, C. (1999). A hierarchical approach to wrapper induction. In *Proceedings of the 3rd International Conference on Autonomous Agents*, Seattle, WA (pp. 190-197).

NCDC. (n.d.). *National Climatic Data Center*. Retrieved from http://www.ncdc.noaa.gov/oa/ncdc.html

NOAA. (n.d.). *National Oceanographic and Atmospheric Administration*. Retrieved from http://www.noaa.gov

NWS. (n.d.). *National Weather Service*. Retrieved from http://www.nws.noaa.gov

OWL. (n.d.). *Web Ontology Language Overview*. Retrieved from http://www.w3.org/TR/owl-features

Preece, A., Gray, P. M. D., & Hui, K. (1999). Supporting virtual organizations through knowledge fusion. In *Artificial Intelligence for Electronic Commerce: Papers from the AAAI-99 Workshop*. Menlo Park, CA: AAAI Press.

QLI. (n.d.). *Quantum Leap Innovations*. Retrieved from http://www.quantumleap.us

Sheth, A., & Larson, J. (1991). Federated database systems for managing distributed, heterogeneous, and autonomous databases. *ACM Computing Surveys, 22*(3).

Sycara, K., Decker, K. S., Pannu, A., Williamson, M., & Zeng, D. (1996). Distributed intelligent agents. *IEEE Expert,* 24-31.

WC. (n.d.). *The Weather Channel*. Retrieved from http://www.weather.com

Widom, J. (1995). Research problems in data warehousing. In *Proceedings of the International Conference on Information and Knowledge Management (CIKM'95)*, Baltimore (pp. 25-30). ACM Press.

Wiederhold, G. (1992). Mediators in the architecture of future information systems. *IEEE Computer*, *25*(3), 38-49.

Wooldridge, M., & Jennings, N. R. (1995). Intelligent agents: Theory and practice. *The Knowledge Engineering Review, 10*(2), 115-152.

Zhou, G., Hull, R., King, R., & Franchitti, J.-C. (1995). Data integration and warehousing using H2O. *Data Engineering Bulletin, 18*, 29-40.

Chapter V

GIME: A Geotechnical Information Exchange Architecture Using Web Services

Wei-Shinn Ku, University of Southern California, USA
Roger Zimmermann, University of Southern California, USA

Abstract

We present an information architecture using Web services for exchanging and utilizing geotechnical information, which is of critical interest to a large number of municipal, state, and federal agencies as well as private enterprises involved with civil infrastructures. For example, in the case of soil liquefaction hazard assessment, insurance companies rely on the availability of geotechnical data for evaluating potential earthquake risks and consequent insurance premiums. The exchange of geotechnical information is currently hampered by a lack of a common data format and service infrastructure. We propose an infrastructure of Web services, which handles geotechnical data via an XML format. Hereafter we report on the design and some initial experiences.

Introduction

Geotechnical information on soil deposits is critical for our civil infrastructure. Local, state, and federal agencies, universities, and companies need this information for a variety of civil engineering and urban policy applications, including land usage and development, and mapping of natural hazards such as soil liquefaction and earthquake ground motions. Foremost examples of geotechnical information, geotechnical boreholes are vertical holes drilled in the ground for the purpose of obtaining samples of soil and rock materials and determining the stratigraphy, groundwater conditions, and/or engineering soil properties (Hunt, 1984). In spite of rather costly drilling operations, boreholes remain the most popular and economical means to obtain subsurface information. These types of data range from basic borehole logs containing a visual inspection report of soil cuttings to sophisticated composite boreholes combining visual inspection and in-situ, laboratory geotechnical and geophysical tests. Figure 1a shows an example transcript of the Standard Penetration Test (SPT), a particular type of geotechnical borehole test. Significant amounts of geotechnical borehole data are generated in the field from engineering projects each year. The data and results of boreholes are usually published and released as hardcopy reports, without the digital data from the field test. Naturally, sharing data via the traditional hardcopy reports is slow and results in errors when the data is converted back to digital form for further processing. With the recent ubiquity of communication networks, particularly the Internet, the trend toward electronic storage and exchange of geotechnical borehole data has accelerated. So far these efforts have often been uncoordinated and ad hoc.

Geotechnical borehole data is complex and sophisticated in that it contains both well-structured and semi-structured elements. In Figure 1a, for example, the *Summary* field contains free-form text, while some of the other columns are well defined. Therefore, an efficient data format for storage and exchange is required that is suitable for the diversity of geotechnical borehole data. Currently, there is no accepted common format for exchanging these data among researchers and practitioners. To date, the most commonly-used formats for representing geotechnical borehole data include the Association of Geo-technical and Geoenvironmental Specialists (AGS, 1999), the Log ASCII Standard (Heslop Karst, Prensky, & Schmitt, 2000) for well logging in petroleum engineering, and the National Geotechnical Experimental Site (Benoit & Lutenegger, 2000) format that adopts the AGS data dictionary and expands it to cover more research-oriented geotechnical tests. Another research project was initiated at the U.S. Army Engineer Waterways Experiment Station (U.S. Army, 1998) to establish a standard electronic data format for geotechnical and geological exploration in order to automate data interchange. In addition, the Pacific Earthquake Engineering Research Center at Berkeley (PEER) and the Consortium of Organizations Strong Motion Observation Systems (COSMOS) commence a

Figure 1. The photographs illustrate the geotechnical boring activities from drilling until the soil samples are examined; the result is a boring log showing stratigraphy, physical sampling record, and SPT blow count: (a) example of boring log; (b) drilling and sampling activities

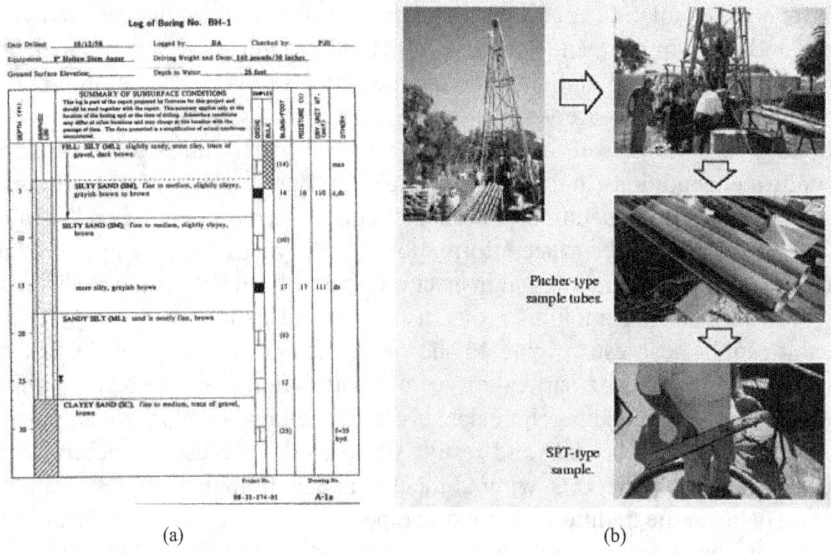

project to create a geotechnical data dictionary and exchange format specifically for the digital dissemination of geotechnical data (COSMOS/PEER, 2002).

Recently, we have proposed the use of XML as the preferred format for storage and exchange of borehole data (Bardet, Hu, & Swift, 2003; Zimmermann, Bardet, Ku, Hu, & Swift, 2003). Similar efforts have been carried out by the W3G (The World Wide Web of Geotechnical Engineers), which proposed the Geotechnical Markup Language (Geotech-XML), a geotechnical engineering version of the eXtensible Markup Language.[1] The eXploration and Mining Markup Language (XMML) project[2] of the SEEGrid Community (Solid Earth and Environment Grid) also proposed an XML-based encoding for geoscience and exploration information. XMML is intended to support exchange of exploration information in a wide variety of contexts. In addition, the Open Geospatial Consortium[3] (OGC) suggested the specification of Geography Markup Language (GML). GML is an XML encoding for the transport and storage of geographic information, which includes features, coordinate reference systems, geometry, topology, time, units of measure, and generalized values. Geographic features in GML include coverage and observations as subtypes.

XML offers many advantages over other data formats for borehole data. Its tree-structure and flexible syntax are ideally suited for describing constantly evolving and annotated borehole data. However, in addition to defining new data formats for borehole data, there is much research to be done to improve the exchange and utilization of geotechnical information over the Internet. There is a need for an infrastructure for *sharing* and *manipulating* this valuable information.

As the data collection and digital technologies improve, more and more geotechnical borehole data from the field, laboratory, or office are directly produced in, or converted to, a digital format. This makes it possible to use, share, and disseminate geotechnical data nationwide by coordinating geotechnical data standard and Internet dissemination activities within large organizations or government agencies. With the recent ubiquity of communication networks, particularly the Internet, the trend towards electronic storage and exchange of geotechnical borehole data has accelerated. The ROSRINE (Resolution of Site Response Issues from the Northridge Earthquake) project has produced an integrated system based on a relational database management system (RDBMS), geographic information system (GIS), and Internet map server (IMS) to disseminate geotechnical data via the Internet (Swift, Bardet, Hu, & Nigbor, 2002). The U.S. Geological Survey (USGS) is continually publishing seismic cone penetration test (CPT) data, which is collected with USGS CPT trucks and then distributed through a Web-based system managed by the USGS Earthquake Hazard Program in Northern California (Holtzer, 2001). All these efforts make it easier, faster, and less expensive for all levels of public and private sectors to access geotechnical information. Hence, these systems try to address the challenges and needs for timely, high-quality data as required in many geotechnical projects.

The architecture of most current geotechnical data archive and distribution systems follows the schematic in Figure 2. The end user utilizes a Web browser to gather the information of interest via the Internet. The data providers host large information sets in their database systems. Using standard Web server technology, a query interface at a URL address is provided to the end user for querying and retrieving data via the Web browser. Since geotechnical data is spatial in nature, a GIS map server is often integrated to provide a more graphical and user-friendly data query ability. This type of interactive data exchange system is designed for human partici-

Figure 2. Traditional client-server architecture with a Web server and a browser-based client; the client is used mostly for information presentation and visualization

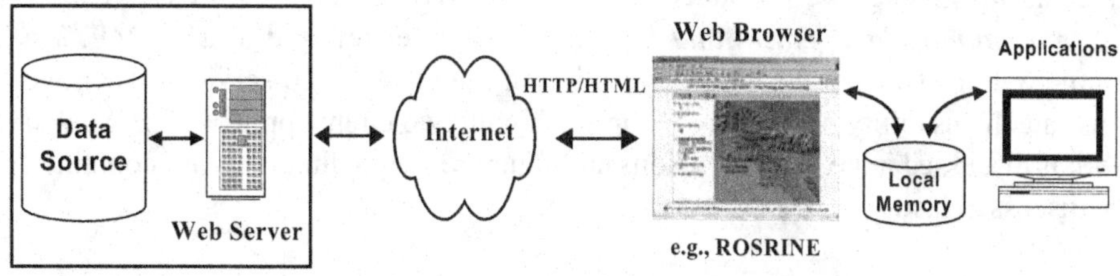

pants since the data flow occurs between the end user (most likely engineers) and the system servers. However, this architecture lacks the flexibility to handle more complex tasks. For instance, how can we streamline the upload of data gathered in the field via digital equipment such as CPT trucks, which not only involve human interaction but also machine-to-machine communication? Furthermore, many times a geotechnical data set is not the end product, but the input to an analysis, simulation, or other computation. With a Web server/browser architecture, no simple, direct programmatic access to remote data is possible. Because many of the data repositories are under different administrative control, it is important that the data exchange format and the communication protocol follow a universally-acceptable standard that is both simple and extensible.

We believe that the emerging standard of Web services (WS) is well suited to alleviate some of these problems.[4] Web services build upon an old idea of accessing resources (storage space, compute cycles, etc.) from a local machine on a powerful remote computer. Unlike earlier attempts to provide this functionality, WS are a broadly-accepted and open standard that is supported by all major industry vendors. The communication protocol to access services is based on the simple object access protocol (SOAP),[5] which uses XML syntax. A Web service interface is formally described with a Web Service Description Language (WSDL) file. A new service can be registered with a universal description discovery and integration (UDDI) server, and it can then be located, explored, and accessed from computers around the Internet. Figure 3 illustrates the Web services paradigm with a geotechnical data repository. Multiple applications, such as soil liquefaction analysis or borehole data visualization can be built in a modular fashion. The next section describes two applications in detail. A traditional, browser-based interface can also be provided if desired.

This chapter describes our efforts to design and implement such an infrastructure based on an extensible set of Web services. The services that are initially required are: (1) *file storage* and (2) *query and exchange*. With these facilities, practitioners in the field can directly store newly-acquired data in a repository while the data customers are able to access these data sets in a uniform way. Beyond these two basic services, we have also designed a (3) *visualization* capability that allows an automated conversion of XML geotechnical data into a graphical view similar to the traditional hardcopy format. The output is presented as *Scalable Vector Graphics* (SVG).[6]

Later in this chapter we introduce the proposed WS architecture for *Geotechnical Information Management and Exchange*, hereafter referred to as GIME. We continue in next with a detailed description of the GIME Web services. Then we illustrate the usability of the GIME approach with two client applications. Related work is discussed in next. Conclusions and future research directions are contained are discussed last.

Figure 3. A Web service architecture enables client applications to access remote information through a machine-level interface for further processing and analysis

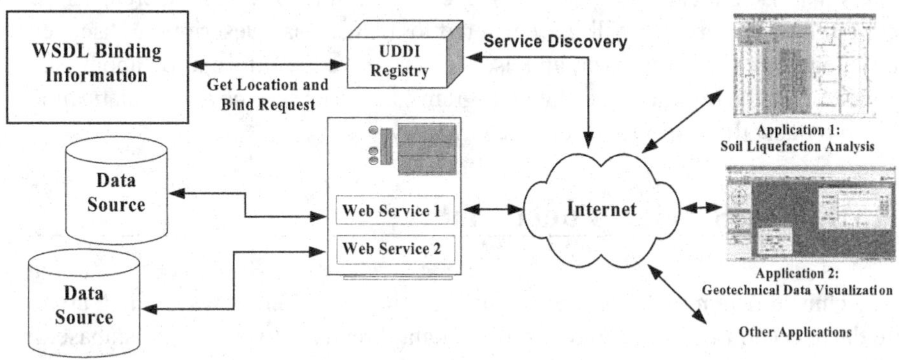

Geotechnical Information Management and Exchange (GIME)

Our proposed architecture for the *Geotechnical Information Management and Exchange* system makes extensive use of Web services to provide access to these valuable data sets for the expert practitioners as well as the general public. We will now describe each component of the system in detail.

GIME Overview

Figure 4 illustrates the architecture of the GIME system. Multiple, distributed geotechnical data archives are accessible via the Internet. These repositories are under different administrative control, for example, the U.S. Geological Survey provides some of their information to the public. We distinguish two types of archives on the basis of what data access they allow: read-write (RW) or read-only (RO). RW archives host three geotechnical Web services, and additionally an XSLT (XSL Transformations) processor for transforming XML files to SVG files, and a database (with XML and spatial data query support). The three Web services that are implemented within the application server provide the interface for distributed applications to store (*File Storage Web Service*, FSWS), query and retrieve (*Query & Exchange Web Service*, QEWS), and visualize (*Visualization Web Service*, VWS) the geotechnical information. RO archives implement only the QEWS Web service to access their database.

The services use the simple object access protocol (SOAP) as the communication protocol between the server and clients. A complete Web Service Description Language (WSDL) file of the system provides two pieces of information: an application-level service description (abstract interface), and the specific protocol-dependent details that users must follow to access the service at a specified concrete service endpoint. These services will be registered to a Universal Description Discovery and Integration (UDDI) server, and users can retrieve the information about these services from the Internet. The client program can use its service proxy (static binding) to request these services from the GIME system.

GIME Web Services Functionality

Geotechnical data may be added to an archive in two different ways. First, an on-site database administrator may insert the data directly into the local database. In

Figure 4. The proposed geotechnical information management and exchange architecture composed of multiple, distributed data archives; some archives are read-only while others allow reading and writing; Web services provide the programmatic interface to the data

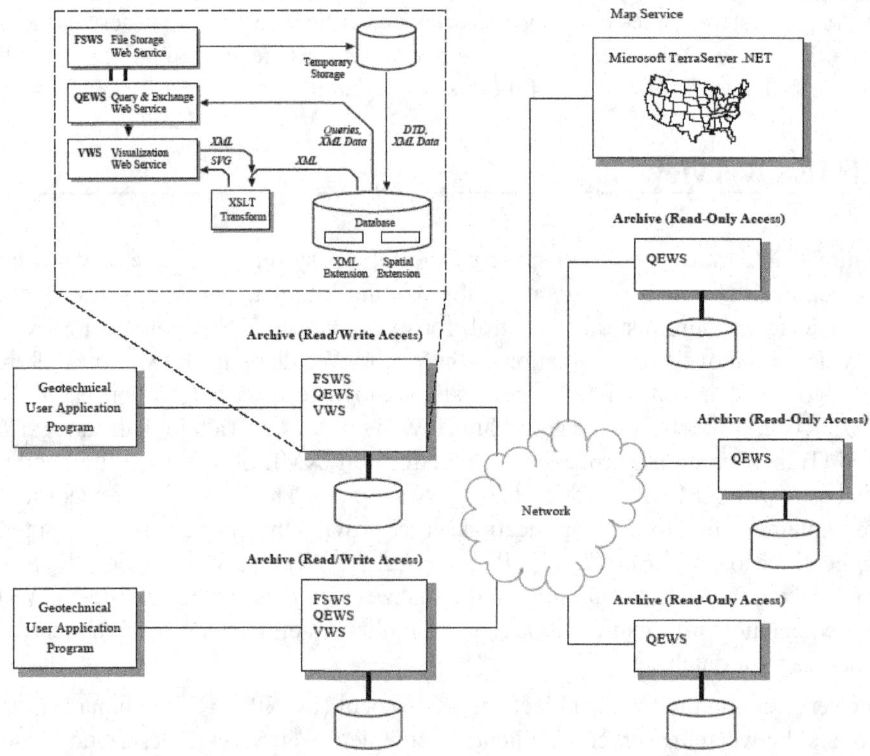

this case, insert operations are not available via Web services, and we consider this archive read-only within the GIME architecture. Second, geotechnical data may be uploaded into a database via the file storage Web service. Hence the repository is considered read-write. Any uploaded XML file is first placed in a temporary space where it is validated against the document type definition (DTD) or XML schema[7] for geotechnical data sets. If the file is accepted, the data is then stored in the main database.

The stored data can be queried and downloaded via the QEWS interface. Currently GIME supports a number of predefined queries that are further described in earlier. Note that each repository may contain a unique set of geotechnical data. To avoid that a user application must contact each repository directly, we implement a distributed query mechanism that automatically forwards queries to other known archives and collects the results before returning the data to the application. Such forwarding mechanisms can be effective as demonstrated earlier by the SkyQuery project (Malik, Szalay, Budavari, & Thakar, 2003) and our own distributed query routing techniques (Zimmermann, Ku, & Chu, 2004). At the current stage the query results are complete borehole data sets. In our local repository, we have added the PostGIS package to support spatial queries on the geotechnical data. For example, users can query boreholes based on their geographical location.

Finally, the visualization Web service, VWS, translates the original geotechnical data files into graphical data images (in SVG format) via an XSLT processor. We use SVG because it is based on XML and is hence easily compatible with the overall architecture.

GIME Access Authentication

The main purpose of geotechnical Web services is to assist in the utilization of geotechnical information by local, state, and federal agencies mandated to develop and sustain our civil infrastructures. For some particular applications, a service may need to control the authentication of the users who want to access geotechnical Web services. Some entry of information into the system database might have to be restricted and controlled to expert members of key organizations. Some other Web services such as data exchange and visualization may not require such stringent security levels and may be anonymously accessed through read-only queries. Some tools (e.g., the Microsoft .NET framework, IBM WebSphere, etc.) may be useful to construct several different levels of a security model for certificate users. Our current GIME prototype does not yet implement fine-grained access control.

Geotechnical Web Service Functionality and Implementation

The three main geotechnical Web services of the system provide a number of specialized methods for programmatic access to the data, and the parameters and variables are described in the GIME WSDL file.[8] These methods follow the W3C

Figure 5. The logical organization of the GIME server components (left) and the architecture for the borehole query (BQ) client application (right); the communication between the client and the server is based on the SOAP and HTTP protocols.

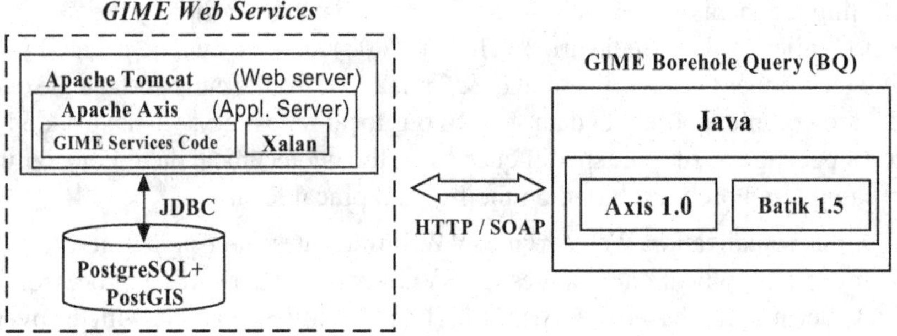

Table 1. Software components and toolkits that are leveraged to build GIME

Name of Component	Description
Apache Axis	Axis is a Web service middleware that acts as SOAP server and client. Axis handles the task of converting Java objects to SOAP requests when they are sent and received over the network.
Apache Tomcat	Tomcat is the official reference implementation for the Java servlet and JavaServer pages technologies. It serves as a servlet engine (mainly for Axis) and a Web server for GIME.
Apache Xalan	Xalan is an XSL Transformation (XSLT) processor for converting XML documents into HTML, SVG or other XML document types. It generates on the fly SVG files from XML borehole files.
Apache Batik	Batik is a toolkit based on Java. It can be used in Java applications or applets for viewing, generating, and manipulating scalable vector graphics (SVG) format images. Batik library is used in one of our Java client applications for viewing SVG files produced by GIME.
PostgreSQL	PostgreSQL is an object-relational database and can be spatially enabled by the PostGIS package. PostgreSQL and PostGIS provide the backend database and spatial functionalities of GIME.

standardized data-types and structures of the SOAP[9] specification to provide an easily-usable interface for client program construction. Web services usually operate from a combination of a Web server and application server; they can be implemented using many available tools and libraries. GIME utilizes the open source software components listed in Table 1. The GIME Web server is Apache Tomcat[10]

Table 2. Description of the GIME application programming interface (API)

Name of Function	Description of Function (client perspective)	Restriction	Related Web Service
GeoPutDTD()	Upload a new DTD file and update the current DTD on server. Input parameters: a DTD identification number and a DTD file	Super user	FSWS
GeoGetDTD()	Send a unique identification number of a DTD file and the server returns a string- type object to the client program. Input parameter: a DTD identification number; return value: a string-type object	All users	FSWS
GeoPutXMLFile()	Upload a borehole XML file and store it in the server. Input parameters: a borehole XML file name and a borehole XML file	Only in write enabled databases	FSWS
GeoGetXMLFile()	Send a unique identification number of a borehole XML file, and the server returns a string-type object to the client program. Input parameter: a XML file identification number; return value: a string-type object	All users	QEWS
GoeQuery()	Execute the input query statement which is parsed by this function to select tuples inside tables. All the result tuples are stored in a result structure and returns to the client. Input parameters: query parameters; return value: a result data object	All users	QEWS
GeoVisualization()	Send unique identification number of a borehole file and display its SVG picture inside a pop-up window. The transformation from XML to SVG format is executed on the fly and the SVG file is rendered in the client. Input parameter: a borehole file identification number; return value: a SVG file	All users	VWS
GeoGetSVGFile()	Send unique identification number of a borehole file and returns its SVG file as string type. Input parameter: a borehole file identification number; return value: a SVG file	All users	VWS

and its application server is Apache Axis.[11] The application code specific to GIME is embedded within Axis, which is convenient to use; when Tomcat starts, Axis automatically compiles the application codes located in its working directory and generates the necessary object class files. Figure 5 shows the components of the GIME Web services and all the application programming interface (API) methods are listed in Table 2. We now describe the overall functionality and implementation of each GIME Web service.

Geotechnical File Storage Web Service

The geotechnical file storage service provides client programs with an interface to upload their geotechnical XML files into the main database. All files are stored in XML format, and at the same time, meta-data is extracted and saved. The meta-data includes specific elements of the imported files to facilitate querying (described earlier). This service is subject to user authentication because only registered expert users are allowed to make changes to the database. We currently utilize the open source PostgreSQL object-relational database with the PostGIS package. To manage the data we implemented two different paradigms to store XML data. The first one extracts elements of interest from an XML file and stores them in table columns as meta-data. The XML file itself is also stored in its entirety in a column of type XML in the main table. Hence, the meta-data columns can be rapidly accessed when users want to query and retrieve XML information in the database. This second approach to store XML data is to completely decompose the elements of an XML file into columns of multiple tables. The second process is bi-directional, which means that the XML files can be regenerated after individual elements have been updated. Furthermore, new XML files can be generated from multiple existing tables.

Verification of the Geotechnical XML Files

Two levels of verification are performed on uploaded files. The first level is executed automatically by checking the XML data against a borehole DTD to ensure that the uploaded file is well formed. The DTD defines geotechnical tags that allow the full description of data provided by our partner organizations (California Department of Transportation, California Geological Survey, Los Angeles Department of Water and Power, etc.). If any file cannot pass the first level of verification, it will be rejected and an error condition will be raised. Otherwise the file will be stored in a temporary directory and a notification e-mail will be sent to an expert of that category of geotechnical files. The expert verifies the content of the uploaded file and decides if it can be stored into the main database or should be returned to the author for clarification. After passing the two levels of verification, the file will be imported into the database and its meta-data will be extracted. Users can download the DTD files from the project Web site for guidance when constructing their geotechnical XML files. They can also use the verification interface on our Web site for remote checks.

Geotechnical Query & Exchange Web Service

The main purpose of the query and exchange Web service is to facilitate the dissemination of the valuable geotechnical data sets and encourage their use in broad and novel applications. Once XML files are uploaded into the main database as described in the previous paragraphs, they are then available for dissemination. A data user can query the geotechnical files in the main database on meta-data attributes such as the name of the data provider, the geographical location of the borehole, and so forth, to find the files of interest. The files can then be downloaded with the *GeoGetXMLFile()* method. A graphical version of the data in SVG format can also be obtained.

Predefined Queries of the Data Exchange Web Service

In the current GIME version, we have identified six parameters for extracting particular sets of geotechnical files from the main database; these parameters are also indexed as meta-data. Client programs can use these parameters in the query interface to find the geotechnical files of interest. At this point we restrict the query interface to these six parameters to gain some experience with our architecture and to simplify the distributed processing of queries. Spatial query constructs are supported within the database management system via a PostGIS package. The six parameters are:

1. **Project Name [Type: string]:** The individual name of geotechnical projects
2. **Site [Type: string]:** The field site name where borehole testing has been carried on
3. **Location [Type: polygon]:** The geographical region within which boreholes have been drilled
4. **Testing type [Type: string]:** Field investigation type (e.g., SPT, CPT, etc.)
5. **Project Date [Type: date]:** The date of the beginning of the project
6. **Data Provider [Type: string]:** The organization or agency who produced the data

Recall that the GIME system is an evolving federation of autonomous and geographically-distributed geotechnical databases on the Internet. To facilitate the querying process, we require a client application program to only contact one of the GIME nodes and then have this node forward the query to and collect results from other GIME databases that are part of the federation. Each node maintains a list of other known GIME nodes. A node recognizes when it receives a query from another GIME node and will not forward the query any further so as to avoid loops in query processing. The result of a query is a list of the borehole data sets that satisfy the query predicate. Each data set is identified with a link descriptor similar to a URL. All the qualifying links are collected from the distributed GIME nodes and returned to the user application to form the result of the query. If the user application decides to perform any processing on the data sets, then it can download the data directly from each individual node via the link descriptor. The details of this query routing mechanism are contained in (Zimmermann et al., 2004).

Using the Web Service of TerraServer

Our query interface allows boreholes to be searched by geographical location. A background map with superimposed borehole locations is a compelling way to present the search results, as illustrated in Figure 6. However, rather than storing aerial maps in the system, the functionality of the Microsoft TerraServer is enlisted

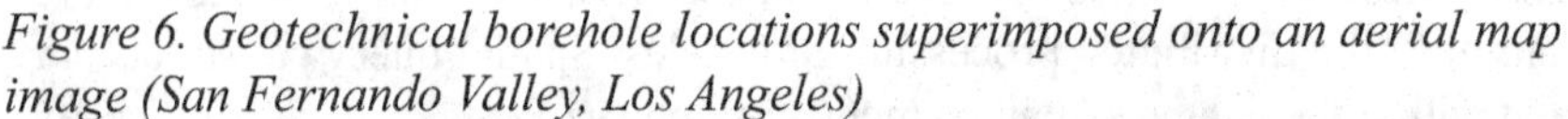

Figure 6. Geotechnical borehole locations superimposed onto an aerial map image (San Fernando Valley, Los Angeles)

Figure 7. Borehole SVG file rendering (the right window) that was automatically generated from a selected XML data file

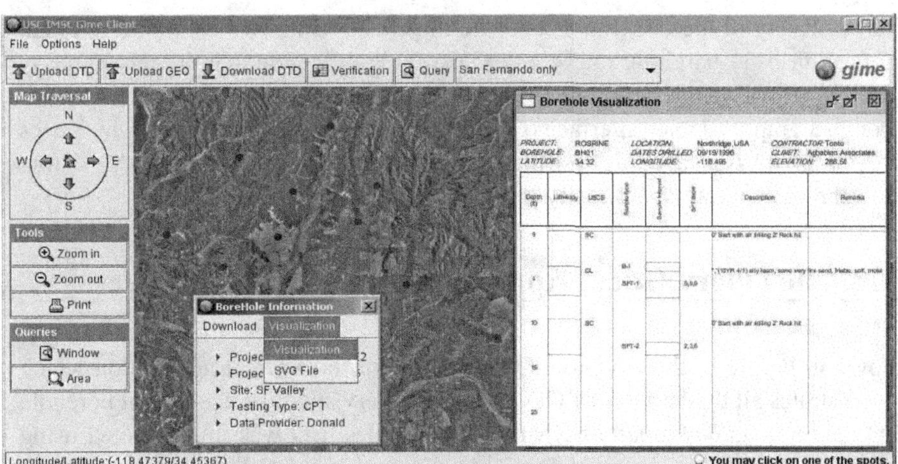

(Barclay, Gray, Strand, Ekblad, & Richter, 2002). The TerraServer provides maps (aerial imagery and topographical maps) covering the United States with up to one-meter resolution. Furthermore, it provides Web service interface methods to obtain these background maps. Our system then plots the geotechnical borehole locations on top of the map according to their longitude and latitude.

Geotechnical Visualization Web Service

XML borehole files, although easily readable by computers, become meaningful to geologists and civil engineers only after they are rendered into SVG images, for example, stratigraphy of soil deposits and geotechnical test results (e.g., CPT and SPT). We use the Apache Xalan parser[12] in combination with Extensible Stylesheet Language (XSL) files for this purpose. The parser translates XML files into SVG descriptions according to a set of XSL rules. After the translation, the SVG data is transmitted to the client, and the user can display and analyze them (Figure 7). Data may not only be visualized from the main database, but also from temporary data provided by users who do not have database write privileges. Again, the user must construct their geotechnical XML files in accordance with the DTD files that are published by our system. They may then upload the data and use the visualization method to translate the file into the SVG format.

GIME Client Application Examples

The feasibility of the GIME concepts are illustrated using two examples of client applications: (1) borehole query and (2) soil classification. The borehole query client is a Java application, which demonstrates all of the GIME functionalities through a graphical user interface (GUI). The soil classification client, which uses the Microsoft Visual Studio .NET framework, demonstrates how to modify existing geotechnical programs to directly import borehole data from GIME.

Borehole Query Client Application

Shown in Figure 8, the Borehole Query (BQ) is a Java client application which demonstrates all the features of GIME, that is, query and visualization of borehole data, and upload/download of XML and DTD files. BQ was implemented using the Java Software Development Toolkit (JDK, version 1.4.1).[13] BQ accesses GIME through the Axis library, and visualizes SVG files using Xerces[14] and Batik15 (Table 1). BQ can be downloaded from the GIME Web site and installed as a standalone Java program along with the Batik Squiggle package (Table 1) which displays SVG files. As shown in Figure 8, five query parameters can be entered into the BQ dialog box with optional AND/OR relations. The other query parameters, that is, the loca-

Figure 8. The sample Borehole Query (BQ) client application is programmed in Java; the dialog box allows the user to input query parameters while the small pop-up display (the left window) illustrates the metadata of a borehole when the user clicks on one of the dots (indicating a borehole location) on the map

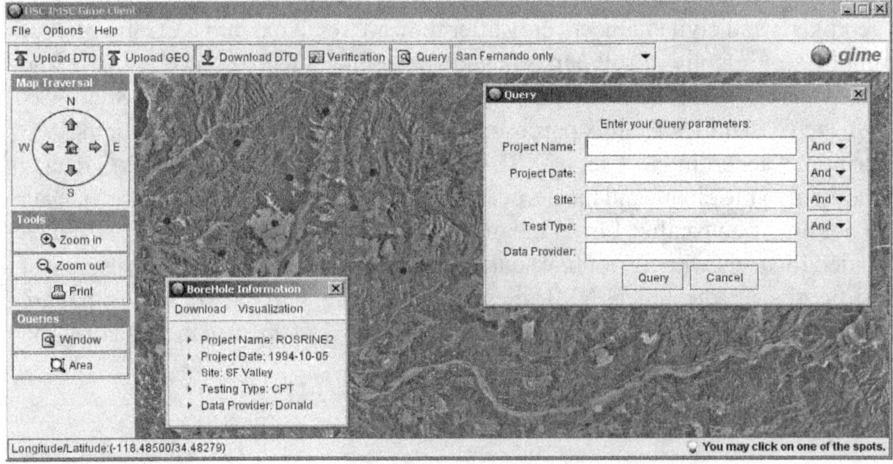

Figure 9. Sample Java code to invoke the "GeoQuery" Web service of the GIME server; this code fragment would typically be executed by GIME clients

```
Import org.apache.axis.client.Call;                        // The class files for SOAP communication
import org.apache.axis.client.Service;
:
:
String endpoint = "http://datalab.usc.edu:8080/axis/jdbc_db2s.jws?wsdl";   // The GIME server URL
Service  service = new Service ();                                        // Create connections to the
call = (Call) service.createCall ();                                      // GIME server
call.setTargetEndpointAddress( new java.net.URL(endpoint) );
:
:
call.setOperationName("GeoQuery");   // Invoke the  GeoQuery  function and preparing the query string
String[] queryString = {  select
BOREHOLE_ID,PROJ_NAME,SITE,LONGITUDE,LATITUDE,TEST_TYPE,PROJ_DATE,DATA_PRO from db2inst1.IDENTIFICATION_TAB
where    . };
Vector result = (Vector) call.invoke(queryString);
```

tion parameters, are defined using an interactive rectangular box displayed over a background map. The background map is assembled from aerial maps downloaded from the TerraServer Web service[16] (Barclay et al., 2002). Figure 9 displays excerpts from the BQ Java code for processing queries through the GeoQuery function of GIME (Table 2). BQ sends the search parameters to GIME, retrieves the metadata of matching borehole files, and displays the search results (i.e., borehole locations) as dots over the background map (Figure 8). Borehole metadata can be viewed by clicking on the dots. BQ allows users to invoke all the functions of GIME (Table 2) through menus and buttons. Borehole XML files can be uploaded to the remote GIME archive using the "Upload Geo" button. BQ prompts users to select the XML file on the local disk before uploading it. After GIME has received a XML file, it compares it to a specific DTD, and if that file conforms, inserts it into the GIME database, and generates and stores the corresponding metadata. Borehole XML files are visualized using the visualization menu, which downloads SVG files from GIME and displays them using the Squiggle package (Figure 7). More details about the functionalities of the Borehole Query Client are available from the GIME Web site.[17]

Figure 10. The block diagram of the visual basic (VBA) client application that implements a core penetration test (CPT) soil classification (CSC)

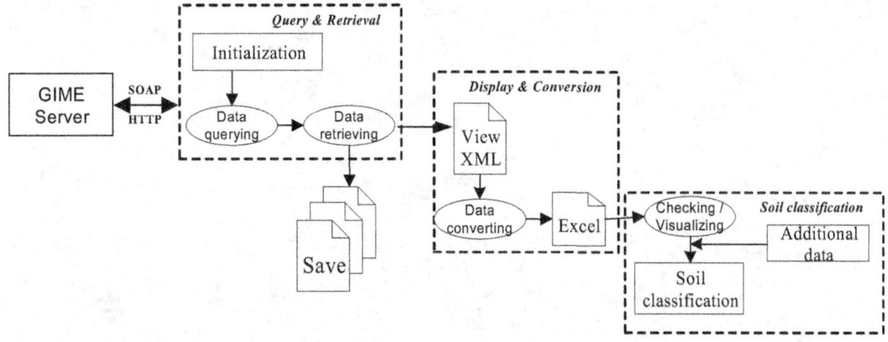

Soil Classification Client Application

GIME can exchange borehole data not only with newly-created Java applications, but also with many existing engineering applications. With minor modifications, stand-alone engineering programs can import information from GIME. This integration of GIME with engineering programs is illustrated with a CPT Soil Classification program, hereafter referred to as CSC. CSC classifies soils based on cone penetration tests (CPT) data and the soil classification method described in Robertson, Woeller, and Finn (1992). CSC was developed starting from an existing Excel Visual Basic Application (VBA), which required importing data manually into spreadsheets. As shown in Figure 10, CSC has three main functions: (1) *query and retrieval* of borehole data via GIME; (2) *display and conversion* of borehole XML data; and (3) *soil classification.* CSC added to the existing VBA application the capabilities of querying and retrieving XML borehole data from GIME and pasting those into spreadsheets. The first modification to the existing VBA application was to import the Web service References Tool 2.0, which is a resource toolkit adding the Web service functionalities to the Excel VBA environment. With the Web service References Tools, VBA can call functions for discovering Web services, select particular Web services, and create proxy classes of Web service objects. With these references, VBA can access the WSDL files of GIME, and the GIME objects defined

Figure 11. The query box (left) and the query results (right) of the CSC client application; the borehole XML data is decomposed in a tree-like structure

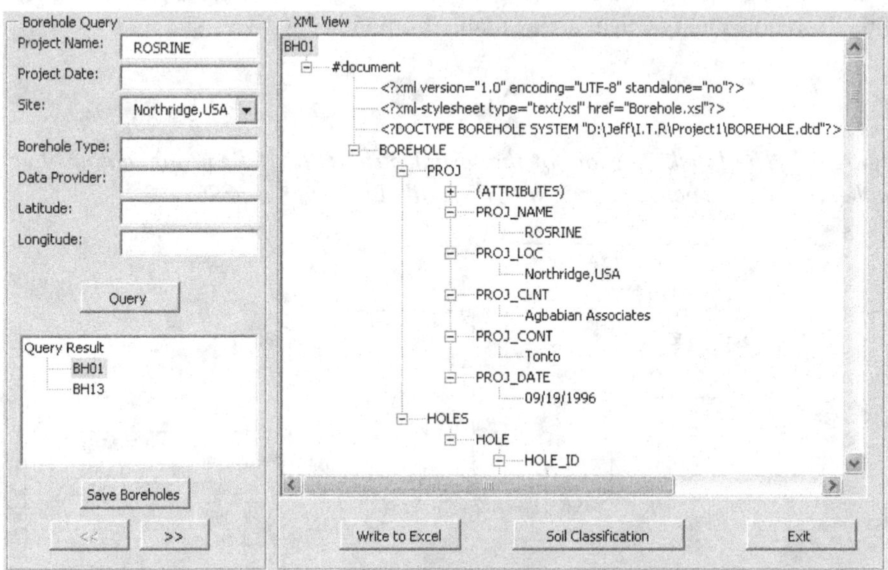

Figure 12. Excerpt from the VBA subroutine DisplayXMLNode that converts the content of an XML file into the Excel tree view shown in Figure 11

```
Sub DisplayXMLNode(ByVal xmlnode As IXMLDOMNode, ByVal root As String, ii As Integer)
' Add a TreeView node for this XMLNode. (Using the node's Name is OK for most XMLNode types)
Dim tvnode As Node
Set tvnode = tvXML.nodes.Add(root, tvwChild, xmlnode.nodeName & ii, xmlnode.nodeName)
tvnode.Expanded = False
tvnode.EnsureVisible
root = xmlnode.nodeName & ii
ii = ii + 1
Select Case xmlnode.nodeType
Case NODE_ELEMENT                              ' This is an element: Check whether there are attributes.
  If xmlnode.Attributes.Length > 0 Then        ' Create an ATTRIBUTES node.
    Dim attrNode As Node
    Set tvnode = tvXML.nodes.Add(root, tvwChild, root & "attr", "(ATTRIBUTES)")
    Dim xmlAttr As IXMLDOMAttribute            ' Add all the attributes as children of the new node.
    For Each xmlAttr In xmlnode.Attributes     ' Each node shows name and value.
      Set tvnode = tvXML.nodes.Add(root & "attr", tvwChild, "", xmlAttr.Name & " = '" & xmlAttr.Value & "'")
    Next
  End If
Case NODE_TEXT, NODE_CDATA_SECTION             ' For these node types we display the value
  tvnode.Text = xmlnode.Text
Case NODE_COMMENT
  tvnode.Text = "<!--" & xmlnode.Text & "-->"
Case NODE_PROCESSING_INSTRUCTION, NODE_NOTATION
  tvnode.Text = "<?" & xmlnode.nodeName & " " & xmlnode.Text & "?>"
Case Else                                      ' Ignore other node types.
End Select
Dim xmlChild As IXMLDOMNode                    ' Call this routine recursively for each child node.
Set xmlChild = xmlnode.FirstChild
Do Until xmlChild Is Nothing
  Call DisplayXMLNode(xmlChild, root, ii)
  Set xmlChild = xmlChild.nextSibling
Loop
End Sub
```

in the proxy class. As shown in Figure 10, CSC checks at first for the availability of GIME services. If the service is available, CSC retrieves metadata about the locations of borehole sites and the number of data sets at each site, and adds this metadata to a list of available sites (site list box in Figure 11). CSC forwards the selection parameters input into its query dialog box to GIME, which replies with a list of selected boreholes (Figure 11). XML borehole files are downloaded using the *GeoGetXMLFile* function of GIME (Table 2). They are loaded into memory using the *LoadXML* function of the XML Document Object Model (DOM), which is detailed in Barwell, Blair, Crossland, Case, Forgey, Hankison, Hollis, Lhotka, McCarthy, and Roth (2002) and Balena (2002). Figure 12 shows excerpts from the subroutine *DisplayXMLNode* which converts XML files into XML document objects and display them as a tree structure (Figure 11). That display is useful to inspect the structure and contents of XML files before pasting them into spreadsheets. The VBA code also uses a DOM function to paste onto spreadsheets the contents of the "CPT" elements of XML borehole files. Each "CPT" element, which contains the values for depth, CPT tip resistance q_c and sleeve friction S_f, is parsed and written sequentially onto spreadsheets (Figure 13). Figure 13 illustrates the final result of the CPT soil classification obtained by CSC. The techniques that CSC uses for

Figure 13. The Excel application display showing the borehole data and the CPT analysis results processed with the CSC client application

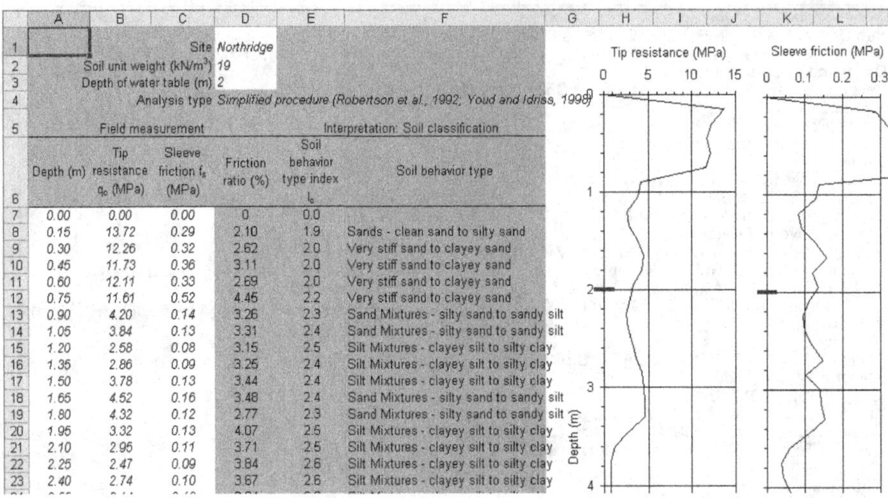

Site Northridge
Soil unit weight (kN/m³) 19
Depth of water table (m) 2
Analysis type Simplified procedure (Robertson et al., 1992; Youd and Idriss, 1998)

Field measurement			Interpretation: Soil classification		
Depth (m)	Tip resistance q_c (MPa)	Sleeve friction f_s (MPa)	Friction ratio (%)	Soil behavior type index I_c	Soil behavior type
0.00	0.00	0.00	0	0.0	
0.15	13.72	0.29	2.10	1.9	Sands - clean sand to silty sand
0.30	12.26	0.32	2.62	2.0	Very stiff sand to clayey sand
0.45	11.73	0.36	3.11	2.0	Very stiff sand to clayey sand
0.60	12.11	0.33	2.69	2.0	Very stiff sand to clayey sand
0.75	11.61	0.52	4.45	2.2	Very stiff sand to clayey sand
0.90	4.20	0.14	3.26	2.3	Sand Mixtures - silty sand to sandy silt
1.05	3.84	0.13	3.31	2.4	Sand Mixtures - silty sand to sandy silt
1.20	2.58	0.08	3.15	2.5	Silt Mixtures - clayey silt to silty clay
1.35	2.86	0.09	3.25	2.4	Silt Mixtures - clayey silt to silty clay
1.50	3.78	0.13	3.44	2.4	Silt Mixtures - clayey silt to silty clay
1.65	4.52	0.16	3.48	2.4	Sand Mixtures - silty sand to sandy silt
1.80	4.32	0.12	2.77	2.3	Sand Mixtures - silty sand to sandy silt
1.95	3.32	0.13	4.07	2.5	Silt Mixtures - clayey silt to silty clay
2.10	2.95	0.11	3.71	2.5	Silt Mixtures - clayey silt to silty clay
2.25	2.47	0.09	3.84	2.6	Silt Mixtures - clayey silt to silty clay
2.40	2.74	0.10	3.67	2.6	Silt Mixtures - clayey silt to silty clay

reading, inspecting, and pasting the contents of XML files can be adapted to many other client applications.

Related Works

During recent years, several geotechnical Web services have been proposed and implemented. The majority of this work focuses on the design of geotechnical information exchange platforms and integration of geotechnical Web services from different providers. Certain design goals of these prototype systems overlap with the GIME system, and we summarize them as follows.

Badard and Braun (2004) proposed a platform named OXYGENE for the development of interoperable geographic applications and Web services. OXYGENE aims at providing users with an open framework for the development of geotechnical research applications and allows for the centralization of code, documentation, and easy maintenance. There are three main characteristics of the OXYGENE platform. First, the architecture and the object-oriented schema of OXYGENE are compliant with OGC/ISO specifications. Second, OXYGENE adopts modularized design and all the components (e.g., DBMS, map server, etc.) can be easily updated. Third, a generic graphical object browser has been embedded in clients of OXYGENE, and most geographical data objects can be visualized by users.

A concrete design and implementation of an integration and interoperation platform that aims to solve heterogeneity and online service for geographical information is presented in Luo, Liu, Wang, Wang, and Xu (2004). This platform aims at providing service integration which takes layers as the basic geographical data organization units, accomplishing data retrieval from multiple GIS data sources, and visualizing digital map data. There are four main Web services provided for achieving the design goals: (1) application integration services, which is the core service of business process scheduling to implement interoperation, (2) metadata service, which maintains the service information, (3) transform service, which can be implemented into platforms of different GIS providers to accomplish data format transformation into Geography Markup Language (GML), and (4) spatial analysis service, which receives GML format data and provides GML-based common spatial analysis functionalities as data clipping, projection, coordinate transformation, and overlapping.

In addition some researches have focused on automated service discovery, binding, and composition of geotechnical Web services. An, Zhao, and Bian (2004) proposed the utilization of patterns with geotechnical Web services based on ontology. Their design employs ontology to advertise geotechnical Web services and uses them for semantics-based discovery of relevant geotechnical Web services. Furthermore, integration of geotechnical Web services can also be implemented based on ontology and system developers can integrate geotechnical functions into their applications without having to host all the functionalities locally.

Conclusion and Future Research Directions

We have presented research results on the development of Web services for exchanging and utilizing geotechnical information across a variety of applications critical to our civil infrastructure systems. The proposed Web services are being presently tested in realistic work environments in collaboration with municipal, state, and federal agencies, as well as international partners. It is likely that our first prototype of geotechnical Web services will evolve in different directions depending on the needs of our research collaborators. It is anticipated that the concepts developed in this research will contribute to pave the way for the creation of a virtual repository of geotechnical information operated by a consortium of local, state, and federal agencies.

Acknowledgments

We would like to thank Jianping Hu, Yu-Ling Hsueh, Chirag Trivedi, and Xiaohui He for their help with the GIME system implementation. We also wish to thank our collaborator on the COSMOS project, Jennifer Swift. The GIME design, implementation, and experiments were made possible by the NSF grants ITR CMS-0219463 and ERC Cooperative Agreement No. EEC-9529152. Any opinions, findings, and conclusions or recommendations expressed in this material are those of the authors and do not necessarily reflect those of the National Science Foundation.

References

AGS (1999). In *Electronic transfer of geotechnical and geoenvironmental data* (3rd ed.). Kent, UK: Association of Geotechnical and Geoenvironmental Specialists.

An, Y., Zhao, B., & Bian, F. (2004). Geo Web services based on semantics. In *ER Workshops, 3289, 139-157*. Shanghai, China: Springer.

Badard, T., & Braun, A. (2004). OXYGENE: A platform for the development of interoperable geographic applications and Web services. In *DEXA Workshops*, 888-892, Zaragoza, Spain: IEEE Computer Society.

Balena, F. (Ed.). (2002). *Programming Microsoft visual basic.net*. Microsoft Press.

Barclay, T., Gray, J., Strand, E., Ekblad, S., & Richter, J. (2002, June). *TerraService. NET: An introduction to Web services* (Tech. Rep. No. MSR-TR-2002-53). Microsoft Research.

Bardet, J. -P., Hu, J., & Swift, J. (2003). Data storage and exchange format of borehole information. *Submitted to Computers & Geosciences*.

Barwell, F., Blair, R., Crossland, J., Case, R., Forgey, B., Hankison, W., Hollis, B. S., Lhotka, R., McCarthy, T., & Roth, J. C. (2002). *Professional VB .Net* (2nd ed.). Wrox Press Ltd.

Benoit, J., & Lutenegger, A. J. (2000, April). National geotechnical experimentation sites (NGES). *ASCE Geotechnical Special Publication, 408*(93), 221-234.

COSMOS/PEER User Survey. (2002). Archiving and Web dissemination of geotechnical data Website. *COSMOS/PEER-LL 2L02, USC*. Retrieved December 1, 2005, from http://geoinfo.usc.edu/gvdc/

Heslop, K., Karst, J., Prensky, S., & Schmitt, D. (2000, June). Log ASCII standard document #1 — file structures, Version 3. *Canadian Well Logging Society*. Calgary, Canada, p. 44.

Holtzer, T. (2001, October). Distribution of USGS CPT data via the Web. In *Proceedings of the COSMOS/PEER-LL Workshop on Archiving and Web Dissemination of Geotechnical Data*. Richmond, CA: U.S. Geological Survey.

Hunt, R. R. (1984). *Geotechnical engineering investigation manual*. New York: McGraw-Hill.

Luo, Y., Liu, X., Wang, W., Wang, X., & Xu, Z. (2004). Web service and geographical information integration. In *Proceedings of the COMPSAC Workshops* (pp. 130-133). Hong Kong, China: IEEE Computer Society.

Malik, T., Szalay, A. S., Budavari, T., & Thakar, A. R. (2003, January). SkyQuery: A Web service approach to federate databases. In *Proceedings of the First Biennial Conference on Innovative Data Systems Research* (pp. 188-196). Asilomar, CA: VLDB Endowment.

Robertson, P. K., Woeller, D. J., & Finn, W. D. L. (1992). Seismic cone penetration test for evaluating liquification potential under cyclic loading. *Canadian Geotechnical Journal, 15*(29), 686–695.

Swift, J., Bardet, J. -P., Hu, J., & Nigbor, R. (2002). An integrated RDBMS-GIS-IMS system for dissemination of information in geotechnical earthquake engineering. Accepted by *Computers & Geosciences*.

U.S. Army Waterways Experiment Station (1998). *Standard data format for geotechnical/geological exploration* (Project 98.005). Retrieved December 1, 2005, from http://tsc.army.mil/products/geotech/geocover.asp

Zimmermann, R., Bardet, J. -P., Ku, W. -S., Hu, J., & Swift, J. (2003, July). Design of a Geotechnical Information Architecture Using Web Services. In *Proceedings of the Seventh World Multi-Conference on Systemics, Cybernetics, and Informatics* (pp. 394-398). Orlando, FL: IIIS Publication.

Zimmermann, R., Ku, W. -S., & Chu, W.-C. (2004, November). Efficient query routing in distributed spatial databases. In *Proceedings of the International Symposium Advances in Geographic Information Systems* (pp. 176-183). Washington, DC: ACM Press.

Endnotes

1 http://www.ejge.com/GML/

2 https://www.seegrid.csiro.au/twiki/bin/view/Xmml/WebHome

[3] http://www.opengeospatial.org

[4] http://www.w3.org/2002/ws/

[5] http://www.w3.org/2000/xp/Group/

[6] http://www.w3.org/Graphics/SVG

[7] http://www.w3.org/XML/Schema

[8] http://datalab.usc.edu/axis/CLS_Services.jws?wsdl

[9] http://www.w3.org/TR/soap12-part0/

[10] http://jakarta.apache.org/tomcat/index.html

[11] http://ws.apache.org/axis/index.html

[12] http://xml.apache.org/xalan-j/

[13] http://java.sun.com/j2se/index.jsp

[14] http://xml.apache.org/xerces2-j/

[15] http://xml.apache.org/batik/

[16] http://terraserver.microsoft.com/

[17] http://datalab.usc.edu/gime/

Chapter VI

ScienceMaps: An Online Resource Portal for Standards-Based Science Instruction Using Geographic Information System Technology

June K. Hilton, Claremont High School, USA
David E. Drew, Claremont Graduate University, USA

Abstract

At the beginning of the 21st century, technology implementation and its effect on student achievement is a topic of much interest and debate. Science education in particular has been criticized for not utilizing the skills of a "techno-savvy" generation and for not effectively integrating technology into the K-12 science classroom. This chapter discusses ScienceMaps, an ongoing research and development effort consisting of an online resource portal for standards-based science instruction using GIS technology. ScienceMaps is unique in that it concentrates on using GIS to teach, not on teaching GIS. Using an Internet-based GIS, ScienceMaps provides access to GIS technology and data to anyone, anywhere, with access to an Internet browser. Assessment, evaluation, and future development directions for ScienceMaps are also discussed.

Introduction

The issue of the effect of technology on student achievement has recently been the subject of much research and debate (J. Hilton, 2003; Hilton, 2005, 2006). Furthermore, as schools are being held more accountable for meeting state and national standards through their performance on standardized tests, the focus on improving student achievement through the use of technology is becoming an even greater issue. As school funding becomes more closely linked to performance on standardized tests, improving student achievement through innovative means, such as technology integration and use, is critical (Hilton, 2006). ScienceMaps is an online resource portal that provides standards-based instructional materials, designed and integrated for use with an Internet-based geographic information system (GIS), that allows for their immediate integration into science lessons. GIS technology is a powerful analytical tool that can help students visualize spatial relationships and supports the spatial analysis of data.

The goals of the ScienceMaps research and development effort are twofold: to support the ongoing development and field-testing of this innovative Internet-based courseware and to promote the integration of technology into the science curriculum so as to develop the problem-solving and critical-thinking skills of students while simultaneously addressing the diverse learning styles of learners.

Background

Archer (1998) believes that computers can raise student achievement and even improve a school's climate. Eliot Levinson (2000) agrees but adds that many factors, such as staff development, infrastructure, and effective instructional materials, influence the effectiveness of technology. Simply put, if schools are to realize benefits from education technology, teachers and students must have adequate and equitable access to hardware and network connections; states and districts must give schools the capacity to use technology well by devising a thoughtful technology plan and offering adequate teacher training and technical support; teachers and students must use technology in effective ways (Jerald, 1998). Thus, not only must teachers be adequately trained in the technology, but they must also understand how to use the technology appropriately in support of students and the curriculum (Hanson & Carlson, 2005). This effective use of technology can only help to "re-excite" students about science. According to Drew (1996), "the number of students who find science interesting seems to shrink as they progress through the school system. Good teaching involves knowing what methods are effective" (p. 6).

Even though GIS is now available to K-12 education, modest budgets for technology and staff development, and limited emphasis on students developing spatial analytical skills, prevent schools from effectively integrating the technology into the classroom curriculum (Joseph, 2004). Thus, if schools are to be effective in utilizing technology, particularly GIS, to raise student achievement, accessibility, professional development, and effective use must be addressed.

Accessibility

Access to computers at school has risen significantly. According to Skinner (2002), "Nationally, in 2001, there were just over four students to every instructional school computer, and the number of students per Internet-connected computer in schools dropped from 7.9 in 2000 to 6.8 in 2001" (p. 53). This trend continues. In 2004, Fox (2005) reports that nationally, there were 3.8 students to every instructional computer and the number of students per Internet-connected computer in schools dropped to 4.1. Rumberger states that, newer and more powerful desktop computers, along with the development of computer networks and the Internet, provide the opportunity for educational technology to transform teaching and learning in more fundamental ways across the curriculum and throughout the educational system (Rumberger, 2000).

The digital divide continues to exist between high (75% or more of the students eligible for the federal free and reduced lunch program) and low poverty schools. While Internet access across all types of schools has shown steady improvement, the actual use of technology in high poverty, high minority, and academically-failing schools lags behind technology use in more advantaged schools (Fox, 2005). In multiple measures of access, schools with a large number of poor students, receiving free or reduced price lunch, rated lower than schools with smaller numbers of poor students (Du, Havard, Olinzock, & Yang, 2004). Students who do not have access to high-quality computer experiences at home or school are not being provided with the opportunities they need to be successful in society. Furthermore, increased access to computers will only have positive results when the educator has a complete grasp of the role and use of computers, and an understanding of the student's home environment and how their deficiencies must be met in order to realize their full potential, thus enhancing society instead of reducing the average achievement (Du et al., 2004).

Professional Development

Another important factor for effective implementation is staff development. Providing sufficient development and training to give staff skills and confidence in the use of technology is widely viewed as an ongoing challenge to schools (Schmitt, 2002). Trotter (1999) reports that nearly four out of every ten teachers who do not use software for instruction say they do not have enough time to try out software, and almost as many say they do not have enough training on instructional software. Adelman et al. (2002) found that although most teachers had participated in multiple professional development opportunities, more than 80% indicated a need for training in how to integrate technology into the curriculum. Ironically, in 2003, 82% of public schools nationwide with Internet access indicated that their school or school district had offered professional development to teachers in their school on how to integrate the use of the Internet into the curriculum (Parsad & Jones, 2005). Interestingly, students believe that professional development and technical assistance for teachers are crucial for effective integration of the Internet into curricula (Levin, Arafeh, Lenhart, & Rainie, 2002). Unfortunately, schools and school districts spend most technology money on hardware and software, and spend relatively little on training, which averages no more than 15% of all technology funds (Hanson & Carlson, 2005). In the technology context, teachers reported having limited time to practice technology skills, to develop new activities, and to conduct activities during a tightly scheduled school day. These were reportedly the most significant barriers to increased integration of educational technology in the classroom (Adelman et al., 2002).

Effective Use

The third important factor to consider is effective use. Technology, it has been argued, helps change teacher-student relationships, encourages project-based learning styles, and supports the acquisition of skills such as "higher order thinking," analysis, and problem solving (Schmitt, 2002). Thus, its integration and effective use is critical to increase student achievement. Although teachers now have the use of an unprecedented amount of technology for their classrooms and schools, there is little evidence to indicate that teachers systematically integrate instructional technology into their classroom curriculum (Wetzel, 1999). Hedges, Konstantopoulos, and Thoreson (2000) found that even though teachers have had increasing access to computers for instruction, very few actually use them. Although 84% of all public school teachers said personal computers were available to them, approximately 60% indicated that they actually used them (U.S. Bureau of the Census, 1998). While 75% of teachers say the Internet is an important tool for finding new resources to meet standards, two-thirds agree that the Internet is not well integrated in their classrooms, and only 26% feel pressure to use it in learning activities (Ely, 2002). Thus even though computer technology may be widely available, in general, it is poorly integrated into the classroom curriculum and is under-used (Hedges et al., 2000).

Unfortunately, the manner in which technology is used in schools also depends on socioeconomic status. Disadvantaged children, even with access to new technologies, are more likely to use them for rote learning activities rather than for intellectually-demanding inquiries (Du et al., 2004). Equally disturbing is the evidence that teachers of students with different ability levels are also using the computer differently. Research indicates that technology use with low-achieving students is mostly skills-based, drill and practice, while more sophisticated programs are used with advanced students (Becker, 2000; Manzo, 2001). While all teachers use technology in multiple areas of their work and believe in technology's potential to positively impact teaching and learning, instructional use (e.g., student projects, accommodations, lesson presentation) is one of the least frequent ways teachers employ technology (Hanson & Carlson, 2005). However, researchers have concluded that technical tools, when used appropriately as instructional supports, have the potential to enhance student learning and teacher instructional success (Bednarz, 2004). Williams believes that education will be affected by how educators and students use the technology to prepare for life-long learning in the face of unrelenting change (Williams, 2002).

The CEO Forum 2001 Report (CEO Forum, 2001) found that while students frequently use computers at school for research (96%) or to write papers (91%), their actual use for learning new concepts or practicing new skills learned in class was significantly lower (60% and 57% respectively). Quintana and Zhang (2004) report that online inquiry activities are important for all K-12 learners to explore substantive driving questions in different areas, especially science.

Geographic Information Systems

Geographic information science is an approach to measuring and understanding the spatial context of the human and physical environment. By combining theories and methods from many disciplines, and use of information technologies, its purpose is to provide geographic representations of our world that allow for visualization and spatial analysis through the use of geographic information system (GIS) technology. For example, the earth's climate, natural hazards, population, geology, vegetation, soils, land use, and other characteristics can be analyzed in a GIS using maps, aerial photographs, satellite images, databases, and graphs. GIS technology is used in many areas such as agriculture, business, earth and space sciences, education, energy, emergency management, health sciences, life sciences, logistics, physical sciences, telecommunications, and transportation.

In education, using GIS to analyze phenomena about the Earth and its inhabitants can help students to better understand patterns, linkages, and trends about our planet and its people (Gutierrez, Coulter, & Goodwin, 2002). Integrating GIS into the school curriculum answers the call for including critical thinking, integrated learning, and multiple intelligences in curriculum design (Joseph, 2004).

Students who are visual learners particularly benefit from the mapping process, as the presentation of the data is consistent with their cognitive strengths (Gutierrez et al., 2002). Research has shown that educators must be attuned to the individual differences in students' strategical information processing styles, and an awareness of the student's style allows for the design of educational experiences that tap into the student's cognitive resources (Farrell & Kotrlik, 2003). Teachers realize that technology enhances science, technology, engineering, and mathematics (STEM) instruction by providing resources for individual students, as well as for the whole class, and serves as a means to address individual learning needs (Hanson & Carlson, 2005). Thus, GIS should be emphasized throughout K-12 education where it can be used to teach concepts and skills in earth science, geography, chemistry, biological science, history, and mathematics.

ScienceMaps

ScienceMaps was created to promote the integration of GIS technology into the science curriculum and to address the aforementioned issues of accessibility, professional development, and effective use. As a result, the ScienceMaps project seeks to:

- Develop standards-based instructional materials for use with an Internet-based GIS and allow for their immediate integration into science lessons *(accessibility and effective use)*
- Reduce the necessary technical skills needed to effectively integrate technology into the science classroom and reduce the time needed to preview/evaluate instructional materials *(professional development and effective use)*
- Provide access to these resources through an online resource portal and in so doing reduce the need for schools to purchase expensive software/hardware for students and teachers to access the instructional materials and applications *(accessibility and effective use)*

Current science learning standards promote inquiry teaching as a means to help students develop a deeper conceptual understanding of science (Borgman et al., 2004). Drawing on the California State Science Standards, numerous science lessons and GIS applications have been developed. California was selected for several reasons:

- California has the largest pre K-12 enrollment (6,356,348) as well the largest number of public school teachers (307,672).
- California ranks fourth in the country in capacity to use technology, that is, number of technology- related policies state has in use, but 30th in the country in use of technology.

- California ranks 47th in the country in access to technology and is one of only five states that have a plan to regularly update technology, but no funding mechanism to ensure that technology is updated (Fox, 2005).
- California was 1 of 7 states to receive an "A" rating on its science standards, receiving top honors for its standards. According to a study by the Thomas B. Fordham Institute, "California has produced an exemplary set of standards for school science; there was no question among readers about the "A" grade" (Gross, Goodenough, Haack, Lerner, Schwartz, & Schwartz, 2005, p. 30).

Until the emergence of GIS and related mapping technologies, constructing maps by hand was an elaborate, time-consuming task that often required good drawing skills. It is not necessary for users of ScienceMaps to "learn GIS" as the online applications are developed in such a manner that the necessary level of technical proficiency for both student and teacher is minimal. However, the spatial analysis performed using the applications is sophisticated and helps to develop students' critical thinking skills through the practice of spatial thinking (Bednarz, 2004). In addition to supporting the visual display of spatial data, students can use the online GIS applications to perform various quantitative analyses. Students can also gain confidence in the use of advanced technologies, giving them additional technology skills for future employment. It has been noted that there is a serious shortfall in professionals and trained specialists who can utilize geospatial technologies in their jobs, which indicates the need for the education, training, and development of these individuals (Gaudet, Annulis, & Carr, 2001).

ScienceMaps Online Resource Portal

Major science education standards call for K-12 students to engage in online, hands-on science activities where they can investigate personally meaningful scientific driving questions. When students learn science through inquiry, they are imitating practicing scientists (Borgman et al., 2004). The use of the Internet has led to a paradigm shift in education from traditional didacticism to technology-rich, constructivist learning where the learner is more active and independent, and the processes of teaching and learning are emphasized (Houtsonen, Kankaanrinta, & Rehunen, 2004).

One aspect of online inquiry involves information seeking. As a result, there is an increased focus on information seeking support for K-12 learners, such as new collections in larger projects like the National Science Digital Library (NSDL) (Quintana & Zhang, 2004). As educators increasingly look to technology to meet the challenges of teaching and learning in a rapidly-changing educational environment, the field of interactive visualization, illustrating educational concepts through visual, interactive applications, and simulations, presents a promising and emerging paradigm for learning and content delivery (Marsh et al., 2005). Research on the use of digital resources among STEM teachers found that digital resources had the added benefit of providing opportunities to supplement limited resources, such as labs (Hanson & Carlson, 2005).

The ScienceMaps Online Resource Portal was developed using the Collection Workflow Integration System (CWIS) a Web-based software application designed to allow groups with collections of information to share that information with others via the World Wide Web and integrate that information into the NSDL (University of Wisconsin - Madison, 2004). CWIS is a software application to assemble, organize, and share collections of data about resources, similar to the Yahoo and Google online directories, but conforming to international and academic standards for metadata. CWIS was funded by the National Science Foundation (NSF) and specifically created to help build collections of STEM resources and connect them into the NSF's NSDL, but it can be (and is being) used for a wide variety of other purposes.

The ScienceMaps version of CWIS has all the features of the standard application including:

- Resource annotations and ratings
- Keyword searching
- Field searching
- Recommender system (similar to the "Amazon" recommender system)
- OAI 2.0 export (a method to allow a "harvester" such as the NSDL, to collect metadata regarding content from the resource portal)
- RSS feed support (a method to "push" a short description of resource portal content and a link to the full version of the content to other Web sites)
- Customizable user interface themes (e.g., large-text version)

Figure 1 is a screenshot of the ScienceMaps online resource portal home page. Users may perform a keyword search to find lessons that pertain to a particular topic (e.g., earthquakes, water, hurricanes, invasive species, etc.) or by California Earth science, biological/life science, or investigation/experimentation standard (e.g., 9a, 6b, 1c, etc.). It is possible to view the entire lesson, including objectives, questions, and so forth, by clicking on "Full Record". It is not necessary to login to access the lessons.

The ScienceMaps online resource portal contains two integrated resources, science lessons and GIS applications. Each science lesson is aligned to California science standards to promote inquiry-based learning as well as investigation and experimentation. Each GIS application is specifically designed and developed to meet the learning objectives contained in the science standards and lessons in such a way as to enhance learning.

Figure 1. ScienceMaps online resource portal — home page

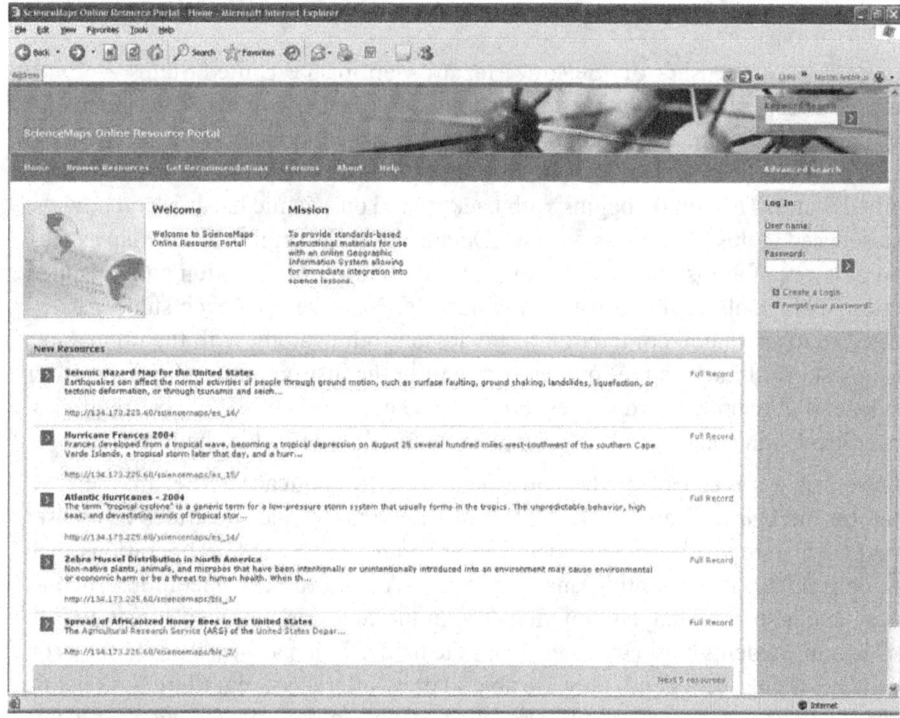

To more effectively meet the requirements for the distribution of ScienceMaps lessons and GIS applications, some of the features of the standard portal application have been customized, and others added, specifically:

- **Description:** background information regarding the lesson topic
- **Objectives:** specific objectives of the lesson
- **Lesson outline:** specific procedures to follow to complete the lesson
- **Classification:** specific content area (e.g., Earth Sciences)
- **Resource type:** type of online resource (e.g., Interactive GIS)
- **Audience:** appropriate grade level (e.g., Grades 10 – 12)
- **Coverage:** geographic region that the lesson covers (e.g., California, United States)
- **California science standards:** specific content standards that the lesson covers

- **California investigation and experimentation standards:** specific standards that the lesson covers

Figure 2 is a screenshot of “Seismic Hazard Map for the United States — Earth Science Lesson 16” illustrating the features described above and the content for this particular lesson. In this lesson, students are asked to analyze the relationship between the occurrences of seismic hazards and topography in California and the United States. This lesson begins with background on seismic hazards and how the dataset used in this lesson was derived. Details about the origins of the map as well as a glossary of terms are provided to the user via links. Information on the United States Geological Survey is also available. The objectives that each student is expected to master upon completion of the lesson follow along with the procedures and questions. It is possible for teachers to print the instructions and questions for students if they prefer hard copies. Each lesson concludes with the coverage area, grade level, and content and investigation standards assessed in the lesson.

Figure 3 is a screenshot of the corresponding GIS application “Seismic Hazard Map for the United States — Earth Science Lesson 16” and illustrates basic user interface features such as a legend and layer control and basic GIS operations such as zoom in/out, pan, identify, and “zoom-to.” Advanced GIS operations such as query and a spatial analysis function (proximity analysis) are also illustrated. In this lesson, students begin by entering a state name, which allows them to focus on one state. Using the legend, they are able to draw inferences regarding the seismic hazard potential as measured by percent of gravity in the selected state. Students are then able to perform queries by comparing other areas that have similar seismic hazard characteristics in the United States by entering a specific percent of gravity. They may also enter a specific address along with search radius, to determine the type of seismic hazard in a particular area (e.g., their home, school, landmark, etc.). In either of these queries, detailed seismic hazard information appears in the box below the map. Many advanced spatial operations, such as routing, overlay analysis, and buffering, can be added to meet the operational requirements of any particular lesson.

ScienceMaps Resource Development Methodology

The ScienceMaps Resource Development Methodology depicted in Figure 4 is being utilized to support the development of the two ScienceMaps resources — science lessons and GIS applications.

Starting with the Content Area Focus activity, the resource developer chooses one of the four major California standards-based science content areas for instructional materials development: biology/life sciences, chemistry, Earth sciences, and physics

Figure 2. ScienceMaps online resource portal — Earth science lesson 8

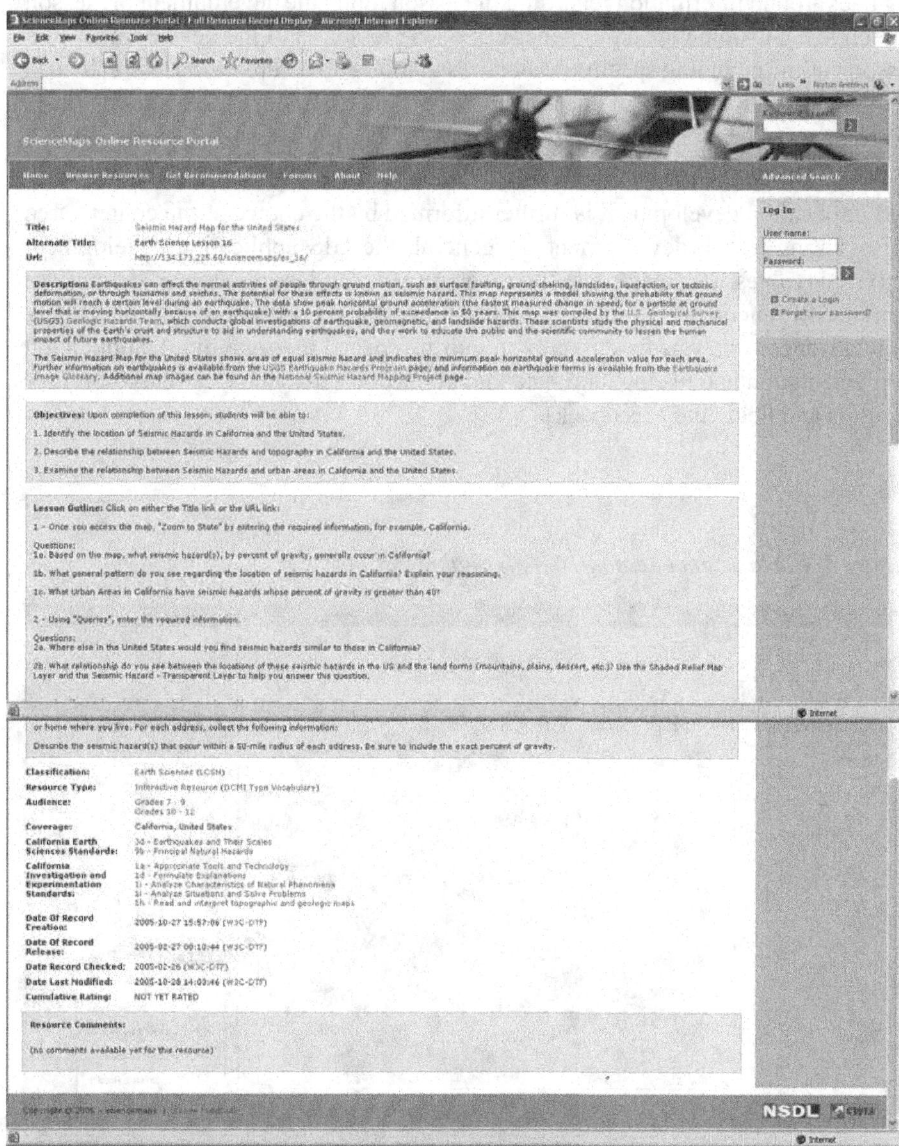

(the investigation and experimentation standards are applicable to all standards-based science content areas). This choice informs and influences both the science lesson development and the GIS application development activities.

Science lesson development involves the development of a lesson description including background information regarding the lesson topic; the development of "lesson objectives" including specific objectives of the lesson; and the development of a lesson outline including specific procedures to follow to complete the lesson. It also involves varying the level of questioning according to Bloom's Taxonomy in order to promote higher order thinking skills (analysis, application, and synthesis) as well as providing all students with a level of success when utilizing the application.

GIS application development is further informed by the choice of the content area focus during lesson development. In general, the GIS application development activity involves four major tasks: data acquisition and manipulation, determination of GIS functionality required (basic and advanced operations as well as possibly advanced analysis functionality requiring special programming), application implementation and testing, and data and application maintenance (based on user requests and field-study feedback).

Figure 3. Earth science lesson 16 — GIS application

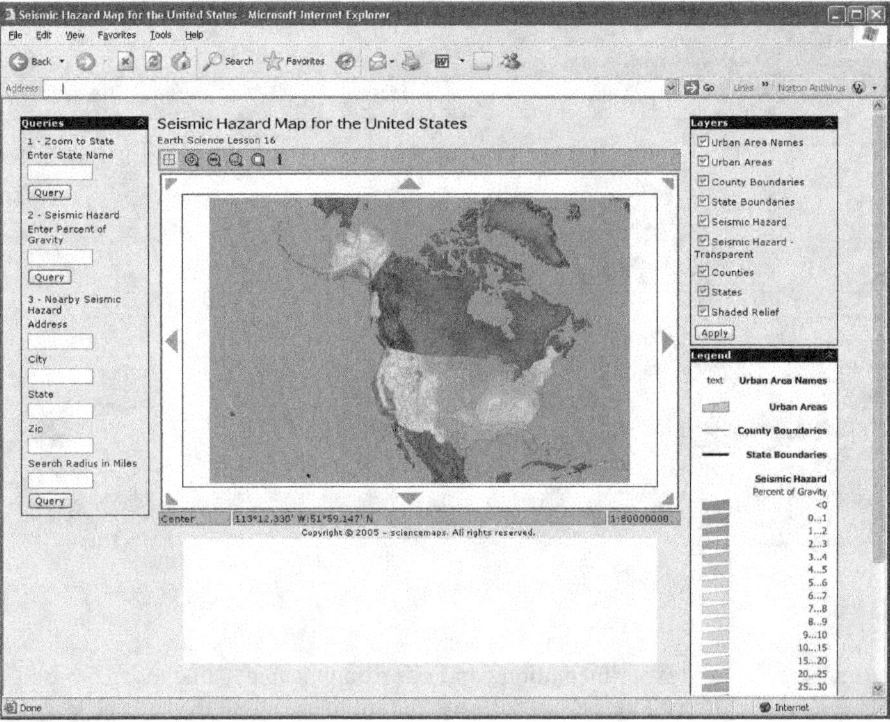

Figure 4. ScienceMaps resource development methodology

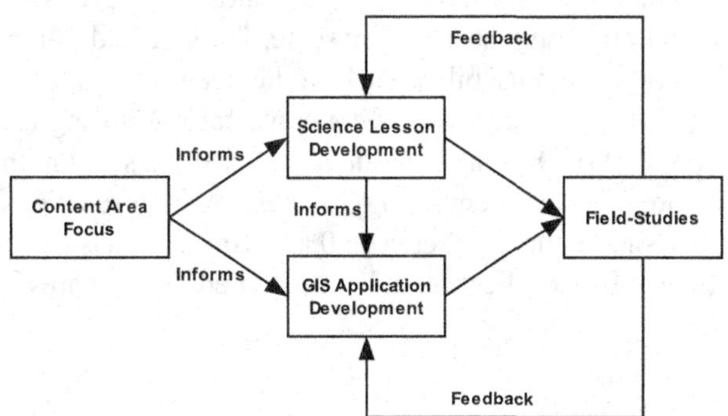

Assessment and Evaluation

There is a tremendous need for the development of a research-based, classroom-tested set of instructional materials for teaching and learning with GIS in order to plan software systems designed to better support student learning (Bednarz, 2004). In keeping with the goals of ScienceMaps, to support the ongoing development and field-testing of this innovative courseware and to promote the integration of technology into the science curriculum, and to validate the efficacy of the ScienceMaps research and development methodology, assessment and evaluation will include quantitative and qualitative data collection and analysis. Field-studies will provide feedback from the various ScienceMaps users (teachers and students) to understand how well participant school districts are integrating GIS technology into their classrooms using the resources available in the ScienceMaps portal. These field-studies will include participant surveys and interviews to assess such system usability issues as ease of navigation and search features of the online portal, as well as how well students interact with the many GIS applications. This feedback will not only inform future resource development, such as new functionality to be added, but will also be used to update existing portal resources. Empirical analyses of this data will provide findings regarding the effective use of technology in the science classroom and will add to the knowledge base in this area.

Initial Results

Data was collected from 17 undergraduate students enrolled in a teacher preparation program at a private university in Southern California. Students completed a system usability scale. The system usability scale (SUS) is a simple, ten-item scale giving a global view of subjective assessments of usability (Brooke, 1996). The SUS was developed by the Digital Equipment Corporation and is a Likert scale, where a statement is made and the respondent then indicates the degree of agreement or disagreement with the statement on a 5-point scale. The selected statements address a variety of aspects of system usability, such as the need for support, training, and complexity, and thus have a high level of coverage for measuring the usability of a system (B. Hilton, 2003). Once a respondent has used the system, they are asked to immediately respond to each item prior to discussing their reactions with others. The SUS provides a single number, between 0 and 100, which is a composite measure of the overall usability of the system being studied. SUS scores are calculated as follows:

1. For questions 1, 3, 5, 7, and 9, the score contribution is the scale position minus 1.
2. For questions 2, 4, 6, 8 and 10, the contribution is 5 minus the scale position.
3. Multiply the sum of these scores by 2.5 to obtain the overall value of System Usability.

Additionally, respondents were asked three open-ended questions regarding their impressions of ScienceMaps.

The mean overall SUS score for this group (N = 17) was 57.21. Table 1 illustrates the descriptive statistics for the group. These statistics are comparable to other studies for first-time use (American Institutes for Research, 2001; B. Hilton, 2003; Musgrave & Ryssevik, 2000). These studies included N = 23 and Mean = 69.13 for Hilton; N = 72 and mean SUS score for the alpha version = 69 and N = 53 and mean = 69.5 in the beta version for Musgrave & Ryssevik; and N = 22 with mean SUS score for Office XP = 91.71 and 51.82 for Office 2000 for American Institutes for Research.

Table 2 outlines the descriptive statistics for the individual SUS questions for the group. The means of the positive questions (1, 3, 5, 7, and 9) ranged from 1.71 to 2.47 while the means of the negative questions (2, 4, 6, 8, and 10) ranged from 1.88 to 2.82. Standard deviations for all questions ranged from 0.81 to 1.17.

Table 1. Descriptive statistics for SUS score

Mean	57.21
Std. Deviation	15.68
Range	55.00
Minimum	35.00
Maximum	90.00

Table 2. Descriptive statistics for individual SUS questions

SUS Questions	Mean	Std. Dev
Q1: I think that I would like to use this system frequently.	1.71	1.05
Q2: I found the system unnecessarily complex.	2.41	1.06
Q3: I thought the system was easy to use.	2.06	1.09
Q4: I think that I would need the support of a technical person to be able to use the system	2.53	1.07
Q5: I found the various functions in this system were well integrated.	2.29	0.85
Q6: I thought there was too much inconsistency in this system.	2.35	1.00
Q7: I would imagine that most pople would learn to use this system very quickly.	1.47	0.94
Q8: I found the system very cumbersome to use.	1.88	0.99
Q9: I felt confident using the system.	2.35	1.17
Q10: I needed to learn a lot of things before I could get going with this system.	2.82	0.81

Subjective responses indicated that generally users liked the visual representation of the maps and thought it provided good background information. Many thought the ability to enter an address, and to find specific information in relation (proximity) to that address, was both useful and informative. Respondents believed that the site addressed California science standards and would be a useful tool for instruction. Suggestions for improvement included adding online help/training as well as making minor improvements to the user interface. These suggestions will be addressed and changes implemented in future versions of the system.

Conclusion

ScienceMaps will continue to utilize the latest cutting edge geospatial technologies to enhance science instruction. The research findings of this effort will inform the ongoing research on the effects of technology on science education. Given the focus on classroom teachers, the resulting impact on K-12 students could be substantial. ScienceMaps can help shape future resource portals, especially those using GIS so that they become more effective instructional tools. The significance of ScienceMaps lies in its ability to address the issue of how to assist educators in developing more in-depth science content knowledge while building a structured approach for teaching science standards using GIS technology. Furthermore, the use of an Internet-based GIS provides the ability to bring geospatial data to anyone with access to an Internet browser. There is no need to run specific GIS software or download data; the science lessons and data layers are already constructed and available for immediate viewing and analysis through the various GIS applications.

The future effort of ScienceMaps is to utilize both the knowledge, gained as well as the lessons and applications developed, to provide the foundation for an initiative that would be replicated nationwide. This would include customized lessons and applications for individual states' science standards, professional development seminars, and evaluation of effectiveness. States with attributes similar to California, large student and teacher populations, high capacity to use technology but low use and access, would be selected first for this initiative.

There is much enthusiasm about ways that these technologies can help shrink the digital divide. ScienceMaps focuses on the integration of technology into the secondary science curriculum by emphasizing effective use while simultaneously addressing accessibility issues and learning styles. Furthermore, it promotes the use of innovative GIS technology in a discipline with which it is not usually associated. While there are programs that exist to promote the use of GIS in education, they require a high level of proficiency in GIS skills and knowledge, expensive software, and a tremendous time commitment. ScienceMaps concentrates *on using GIS to teach, not on teaching GIS.*

References

Adelman, N., Donnelly, M. B., Dove, T., Tiffany-Morales, J., Wayne, A., & Zucker, A. (2002). *The integrated studies of educational technology: Professional development and teachers' use of technology* (Tech. Rep. No. SRI Project P10474). Menlo Park, CA.

American Institutes for Research. (2001). *Microsoft Office XP vs. Office 2000 comparison test public report* (Tech. Rep. No. AIR Project No. 01674.001). Washington, DC.

Archer, J. (1998). The link to higher scores. *Education Week— Technology Counts, 1998* (p. 18).

Becker, H. J. (2000). *Findings from the teaching, learning, and computing survey: Is Larry Cuban right?* Paper presented at the Council of Chief State School Officers Annual Technology Leadership Conference, Washington, DC.

Bednarz, S. W. (2004). Geographic information systems: A tool to support geography and environmental education? *GeoJournal, 60*(2), 191–199.

Borgman, C. L., Leazer, G. H., Gilliland-Swetland, A., Millwood, K., Champeny, L., Finley, J., et al. (2004). How geography professors select materials for classroom lectures: Implications for the design of digital libraries. In *Proceedings of the 4th ACM/IEEE-CS Joint Conference on Digital Libraries* (pp. 179-185). Tuscon, AZ: ACM Press.

Brooke, J. (1996). SUS: A 'quick and dirty' usability scale. In I. McClelland (Ed.), *Usability evaluation in industry* (pp. 189-194). London: Taylor & Francis Ltd.

CEO Forum. (2001). *Year 4 StaR Report*, 2003. Retrieved from http://www.electronicschool.com/2001/09/0901ewire.html#forum

Drew, D. E. (1996). *Aptitude revisited: Rethinking math and science education for America's next century*. Baltimore, MD: The Johns Hopkins University Press.

Du, D., Havard, B. C., Olinzock, A., & Yang, Y. (2004). *The impact of technology use on low-income and minority student academic achievements.* Paper presented at the American Educational Research Association 2004 Annual Meeting, San Diego, CA.

Ely, D. P. (2002). *Trends in educational technology* (5th ed.). Syracuse, NY: ERIC Clearinghouse on Education and Technology.

Farrell, B. A., & Kotrlik, J. W. (2003). Design and evaluation of a tool to assess strategical information processing styles. *Journal of Vocational Education Research, 28*(2), 141-160.

Fox, E. (2005). Technology counts, 2005: Tracking U.S. trends. *Education Week, 24,* 40-79.

Gaudet, C., Annulis, H., & Carr, J. (2001). *Workforce development models for geospatial technology*. Hattiesburg, MS: The University of Southern Mississippi, Geospatial Workforce Development Center.

Gross, P., Goodenough, U., Haack, S., Lerner, L., Schwartz, M., & Schwartz, R. (2005). *The state of state science standards*. Washington, DC: Thomas B. Fordham Foundation.

Gutierrez, M., Coulter, B., & Goodwin, D. (2002). Natural disasters workshop integrating hands-on activities, Internet-based data, and GIS. *Journal of Geoscience Education, 50*(4), 437-443.

Hanson, K., & Carlson, B. (2005). *Effective access: Teachers' use of digital resources in STEM teaching*. Newton, MA: Gender, Diversities, and Technology Institute at the Education Development Center.

Hedges, L. V., Konstantopoulos, S., & Thoreson, A. (2000). *Designing studies to measure the implementation and impact of technology in American schools.* Paper presented at the Conference on The Effectiveness of Educational Technology: Research Designs for the Next Decade, Menlo Park, CA.

Hilton, B. (2003). *The impact of open source software and Web services on information system development: An investigation of proximate computing.* Claremont, CA: School of Information Science, Claremont Graduate University.

Hilton, J. (2003). *The effects of technology on student science achievement.* Claremont, CA: School of Educational Studies, Claremont Graduate University.

Hilton, J. (2005). Narrowing the digital divide: Technology integration in a high-poverty school. In D. Carbonara (Ed.), *Technology literacy applications in learning environments* (pp. 385). Hershey, PA: Idea Group Publishing.

Hilton, J. (2006). The effect of technology on student science achievement. In E. M. Alkhalifa (Ed.), *Cognitively informed systems: Utilizing practical approaches to enrich information presentation and transfer* (pp. 346). Hershey, PA: Idea Group Publishing.

Houtsonen, L., Kankaanrinta, I.-K., & Rehunen, A. (2004). Web use in geographical and environmental education: An international survey at the primary and secondary level. *GeoJournal, 60*(2), 165 - 174.

Jerald, C. D. (1998). By the numbers. *Education Week — Technology Counts* (Vol. 18).

Joseph, E. (2004). *Community GIS: University collaboration and outreach with K-12 teachers.* Paper presented at the ESRI 2004 Users Conference, San Diego, CA.

Levin, D., Arafeh, S., Lenhart, A., & Rainie, L. (2002). *The digital disconnect: The widening gap between Internet savvy students and their schools*. Washington, DC: The Pew Internet & American Life Project.

Levinson, E. (2000). Technology and accountability: A chicken-and-egg question. *Converge, 3*(11), 58-59.

Manzo, K. K. (2001). Academic record. *Education Week — Technology Counts* (Vol. 20, pp. 22-23).

Marsh, T., Wong, W. L., Carriazo, E., Nocera, L., Yang, K., Varma, A., et al. (2005). *User experiences and lessons learned from developing and implementing an immersive game for the science classroom.* Paper presented at the HCI International 2005 — 11th International Conference on Human-Computer Interaction, Las Vegas, NV.

Musgrave, S., & Ryssevik, J. (2000). *NESSTAR final report.* Brussels: Networked Social Science Tools and Resources.

Parsad, B., & Jones, J. (2005). *Internet access in U.S. public schools and classrooms: 1994–2003* (Rep. No. NCES 2005015). Washington, DC: National Center for Education Statistics.

Quintana, C., & Zhang, M. (2004). *IdeaKeeper notepads: Scaffolding digital library information analysis in online inquiry.* Paper presented at the Conference on Human Factors in Computing Systems (CHI 2004).

Rumberger, R. W. (2000). *A multi-level, longitudinal approach to evaluating the effectiveness of educational technology.* Paper presented at the Design Meeting on Effectiveness of Educational Technology, Menlo Park, CA.

Schmitt, C. (2002). *Technology in schools: Suggestions, tools, and guidelines for assessing technology in elementary and secondary education* (Rep. No. NCES 2003313). Washington, DC: National Center for Education Statistics.

Skinner, R. A. (2002). Tracking tech trends. *Education Week — Technology Counts* (Vol. 22, pp. 53-56).

Trotter, A. (1999). Preparing teachers for the digital age. *Education Week —-Technology Counts* (Vol. 19, pp. 37-43).

U.S. Bureau of the Census (1998). *Statistical Abstract of the United States: 1998* (118th ed.). Washington, DC: U.S. Government Printing Office.

University of Wisconsin - Madison. (2004). *The Internet Scout Project, 2005.* Retrieved from http://scout.wisc.edu/Projects/CWIS/index.php

Wetzel, D. R. (1999). *A model for the successful implementation of instructional technology in science education.* Paper presented at the Mid-South Education Research Association Annual Conference, Point Clear, AL.

Williams, R. S. (2002). *Future of education = Technology + teachers.* Washington, DC: U.S. Department of Commerce Technology Administration.

Section III

Decision-Making Environments

Chapter VII

Flexible Spatial Decision-Making and Support: Processes and Systems

Shan Gao, University of Auckland, New Zealand
David Sundaram, University of Auckland, New Zealand

Abstract

Spatial decision-making is a key aspect of human behaviour. Spatial decision support systems support spatial decision-making processes by integrating required information, tools, models, and technology in a user-friendly manner. While current spatial decision support systems fulfill their specific objectives, they fail to address many of the requirements for effective spatial problem solving, as they are inflexible, complex to use, and often domain-specific. This research blends together several relevant disciplines to overcome the problems identified in various areas of spatial decision support. We proposed a generic spatial decision-making process and a domain-independent spatial decision support system (SDSS) framework and architecture to support the process. We also developed a flexible SDSS to demonstrate an environment in which decision-makers can utilize various tools and explore different scenarios to derive a decision. The use of the system is demonstrated in a number of real scenarios across location, allocation, routing, layout, and spatio-temporal problems.

Introduction

Decision-making is an essential element of our lives and critical for business success, because many natural phenomena and socio-economic activities take place in a spatial context. Spatial decision-making (SDM) becomes one of the important aspects of human behaviour. SDM activities are either dependent or influenced by geographical information. They are based on spatial problems that are normally semi-structured or ill-defined. Spatial problems are also multi-dimensional as they contain both spatial and non-spatial aspects. It is not easy to measure or model all the aspects of a spatial problem in a single step. Therefore, a sophisticated modelling process is needed for solving these spatial problems.

Spatial decision-making usually involves a large number of alternative solutions, and these alternatives need to be managed using an appropriate scenario management facility. The multi-criteria decision-making (MCDM) method helps the decision-maker to select a solution from the many competitive alternatives. It facilitates the evaluation and ranking of the alternative solutions based on the decision- maker's knowledge or preference with respect to a set of evaluation criteria.

Decision support systems (DSS) have been proposed to support decision-making. Silver (1991) broadly defines a decision support system as a computer-based information system that affects or is intended to affect the way people make decisions. A focused DSS definition given by Sprague and Carlson (1982) states that a decision support system is an interactive computer-based system that helps decision-makers to solve unstructured problems by utilising data and models. To support spatial decision-making, a variety of systems have been developed: These include geographic information systems (GIS) and spatial decision support systems (SDSS). Our focus is on SDSS in this research. Peterson (1998) defines a spatial decision support system as an interactive and computer-based system designed to support a user or a group of users in achieving higher effectiveness for solving semi-structured or non-structured spatial decision problems.

As technology progresses, there is increasing opportunity to use SDSS in a variety of domains. Flexible support of decision-making processes to solve complex, semi-structured or unstructured spatial problems can offer advantages to individuals and organisations. We synthesise ideas, frameworks, and architectures from GIS, DSS, and SDSS. In addition, concepts from spatial modelling, model life cycle management, scenario life cycle management, knowledge management, and MCDM methodology are explored and leveraged in the implementation of a flexible spatial decision support system using object-oriented methodology and technology.

Background

Moloney, Lea, and Kowalchek (1993) observe that about ninety percent of business information are geographically related and cover diverse domains, for example, resource management, environmental modelling, transportation planning, and geo-marketing. Spatial problems are normally categorised into allocation, location, routing, and layout problems based on their geographical features. The primary goal of SDSS is to support decision-making activities using its flexible modelling capabilities and spatial data manipulation functions. SDSS encompass spatial analytical techniques and enable system output in a variety of spatial forms. The characteristics of the spatial data, models, and operations as well as the integration processes of non-spatial systems with spatial systems make SDSS more complex. Currently- available SDSS frameworks and architectures are suitable for their specific objectives. However, they fail to properly address many of the requirements of a generic, flexible, and easy-to-use SDSS. As we have noted earlier, incorporating a GIS with a DSS develops some of SDSS frameworks and architectures. However, the existing SDSS frameworks and architectures are neither comprised of all the DSS components, nor are they generic. Fedra's (1995) framework is good for analytical modelling, but the solver is tightly integrated within the model, which does not provide flexibility in using a solver with different models. It does not provide any mapping instrument for flexible integration of model and data; rather it uses a pre-customised integration system that is limited to a specific domain. The model management framework of Yeh and Qiao (1999) supports the modelling life cycle but overlooks spatial presentation functionalities. The dynamic environmental effects model (DEEM) is a software framework that provides optimal interoperability among environmental models, supports flexible decision-making, but fails to address scenario development and run-time model generation. The SDSS framework proposed by Armstrong and Densham (1990) does not separate model and solver. The knowledge management system framework of Mennecke (1997) does not pay attention to spatial visualisations, but rather focuses on the queries and reports. Some implemented SDSS are good in modelling systems, for example, Illinois River Decision Support System (ILRDSS) and Environmental Decision Support System (EDSS). Some are good in spatial data analysis and visualisation, for example, GRASSLAND, but none of these systems is generic and domain-independent.

The scenario-based SDSS architecture of Hall, Bowerman, and Feick (1997) is the only one that supports scenario management and facilitates the multiple scenario development. The system allows the decision-makers to generate, save, and recall solutions and supports comparing different scenarios. It is well developed for solving domain specific spatial problems, but the scenario evaluation has not been fully explored in this system as a non-spatial model; for example, the evaluation model has been absent in this framework. None of these frameworks and architectures addresses multi-criteria decision-making.

Issues, Controversies, Problems

Though significant progress has been made in the context of decision-making and decision support systems, there has not been sufficient emphasis on SDM nor on SDSS. Densham (1991) argues that the main objective of a SDSS is to support decision-makers to make well-informed decisions based on complex spatial tasks. The processes and the various mechanisms used for solving spatial problems are also complex. The available technologies related to spatial decision-making are neither quite sufficient nor easy-to-use for managing this complexity.

Decision-makers often perceive the decision-making process adopted to solve complex multi-dimensional spatial problems as unsatisfactory. Decision-makers have been using the decision-making frameworks and processes for many years, but the general approaches proposed by Simon (1960) and others were not particularly developed for solving spatial problems; rather they provide a guideline for development of decision-making processes. Though Malczewski (1999) has proposed a multi-criteria decision-making framework, the implementation of the process has not been fully explored in the spatial context. A generic process to guide decision-makers to solve spatial problems is lacking. Decision-makers have to rely on their own processes and experience for spatial decision-making.

On the other hand, existing GIS, DSS, and SDSS that support decision-makers have their limitations in solving spatial problems. GIS do well in managing spatial data, but lack flexible modelling capacity. DSS are typically used in the non-spatial domain. SDSS encompass analytical techniques inherited from DSS and spatial modelling and various spatial input and output mechanisms provided by GIS to support decision-makers to make well-informed decisions. Densham (1991) argues that SDSS should facilitate a number of functions such as spatial data input, model-based analyses, and powerful visual presentations. Furthermore, these systems generally do not facilitate flexible spatial data manipulation mechanisms and lack output facility for presentation of the result of the decision-making process. They do not provide knowledge storage facility and lack a process-oriented user interface, thus enlarging the complexity of using the systems. A review of SDSS frameworks and architectures led us to conclude that current approaches fulfill their specific objectives, but fail to address many of the requirements of a generic, flexible, and easy-to-use SDSS.

In addition, model and scenario management processes have not been well developed in SDSS. The modelling process is ad hoc rather than generic and does not address the need of separation and integration of spatial and non-spatial models. Research indicates that the difficulties in synthesising various decision alternatives are primary obstacles to spatial problem-solving (Ascough II et al., 2002). Some SDSS support the development of single spatial or non-spatial scenario at one time, but few systems support integration of spatial and non-spatial scenarios to develop numerous multi-attribute spatial scenarios simultaneously. And also, spatial problems often have numerous alternative solutions, and use multiple criteria upon which they are evaluated. These complex spatial problems can be solved efficiently by incorporating the analytic modelling capabilities of the application specific spatial decision support system. The multi-criteria decision-making helps in screening alternatives and identifying the best solution. At this point many strategic requirements of SDSS have not been implemented completely. Their capability to solve complex multi-dimensional spatial problems is very limited.

Based on the problem areas identified in the field of spatial decision-making, we believe that a generic process for solving complex spatial problems is needed for achieving high effectiveness in spatial decision-making. The ideas from related disciplines (i.e., spatial modelling, model and scenario life cycle management, knowledge management and MCDM) need to be addressed in this process. Current SDSS frameworks and architectures address or implement one or a combination of requirements that are needed for complex spatial problem-solving, but they are incapable of managing all the issues required in a single coherent way. Synthesising ideas, frameworks, and architectures from related disciplines helps to overcome some of the problems identified in spatial decision support systems. A generic spatial decision-making process and a domain-independent SDSS framework and architecture will improve spatial decision quality and provide more opportunities for the use of SDSS.

Solutions and Recommendations

To address the issues of spatial decision-making and spatial decision support systems, we first propose a spatial decision-making process that allows the decision makers to better use SDSS to solve spatial problems in a generic way, thus resulting in a better decision. We then develop a flexible spatial decision support system (FSDSS) framework and architecture to support this spatial decision-making process. The FSDSS provides flexible spatial data manipulation facility and supports integration of spatial and non-spatial data; it also facilitates the entire model and scenario management life cycle process, as well as support for multi-criteria spatial problem solving. We further implement a prototypical FSDSS that acts as a proof-of-concept for these proposals.

Spatial Decision-Making Process

Malczewski (1997) identifies *complexity, alternatives,* and *multi-criteria* characteristics as key features of spatial problems. Spatial problems are complex because they are semi-structured or ill-defined in the sense that the goals and objectives are not completely defined. Spatial problems are multi-dimensional and often related to non-spatial information. Each spatial problem can have a large number of decision

Figure 1. Spatial decision-making process

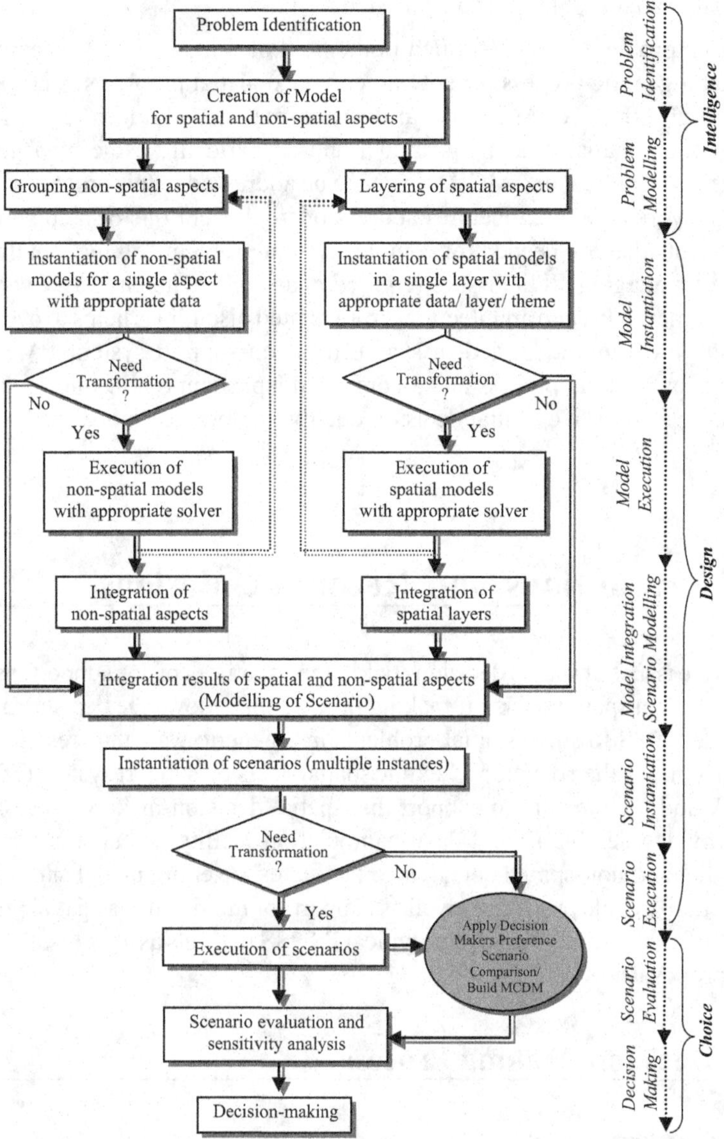

alternative solutions. These alternative solutions to the spatial decision problems are normally characterised by multiple criteria upon which they are judged.

Model building is critical in decision-making as it clarifies thinking and improves the decision-making quality (Georgantzas & Acar, 1995). Spatial modelling techniques are used for finding relationships among geographic features and helps decision-makers to address the spatial problem clearly and logically. Spatial aspects and non-spatial aspects can be coexistent in a spatial problem, so that we need to consider both aspects at the same time. It is difficult to model a complex spatial problem in a single step, but it is possible to model one aspect of a complex problem at a time. For example, create a spatial model to deal with spatial aspects and a non-spatial model that caters to the non-spatial aspects of the problem, and then integrate them.

A spatial model contains spatial parameters that refer to the geographical features of a spatial problem. Vector-based spatial data can be categorised into three major groups, that is, spatial objects, spatial layers, and spatial themes. A spatial object represents a single spatial item, for example, a point, a line, or a polygon. A spatial layer contains a collection of spatial objects similar in nature, and every spatial object belongs to a certain layer. A spatial theme comprises a number of spatial objects and/or spatial layers that represent a particular meaning to a particular spatial problem. Vector data is linked to non-spatial domain data through a spatial reference system; a point could be associated with a residential location, and a line may represent a running path. Each aspect of a spatial problem can be modelled in one layer. These layers are then integrated into a complex model that represents the many facets of the problem.

We propose a spatial decision-making process (Figure 1) by synthesising ideas of decision-making processes (Simon, 1960) and the multi-criteria decision-making process (Malczewski, 1999). It also integrates concepts from spatial modelling, model, scenario, and knowledge management. The process contains nine specific steps, namely, problem identification, problem modelling, model instantiation, model execution, model integration, scenario instantiation, scenario execution, scenario evaluation, and final decision-making.

The decision-making process begins with the recognition of a real-world problem that involves searching the decision environment and identifying comprehensive objectives that reflect all concerns relevant to a decision problem. The problem is then put into a model by specifying the relevant attributes and behaviours. The parameters in a model structure are instantiated with appropriate data. Decision-makers select a solver for execution of a model instance and generate a result, that is, the scenario. A scenario improves cognition by organising many different bits of information (De Gues, 1997). Multiple scenarios are needed to explore different ways of seeing problems and enhancing the decision-making quality (Forrester,

1992). The scenario evaluation process evaluates many competitive alternatives simultaneously and helps to identify the best solution.

The process is iterative in nature so that multiple scenarios instances can be generated using the same scenario structures. The scenario integration process enables the decision-maker to combine both spatial and non-spatial scenarios to create a complex multi-criteria spatial scenario that addresses all the requirements of a complex spatial problem. When required, the instantiated scenarios are called for execution using different solvers. The execution of the scenario allows the decision-maker to further develop a more desirable solution to a particular problem. Scenario evaluation ranks the many alternative scenarios based on decision-makers' preferences. Sensitivity analysis is employed as a means for achieving a deeper understanding of the structure of the problem by changing the inputs, for example, data, solver, or evaluation model. This helps decision-makers learn how the various decision elements interact and allows them to determine the best solution. In completing the above processes, the best-evaluated scenario is selected. As there is no restriction on how the user chooses to solve a problem, decision-makers can select the phases to follow based on the nature of the specific problem and their specific purposes.

The FSDSS Framework

We propose a flexible spatial decision support system (FSDSS) framework (Figure 2) to support the decision-making process and overcome the problems identified earlier. The FSDSS framework is comprised of six major DSS objects or components namely, data, models, solvers, visualisations, scenario, and knowledge. These objects are stored in the object repository independently, and they communicate through the kernel, the programmatic engine that makes the system run. The framework accommodates spatial data (spatial objects, layers, and themes) and non-spatial data. It contains both spatial and non-spatial models, solvers, scenarios, and visualisations. The knowledge is the output of the decision-making process and can be stored in the system for future reference. The decision-maker interacts with the system through the user interface. Different data, model, and solver can be selected from the object repository and mapped together to generate a scenario, or a specific decision support system that is tailored for a particular problem domain.

This framework allows generating multiple scenarios at one time and stores them in the scenario pool. The framework supports the integration of several simple scenarios into a complex multi-attribute scenario that contains both spatial and non-spatial aspects through the scenario integration process. The multiple scenarios and the evaluated scenarios can be presented using the appropriate visualisation component. The output of the decision-making process can be saved in the object repository as knowledge.

Figure 2. The FSDSS framework

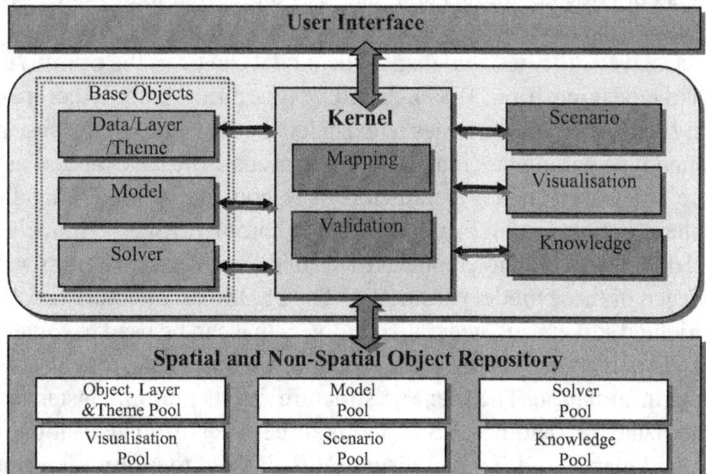

The FSDSS Architecture

We propose an architecture that implements the FSDSS framework and supports the proposed decision-making process, as shown in Figure 3. The FSDSS architectural components are organised into five distinct layers; these are persistence layer, object services layer, DSS objects layer, integration layer, and presentation layer. These layers and their components are briefly described as follows.

The *persistence layer* contains the object library used to store the system objects. This includes the storage of non-spatial data and a variety of spatial data (objects, layers, themes, and map). It is also responsible for the storage of models, solvers, visualisations, scenarios, and knowledge, either spatial or non-spatial in nature, using the object-oriented database management system.

The *object services layer* manages the system objects through the component control that contains several parameters and methods to coordinate the component pool and the application. It exports objects from the object library to the DSS objects layer, as well as importing the resulting scenarios and knowledge from the DSS objects layer back to the object library. It also facilitates dynamic creation, updating, and deletion of the objects.

The *DSS objects layer* supports independent development and use of the decision-support components including spatial and non-spatial data, models, solvers, and visualisations, for generating basic spatial and non-spatial scenarios. It is responsible for integrating scenarios to develop complex spatial scenarios. It supports the evaluation and ranking of multiple scenario instances using the evaluation model. This layer also facilitates the storage and reuse of the result from the decision-making process. It also provides graphical and map-based presentation of data, scenarios, and knowledge. The data component includes non-spatial and spatial data, that is, spatial objects, layers, themes, and maps. The model can be of the primitive type or the compound type (Geoffrion, 1987). Primitive type model parameters are directly derived using base data type variables or executed model values of the base models. The compound type parameters inherit and/or aggregate the base models as well as adding some other user-defined parameters. The non-spatial model handles non-spatial problems or non-spatial aspects of a spatial problem. Spatial models cater to spatial problems. The evaluation model is made of different parameters as well as the weights for each of these model parameters. The FSDSS architecture has a number of spatial-oriented solvers and generalised solvers that can be used to solve/execute both spatial and non-spatial models. The scenario combines data, model, solver, and other relevant information. The scenario structure and its multiple instances can be stored in the database. The FSDSS supports three types of visualisation: spatial, non-spatial, and map-based. Spatial visualisation is used to represent spatial data, scenarios, and knowledge. Non-spatial visualisation, for example, 3D graphs, are used to present the output of analytical results. In addition to the general graphical report functions, the FSDSS visualisation is particularly important when used with maps. Different spatial objects, layers, or themes are overlaid to generate a new map. The knowledge component contains the final results of the decision-making process, including information about the decision-maker, the rules that were applied, alternative scenarios, the final decision, as well as the system components used in reaching a particular decision.

The *integration layer* contains the communication components, that is, kernel, mapping, and validation components. In addition to activating and using the component functions, the kernel works as a user interface and is responsible for the communication and integration of system components. Mapping enables the model component to communicate with data and solver components properly through model-data and model-solver mapping processes. The model parameter or attributes are fixed; the user selects the data attributes for model-data mapping and selects the solver name and solver attributes for model-solver mapping. Validation enables proper communication between system components. The validation module is responsible for checking the input data type to the model and to the solver during the mapping process. The model-data validation tests whether the data type of the model attributes is similar or convertible to the data attributes, while model-solver validation checks whether the data types of the attributes of the model instance are similar or convertible to the data type of the solver attributes.

The *presentation layer* or user interface supports all the interactions between users and the system. It provides a flexible environment where spatial and non-spatial components are used together to solve complex spatial problems. The architecture

Figure 3. The FSDSS architecture

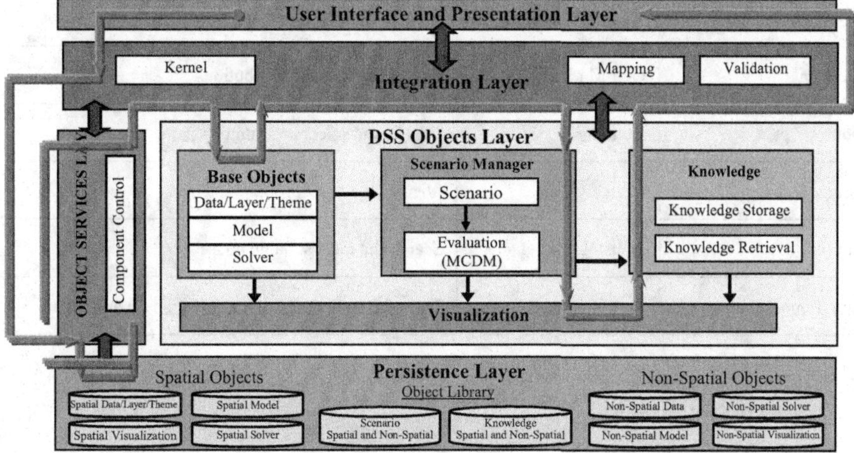

as a whole is technology independent so that it can be implemented using commonly-available platforms.

A simple decision-making flow in Figure 3 illustrates how the FSDSS architecture supports the decision-making process. The decision-maker initiates the decision-making process at the interface layer and interacts with the system through the kernel. The component control picks up the relevant components from the persistence layer. The selected data, models, and solvers are combined in the integration layer to develop scenarios using the mapping component. The scenario manager manages these scenarios, and the evaluated scenarios can be presented using the appropriate visualisation component. The interaction between the DSS objects layer and the persistence layer are bi-directional. On the one hand, the architecture allows flexible selection of objects from the object library. On the other hand, the executed results (e.g., scenarios generated) can be stored back to the object library.

The FSDSS Implementation

A prototypical FSDSS was implemented to prove the validity of the proposed spatial decision-making process as well as the FSDSS framework and architecture. Object-oriented concepts, object-oriented database management system, and the object-oriented programming language were the tools and technologies used to develop the FSDSS prototype. *Jade* (www.jadeworld.com), a fully integrated development environment (Post, 2000) with its own object-oriented database and programming language, was selected as the implementation platform. The complete prototype

Table 1. Spatial problems and implementation domains

Spatial Problem	Application Domain	Example Spatial Problems
Allocation	Geo-Marketing	Find geographical distributions
Layout	Running	Design and select best running path
Routing	Delivery	Identify the fastest route
Location	Housing	Search the most suitable house
Spatio-Temporal	Health	Trace the spread of a disease over space and time

was developed within Jade without recourse to any other tool. The proposed spatial decision-making process and the implemented FSDSS were evaluated through five scenarios across different spatial decision problem domains including location, allocation, routing, and/or layout. Table 1 details of the type of spatial problems and the specific domains where we tested the prototype. The same environment was used in the testing, but with different data, model, and solver sets.

Sample Sessions with the FSDSS

In the following sections, we explore the interaction with the FSDSS to solve three of the spatial problems mentioned above. We first use the problem of the design of a running track to introduce some of the core spatial modelling concepts such as objects, layers, and themes. The second example explores in detail the use of the FSDSS, following the proposed spatial decision-making process, in the context of the purchase of a house. To highlight the generic applicability of the system we show its use in the context of solving a spatio-temporal problem in health care.

Design of a Running Track

The first scenario we explore is the design of a path for a particular running event that takes into consideration the required amenities like drink points and toilets, as well as the distance. This example introduces some of the basic spatial concepts and functionality of the system. The decision-makers can plot a number of paths by clicking points on the map. These paths are then saved in the database as *running path 1* and *running path 2* (see Figure 4).

Figure 4. The two alternative paths for running event

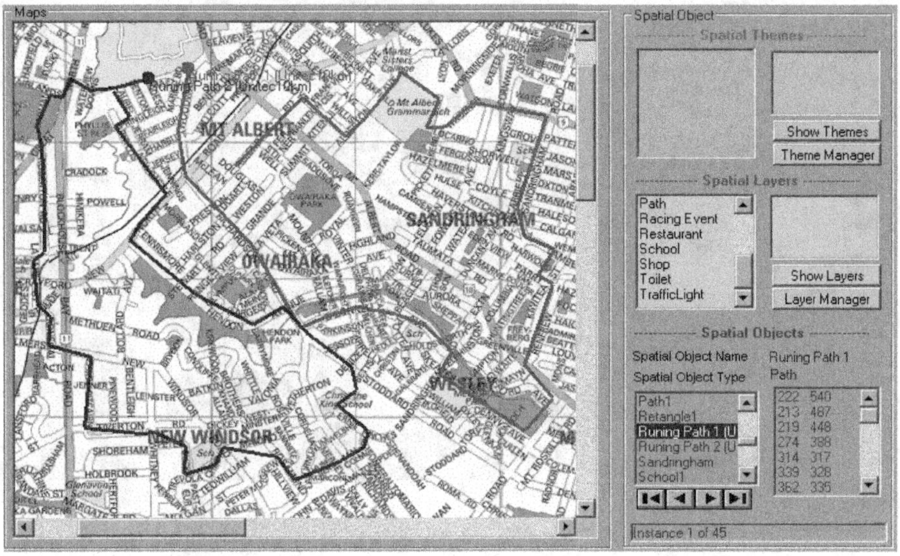

Figure 5. Spatial layer manager

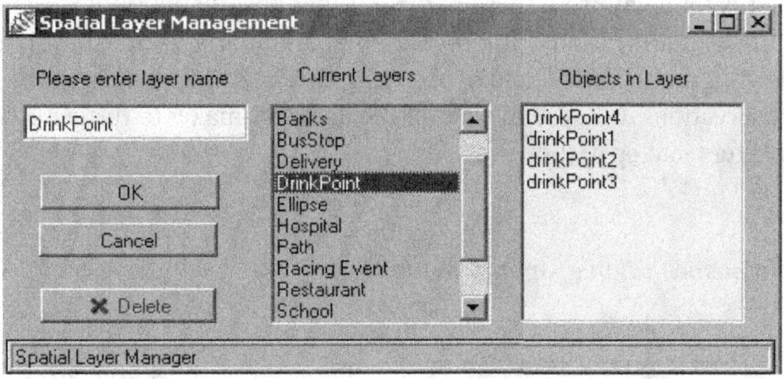

In addition to these two paths, the decision-makers need to consider other facilities that might be useful to this event, for example, drink points and toilets. These objects are stored in the database as individual objects or as a layer. The spatial layer manager manages these layers. As we can see from Figure 5, there are four drink points in the *drink point* layer.

Figure 6 presents the map layout of the two paths (running path 1, running path 2) and the relevant layers, that is, the four toilets in the toilet layer and four drink points in the drink point layer.

Figure 6. Spatial layers (toilet and drink point layer)

It also shows that some of the facilities are not useful for the event, for example, *toilet 4*, as it is far away from these paths. Further observation indicates that *toilet 1, toilet 2, drink point 1,* and *drink point 2* are particularly useful for running *path 1*, while *toilet 3, drink point 3,* and *drink point 4* are useful to *running path 2*. Based on these observations, the system enables the decision-maker to further group these objects or layers into spatial themes.

Figure 7. Implementation of spatial modelling

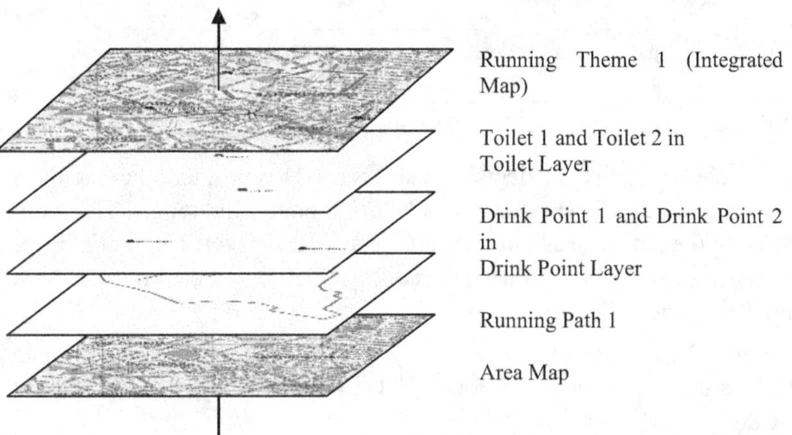

A spatial theme contains a group of spatial objects and/or spatial layers and presents a particular meaning to the decision-maker. In this illustration, *running path 1, toilet 1, toilet 2, drink point 1,* and *drink point 2* are grouped together to form a theme, that is, *running theme 1*. Similarly, *running path 2* along with *toilet 3*, *drink point 3,* and *drink point 4* forms *running theme 2*. The spatial objects and layers used for creation of *running theme 1* are presented in Figure 7. Integration of these spatial items from different layers through map overlay allows viewing the whole picture of a spatial problem from different perspectives.

The spatial theme manager provided by the FSDSS manages the spatial themes. It allows the decision-makers to save themes to the database and retrieve themes from the database. The interface for the spatial theme manager is given in Figure 8.

The spatial theme manager facilitates the creation and deletion of themes as required. In addition, it facilitates the updating of themes, for example, add new objects or layers to the theme, or delete spatial objects or spatial layers from the theme. Figure 9 shows the map presentation of *running theme 1* and *running theme 2*.

Decision makers can also perform other tasks using appropriate models and solvers to further investigate the problem, for example, calculate the distance of each of these running paths using the *path* model and *distance* solver. The following illustration shows two different scenarios for the above-mentioned themes. These scenarios are compared with each other to decide the best path for this running event.

Figure 8. Spatial theme manager

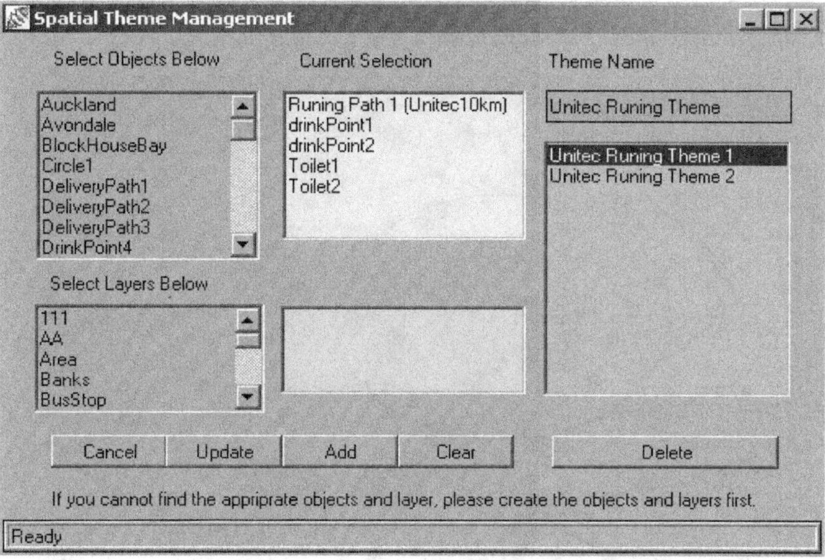

Running Path 1 Distance: 10011M	Toilets: 2	Drink Points: 2
Running Path 2 Distance: 9912 M	Toilets: 1	Drink Points: 2

In this case, *running path 1* is better than *running path 2* for two reasons. Firstly, *running path 1* has additional facilities (one more toilet) along its path compared with *running path 2*. Secondly and most importantly, the geographical layout of *running path 1* is better than *running path 2* since all available facilities are more evenly distributed along the track.

Purchase of a House

This section illustrates the implemented FSDSS to solve a location problem using the proposed spatial decision-making process. The application of each step of the process shown in Figure 1 is described in detail.

Step 1: Problem Identification

The problem presented in this session is to identify the optimal location of a property that maximises "return," that is, the satisfaction level that is measured on the

Figure 9. Spatial themes (Running theme 1 and running theme 2)

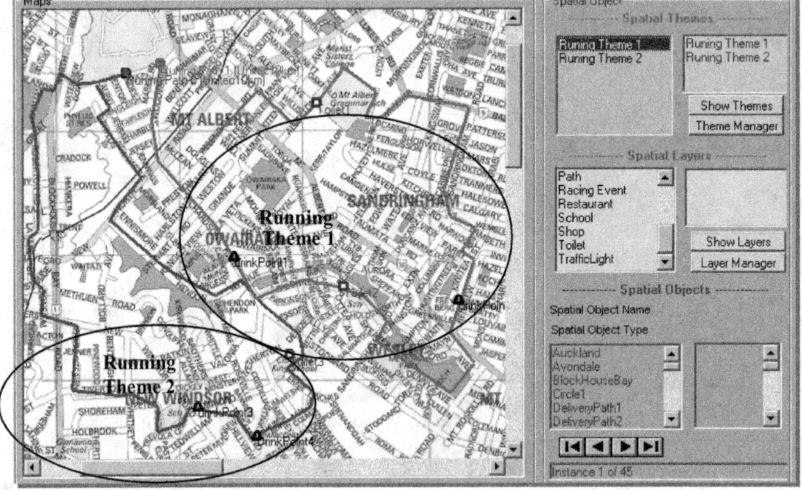

Figure 10. Value tree of location problem

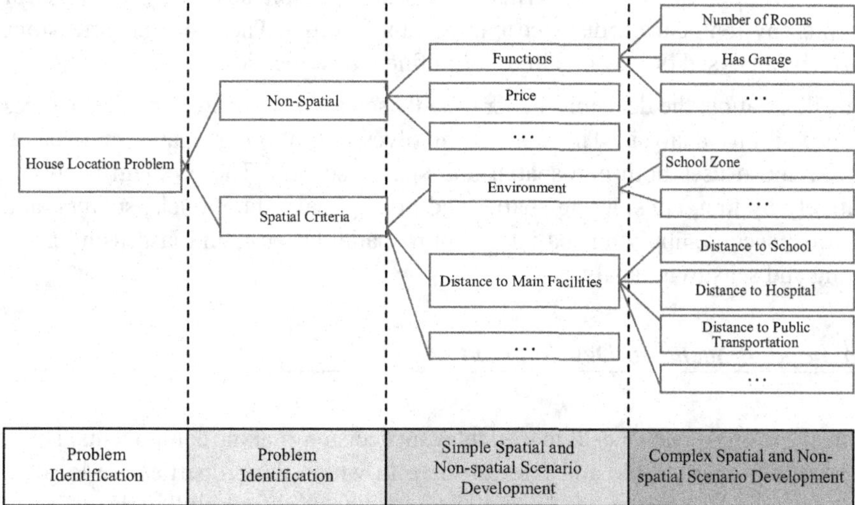

basis of the following three criteria. The value tree of after-analysis of the problem is presented in Figure 10.

- **Quality criteria:** for example, construction material, year built, size, function, and number of rooms
- **Economic criteria:** such as market price or rental cost
- **Location:** for example, property accessibility, vicinity, and environmental conditions

Some of these factors are difficult to evaluate or predict, as relative impacts for some of these factors on return remain unknown. It is hard to structure the problem in its entirety at one time, that is, precisely define and measure the objective for every possible solution. In the next step, the decision-maker models this problem using the proposed modelling approach by separating the spatial and non-spatial aspects of a complex spatial problem.

Step 2: Problem Modelling

The problem modelling involves both spatial and non-spatial aspects. Quality and economic factors are non-spatial in nature whereas accessibility criteria are of a spatial nature. On the non-spatial side, cost and quality of the property can be analysed using non-spatial models and solvers. The spatial aspect of the problem focuses on the location of the property, as it is an important criterion when people rent or buy a house. Location is a complex criterion that has multiple spatial dimensions, for example, environment and distance to important facilities. These spatial dimensions need to be analysed one by one in order to find a best location.

In this illustration, the decision-maker broadly selects a target area and then carries out accessibility analysis. The analysis involves both the non-spatial and spatial models, and it uses both non-spatial and spatial solvers. The problem is solved iteratively by first, considering spatial and non-spatial data, models, solvers, and scenarios; second, applying spatial and non-spatial criteria; and last, using goal-seeking and sensitivity analysis.

Step 3 and 4: Scenario Development

The decision-maker now needs to load relevant decision-making components. These include the property table and relevant map in which the properties are located, the various models, solvers, and visualisations to be used for building the different scenarios. A simple non-spatial scenario and a simple spatial scenario are developed separately at first; they are then integrated into a combined scenario. These scenarios are then transformed into a complex multi-criteria scenario through a structural integration process. The scenario development process is illustrated as follows:

Simple Non-Spatial Scenario

The non-spatial scenario is created using the non-spatial *filtering* model and the *range* solver. In this example, we have specified that we need a 3-bedroom flat with a price range between $300,000 and $400,000. Several properties are identified through this filtering process (see Figure 11). These are then stored in the database as *scenario 1* (4 instances).

Simple Spatial Scenario

The decision-maker has selected a buffer zone (a 500-meter radius circle) around a particular location (e.g., x, y coordinates: 200,200). The *filtering* model is instantiated with the *property* data and executed using the *distance* solver to find the properties within the defined circle. This process develops many scenario instances as shown in Figure 12. These scenario instances are then stored in the database as *scenario 2* (14 instances).

Figure 11. Simple non-spatial scenario creation

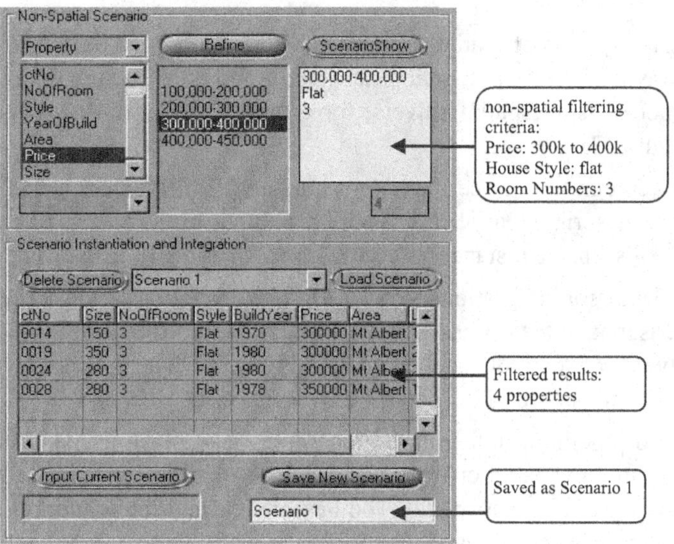

Figure 12. Simple spatial scenario creation

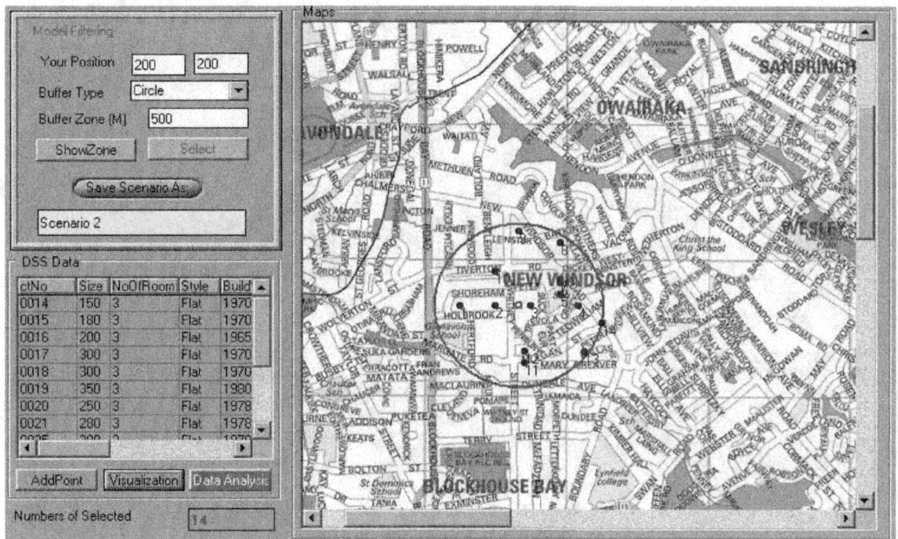

Combined Scenario (Pipelining Integration)

Pipelining integration of spatial and non-spatial scenarios can be done in two ways. The first way is to create non-spatial *scenario 1* and then execute the geographical filtering model using spatial solvers, for example, d*istance* or *point-in-polygon* solver (Figure 13).

During this integration process, the four non-spatial filtered scenario instances of *scenario1* as described earlier are supplied as input to the spatial filtering model. The resulting scenario instances are stored as *scenario 3* (3 instances).

The second way for integration of *scenario 1* and *scenario 2* is to supply the spatial *scenario 2* as input into the non-spatial filtering model and then apply the non-spatial Range solver for execution, as illustrated in Figure 14. The process develops three instances that are stored in the database as Scenario 3.

The scenario pipelining integration process can take place in many ways, either from non-spatial to spatial or from spatial to non-spatial or from spatial to spatial or from non-spatial to non-spatial. The flexible use and integration of spatial and non-spatial models, solvers, and scenarios is one of the most important features of the FSDSS. The above process helps the decision-maker to choose the properties

Figure 13. Integration of non-spatial with spatial scenarios

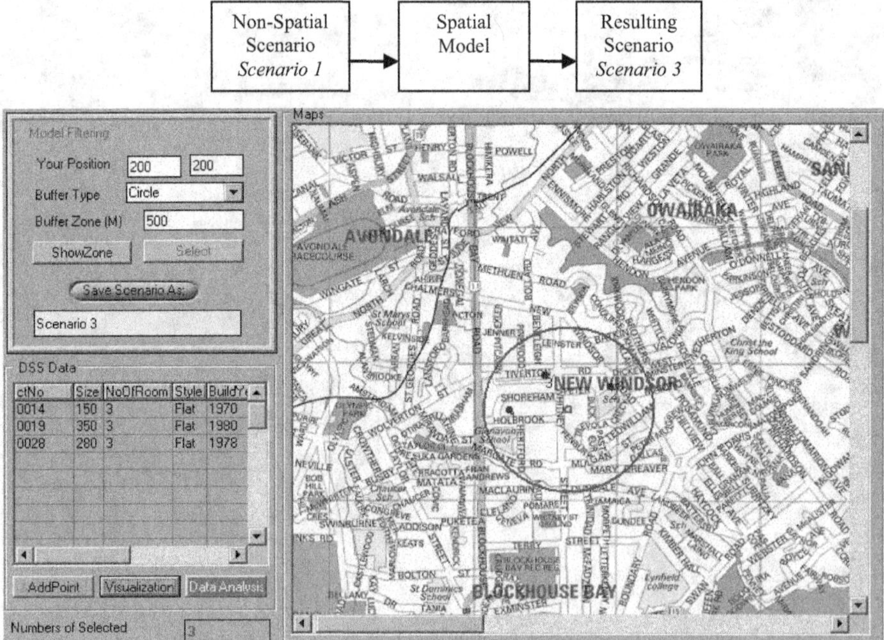

Figure 14. Integration of spatial with non-spatial scenarios

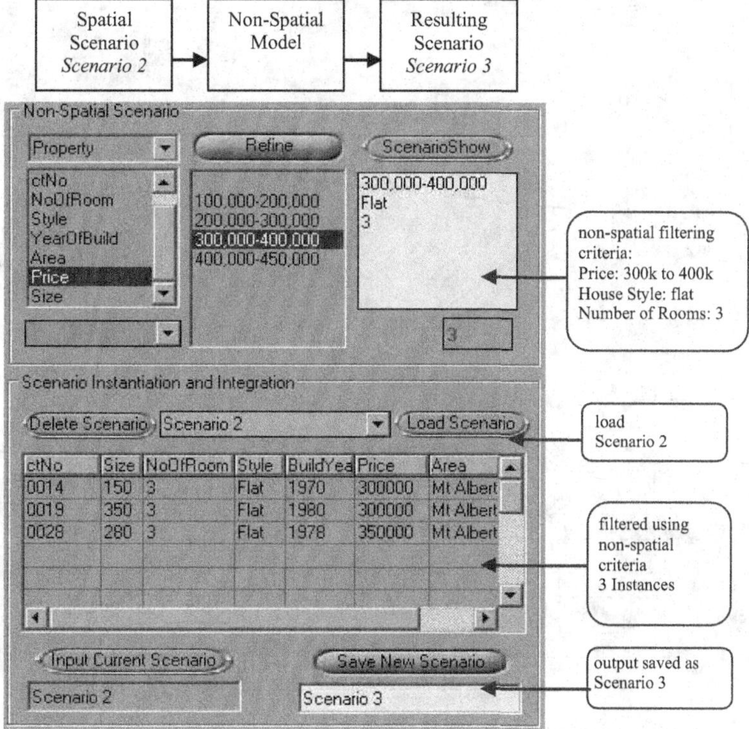

that satisfy the non-spatial criteria, for example, quality, cost, and the basic location requirements such as area. The following section illustrates another aspect of the location problem, namely, accessibility analysis.

Complex Spatial Scenario (Structural Integration)

The complex spatial scenario is generated using the *property* data, *distance* model, and *distance* solver as shown in Figure 15. The previously created *scenario 3* and its three instances are loaded from the scenario pool. Now, the decision-maker focuses on distance to major facilities for accessibility analysis.

Distance has multiple dimensions. It includes the distance from a particular spatial object (e.g., *property 0014*) to another object (e.g., *hospital 2*). The distance from one object to a spatial layer (e.g., *school layer*) returns multiple values, in this case the system returns the shortest distance from the target object to a single object (e.g., *school 1*) in that layer.

Figure 15. Multi-attribute spatial scenario creation

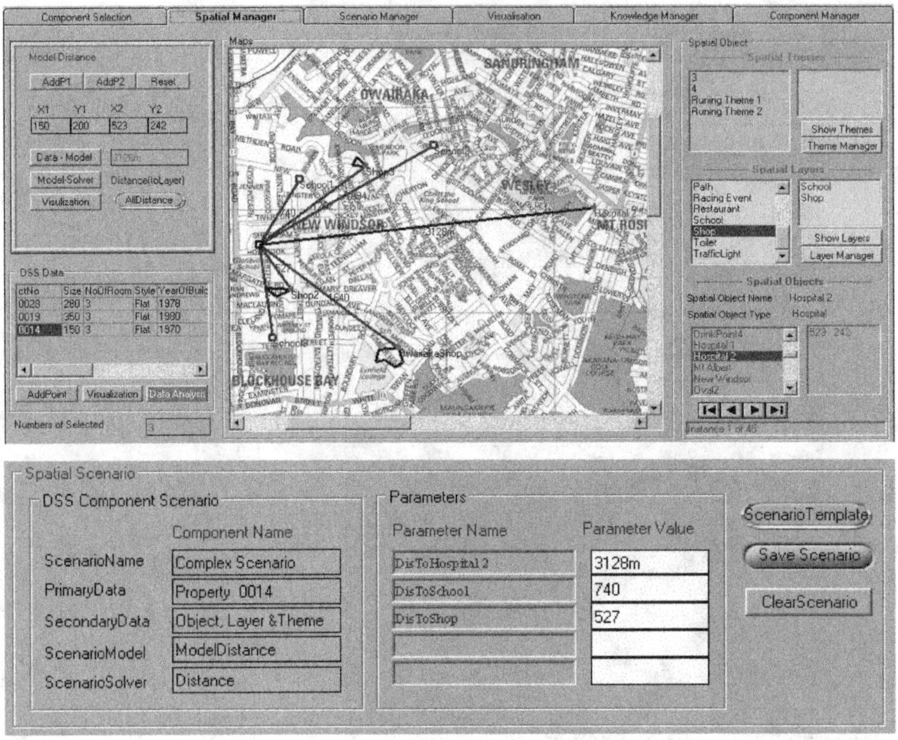

Step 5 and 6: Scenario Integration and Instantiation

The decision-maker integrates the simple combined scenario (*scenario 3*) structure with these newly- developed distance parameters to develop a more complex scenario that contains all the criteria for the problem.

The structural or permanent scenario integration takes place in two steps. First, a bare scenario template is created as shown in Figure 16. Then multiple scenario instances are created (Figure 17).

The scenario integration process is iterative in nature until all scenario instances have been generated. The scenario template and its multiple instances are stored in the database as a complex scenario, and they can be retrieved for further analysis or evaluation. The distance to the schools and shops are calculated on a spatial layer, rather than a single spatial object. The system picks up the distance to the closest object in the layer for instantiation of the scenario parameter. The decision-maker

Figure 16. Scenario template for integration of spatial and non-spatial scenarios

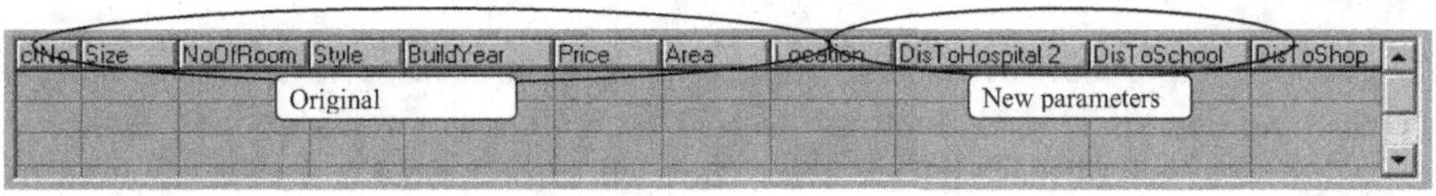

ctNo	Size	NoOfRoom	Style	BuildYear	Price	Area	Location	DisToHospital 2	DisToSchool	DisToShop
			Original					New parameters		

Figure 17. Multi-criteria spatial scenarios

ctNo	Size	NoOfRoom	Style	BuildYear	Price	Area	Location	DisToHospital 2	DisToSchool	DisToShop
0014	150	3	Flat	1970	300000	Mt Albert	150,200	2860	406	685
0019	350	3	Flat	1980	300000	Mt Albert	235,220	2407	569	663
0014	150	3	Flat	1970	300000	Mt Albert	150,200	3128	740	527

can select any spatial object, layer, or theme for integration of scenarios using the spatial manager as shown in Figure 18.

Step 7: Scenario Execution

Scenarios can be instantiated with the relevant data, model, and a number of solvers can be applied for execution of the scenarios. The scenario can be executed in a simple process or using multiple steps. The integration of executed models (scenarios) is also the process of modelling the scenario. During the scenario execution process, one scenario is instantiated and executed using different solvers.

Figure 18. Multiple spatial scenario generation

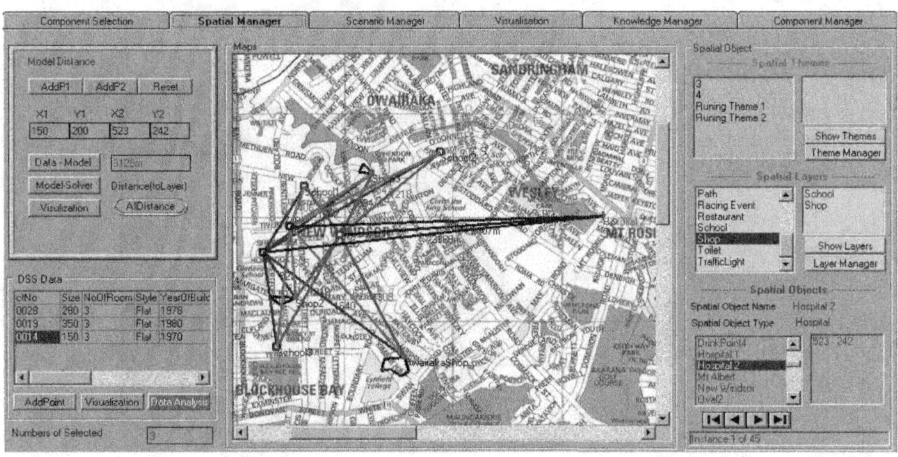

Step 8: Scenario Evaluation

The FSDSS supports the MCDM scenario evaluation process. The decision-maker needs to build a MCDM evaluation model by specifying parameters and assigning weights to each of these parameters. The evaluation model is instantiated with alternative scenario instances. These scenarios are executed using the solver that is tightly coupled within the evaluation model. The results are then ranked for selection. The sequence of the steps taken in this process is shown in Figure 19. The decision-maker selects the scenarios for evaluation to the scenario table as indicated in step 1. Then, an evaluation model is built by selecting the appropriate criteria from the input scenario. In step 3, the decision-maker assigns a weight to each of the criteria. Step 4 evaluates the scenarios using the model template created in step 2 and step 3. The built-in solver not only calculates values according to the formula but also ranks these values. The highest value is given as 100%, and other scenarios are calculated on a ratio basis by comparing the highest value.

Step 9: Decision-Making

As we can see from the results, *property 0014* (Figure 19) is ranked highest. Furthermore, the decision-maker can apply different evaluation models to explore alternative scenarios by considering the uncertainty involved in the decision-making process. Uncertainty may be caused by the error in available information to the decision-maker, or improper judgment regarding the relative importance of evaluation criteria.

Sensitivity analysis is employed as a means for achieving a deeper understanding of the structure of the problem. Sensitivity analysis is done through changing data, model, solver, scenario, and evaluation models. The decision-maker can change

Figure 19. Multi-criteria spatial scenarios

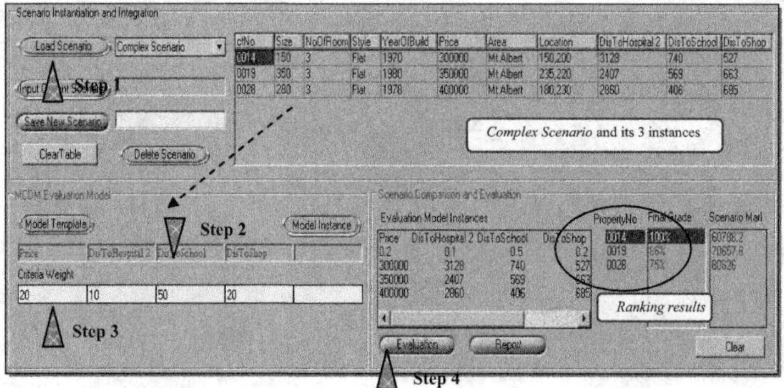

any one of these aspects and then re-evaluate these scenarios. This process can be repeated until all the scenarios relevant to the decision-maker are explored.

Trace the Spread of a Disease

The problem presented in this section is to identify the spread of the SARS epidemic in Hong Kong. We try to understand, analyse, and manage geographically distributed data using spatial functions. Overlaying quantitative graphics on a map enables the viewer to realise potential information in an extremely clear manner so that spatial patterns can be discovered.

We have aggregated a case database that includes the date, the number of cases confirmed, and the places they were found. Through the geo-coding process, each case was mapped to a geographical object, for example, a building or a hospital. These spatial objects can then be referenced by the geo-coding locations on the map. Figure 20 presents an overall picture of the geographical distribution of SARS cases and the population density; this gives us information about the number of SARS cases among different population groups at any given time. The visual representation would be useful for developing hypotheses about relationship between the distribution of SARS and population density or groups (Chu, Gao, & Sundaram, 2005). It could provide useful pointers for further analysis and investigations.

Figure 20. Case occurrences and population density (Source: Chu, Gao, & Sundaram, 2005)

Figure 21. Time series presentation of SARS spread period 1

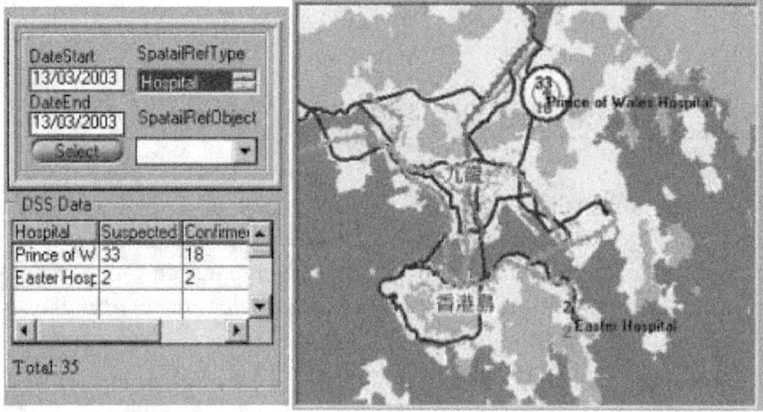

We explore the above scenario one step further by applying a time frame, to give pictorial views of the rate of case increases in various hospitals over time. As we can see from Figure 21, on the 13th of March, 2003, 33 SARS patients were admitted by the Prince of Wales Hospital (PWH); among them, 18 were confirmed. There were also two confirmed patients in Pamela Youde Easter Hospital (PYEH). The total number of patients admitted in Hong Kong hospital was 35 (20 confirmed).

On the 20th of March, the total number of admissions increased to 99 (58 were confirmed). The number of suspected patients in PWH jumped to 77, and PYEH cases increased to ten. New suspected patients were also found in Princess Margaret Hospital and Queen Elizabeth Hospital (Figure 22).

Figure 22. Time series presentation of SARS spread 2

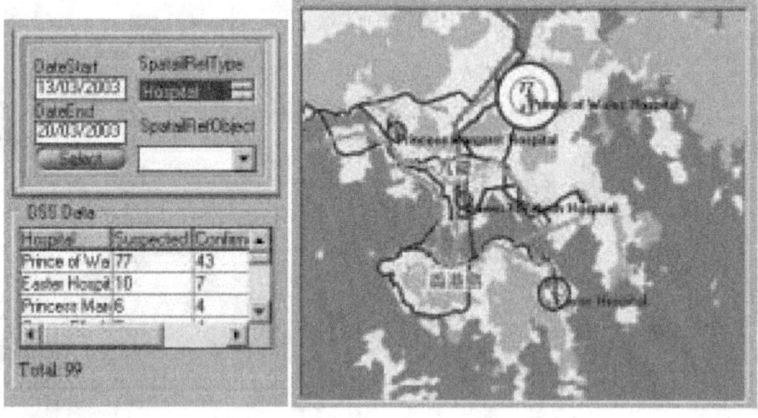

Figure 23. Infected buildings, school, and others

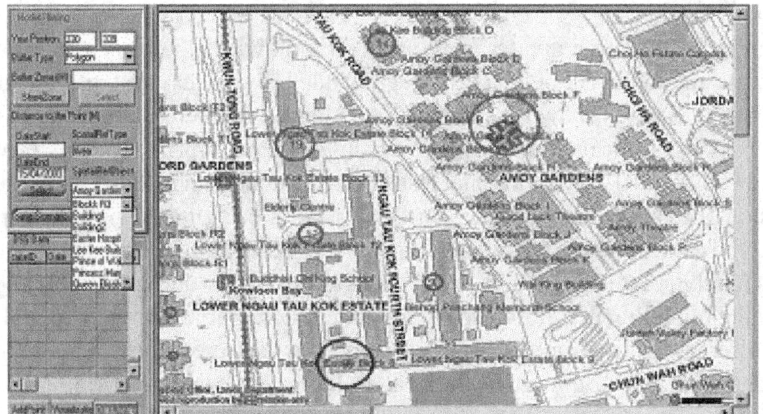

Using the time series mapping, we were able to map the number of patients admitted with suspected SARS symptoms and compare the number of these cases being confirmed as SARS patients subsequently at later times. Similarly, we can use the FSDSS to map the spread of SARS infections in the community. The system modules are inter-connected, and new entry of data dynamically changes other modules. An example of this is the dynamic refresh of collection of spatial objects where there is an infection (as seen in the drop-down combo box that appeared in the left-hand side in Figure 23). These spatial objects could include residential buildings, schools, shops, and any other objects that have a spatial reference.

Visual overlay of spatial objects over time allows us to ask a question such as "why has one block (in Lower Ngau Tau Kok Estate, quite far away from the Amoy Gardens) a much higher rate of infection than any other building?" Demographic analysis later reviewed that residents in this block comprised mostly senior citizens and that they passed through the Amoy Garden shopping mall each day to do their shopping.

Future Trends

Advances in MCDM, GIS, other relevant technologies, and their integration will have major impacts on the future development of SDSS. Multi-criteria spatial decision support is clearly the appropriate paradigm because it is such an adaptable and comprehensive concept. Multi-criteria spatial analysis is moving to a more exploratory, interactive emphasis with new decision analysis tools. There is also an increasing emphasis on the study of complex systems through simulation (Ascough II et al., 2002).

GIS itself is moving to a greater level of integration with other types of software. Spatial data and tools will be ubiquitous, embedded in business systems, and transparent to most users as shown in Figure 24. GIS can be an interoperable part of most critical business information systems including ERP/enterprise systems (such as SAP and PeopleSoft), environmental, asset, financial, human resource, emergency, and customer relationship management systems, thus bringing the power of spatial analysis and data mining to bear to measure results (business intelligence) and future impacts (analytic intelligence). A major focus is the design and implementation of true strategic intelligence frameworks that integrates spatial and non-spatial data across different information systems and business units to create broader knowledge and understanding within organisations at all levels of decision-making (Holland, 2005).

The design of an intelligent SDSS by coupling a GIS with an expert system is discussed by Zhu and Healey (1992). Spatial decision-making is based on two streams: the quantitative, which includes data analysis and modelling, and qualitative, which includes experience, intuition, judgment, and expertise. Current GIS systems focus

Figure 24. Historical and future trends of GIS (Source: Holland, 2005)

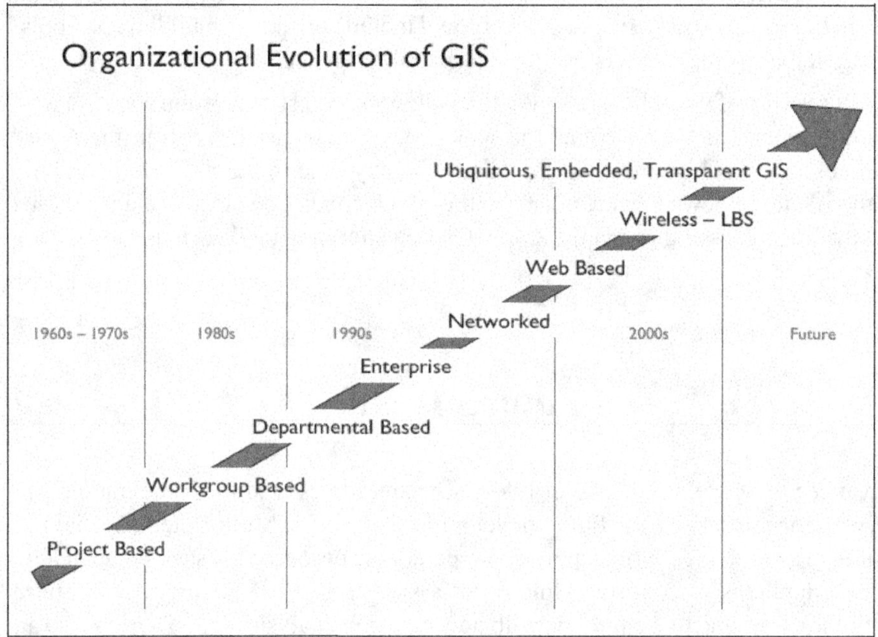

on quantitative information and largely ignore the qualitative aspects of the process. The inclusion of expert systems, which perform decision-making tasks by reasoning, using rules defined by experts in the relevant domain, would greatly aid qualitative spatial decision-making within GIS, and thus SDSS.

Conclusion

Decision-makers perceive the decision-making processes for solving complex spatial problems as unsatisfactory and lacking in generality. Current SDSS fulfil their specific objectives, but fail to address many of the requirements for effective spatial problem-solving, as they are inflexible, complex to use, and often domain-specific. This research blends together several relevant disciplines in a unique way and attempts to overcome the problems identified in the fields of spatial decision-making and SDSS.

We proposed a spatial decision-making process. Within the context of the spatial decision-making process, we have proposed a modelling approach by addressing the need of differentiating the spatial and non-spatial elements for multi-dimensional complex problem modelling. We then developed a flexible spatial decision support system framework and architecture to support this process. We also implemented a prototypical FSDSS that acts as a proof-of-concept for the spatial decision-making process, FSDSS framework, and architecture. The proposed spatial decision-making process and the implementation of FSDSS have been evaluated through a number of scenarios across diverse domains. The evaluation results indicate that the proposed spatial decision-making process is generic, and it is effective in solving complex spatial problems in different domains. Furthermore, the flexible use across domains and different types of problems was due to the generic nature of the architecture and design that leveraged spatial modelling and object-oriented concepts.

References

Armstrong, M. P., & Densham, P. J. (1990). Database organisation strategies for spatial decision support systems. *International Journal of Geographical Information Systems, 4*(1), 3-20.

Ascough II, J. C., Rector, H. D., Hoag, D. L., McMaster, G. S., Vandenberg, B. C., Shaffer, M. J., et al. (2002). Multi-criteria spatial decision support systems: Overview, applications, and future research directions. In *Online Proceed-*

ings of the iEMSs (Vol. 3, pp. 175-180). Retrieved from http://www.iemss.org/iemss2002/proceedings/pdf/volume%20tre/290_ascough%202.pdf

Chu, S., Gao, S., & Sundaram, D. (2005). A flexible multi-criteria spatial decision support architecture: Design and evaluation by healthcare test cases. *The Journal on Information Technology in Healthcare, 2005, 3*(1), 5–20.

De Gues, A. (1997). *The living company: Habits for survival in a turbulent business environment*. Boston, MA: Harvard Business School Press.

Densham, P. J. (1991). Spatial decision support systems. In Maguire, D. J., Goodchild, M. F., & Rhind, D. W. (Eds.): *Geographical information systems: Principles and applications* (pp. 403-412). Burnt Mill, UK: Longman.

Fedra, K. (1995). Decision support for natural resources management: Models, GIS and expert systems. *AI Applications, 9*(3), 3-19.

Forrester, J. W. (1992). Policies decisions and information sources for modeling. *European Journal of Operational Research, 59*(1), 42-63.

Geoffrion, A. M. (1987). An introduction to structured modeling. *Management Science, 33*(5), 547-588.

Georgantzas, N. C., & Acar, W. (1995). *Scenario-driven planning: Learning to manage strategic uncertainty*. Westport, CT: Greenwood Press.

Hall, G. B., Bowerman, R. L., & Feick, R. D. (1997). GIS-based decision support architecture and applications for developing countries. *South African Journal of Geo-Information,17*(3), 73-80.

Holland, W. S. (2005, April 10-13). Integration of SAS® data warehousing/mining and enterprise collaboration and data acquisition portals with ESRI-based geographic information systems and public sector business systems. In *SUGI 30 Proceedings*, Philadelphia (Paper 188-30).

Malczewski, J. (1997). Spatial decision support systems. *NCGIA Core Curriculum in Geographic Information Science*. Retrieved from http:// www.ncgia.ucsb.edu/giscc/units/u127/u127.html

Malczewski, J. (1999). Spatial multi-criteria decision analysis. In J.-C. Thill (Ed.), *Spatial multi-criteria decision-making and analysis: A geographic information sciences approach* (pp. 11-48). Brookfield; New York: Ashgate.

Mennecke, B.E. (1997). Understanding the role of geographic information technologies in business: Applications and research directions. *Journal of Geographic Information and Decision Analysis, 1*(1), 44-68.

Moloney, T., Lea, A. C., & Kowalchek, C. (1993). *Manufacturing and packaged goods in profiting from a geographical information system*. Fort Collins, CO: GIS World Books Inc.

Peterson, K. (1998). Development of spatial decision support systems for residential real estate. *Journal of Housing Research, 9*(1), 135-156.

Post, E. (2000). *Jade for developers* (2nd ed.). Auckland, New Zealand: Pearson Education.

Silver, M. S. (1991). *Systems that support decision makers: Description and analysis*. Chichester, UK: Wiley Series in Information Systems, John Wiley and Sons.

Simon, H. A. (1960). *The new science of management decision*. New York: Harper and Row.

Sprague, R. H. Jr., & Carlson, E. D. (1982). *Building effective decision support systems*. Englewood Cliffs, NJ: Prentice-Hall.

Yeh, G. -O. A., & Qiao, J. (1999). An intelligent solution support system for spatial modeling and decision support. *Proceedings of the 32nd Annual Hawaii International Conference on System Sciences* (Vol. 6, CD-ROM). January 5-8, Maui, HI.

Zhu, X., & Healey, R. (1992). Toward intelligent spatial decision support: Integrating geographical information systems and expert systems. In *Proceedings GIS/LIS '92 Annual Conference* (Vol. 2, pp. 877-886). San Jose, CA: ACSM-ASPRS-URISA-AM/FM.

Chapter VIII

Development of a Web-Based Intelligent Spatial Decision Support System (WEBISDSS): A Case Study with Snow Removal Operations

Ramanathan Sugumaran, University of Northern Iowa, USA
Shriram Ilavajhala, University of Maryland, USA
Vijayan Sugumaran, Oakland University, USA

Abstract

A SDSS combines database storage technologies, geographic information systems (GIS), and decision modeling into tools which can be used to address a wide variety of decision support areas (Eklund, Kirkby, & Pollitt, 1996). Recently, various emerging technologies in computer hardware and software such as speedy microprocessors, gigabit network connections, fast Internet mapping servers along with Web-based technologies like eXtensible Markup Language (XML), Web services, and so forth, provide promising opportunities to take the traditional spatial decision support systems one step further to provide easy-to-use, round-the-clock access to spatial data and decision support over the Web. Traditional DSS and Web-based spatial DSS can be further improved by integrating expert knowledge and utilizing intelligent software components (such as expert systems and intelligent agents) to emulate the human intelligence and decision-making. These kinds of decision support systems are classified as intelligent decision support systems. The objective of this chapter is to discuss the development of an intelligent Web-based spatial decision support system and demonstrate it with a case study for planning snow removal operations.

Introduction

Spatial Decision Support Systems

The past decade witnessed an explosive growth of spatial data and various applications that utilize spatial data. Geographic information systems (GIS) have been developed to facilitate storing, retrieving, editing, analyzing, and displaying spatial information. The increasing complexity of spatial data and a need for better modeling requires decision support systems that can handle spatial data. This led to the idea of spatial decision support systems (SDSS). Since the early 1980s, SDSS have been used in several applications that provide spatial functionalities such as routing, allocation modeling, and so forth.

Most of the existing SDSS do not employ any intelligent software components to enhance decision support. Only a very few researchers have explored the possibility of integrating intelligent software components with an SDSS for applications like multi-criteria decision analysis, routing, and weather-based decision-making. Most of the literature reviewed for Intelligent GIS systems deals with architectural as well as implementation issues of GIS-based decision support systems and integrating them with agents. The use of software agents for GIS-based systems is well documented (Odell, Parunak, Fleischer, & Brueckner, 2003; Sengupta, Bennett, & Armstrong, 2000; Shahriari & Tao, 2002; Tsou, 2002). Most of these systems are not Web-based, and they lack the advantages of Web-based systems like ease-of-use, cross platform functionality, low maintenance costs, centralized data storage, and so forth.

Also, recent advances in Web technologies like rich site summary (RSS), XML feeds, and asynchronous JavaScript and XML (AJAX) can help us device a seamless interface by providing real-time access to data over the World Wide Web. Therefore, integrating the process of decision-making with an intelligent component and Web-based technologies proves to be very beneficial. When integrated with encoded human intelligence, the spatial decision support systems can rival a human expert in a particular domain (e.g., snow removal, traffic management, logistics, etc.).

This chapter explores and discusses the development of a Web-based intelligent spatial decision support system for planning snow removal operations. Specifically, this chapter addresses the existing problems with snow removal decision-making in the USA. The SDSS discussed here integrates knowledge from snow removal experts and real-time weather information into a Web-based interface. The system is intended to provide advised decision support for officials at various departments of transportation across the country, and to serve as a guideline for development of a snow removal DSS for the decision-makers and stake-holders around the world.

Background on Snow Removal Operations

Snow removal operations during the winter are of prime importance in avoiding traffic accidents and providing safe travel conditions on the nation's highways and city streets. Quality snow and ice control service is critical for preserving traffic safety, maintaining city commerce, and allowing residents access to schools and medical facilities (Hintz, Kettlewell, Shambarger, & Sweeney, 2001). Department of Transportation (DOT) of each state is responsible for snow removal on all interstates, and primary highways like the U.S. Federal highways and state highways. The city streets are snowplowed by the Street Department of that city, or sometimes by the DOT itself (Iowa Department of Transportation (IDOT), 2005). Snowplowing is done according to a set priority assigned to each road depending upon the annual average daily traffic (AADT). Higher priority roads like the interstates are cleared before the lower priority routes like city streets.

Managing snow removal operations necessitates activities ranging from the preparation of roads before the snowfall by pre-wetting by salt (e.g., most roads and bridge decks are pre-wetted with salt before the snow to avoid bonding of ice to the pavement in order to prevent slippery road conditions) to the timely clearing of the snow off the roads after the snowfall. The personnel in charge of snow removal operations keep tabs on weather forecasts to verify conditions that require snowplowing. These conditions include snow, flurries, freezing rain, and sleet. Once the weather forecast predicts these conditions, routes that need snow removal or salt-treatment are determined, and the snowplowing vehicles are loaded with material. These vehicles are then sent out to the roads, both before and after the snowfall. Considering the number of managerial aspects like monitoring weather information, allocating resources like vehicles, drivers, and material, it is an overwhelming task for the personnel in charge of snow removal operations to administer timely deployment of snowplows and manage efficient resource allocation. Therefore, maintaining snow removal operations efficiently and optimally during the winter is a major challenge for many governmental as well as non-governmental agencies and prove to be a big budgetary burden (Hintz, Kettlewell, Shambarger, & Sweeney, 2001; Salim, Timmerman, Strauss, & Emch, 2002).

Existing Methods for Snow Removal Operations and Their Disadvantages

Most of the existing methods for snowplowing management such as resource allocation, inventory management, and routing are performed manually by a person or persons in charge of snow removal operations. These methods, in most cases, are based on a pre-determined set of static rules that are inefficient for snow plowing and resource allocation under constantly-changing weather conditions. They often result in inefficient and non-optimal results and tend to increase the cost of snow removal. Moreover, the reaction time and the margin of error during heavy storm conditions can prove deadly, and human-based methods are always prone to such errors.

In addition, our observations with various snowplowing stations showed that there is no substantial use of analytical methods before planning snowplowing operations to reduce cost and maximize overall effectiveness. For example, the methods used for most local government agencies (e.g., the DOT) do not use any special measures for efficient routing and resource allocation. Many of the existing methods do not choose the shortest or the quickest path from the snowplow station to reach the snowplow route. Neither do they optimize resource allocation by taking into consideration various important factors like the cost of operation of a vehicle, availability of drivers or vehicles, and so forth. Such methods have a severe limitation of being inefficient; even a very slight change in weather conditions would almost demand double the amount of resources and unplanned travel for a different, non-predetermined route, and thus result in waste of time and money. Moreover, the existing manual methods cannot deal efficiently with resource allocation for newly-added routes and changing weather conditions .

Also, existing methods do not use automated inventory management and control. Inventory management is very important, and analytical tools must be used to keep up with the demand of snow removal. Various factors like the lead time for order, reorder point, stock levels, and so forth, must always be monitored to keep the necessary materials (e.g., salt) in stock. Keeping in mind the importance of providing speedy response after a snowstorm, inventory management tools are indispensable for planning snow removal operations. In addition, the existing methods do not provide any visual feedback when it comes to routing and resource allocation. Visual feedback not only improves the perception of the current assignments, but also helps review the allocations for better planning in future allocations. Also, there is no integrated use of weather information that could alert the snow removal crews and provide a scenario-based decision support. Thus, snowplowing operations must be carefully planned to provide optimum resource allocation and efficient routing.

Further, a literature review reveals that there is lack of extensive research in the field of GIS-based winter maintenance decision support systems. One of the existing

SDSS for snow removal planning is the "snow removal asset management system," SRAMS for short. Salim, Timmerman, Strauss, and Emch (2002) developed a SDSS called "snow removal asset management system"(SRAMS). SRAMS is a stand-alone, personal computer-based program that utilizes a rule-based expert system for decision support. The test runs of SRAMS concluded that snow removal can be planned efficiently, by reducing the deadhead times and optimizing resources for snow removal. While this system is useful to a certain extent, it ignores many aspects of resource allocation like the availability of drivers for a certain shift, the ability of a driver to drive a specific category of a vehicle, inability to read live weather data, providing scenario-based solutions, and so forth. Being a stand-alone program, SRAMS cannot be accessed from any other computer. Also, SRAMS was developed bearing a non-technical user in mind and therefore, there is a significant need to develop strong winter operations maintenance system that offers expert advice and decision support, while being easy-to-use for even a non-GIS professional.

Another decision support system for snow removal is the winter road maintenance decision support system (Mahoney & Myers, 2003). The maintenance decision support system (MDSS) focuses mainly on using weather data to design a decision support system for maintaining roads during winters. While MDSS uses advanced weather data, it lacks the ability to calculate the amounts of snow removal material which are needed. Also, MDSS lacks an asset management module that would have made the system much more efficient.

Similarly, a winter maintenance decision support system developed by the U.S. Department of Transportation (USDOT) allows viewing road-wise weather data, and various weather parameters like Visibility, Air Temperature, Snow Rate, Snow Accumulation, and so forth (U.S. Department of Transportation, 2004). Also, another system called "weather support to de-icing decision-making" (WSDDM) uses commercial weather data in the form of Next Generation Radar WSR-88D and METAR surface weather reports from automated surface observing system stations and observers. The system also uses snow gauges on the ground to measure the precipitation to provide decision support. The WSDDM essentially provides decision support for de-icing operations that take place at airports. The drawbacks of this system are the usage of commercial data and the lack of an intelligent component (e.g., expert system) for making crucial decisions.

In summary, there are no well established intelligent SDSS available for snow removal operations that integrate automatic routing, asset management, and real-time weather data. Further, the systems discussed in the literature do not leverage the potential of GIS using Web-based architectures and integrate expert system components for intelligent decision support. Therefore, there is a significant need for an intelligent system that provides analytical tools and decision support through visual feedback for managing snowplowing operations with optimal resource allocation and efficient routing.

Methodology

The methodology for developing WebISDSS encompassed the following four steps (shown in Figure 1): (a) data collection, (b) data analysis and modeling, (c) GIS and intelligent software component integration, and (d) providing results and obtaining feedback. Each of these steps is briefly described below.

The first step in developing WebISDSS is data collection. During data collection, three categories of data were collected. These categories are expert knowledge, spatial data, and non-spatial data. The aim of expert knowledge elicitation is to gather knowledge of various snow removal operations like resource allocation, routing, and so forth, from the officials responsible for handling snowplowing operations.

Figure 1. Overall methodology adapted for developing WebISDSS (Source: Ilavajhala, 2005)

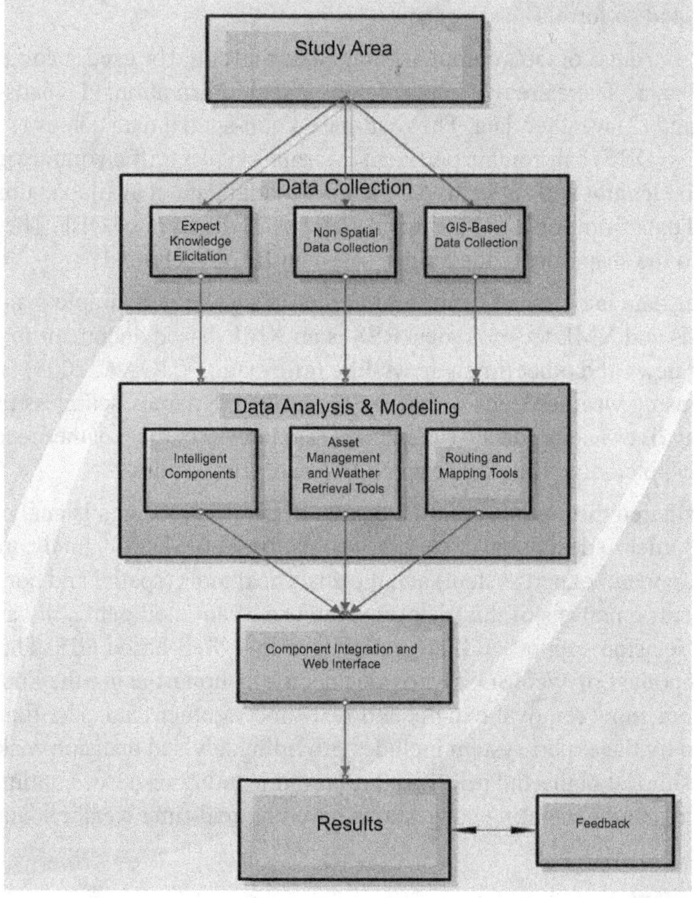

Officials from the Street Departments of Cedar Falls and Waterloo, IA, along with the county and Iowa DOT's highway maintenance supervisor in Waterloo were consulted to obtain the knowledge about snow removal in the study area of Black Hawk County. Through a series of direct interviews, a variety of information regarding the existing snow removal procedures was gathered.

The spatial data gathered is the county-wide roads and street dataset of Black Hawk County, IA. This data is available from the Iowa DOT's maps Web site (IDOT, 2005). The dataset essentially contains the centerlines for public roads including interstates, U.S. and state Highways, county roads, city streets, park roads, and institutional roads. For providing effective routing solutions like providing shortest or quickest path from the snowplow station to the snowplow route, the optimized road data set from GDT Inc., was purchased. This data set is commercially available in a format called spatial data engine (SDE). SDE is a format optimized to provide quick routing solutions. ArcIMS utilizes the SDE data through its RouteServer extension. The SDE data, in combination with ArcIMS, can be used to provide various kinds of routing and logistics options such as vehicle routing with multiple stops, interstate preference, and so forth.

The non-spatial data contains complementary data that could be used in combination with spatial data. There are two kinds of non-spatial information: (1) roads-related asset data, and (2) weather data. The road-based non-spatial data comes as a set of database files (DBF) that contain pertinent information like traffic volumes, number of lanes, lane length, and so forth. All the non-spatial data is available along with spatial road data from Iowa DOT's maps Web site in the form of DBF. These DBF are linked to the shapefile by the unique segment ID of each road.

The weather data is obtained from the Internet using the rich simple syndication or RSS feeds and XML technologies. RSS is an XML-based document format for syndicating news and other timely news-like information (NOAA, 2003). The reason for choosing weather feeds is that they provide a dynamic, seamless interface for obtaining live weather data without page reloads. Also, the weather feeds from most sources, including the ones from NOAA, are free of cost.

The data gathered through the various data collection procedures is analyzed and modeled in order to design the core components for WebISDSS, namely, the intelligence component (expert system) and the analytical tools (spatial and non-spatial tools). A major emphasis of this chapter is the use of an intelligent software component for decision support and integrating it with a Web-based GIS. The expert system component of WebISDSS provides decision support using the knowledge gathered from snow removal experts and real-time weather data. The functionality provided by the expert system includes providing advised decision-making for generating shortest paths and prioritized routes, allocating resources optimally for snow plowing, and generating suggestions based on real-time weather data.

The analytical tools available in WebISDSS provide functionality such as basic navigation, routing, resource management, and so forth. These tools utilize spatial and non-spatial data. The intelligent component and the analytical tools are integrated into a single interface that could be accessed through the World Wide Web. Therefore, a Web site is designed for publishing the road (street) map of Black Hawk County, IA. The Web site, in effect, will serve both as a user interface and a way to publish the resultant maps and show the results. Various routes are color coded for effectively presenting the route information visually for better understanding.

Architecture and Implementation

WebISDSS is designed using Web-based client/server architecture and rule-based artificial intelligence techniques. The implementation combines GIS and Web-based programming components from two leading technologies, Environmental Systems Research Institute (ESRI) and Microsoft. For developing the current prototype, ESRI ArcIMS ActiveX Connector is used in combination with Microsoft Internet information server and active server pages technology. The overall architecture of WebISDSS is shown in Figure 2. It contains the following two main components: (a) Web-based client interface, and (b) the server. These two components are briefly described as follows.

The Web-Based Client Interface

The primary functions of the Web-based client are providing the user interface and facilitating communication between the user and the server components. WebISDSS offers user interface by the means of a Web browser. The client corresponds with the server through requests; the server processes clients' requests and sends back a response.

The Server

The server is the "backbone" of the entire system and is composed of a set of components that work in tandem to process the user requests and provide a response. The server has the following components: (a) Web server, (b) spatial server, (c) non-spatial databases, (d) intelligent component, and (e) real-time weather retrieval component. A brief description of these components is given as follows.

The primary component on the server-side is the Web Server. It is the "central location" from where the user requests are received and processed or delegated further to other components like the spatial server or analytical tools, and so forth.

The Web server for WebISDSS is the Microsoft Internet information server (IIS). The server is hosted on a Microsoft Windows XP Professional machine. All server side programming to create the analytical tools is accomplished using Microsoft active server pages (ASP) technology. The primary reason for choosing Microsoft technologies is their tight integration and ease-of-use.

The Spatial server is responsible for processing client requests that involve rendering and presenting maps and map-related information to the user. The spatial server is implemented using ESRI ArcIMS, the most popular Internet mapping software. The communication between the map display (client) and the spatial server components is performed via a standardized and proprietary XML format called ArcXML. WebISDSS utilizes ArcIMS ActiveX Object Connector v. 4.1. The ActiveX connector acts as an intermediary between the Web server and the spatial server by converting the user requests over HTTP into ArcXML statements, the language that the spatial server understands.

For providing routing solutions, the ArcIMS RouteServer extension is used. ArcIMS RouteServer comes as an additional component with ArcIMS and provides routing by using commercial data from TeleAtlas, Inc. This data is available in an optimized format called Spatial Data Engine (SDE) format. Advantages of using RouteServer are quick and efficient routing, complete integration with ArcIMS for use over the

Figure 2. The overall architecture of WebISDSS (Source: Ilavajhala, 2005)

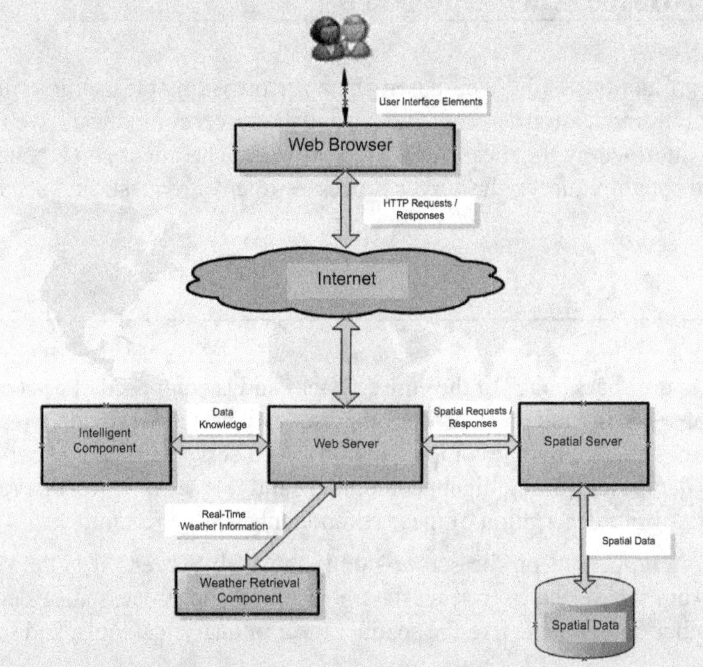

Web, and provision for obtaining fully-customized routes (e.g., percentage of interstates of travel, addition of multiple stops, etc.). All the routes are color-coded, according to a pre-determined priority, to take advantage of the visualization that GIS-based systems provide.

ESRI software was chosen over other vendors' products because we found ESRI products to be stable, scalable, and reliable. A detailed comparison of various Internet mapping software products from different vendors is beyond the scope of this chapter. Also, ESRI ArcIMS provides a programming model (object model) that is compatible with our server-side scripting language (ASP) and Web server (IIS), respectively.

The intelligent component developed for WebISDSS is a rule-based expert system. The knowledge gathered from the snow removal experts was carefully sifted and categorized into three knowledge categories, routing, resource allocation, and weather data. Categorizing the knowledge provided modularity and structure for storing the knowledge. The knowledge gathered was entirely conditions-based, in the form of a set of "actions" resulting from a set of "conditions." This sort of knowledge can be best represented as "if-then" structures. The intelligent component thus incorporates the expert knowledge and an inference engine. The expert knowledge is stored in a repository called the "knowledge base" and fed into the inference engine that provides a set of results or suggestions.

Rule Machine Corporation's Visual Rule Studio offers an easy and efficient way to code knowledge as "business rules", providing for encoding expert knowledge in the form of "if-then" rules. Each rule has a left-hand side (LHS) or conditions, and right-hand side (RHS) or results. The RHS is evaluated only when the LHS is true. These rules can be "fired" depending upon various data that is supplied and can help make a decision, rivaling a human expert. The knowledge-base is coded using Procedural Rule Language (PRL), a proprietary language of Rules Machines Corporation.

The asset databases contain information about various transportation assets that are utilized in snow removal activities such as characteristics of snowplows, capacity, mileage for equipment maintenance, odometer reading prior to assignment of the machine, details of the materials available at the central storage for snow removal, available quantity, unit cost of the material, reorder point, assignment of the operator to preferred machines, and so forth. All the asset databases are implemented in DBASE IV database file (DBF) format and are managed through the Web-based client.

As mentioned previously, the weather data for WebISDSS is obtained using the RSS and XML feeds technology. The weather data is embedded into the system by reading the free RSS and XML Weather feeds provided by www.weatherroom.com and NOAA's National Weather Service (http://www.nws.noaa.gov). These XML feeds essentially provide an XML document that encodes various weather parameters including the air temperature, wind speeds, wind direction, wind-chill, and visibility. Live as well as the forecast weather data can be obtained and presented to the user in this fashion by reading a particular weather feed from the Internet , and loading the information contained in the weather feed document. The current weather conditions help generate suggestions for material assignment and help determine the allocation of resources. The forecast data is used to generate alerts. The weather information can also be used for generating scenario-based solutions. Further, the live weather data, in combination with the encoded rules, help make intelligent decisions for snow removal and resource management and allocation.

Results

Application Example: Planning Snow Removal Using WebISDSS

One of the main objectives of WebISDSS is to provide easy-to-use Web-based interface and intelligent decision support for planning snow removal operations. To achieve this goal, the system uses the knowledge gathered from snow removal experts as well as real-time weather data. It provides an uncluttered interface, divided neatly into various "areas." For example, the menu and the tool bar appear on top, and the map and map layers area are beneath the menu, and a "message area" displays detailed messages to the users. The interface is mainly menu-driven, making it very easy to use. All the menu options are given appropriate, non-technical names so that a naïve computer user can also utilize the system. Figure 3 shows the main interface of WebISDSS and its organization into various "areas."

The system generates verbose and detailed alerts, warnings, tips, and other messages that help a non-technical user better understand the system. Most of the commonly-used menu options are provided as tools on a separate tool bar and can be used by clicking on the appropriate icon. When the user clicks on a particular tool, a message is displayed in the message area of the window. A detailed help system is available, which avoids technical jargon and provides the user with an easy guide to use the system. The salient features and functionalities of the menu interface of WebISDSS are briefly described as follows.

- **Weather menu:** The Weather menu lets the user set and view real-time weather information. The weather menu is shown in Figure 4. The user can choose to view live or forecast weather information and also store it. Weather conditions can be set either manually by entering a set of parameters or by automatically

Figure 3. The main interface of WebISDSS (Source: Ilavajhala, 2005)

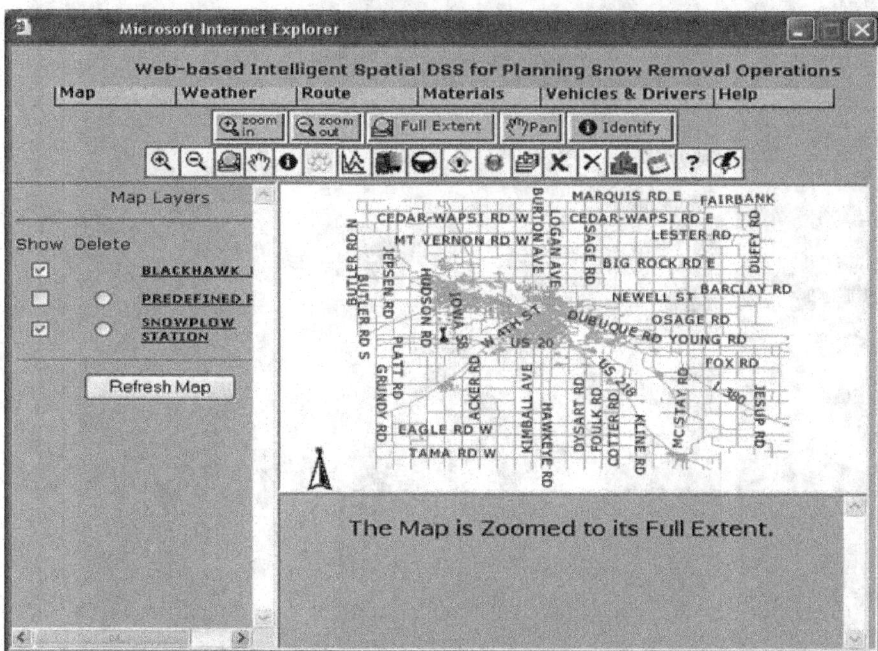

Figure 4. The "Weather" menu interface of WebISDSS

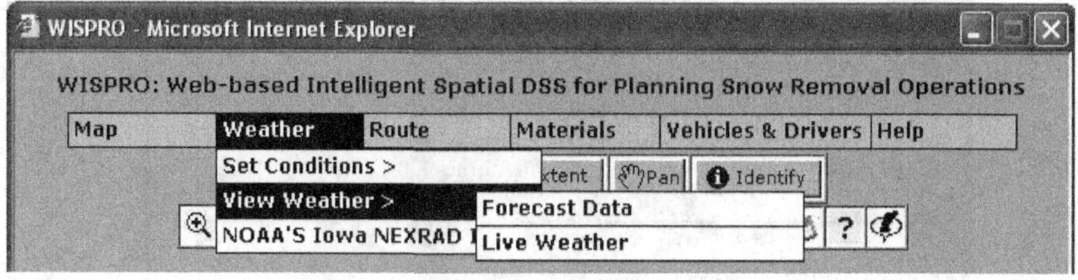

obtaining them from the Web. The weather menu also provides an option to view live weather through NOAA NEXRAD radar image for the state of Iowa (Figure 5) or Forecast data. Figure 6 shows a screenshot of forecast weather retrieved by WebISDSS.

- **Route menu:** Route menu provides options for creating, deleting, and loading route information. The user can choose to create a route by clicking on the "start route" option, and then clicking on the road segments to snowplow. Clicking "end route" menu item will save the route, and generate driving directions from the station to the route by creating the shortest or quickest

Figure 5. NEXRAD radar image obtained from NOAA

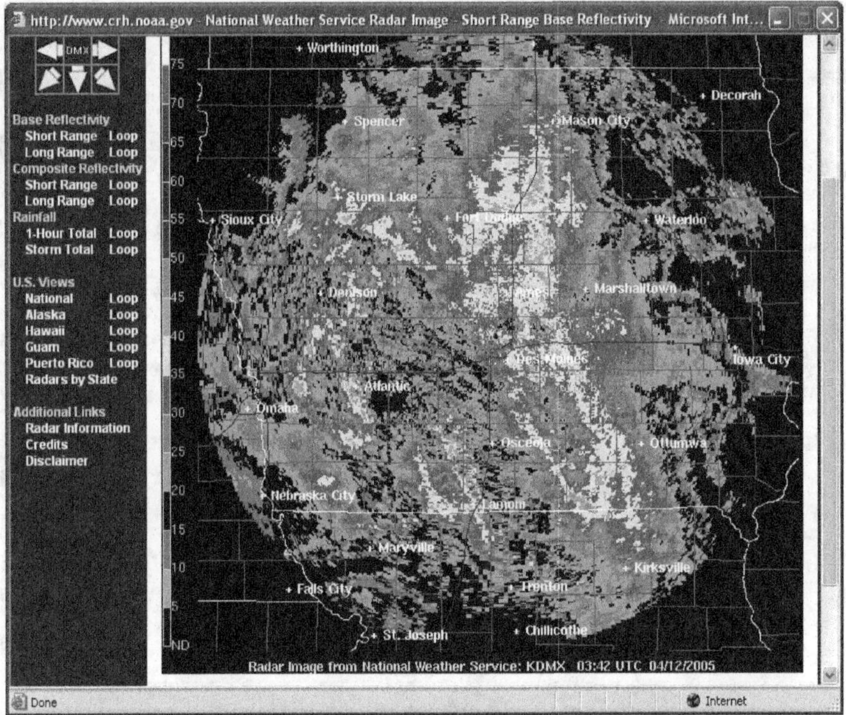

Figure 6. Screenshot of weather forecast information retrieved by WebISDSS

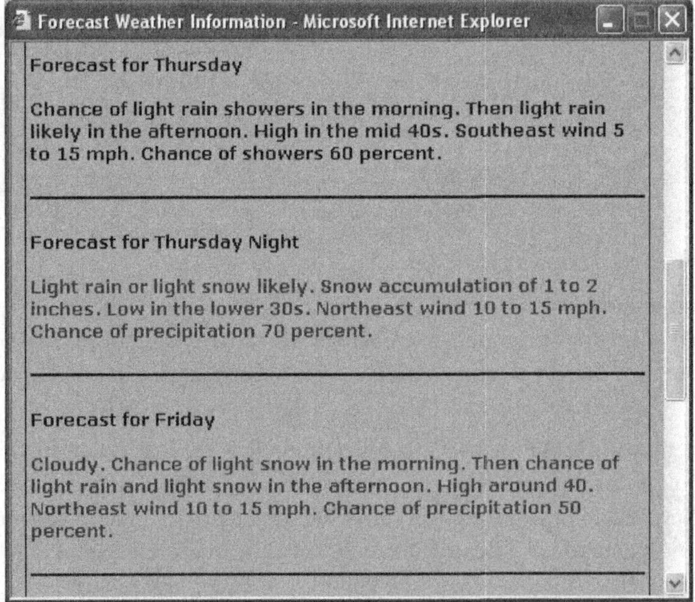

route, as chosen by the user. The user can also delete a route or a route segment. Deletion of route can either be temporary (deletion from the map) or permanent (deletion from the disk).

- **Vehicles and Drivers menu:** The Vehicles and Drivers menu provides options to assign drivers and vehicles. Also available from this menu is an option to manage drivers and vehicles by adding, deleting, or editing driver or vehicle information.
- **Materials menu:** Materials menu gives options related to materials management and control. Options include inventory analysis, material assignment, addition/deletion/editing snowplowing materials such as salt, sand, and so forth.
- **Help menu:** The Help menu lets the user obtain information about how to use the system. The "Using WebISDSS" option shows the user the "Help central" screen with various options for getting help. Also, the help menu shows the product and copyright information.

System Walkthrough

The expert system provides suggestions based on user input. These suggestions include initiation of snow plowing operations, material to utilize for snowplowing, amount of material that must be used, number of lines to snowplow, and material assignment. To begin with, the user sets the weather conditions either by entering weather parameters like current conditions, temperature, dew point, wind speed, and so forth, or by using the system to read weather conditions from the Internet. The real-time weather retrieval component reads the encoded current and forecast weather data through the Web and provides a readable output to the user. Further, these suggestions are used for assisting and planning resource allocation, initiating snowplowing operations, and so forth. Thus, the real-time weather retrieval component works with the Web server and the intelligent component to provide suggested actions depending upon real-time weather information retrieved from the Web. These weather conditions are stored in a database file (DBF).

The expert system's inference engine examines the weather conditions stored in the database. The inference engine then produces a set of suggestions and stores these suggestions on the server's hard drive. These suggestions advise the user whether to initiate a snowplowing operation, which materials to use for snowplowing, and how much of each material should be used. Depending on the precipitation, the expert system also produces suggestions to either initiate anti-icing or de-icing operations. Other parameters that are used in producing suggestions are visibility and dew point. The system advises the exercise of caution if the visibility is less than a

Figure 7. Sample rules for material allocation

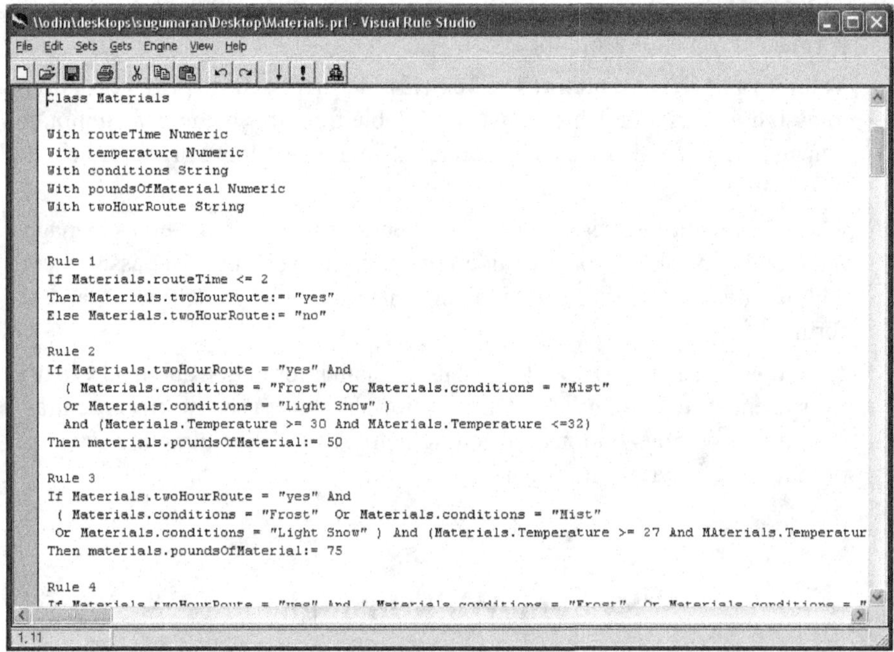

mile. The dew points are used to forecast precipitation and to caution the users to wet the bride decks to prevent icing.

\\odin\desktops\sugumaran\Desktop\Materials.prl - Visual Rule Studio
File Edit Sets Gets Engine View Help
Class Materials
With routeTime Numeric
With temperature Numeric
With conditions String
With poundsOfMaterial Numeric
With twoHourRoute String
Rule 1
If Materials.routeTime <= 2
Then Materials.twoHourRoute:= "yes"
Else Materials.twoHourRoute:= "no"
Rule 2
If Materials.twoHourRoute = "yes" And
(Materials.conditions = "Frost" Or Materials.conditions = "Mist"
Or Materials.conditions = "Light Snow")
And (Materials.Temperature >= 30 And MAterials.Temperature <=32)
Then materials.poundsOfMaterial:= 50
Rule 3
If Materials.twoHourRoute = "yes" And
(Materials.conditions = "Frost" Or Materials.conditions = "Mist"
Or Materials.conditions = "Light Snow") And (Materials.Temperature >= 27 And MAterials.Temperatur
Then materials.poundsOfMaterial:= 75
Rule 4
1, 11

Once the weather conditions are accessed and stored in the database, routes can be created. The WebISDSS calculates route parameters needed for snowplowing such as the number of lane miles, total route length, and so forth. These parameters are stored in a database along with other route parameters like route identification number, and so forth. These parameters are further used for making suggestions for material allocation.

After the routes are created, material can be assigned to these routes. Based on the weather conditions stored in the database, and various route parameters such as the route length, and so forth, the expert system provides suggestions on how much material should be used for snowplowing. Figure 7 shows part of the "rules" that the expert system uses to provide suggestions on material allocation and Figure 8 shows the material allocation interface of WebISDSS. Also, the expert system calculates the amount of material needed per route depending upon the precipitation levels. These calculations are based on a set of guidelines that the Iowa DOT uses to calculate material allocation.

WebISDSS also provides a quick way to view all current assignments in one screen. The menu option "Map > Show Current Assignments" provides a screen with cur-

Figure 8. Material assignment interface of WebISDSS

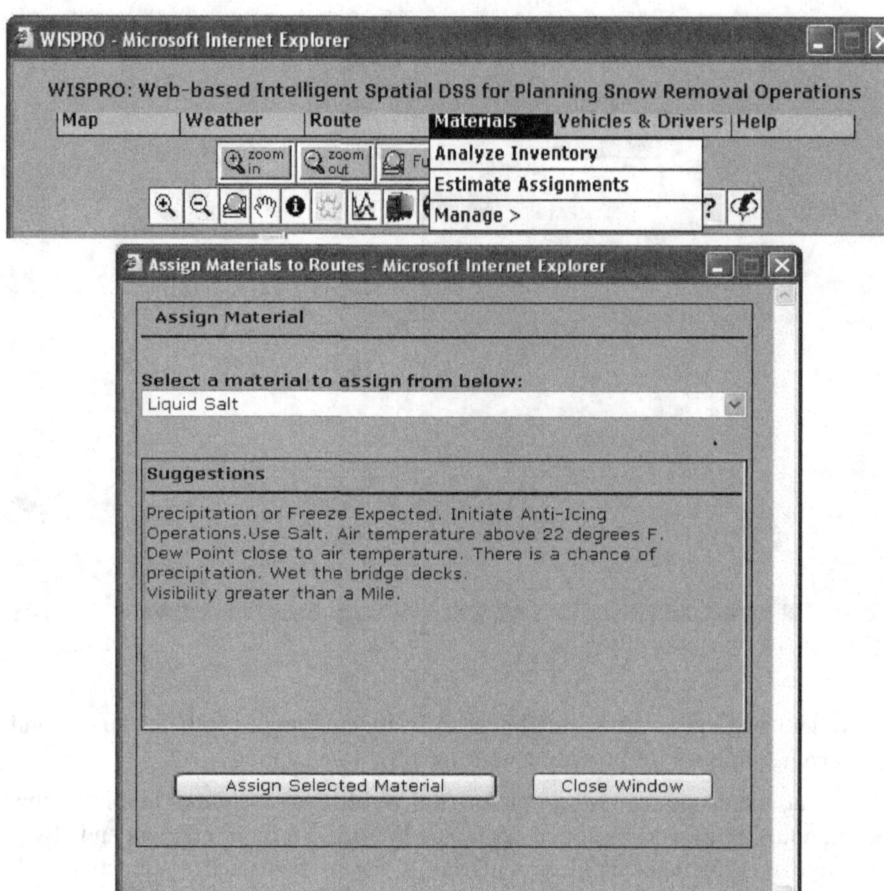

rent vehicle assignments, driver assignments, weather conditions, and material estimations. Figure 9 shows one such screenshot.

Summary and Future Work

We have presented a Web-based intelligent spatial decision support system (WebISDSS) in this chapter that overcomes the disadvantages of existing systems by providing intelligent decision support for effectively planning snow removal operations. The system has been designed using ArcIMS ActiveX Connector with ArcIMS RouteServer extension and Web technologies such as ASP, XML, and RSS.

Figure 9. Viewing all current assignments

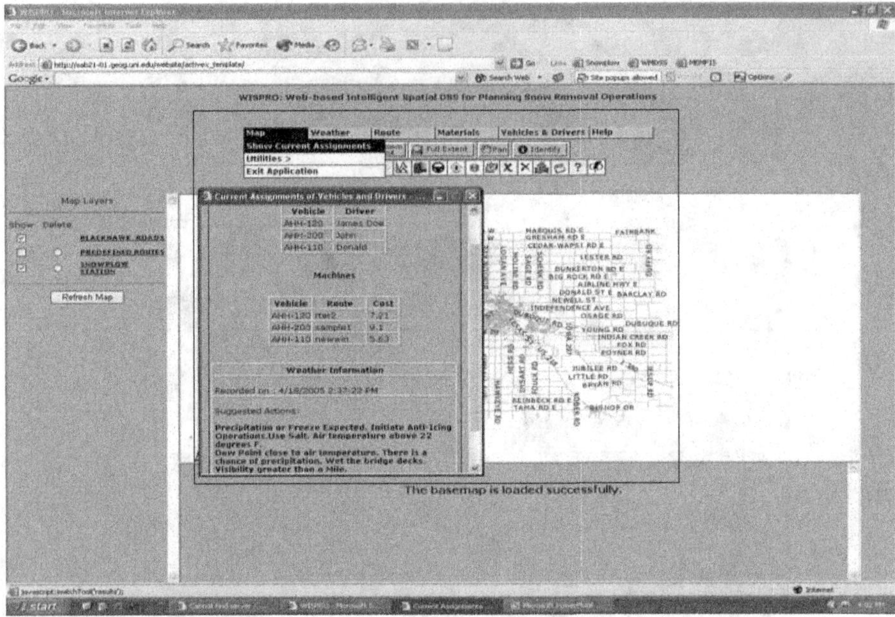

The system also integrates an intelligent software component with geo-spatial and analytical techniques for providing real-time decision support.

There is ample scope for further refining the WebISDSS system described in this chapter. Our future work is aimed at making WebISDSS more efficient and effective. For extending WebISDSS, ArcGIS Server 9.x can be used in conjunction with ArcObjects to provide advanced functionality like adding new features (e.g., new roads) and advanced geo-analytical tools. Additional solutions based on "intelligent technologies" such as intelligent software agents can be explored to extend the fundamental rule-based system to a full-scale "intelligent agent" based system. Also, the use of commercial weather data service that provides frequent updates and segment-wise conditions can improve the efficiency of the current prototype by generating very accurate snowplow routes and by cutting costs further. The weather conditions can also be shown on the map to provide a visual display of various road weather conditions around the county. Furthermore, advanced algorithms can be implemented for sophisticated inventory analysis for better management of materials. Similarly, improved algorithms can be employed for driver and vehicle assignment purposes. Currently, the prototype is optimized to work with the Microsoft Internet Explorer browser. It can be expanded to work with other browsers such as Netscape, Mozilla, and Firefox by carefully considering the cross-browser functionality issues.

There is plenty of research and development yet to be done in the field of Web-based intelligent decision support systems. The prospect of employing intelligent autonomous agents for decision support is very promising. Advances in the fields of artificial intelligence and human computer interaction will have a big impact on how spatial decision support systems behave. Another emerging trend is the availability of decision support systems though a Web-based interface. This ensures cross-platform compatibility and ease-of-use. Further, these interfaces can be extended to work from portable devices like palmtops, cell phones, and so forth. In the coming years, the Web will change dramatically, reaching a wide population via a variety of handheld, smart devices. The future will also usher us into new ways of interaction with computing devices in a radically different way from today's interfaces.

The future for spatial decision support systems is promising considering the explosion of spatial data that we are experiencing. These spatial decision support systems provide many types of scenario-based decision support for governmental and non-governmental organizations (e.g., utility installation planning, right-of-way management, demographic research, etc.) and will be capable of providing advanced spatial analysis to further assist in decision-making. For example, the future spatial decision support systems will include active raster and vector data processing to provide instant results. This is a huge improvement from the various online mapping systems that use only raster data for providing driving directions, locations, and aerial photography.

Acknowledgments

The authors would like to thank Midwest Transportation Consortium (MTC), Iowa DOT, and the University of Northern Iowa for sponsoring this research. We further extend our thanks to Mr. Russ Frisch, Highway Maintenance Supervisor 3 of Iowa DOT, Mr. Steve Decker of Waterloo Street Department, and Mr. Darrell Fanning and Mr. Steve Ravn of Cedar Falls Streets Department for their time and input.

References

Eklund, W. P., Kirkby, S., & Pollitt, S. (1996). A dynamic multi-source Dijkstra's algorithm for vehicle routing. In *Proceedings of the Australian and New Zealand Conference on Intelligent Information Systems (ANZIIS '96)* (pp. 329-333). Adelaide, Australia: IEEE Press.

Hintz, G., Kettlewell, A., Shambarger, E., & Sweeney, T. (2001). Milwaukee's snow and ice control service. *La Follette Policy Report*, *12*, 16.

Iowa Department of Transportation (IDOT). (2005). *IDOT digital maps.* Retrieved August 29, 2004, from http://www.dot.stae.ia.us/

Ilavajhala, S. (2005). *A Web-based intelligent spatial decision support system for planning snow removal operations*. Unpublished master's thesis, submitted to the Computer Science Department at the University of Northern Iowa, Cedar Falls, Iowa.

Mahoney, P. W., & Myers, W. (2003). The winter road maintenance decision support system (MDSS) project update and future plans. In *Proceedings of the 19th Conference on IIPS, 2003*. Retrieved June 17, 2004, from http://ams.confex.com/ams/annual2003/techprogram/paper_51856.htm

NOAA (National Oceanic and Atmospheric Administration). (2003). *NOAA's NWS RSS Library*. Retrieved February 25, 2005, from http://www.nws.noaa.gov/

Odell, J. J., Parunak, V. D. H., Fleischer, M., & Brueckner, S. (2003). Modeling agents and their environment. *The Physical Environment Journal of Object Technology*, *2*, 43-51.

Salim, M. D., Timmerman, A. M., Strauss, T., & Emch, M. (2002). *Artificial-intelligence-based optimization of the management of snow removal assets and resources* (MTC Final Report). Cedar Falls, IA: University of Northern Iowa.

Sengupta, R., Bennett, A. D., & Armstrong, P. M. (2000). Agent-oriented modeling environment for spatial decision support. In *Proceedings of the First International Conference on Geographic Information Science.* Retrieved December 26, 2004, from http://www.giscience.org/GIScience2000/papers/188-Sengupta.pdf

Shahriari, N. & Tao, C. V. (2002). Applications of agent technology in GIS. *Journal of Geographic Information Science*, *8*, 78-85.

Tsou, M. (2002). Adopting software agents for Internet mapping and distributed GIServices. In *Proceedings of the ESRI International User Conference, 2002* (pp. 234). San Diego, CA: ESRI.

Chapter IX

Conservation Studio: Dynamically Modeling and Mapping Habitat Suitability

Todd G. Olson, Landix, Inc., USA
Brian N. Hilton, Claremont Graduate University, USA

Abstract

Habitat suitability modeling in some form is required for virtually every regulatory action and conservation planning process that involves rare and/or endangered species or habitat types. Conservation Studio is a spatial information system that automates the entire process of conservation modeling, simulation, and planning. Conservation Studio consists of four software modules: data acquisition interface, habitat suitability analyst, conservation criteria developer, and implementation modeler, the latter of which has been developed as a working prototype. The implementation modeler models the outcome of using tradable conservation credits to conserve habitat resources in a specified geographical plan area. Future design and development activities for this spatial information system are discussed.

Introduction

Habitat suitability modeling in some form is required for virtually every regulatory action and conservation planning process that involves rare and/or endangered species or habitat types, yet no software application currently exists that automates the entire process of developing such models. Consequently, such modeling efforts are costly, and the answers that they are intended to provide can be long-delayed when they are most in demand, at the beginning stages of a conservation project as the interested parties are attempting to assess the scope of the project. The following sections describe an ongoing research and development project entitled "Conservation Studio," a spatial information system for conservation modeling, simulation, and planning, to overcome these problems.

Conservation Studio guides non-experts through the entire process of generating habitat suitability models; no current spatial information system performs this comprehensive function. This spatial information system can be used to support decision-makers in various earth science applications, such as invasive species management, community growth, and water quality management (NASA, 2005). It can also be used by conservationists, environmental regulators, parties subject to environmental regulation, forest managers, and others who need to generate habitat suitability models relevant to their activities.

Furthermore, this spatial information system provides an example of how remotely-sensed earth observation data can be made useful to practitioners who are not specialists in geospatial data management or geostatistical analysis.

The significance of this spatial information system is that it:

- Automates the creation of habitat suitability models, making it possible for practitioners to perform this task without the need for expertise in various technical disciplines
- Dramatically decreases the time and expense required to generate such models
- Brings scientific rigor to a process that is often completed in an ad hoc fashion due to the difficulty and expense of completing it in a more scientifically-defensible manner

No existing software application automates the entire process of developing habitat suitability models. Currently, several different software tools are required to perform such analyses, and the user must assemble these tools. Even after the tools have been assembled, they are not wholly integrated, and they are not specific to the task of developing habitat suitability models. Furthermore, the data available for use with these tools is often disparate and exists in various incompatible formats. Consequently, significant expertise in the disciplines of geographic information systems (GIS), database management, geostatistics, and conservation biology is currently required to perform habitat suitability analyses.

Conservation Studio converts a task that requires an entire team of experts into a task that can be performed by a non-expert with moderate experience in conservation planning and conservation biology. Consequently, the time and expense of performing these analyses are dramatically reduced, while the quality of such analyses are greatly increased by helping the user focus on conservation issues rather than on numerous technical problems involved with performing the task.

Background

Habitat Suitability Modeling

Two approaches to habitat suitability modeling have been employed widely in the United States: (1) the Habitat Suitability Index (HSI) approach, based on the Habitat Evaluation Procedures developed by the U. S. Fish and Wildlife Service in 1980, and (2) the correlation of vegetative cover and vertebrate species occurrences used by the National Gap Analysis Program (Scott & Jennings, 1998), which is sponsored and coordinated by the Biological Resources Division of the U.S. Geological Survey. The HSI approach was developed in 1980 before the ready availability of GIS tools, and therefore relies heavily on manual processes that require expert input. The gap analysis approach, developed in 1987, was designed to identify biodiversity correlates on a very large scale; however, its methods are not typically suited to predictive modeling on a finer scale. In spite of the limitations of these two approaches, the documented experience gained through their application over the years is instructive and has guided the design and development of Conservation Studio.

Besides the two major, systematic habitat suitability modeling efforts described above, numerous habitat suitability modeling projects have been documented that take varying approaches to data selection, data acquisition, and data analysis. These cases have also been studied for their unique perspectives on the problem.

Geostatistical Analysis Applied to Habitat Suitability Models

With the maturation of GIS software, the ability to perform computerized geostatistical analysis to develop and test habitat suitability models is rapidly increasing (Larson &

Sengupta, 2004; Nikolakaki, 2004; Store & Jokimäki, 2003). Consequently, the body of literature in this area is growing quickly (Goovaerts, 1997; Guisan, Edwards, & Hastie, 2002; Scott, Heglund, & Morrison, 2002). For instance, NatureServe has a project under way to evaluate various approaches to what it refers to as "predictive range mapping" (NatureServe, 2005b). Also, geostatistical software that interoperates with GIS software is becoming increasingly available, as exemplified by such packages as FRAGSTAT, Variowin, GEOEas, Surfer, Gstat, GSLIB, SpaceStat, S-PLUS, and Spatial Statistics Toolbox for Matlab.

Data Model

NatureServe has published a "biodiversity data model" that is used extensively across the United States and in other parts of the Western Hemisphere for purposes of representing ecological data of many types and at many scales (NatureServe, 2005a). Such data are gathered and made available through "Natural Heritage Programs" that are administered by states and other units of government. This data model has informed the design of both the input and output formats for Conservation Studio to facilitate the acquisition of species occurrence and other relevant data, as well as to be able to produce output that can be readily used by others.

Data Interoperability

The implementation of interoperable solutions and applications for geospatial services, data, and applications is the focus of the ongoing work of the OpenGIS Consortium (OGC) (Open GIS Consortium Inc., 2003b). The OGC has specified multiple data services that provide ready access to collections of spatial data over the Web. These services include the Web map service (WMS), the Web feature service (WFS), and the Web coverage service (WCS) to access spatial data. These services are enabled by a number of underlying technologies such as registry, portrayal, processing, and data services. Additional OGC services also support privacy and access controls based on authenticated user identity.

Two key issues outlined in the Decision Support Priority Application Theme of the OGC are: (1) defining methods for decision analysts to organize, store, and share geo-analysis projects; and, (2) extending the access of decision support clients to predictive modeling in addition to observations (Open GIS Consortium Inc., 2003a). The OGC Web Services described above address these issues and would enable the development of Web-based decision support tools. The OGC defines decision support tools and systems as "interactive computer-based systems designed to help people and organizations retrieve, summarize, analyze data/information and conduct predictive analysis on scenarios that enable enhanced capacity to make better decisions" (Open GIS Consortium, Inc., 2003a). In a similar manner, Conservation Studio will serve as a decision support tool built on these services.

Conservation Studio

Conservation Studio consists of four software modules: data acquisition interface, habitat suitability analyst, conservation criteria developer, and implementation modeler. The first module, currently under development, would allow the user to easily acquire data over the Internet that is relevant to a specified project. The second module would apply geostatistical analyses to the acquired data and other data supplied by the user to identify correlates of habitat suitability and map predicted suitable habitat. The third module would assist the user in establishing quantitative criteria that can be said to meet specified conservation objectives for a resource. The fourth module, which has been developed to a working prototype, assists the user in describing and modeling an implementation plan for the resource.

The combination of these four modules, when fully developed, would extend the use of remotely-sensed earth observation and other spatial data beyond the habitat suitability modeling process. It would assist a user step-by-step through the entire conservation planning process to create a practical, science-based plan for conserving a given species, set of species, or natural community. This spatial information system would provide not only habitat suitability analyses for various earth science applications, but also tools to assist decision-makers in developing and implementing plans for the conservation of species and natural communities. Figure 1 below illustrates the relationship among the four software modules.

Furthermore, Conservation Studio could be extended for use in a GPS-enabled hand-held device to allow for real-time analysis in the field. Through the habitat suitability analyst, a field biologist could obtain instant feedback and suggestions for furthering the fieldwork to refine the habitat suitability model. Development of this capability will also be part of future research and development activities.

Data Acquisition Interface

Based on a specified geographical area (a "study area") as the only required user input, the data acquisition interface will: (1) directly acquire over the Internet (without needing to use a separate Web browser) spatial data layers from NASA and other diverse sources that are specifically relevant to creating predictive habitat suitability models for species or natural communities ("resources") in the study area; (2) directly acquire over the Internet any available species-specific data for biological resources known to exist in the study area or specified by the user; and

Figure 1. Conservation studio system architecture

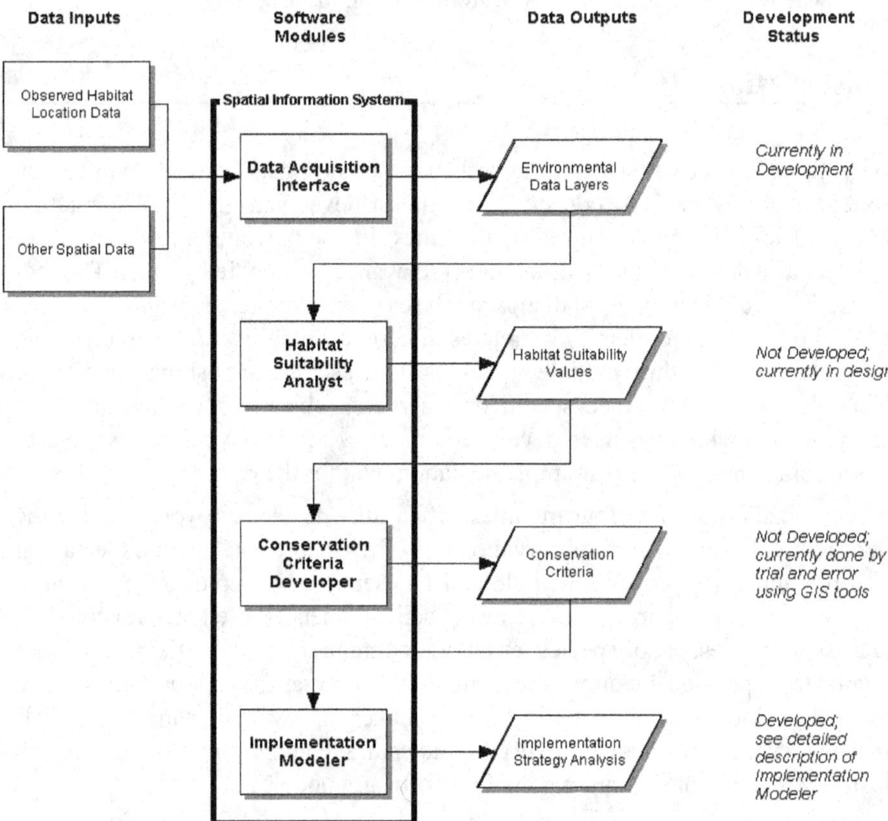

(3) convert the acquired data into a raster format that is easily manipulated in the habitat suitability analyst module described next.

Habitat Suitability Analyst

The habitat suitability analyst will automate the process of: (1) performing geostatistical analyses on the data obtained using the Data Acquisition Interface to find correlates of habitat suitability for a given resource in the plan area; (2) suggesting geographic locations for new field work based on analytical results; (3) incorporating new field data and repeating steps #1 and #2 in an iterative fashion until the statistical errors are reduced to an acceptable level of tolerance; and (4) creating a spatial model based on the statistical analyses that predicts the locations and quality of suitable habitat for the resource.

Conservation Criteria Developer

Conservation criteria developer will assist the user in establishing quantitative criteria that can be said to meet specified conservation objectives for a resource. The criteria may include such factors as quantity and quality of habitat to be preserved (quality being based on the habitat suitability model developed using habitat suitability analyst), the patch sizes of the preserved habitat, the shape of the preserved patches, the edge effect on the preserved patches, the distribution of the habitat across the historic or extant range of the resource, and so forth. The criteria will be based on a combination of generalized principles of: (1) species and habitat needs inferred from the habitat suitability results, (2) general principles of conservation biology, and (3) species-specific habitat requirements supplied from available databases and by the user. This component could incorporate a population viability analysis tool.

Implementation Modeler

Implementation modeler assists the user in describing and modeling an implementation plan for the resource. The modeling is conducted in two steps. First, the user describes an implementation strategy for testing using tools provided in the software. Second, the software analyzes the specified strategy using "Monte Carlo" analysis techniques to generate multiple outcomes with given ranges of variability in input variables. Each outcome consists of a grid of cells in which some cells are conserved and others are developed for economic uses. Statistical analyses can be performed on the outcomes to assess the likelihood that the various conservation criteria developed using conservation criteria developer will be achieved, the economic efficiency of the plan, and so forth. Various implementation strategies can be modeled for the same project to compare the tendencies of the different strategies to produce different conservation and economic outcomes. The next section describes, in detail, the implementation modeler.

Implementation Modeler

The "Habitat Transaction Method" and Implementation Modeler Software

The lead author, along with others, has developed a conservation planning implementation methodology known as the "habitat transaction method," which employs tradable conservation credits to implement large-scale, multiple-landowner conservation plans (Glickfeld, Jacques, Kieser, & Olson, 1995; Olson, 1996; Olson, Murphy, & Thornton, 1993; Sohn & Cohen, 1996). The lead author has also co-developed, in concert with software engineer Andrew Morgan, a prototype of the implementation modeler, which models the outcome of using tradable conservation credits to conserve habitat resources in a specified geographical plan area. He has used the software in his conservation planning consulting practice both to demonstrate the tradable credit concept and to model outcomes of conservation plans under consideration. Implementation modeler utilizes grid-based geospatial data layers that represent habitat values and economic development values for each cell in the plan area, and it graphically models potential patterns of development and conservation, resulting in an outcome data layer. The current version is written in Java and runs on Windows, Mac OS X, and Linux.

As it is further developed, implementation modeler will allow the user to model the use of several different implementation strategies for meeting a specified set of conservation objectives. In addition to tradable conservation credits, other strategies that could be modeled include direct regulation, development fee, transferable development rights, and combinations of techniques. The user could then compare outcomes of the different strategies both in terms of likelihood of meeting the conservation objectives and the economic efficiency in meeting the conservation objectives.

The implementation modeler allows the user to describe: (1) existing land use and open space patterns within the study area, (2) the relative development value of the remaining undeveloped land, (3) the relative conservation value of the remaining developed land, and (4) a set of rules governing future development and conservation that describe the conservation strategy. The implementation modeler then models future land development and conservation patterns based on: (1) the relative development value of land, (2) the conservation rules that apply to new development under the specified strategy, (3) the cost of complying with the rules in order to develop land, and (4) a degree of randomness in decision-making to take into account factors that the model does not address explicitly. Because of the randomness introduced into the model, each outcome will be different. Each outcome consists of both a map of lands projected to be protected, developed, and conserved as well as a set of statistics to provide a quantitative analysis of the conservation and economic results. Performing much iteration allows patterns of new development and new conservation to emerge that can be subjected to statistical analysis and comparison among conservation strategies.

Once the user has provided the map-based information described above, the user is then able to make parameter selections for a model run that include:

1. Conservation rules that apply to new development under the specified strategy, such as conservation set-aside requirements and/or development fees that must be paid, and so forth
2. Factors that affect the value of land for development over time, such as adjacency to other development and associated infrastructure
3. Factors that affect the conservation value of conserved or undeveloped land over time, such as habitat fragmentation and edge effects
4. A degree of randomness to be assumed in decision making to take into account factors that the model does not address explicitly

The current version of implementation modeler utilizes an elementary version of the parameter inputs; a key priority for further development is to increase the robustness of the model with respect to the input and modeling of the above input parameters.

Figure 2 is a screenshot illustrating future habitat conditions as predicted by specified parameter selections using the implementation modeler (Map tab); areas shaded green are protected/conservation areas while those shaded blue are developed areas.

Figure 2. Conservation Studio implementation modeler — results of simulation

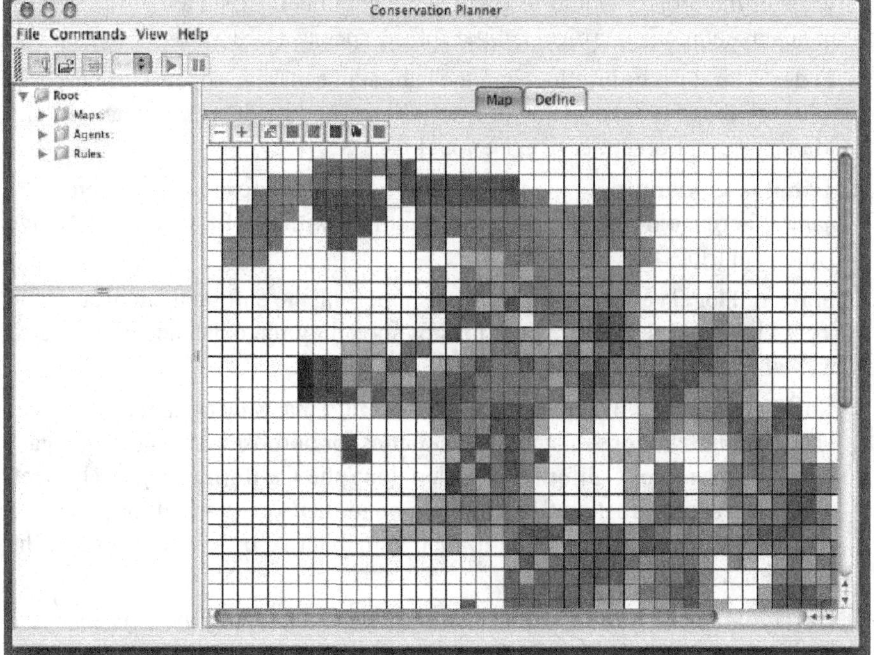

Applications of Conservation Studio

Conservation Studio should be useful to conservation planning practitioners in both governmental and non-governmental sectors. Potential applications for each sector are discussed in detail below.

Governmental

Government agencies have a need to determine the location of the habitat of sensitive species and habitat communities on a regular basis. Specific government applications that would benefit from Conservation Studio include:

- **Endangered species range modeling:** developing range maps for species to be listed as threatened or endangered under the Federal Endangered Species Act (the "ESA") and some state endangered species acts (U.S. Fish and Wildlife Service, or "USFWS")
- **Critical habitat designations:** designating "critical habitat" for threatened and endangered species as required by the Federal ESA (USFWS)
- **Jeopardy determinations:** analyzing the threat to the habitat of a threatened or endangered species caused by a proposed Federal project to determine whether the project would jeopardize the continued existence of the species or adversely modify critical habitat for the species (USFWS)
- **Federal land planning:** locating the habitat of sensitive species for purposes of developing land use plans for Federally-owned land (e.g., Bureau of Land Management, Forest Service, National Park Service)
- **Tribal land planning:** mapping sensitive biological resources to protect the natural heritage of tribal lands and to comply with the ESA (various Native American tribes)
- **State and local resource regulation:** supporting the enforcement of state and local biological resource regulations by modeling the existence of protected habitat (states, counties, and cities)
- **Non-Federal regional conservation planning:** mapping of habitat resources under the jurisdictions of states and counties for purposes of long-range planning; for example, California is undertaking the California Legacy Project, which has approximately $10 billion in bond funds earmarked for parks and conservation and is attempting to map its habitat resources to prioritize the use of these funds
- **Development of habitat conservation plans:** analyzing the existence and location of suitable habitat for the species for purposes of developing "habitat

conservation plans" (HCPs) under the ESA; in exchange for developing an HCP, the applicant can obtain authority to "take" a certain amount of endangered species habitat so long as the species in question is sufficiently conserved by the plan (counties and cities; see also private sector HCPs as follows)

- **Evaluation of habitat conservation plans:** evaluating HCPs that are proposed under the ESA by either public (see bullet immediately previous and "Non-Governmental" described later) (USFWS)

Habitat suitability modeling is necessary or useful in various earth science applications. Some examples of how Conservation Studio would support this include:

- Modeling habitat for both invasive non-native species and the native species that are threatened by such invasive species
- Modeling the location of habitat that may be impacted by community growth
- Discovering correlations between habitat suitability and water availability/quality

Non-Governmental

The private sector also has regular need to perform habitat suitability modeling, such as in the following applications:

- **Development of habitat conservation plans:** performing analysis in support of private HCPs under the ESA (landowners, industry groups)
- **Development of conservation banks:** analyzing the quality and importance of habitat in a proposed "conservation bank" to establish the number of mitigation "credits" that the bank owner will obtain in exchange for protecting sensitive habitat; such credits can be used under programs administered by the USFWS (for endangered species habitat), the Army Corps of Engineers (for wetlands habitat), and other regulators to mitigate project impacts or sold to third parties as mitigation for their project impacts (landowners)
- **Prioritization of land conservancy acquisitions:** mapping of the habitat of rare and endangered species and natural communities for purposes of prioritizing land acquisitions and other conservation activities (private, non-profit land conservancies)
- **Environmental consulting:** supporting as a private environmental consultant to any of the activities listed above (consultants)

The previous examples illustrate how Conservation Studio can make earth science observations accessible to practitioners who do not have necessary technical expertise by automating the entire process from data acquisition through data analysis and map-based data presentation. The concept of habitat suitability modeling is intuitive, and both the data inputs into the analysis and the data outputs from the analysis are visual. As a result, Conservation Studio demonstrates how the use of remotely-sensed data in a visual manner can be easily grasped.

Future Design and Development Activities

In its current phase of development Conservation Studio consists of a prototype of the implementation modeler module described above. The goal of this project is to fully develop the four application modules of Conservation Studio, data acquisition interface, habitat suitability analyst, conservation criteria developer, and implementation modeler, into a complete, unified spatial information system. However, spatial information system development, and indeed all information system development, is impacted by the rapid development of emerging technologies and various governmental regulations. As a result, the objectives of this project will address these issues by:

- **Applying standards-based technologies:** Selection of standards-based technologies to facilitate interoperability with software and systems external to Conservation Studio (International Organization for Standardization, 2000; Open GIS Consortium Inc., 2002, 2003b);
- **Incorporating open source software:** Integration of open source software whenever possible to minimize the deployment cost of the Conservation Studio (Bollinger, 2003; Câmara & Onsrud, 2004; Open Source Initiative, 2005; The GNU Project, 2005); and
- **Developing an easy-to-use interface:** Emphasis on system usability and quality in use in the design of the Conservation Studio user interface in order to make its component modules useful to a wide variety of users with varying levels of expertise in its underlying technologies and processes (Bevan, 1999; Brooke, 1996; International Organization for Standardization, 1997; Losavio, 2002).

The following is the research and development methodology that will be used in the design and development of Conservation Studio.

1. Conservation Studio Spatial Information System

Design the overall Conservation Studio spatial information system to incorporate the data acquisition interface, the habitat suitability analyst, the conservation criteria developer, and the implementation modeler modules, including the following components:

- Graphical user interface
- File system
- Map data display
- Statistical graphing display
- Method for integrating component software such as the data acquisition interface and habitat suitability analyst
- Potential deployment under a Web services model

2. Data Acquisition Interface

Design the data acquisition interface software module, including the following components:

- Spatial data server for locating, previewing, and downloading spatial and other data relevant to the user project
- E-commerce tool to facilitate the direct purchase of data through the proposed client software
- Conversion utility for reading necessary data types and converting them to the native format that will be used in the habitat suitability analyst

3. Habitat Suitability Analyst

Design the habitat suitability analyst software module, including the following components:

- Internal data format(s)
- Project set-up (with "interview" of user on project characteristics, information about the data sets, project definition of habitat suitability, etc.)
- Geostatistical query strategy for finding habitat suitability correlates

- Geostatistical analysis functions
- Analysis and presentation of geostatistical results, including tabular and graphical presentations, and suggestions for additional field surveying
- Interactive habitat suitability modeler that allows the user to combine the geostatistical results with other input to define a habitat suitability model
- Habitat suitability mapper and GIS data exporter

4. Conservation Criteria Developer

Design the conservation criteria developer software module, including the following components:

- Raster map display and interface
- GIS data acquisition and rasterization
- Interface for describing implementation strategy rules
- Interface for describing landowner and government behavioral assumptions
- Monte Carlo modeler and data capture with animated display of model in progress over time
- Outcome description in the form of both maps and statistics
- Outcome analysis for multiple implementation strategy variations

References

Bevan, N. (1999). Quality in use: Meeting user needs for quality. *The Journal of Systems and Software, 49*, 89-96.

Bollinger, T. (2003). *Use of free and open source software (FOSS) in the U.S. Department of Defense* (No. MITRE Report Number MP 02 W0000101 v1.2.04). The MITRE Corporation.

Brooke, J. (1996). SUS: A 'quick and dirty' usability scale. In P. Jordan, B. Thomas, B. Weerdmeester, & I. McClelland (Eds.), *Usability evaluation in industry* (pp. 189-194). London: Taylor & Francis Ltd.

Câmara, G., & Onsrud, H. (2004). *Open-source geographic information systems software: Myths and realities.* Paper presented at the Open Access and the Public Domain in Digital Data and Information for Science, Washington, DC.

Glickfeld, M., Jacques, S., Kieser, W., & Olson, T. (1995). Implementation techniques and strategies for conservation plans. *Land Use & Envirornment Forum, 4*, 12-28.

Goovaerts, P. (1997). *Geostatistics for natural resources evaluation.* New York: Oxford University Press.

Guisan, A., Edwards, T. C., & Hastie, T. (2002). Generalized linear and generalized additive models in studies of species distributions: Setting the scene. *Ecological Modelling, 157*, 89-100.

International Organization for Standardization. (1997). *Human-centered design processes for interactive systems* (No. ISO 13407). Geneva.

International Organization for Standardization. (2000). *Draft business plan of ISO/TC 211 — Geographic information/geomatics*. Geneva.

Larson, B. D., & Sengupta, R. R. (2004). A spatial decision support system to identify species-specific critical habitats based on size and accessibility using U.S. GAP data. *Environmental Modelling and Software, 19*(1), 7-18.

Losavio, F. (2002). Standard quality model to design software architecture. *Journal of Object Technology, 1*(4), 165-178.

NASA. (2005). *Applied sciences directorate — national applications*. Retrieved from http://www.asd.ssc.nasa.gov/aaps.aspx

NatureServe. (2005a). *Biodiversity data model.* Retrieved from http://www.natureserve.org/prodServices/biodatamodel.jsp

NatureServe. (2005b). *Predictive range mapping*. Retrieved from http://www.natureserve.org/aboutUs/northamerica.jsp

Nikolakaki, P. (2004). A GIS site-selection process for habitat creation: Estimating connectivity of habitat patches. *Landscape and Urban Planning, 68*(1), 77-94.

Olson, T. G. (1996). Biodiversity and private property: Conflict or opportunity? In W. J. Snape (Ed.), *Biodiversity and the law* (pp. 67–79). Washington, DC: Island Press.

Olson, T. G., Murphy, D. D., & Thornton, R. D. (1993). The habitat transaction method: A proposal for creating tradable credits in endangered species habitat. In H. Fischer & W. E. Hudson (Eds.), *Building economic incentives into the endangered species act* (pp. 27–36). Washington, DC: Defenders of Wildlife.

Open GIS Consortium, Inc. (2002). *The OpenGIS Abstract Specification, Topic 12: OpenGIS Service Architecture, Version 4.3*. Wayland, MA: Open GIS Consortium, Inc.

Open GIS Consortium, Inc. (2003a). *Decision support priority application theme*. Wayland, MA: Open GIS Consortium, Inc.

Open GIS Consortium, Inc. (2003b). *OpenGIS reference model.* Wayland, MA: Open GIS Consortium, Inc.

Open Source Initiative. (2005). Retrieved from http://www.opensource.org/index.php

Scott, J. M., & Jennings, M. D. (1998). Large-area mapping of biodiversity. *Annals of the Missouri Botanical Garden, 85*(1), 34–47.

Scott, M. J., Heglund, P. J., & Morrison, M. L. (2002). *Predicting species occurrences: Issues of accuracy and scale.* Covelo, CA: Island Press.

Sohn, D., & Cohen, M. (1996). From smokestacks to species: Extending the tradable permit approach from air pollution to habitat conservation. *Stanford Environmental Law Journal, 15*(2), 405–451.

Store, R., & Jokimäki, J. (2003). A GIS-based multi-scale approach to habitat suitability modeling. *Ecological Modelling, 169*, 1-15.

The GNU Project. (2005). Retrieved from http://www.gnu.org

Chapter X

GIS-Based Site Suitability Decision Support System for Planning Confined Animal Feeding Operations in Iowa

Ramanathan Sugumaran, University of Northern Iowa, USA
Brian Bakker, Aerial Services, Inc., USA

Abstract

Confined animal feeding operations (CAFOs) are becoming increasingly common on the Iowa landscape. They produce large amounts of byproducts that can cause a threat to the surrounding environment of the areas of production. Thus, there is a need for careful planning, particularly the selection of suitable locations for future CAFO development. In addition to Iowa state regulations, selection of locations for CAFOs require multiple parameters like, locations of manmade structures that include roads, residences, businesses, wells, and so forth, and location of natural features such as rivers and lakes. Currently, locations for CAFOs are chosen manually using paper hard copies with producer's preference and are restricted by state of Iowa guidelines. There is no decision support system available to aid in selecting an appropriate location for the development of future CAFO structures. The purpose of this chapter is to demonstrate how a decision support tool was developed to aid CAFO managers and producers in selecting appropriate locations for animal confinements using geographic information system (GIS) technology and CAFO regulations in Iowa.

Background

In the past half century, the production of livestock has gone from being an activity carried out on small family farms, to an industrialized activity completed by very large corporations using specialized labor and confinement facilities. The number of farms in America has been reduced drastically from over 5,500,000 in 1950, to just over 2,000,000 at the end of the 1990s (Hallberg, 2001). While the number of farms decreased, production per farm increased to keep up with food demands. Much animal production is now carried out in CAFO facilities. These confinement facilities are generally very large and are often hundreds of feet long and can contain hundreds or even thousands of animals. It is commonly known throughout the Midwest United States that these large factory-style CAFOs create many benefits to local economies while also creating many threats to the environment where they are located. Rural areas are in desperate need of the economic benefits that animal feeding operations bring to local communities. Research shows that an estimated 89,000 jobs in the state of Iowa are directly or indirectly related to the hog industry, and an estimated $700 million of income is earned by farmers and workers directly employed in the hog production and processing industry, while an additional $1.4 billion of personal income is indirectly linked to Iowa's hog industry (Otto, Orazam, & Huffman, 1998).

Despite the positive economic benefits created by CAFOs, many environmental concerns have been raised. Many individuals are concerned about air and water pollution created by animal confinements. Several studies have examined and reported the environmental impacts of livestock production on neighboring communities (Abeles-Allison, 1990; Kim, Goldsmith, & Thomas, 2005; Taff, Tiffany, & Weisberg, 1996). Researchers have also found various problems associated with air pollution caused by CAFOs (Wing & Wolf, 1999). Their results show that persons living near the hog farms where smell is noticeable had increased feelings of tension, depression, anger, fatigue, and confusion as compared to a control group (Schiffman, Miller, Suggs, & Graham, 1994). Physical symptoms have also been linked to air pollution from CAFOs, showing that persons living near large hog farms suffer from significantly higher levels of upper respiratory and gastrointestinal ailments than people living near large cattle farms or in non-livestock farming areas (Wing & Wolf, 1999). Surface and ground water is also impacted by the CAFO.

From 1995 to 1998, there were at least 1,000 spills or other pollution incidents at livestock feedlots in ten states, and 200 manure-related fish kills that resulted in the death of thirteen million fish (Frey, Hopper, & Fredregill, 2000). Studies from Illinois showed that the *streptococcus* bacteria were detected at least once from groundwater wells located below manure pits (Krapac et al., 2002).

These above-mentioned issues clearly show the need for proper planning of CAFO locations. The result of poor planning of CAFO locations was most strongly demonstrated in September of 1999, when Hurricane Floyd produced nearly 20 inches of rain over North Carolina, the second largest hog producing state in the United States. Fifty CAFOs were flooded, and thirty thousand swine and nearly 3 million poultry were reported dead. The catastrophe drew attention to 185 animal operations that were built within a 100-year floodplain prior to 1997 rules which outlawed such construction ("Hurricane Floyd," 2000).

Since CAFO facilities create benefits and risks in the locations where they are constructed, careful and intelligent planning of the facilities is the only solution that protects the environment, local economies, and a farmer's right to produce. Selection of locations for CAFO require integration and analyses of multiple parameters like, manmade structures including roads, residences, businesses, wells, and so forth, and also requires natural features like rivers and lakes. Recently, GIS proved to be an excellent decision support tool to help evaluate general land suitability by integrating multiple location information. GIS is an information system that is used to manipulate, analyze, and output geospatial data, in order to support decision-making for planning and management purposes (Warren County, 2005). *Only a couple researchers have attempted to show the importance of GIS in CAFO site selection. These studies are explained in the next section.*

Site Suitability Studies for Confined Animal Feeding Operations

An early decision support system for livestock facility planning was created by Jain, Tim, and Jolley (1995) at Iowa State University (ISU). This system was created using ARC/INFO to aid in determining land areas that are suitable for various livestock production strategies. Factors taken into account by the decision support system (DSS) included environmental, aesthetic, and economic constraints in the study area of the Lake Icaria watershed in southern Iowa. The ISU system used a point analysis technique to determine how far a set of acceptable solutions, weighted according to a specified criterion, deviated from a set of ideal solutions or feasible regions. Since the ideal solution is rarely available, the technique involves the use of a best compromise solution that minimizes the distance from the theoretical ideal solution

(Jain, Tim, & Jolley, 1995). Parameters taken into effect in the model included: soil drainage class, stream proximity, soil permeability, road proximity, land slope, and aspect. When run, the ISU model selected parcels of land which were best suited for various livestock production strategies including small, medium, and large beef and hog operations. The ISU study did not take into account current state or federal regulation placed on confined feeding operations. It also focused on physical land features, and not manmade features. Furthermore, instead of focusing simply on CAFOs, it looked at animal production on a broader level, including small, medium, and large livestock production operations. It did not focus on large confined animal feeding operations.

GIS tools for siting animal feeding operations have also been developed by Covington, Kloot, and Atkins (2000) in conjunction with the USDA and University of South Carolina. The system can be used to identify whether an area meets legal requirements for siting a CAFO or for manure application according to South Carolina regulations. The system can also qualify legally-sited areas based on environmental factors, and can assist in managing the relocation of facility byproducts. The South Carolina DSS was created using ArcView GIS. Instead of looking at area-wide suitability, the DSS tool is designed to evaluate a specific location. It primarily takes into account setback distances which are individually entered by the user. The setback distances are then used to create a grid for the selection of CAFO locations, and waste utilization areas. The South Carolina DSS includes an economic component, allowing the user to input information about animal weight and waste management. It is designed to help producers make economic decisions about livestock production. A later version was developed to help in manure management, specifically to aid in determining field areas, land-application areas, and volume of manure that could be applied to a location (Covington, Kloot, & Taduri, 2000).

A study by Worley, Rupert, and Risse (2001) addressed the effects of property line and water buffers on land availability for animal feeding operations. Using GIS, the authors found that available land was decreased to 63% of total land with a 100-foot buffer, and as little as 7% of total land was available with a 500-foot buffer. The study used a simple buffer analysis to determine where 1,000 or more animal-unit swine production facilities could be constructed. The study assumed that a 1,000 unit swine facility requires 5 acres for the facility and 100 acres of crop land to effectively apply manure. Property boundaries were buffered at 30.5 and 152.5 meters, and water boundaries were buffered at 30.5, 61, and 152.5 meters. The study made some broad assumptions, including the notion that all waste had to be spread onto one field, and that setback distances applied to fields where application of manure would occur. The study also did not incorporate many other objects that must have a buffer zone under State of Iowa regulations, including homes, public areas, and schools.

Each reviewed system failed to fully meet the current needs of a producer selecting a location for a new CAFO facility. While the ISU system failed to consider state laws when selecting suitable locations for CAFOs, the Worley et al. (2001) study was not designed to aid in specific site selection. The South Carolina system was exceedingly broad and reached far beyond simple site selection. It also required user input of setback distances. The main goal of this research is to create a GIS-based suitability tool to aid in CAFO site selection, while also aiding in the understanding of how CAFO sites impact neighborhoods and are impacted by state regulations.

CAFO Decision Support System Development

Study Area and Data Used

In order to understand the effects of CAFO regulation, it is important to look at a rural and urban county to compare how the amount of urban space affects the land available for CAFO development. It is also important to consider how the types and amounts of natural resources affect land availability for animal feeding operations. In this study, a case study using data from two Iowa counties: Black Hawk (an urban county) and Grundy (a rural county) were selected. Figure 1 shows a map of the study area. The primary data provider for both counties was the county government itself. Other data providers include the Iowa DNR and Iowa DOT. In addition, 2004 USDA National Agriculture Imagery Program (NAIP) photography was also used to analyze and verify the county data sources. Much of the data needed were preprocessed due to compatibility issues between the decision support tool and the original county data.

Decision Support Tools Development

The GIS-based analysis tools were developed using ArcGIS software. ArcGIS software is the industry standard GIS software developed by Environmental Systems Research Institute (ESRI). ArcGIS allows users to customize the GIS interface using Visual Basic for Applications (VBA), a simple object-oriented programming language. VBA is a very popular programming language because of its ability to be used in rapid development of applications. Furthermore, ESRI has written a special VBA library of functions, called ArcObjects, which allows a user to automate commands and functions available through the regular ArcGIS interface. By automating complex spatial analyses, novice GIS users can complete tasks that would otherwise require advanced GIS knowledge. In addition, the ArcGIS platform was chosen because it is the standard GIS application used by most government agencies, such as many of the anticipated users of this application, including county governments, USDA service offices, and Iowa DNR.

Figure 1. Study area — Black Hawk and Grundy County

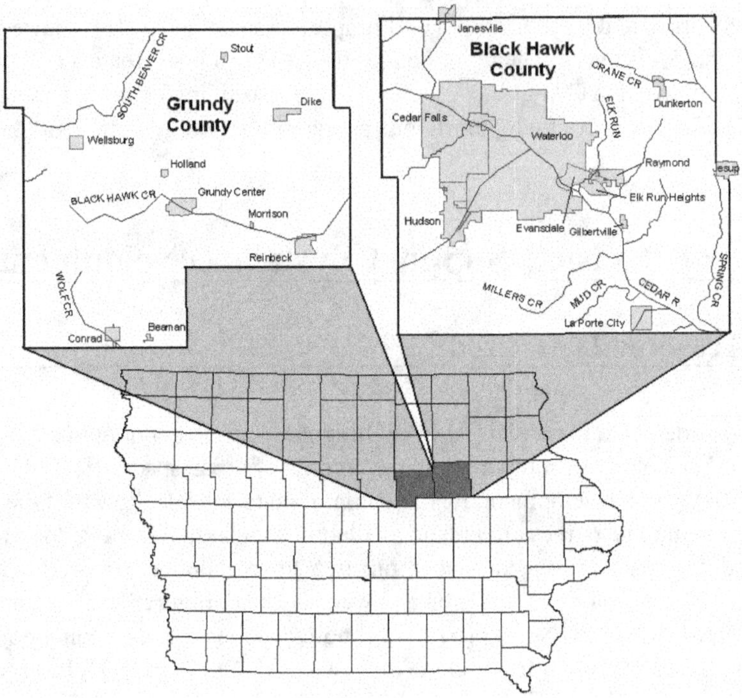

Analysis Techniques

To determine the most appropriate location for animal feeding operations, two methods, the setback analysis and multi-criteria decision analysis, were developed. Figure 2 shows the flowchart for the overall GIS-based site suitability analysis.

Setback Analysis

Prior to selecting a suitable location for a CAFO, a developer must understand which locations would be legally eligible for a confinement facility. As mentioned previously, CAFOs must be constructed beyond state-mandated distances from various objects. Therefore, a logical first step to selecting a CAFO location must include a setback analysis to determine legal locations for CAFO construction. To complete the setback analysis, a GIS-based buffer analysis was chosen in this study. A buffer is a map feature that is created at a specific distance around other features on a map (Wyatt & Ralphs, 2003). Using buffers, an exclusionary method of analyzing

Figure 2. Flowchart for GIS-based site suitability analysis

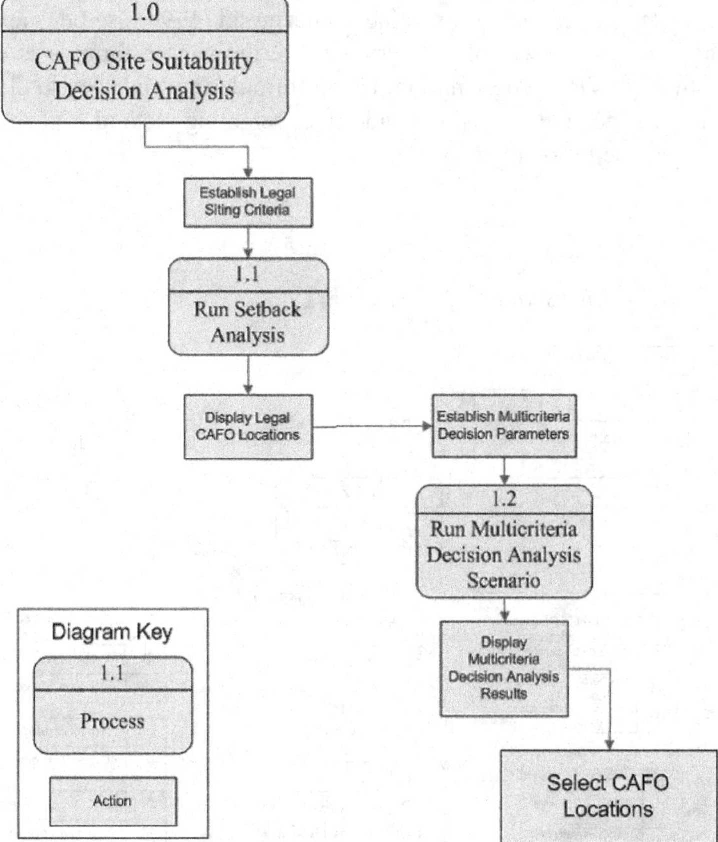

potential CAFO locations can be completed where locations within state-mandated setback distances can be excluded from consideration for CAFO development. Figure 3 shows the steps involved in completing the setback analysis to determine locations that are legally eligible for a CAFO facility in Iowa. The analysis starts with State's distance requirements, followed by checking appropriate GIS layers, creating buffers, and displaying the results.

Multi-Criteria Decision Analysis

Once legal locations have been determined by the setback analysis, a multi-criteria evaluation (MCE) can then be run on the remaining locations to better understand which legal locations are best suited for CAFO development. For this study, a simple weighting MCE has been chosen. This weighting method was chosen because it is simple to understand even by novice users and also widely used for the similar type of site suitability study. For example, Malczewski (1999) used this approach for locating a nuclear power plant. Furthermore, the simple formula is easy to implement through VBA programming. Using formulas by Malczewski (1999) to compare suitable locations, the simple additive weighting method evaluates each alternative A_i by the following formula:

Figure 3. Flowchart for setback analysis

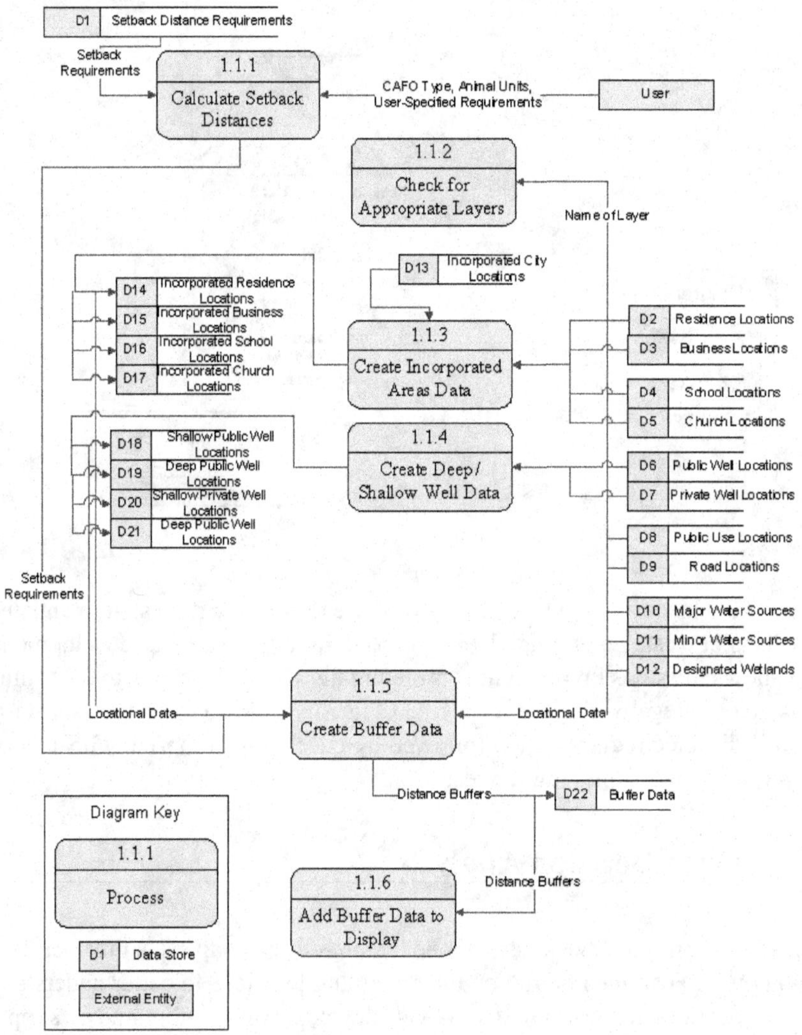

$$A_i = \Sigma_j [w_j * x_{ij}]$$

where x_{ij} is the score of the $_i$th alternative with respect to the $_j$th attribute, and weight w_i is a normalized weight, so that $\Sigma [w_j] = 1$.

Two simple weighting methods: (a) rank sum and (b) ratio estimation procedure have been selected to determine the weights to be applied to the simple additive

Figure 4. Flowchart for multi-criteria analysis

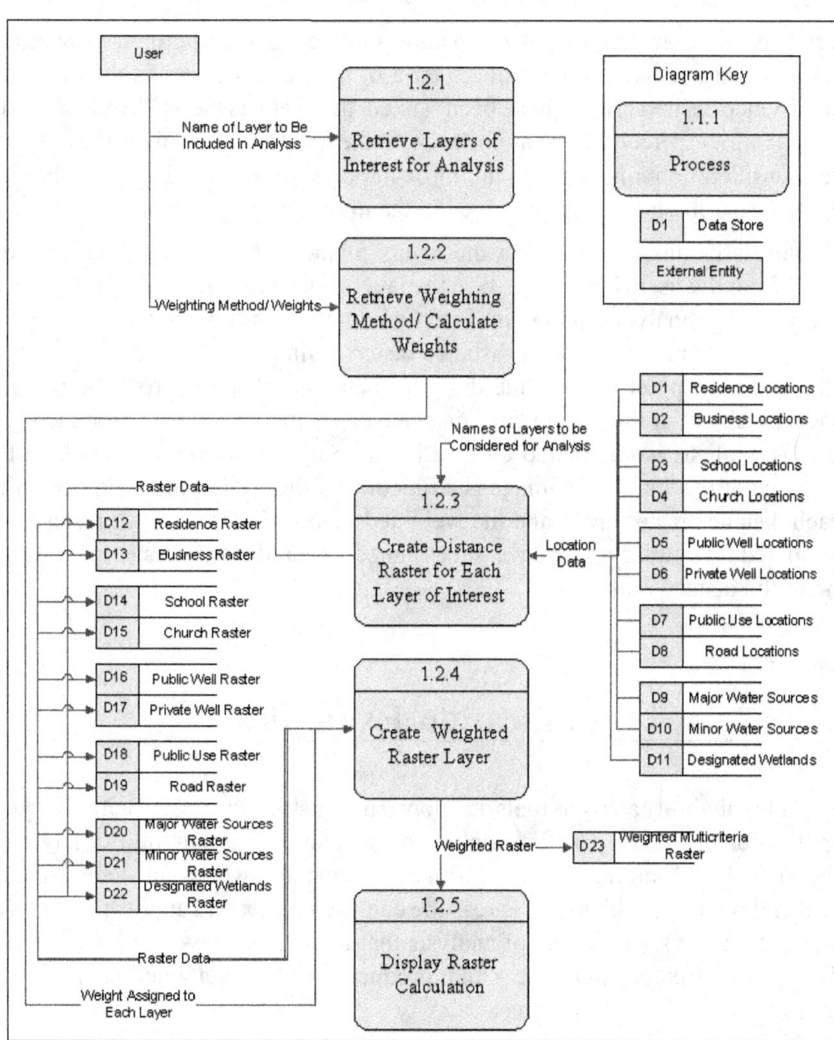

weighting evaluation. The rank sum weighting method assigns weights by ranking each criterion in order by a decision-maker's preference. Using rank sum, a user would select the most important criteria, followed by the second most important criteria, and so on, until all criteria under consideration has been selected. The weight is then calculated by the following formula:

$$W_j = n\text{-}r_j + 1/\Sigma\ (n\text{-}r_k + 1)$$

where w_j is the normalized weight for the $_j$th criterion, n is the number of criteria under consideration, and r_j is the rank position of the criterion. The criterion under consideration is normalized by the sum of all weights.

The ratio estimation weighting method allows for additional user input. To use this method, the user must first rank the criteria in the same manner as the rank sum method. Once desired criteria have been ranked, the user has the ability to assign the criteria a ratio or percentage of importance, at the level he or she feels the criterion under consideration compares to the most important criterion. Figure 4 shows a flowchart describing the steps involved in the multi-criteria evaluation.

The analysis begins by retrieving the layers of interest, weighting method, and weights from the user (Figure 4). Once the layers and weighting criteria have been determined, the analysis can begin. Upon completion of the analyses, the results are displayed as raster layers. A distance raster is simply an image comprised of pixels, and each pixel has a value that represents the distance from the pixel to the nearest object of interest. Once a distance raster image is created for each GIS layer, the analysis is completed by creating a composite raster image where the pixel value of the composite image is a function of the sum of the weighted value of each distance raster layer, and the weighted value of each distance raster layer is computed by multiplying the weight assigned to that distance raster layer by the value of the distance raster.

Application Examples

The CAFO suitability analysis tools developed in this study was tested with two types of application examples. The first application, a county-wide suitability analysis, is a type of analysis that might be used by a county planner who wants to understand the general picture of suitability across the county. The second application, a location-specific analysis, is a type of analysis that a farm service organization like a USDA Service Center might use with a producer to find a suitable location at the farm level for a CAFO development.

County-Wide Suitability Analysis

As shown in Figure 2, two types of analysis tools (setback and multi-criteria) need to be run to determine the availability of suitable lands for CAFO development.

Setback Analysis

The setback analysis user interface developed in this study is given in Figure 5, and that can be launched from ArcMap software. A setback analysis uses various

Figure 5. Legal locations setback analysis user interface

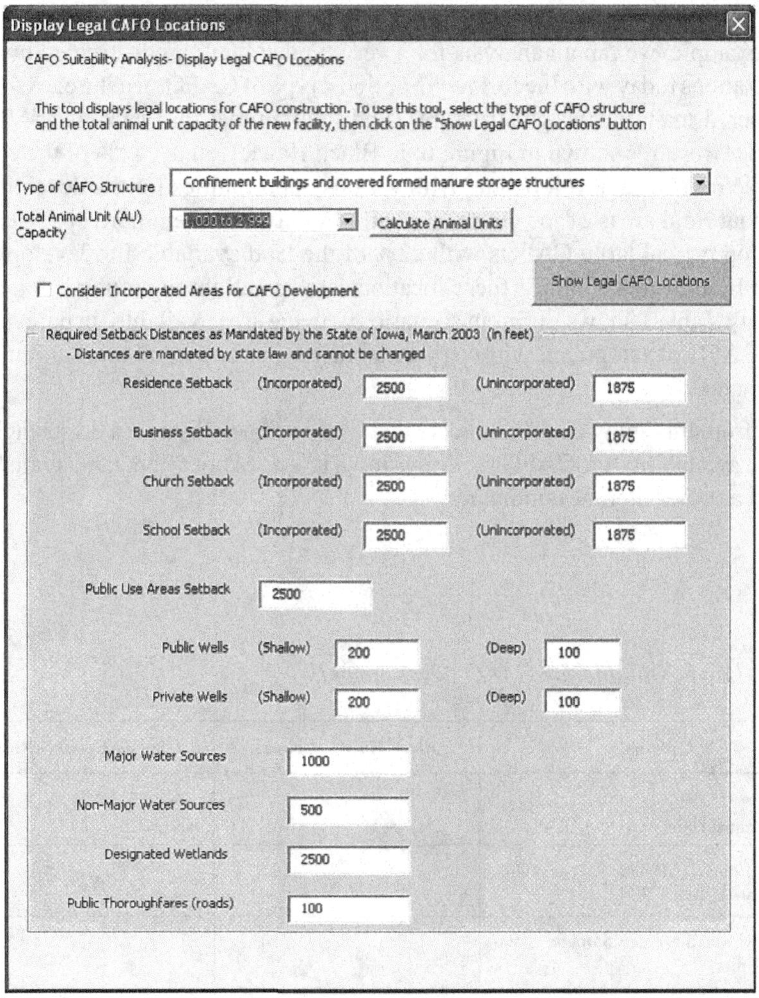
Display Legal CAFO Locations
CAFO Suitability Analysis- Display Legal CAFO Locations
This tool displays legal locations for CAFO construction. To use this tool, select the type of CAFO structure and the total animal unit capacity of the new facility, then click on the "Show Legal CAFO Locations" button
Type of CAFO Structure
Confinement buildings and covered formed manure storage structures
Total Animal Unit (AU) Capacity
1,000 to 2,999
Calculate Animal Units
Consider Incorporated Areas for CAFO Development
Show Legal CAFO Locations
Required Setback Distances as Mandated by the State of Iowa, March 2003 (in feet)
- Distances are mandated by state law and cannot be changed
Residence Setback (Incorporated) 2500 (Unincorporated) 1875
Business Setback (Incorporated) 2500 (Unincorporated) 1875
Church Setback (Incorporated) 2500 (Unincorporated) 1875
School Setback (Incorporated) 2500 (Unincorporated) 1875
Public Use Areas Setback 2500
Public Wells (Shallow) 200 (Deep) 100
Private Wells (Shallow) 200 (Deep) 100
Major Water Sources 1000
Non-Major Water Sources 500
Designated Wetlands 2500
Public Thoroughfares (roads) 100

CAFO facility types and numbers of animal units. Firstly, the user must select the type of CAFO structure to be constructed. Five types of structures are listed in the drop-down menu corresponding with state regulations. Secondly, the user enters the number of animal units (AU) to be housed in the CAFO facility. Once both drop-down boxes have been populated, the setback analysis form populates all remaining setback distance textboxes based on the state legal requirements (Figure 5). In the final choice, the user must decide whether to consider locations within incorporated areas for development or not. In general, the user will not be able to construct a CAFO facility within incorporated areas due to zoning laws; however, in the rare case a person would actually want to develop within an incorporated area, this tool gives the user the power to create such an analysis. Once the decision parameters have been entered, the user must simply select the "Show Legal CAFO Locations" button to complete the setback analyses. The results of suitable locations will be displayed in ArcGIS.

In this example, we ran an analysis for a very typical facility constructed by large hog operations today with the following options: type of CAFO structure: "a formed and covered manure storage structure", and total animal unit capacity = "1000-2999". The result is shown in Figure 6. In Black Hawk County, 11% of the county is eligible for such a development, with various opportunities for the development throughout rural areas of the county. Grundy County has even more opportunities to develop typical large CAFOs with 22% of the land available for development. As with Black Hawk County, these locations are spread throughout rural areas of the county. Table 1 shows different scenarios with the area available (in percentage) for the CAFO development with various facility types and number of animals for both counties.

Results from this study clearly indicate that while setback distances do strongly affect land availability for CAFO facilities, Iowa law does not affect land availability as much as other literature indicates.

Table 1. Land available for CAFO development

Options	Black Hawk (Urban)	Grundy County (Rural)
Earthen Lagoon, 3000+ Animal Units	0.4%	1.7%
Formed, Covered Manure Storage, 1000-2999 Animal Units	11%	22%
Formed, Covered Manure Storage, < 500 Animal Units	67%	85%

Figure 6. Land available for a typical large CAFO (Black Hawk County top, Grundy County bottom)

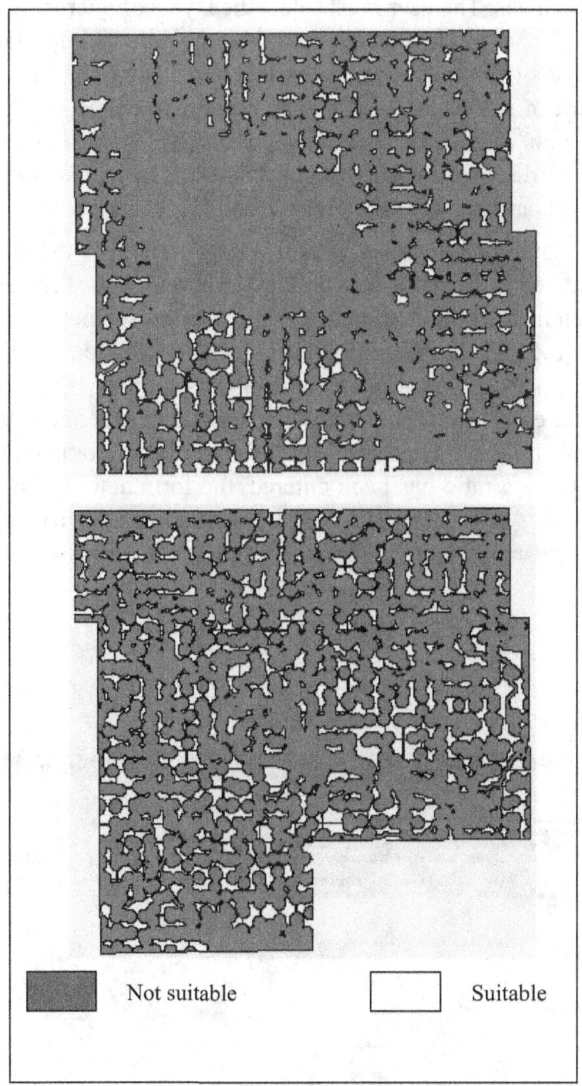

Multi-Criteria Analysis

The "Weighted Distance Analysis" tool (Figure 7) allows the user to apply weights to individual layers. To complete this analysis, the user must begin by selecting the layers to be included in the analysis. By double-clicking on a layer listed in the left text box, the layer name disappears from the textbox, and is placed by a number under the "Layer" column. The user can select as many layers as he or she wants to include in the analysis. The user must select the layers of interest in a rank order, selecting the most important layer first, then the second most important layer, and so on until all layers of interest have been selected. Once the layers have been selected, the user can select one of two weighting methods to weight the layers, either the rank weight method or ratio weight method. The formulas behind these weighting methods, discussed in the previous section, assign each layer a weight of importance less than one, and all weights of all layers add to one.

The rank-weight method requires no input from the user. Once the user selects the layers to be considered in the analysis in order of importance, the form automatically calculates the weights. To run this analysis, the user must select the rank weight tab, and click on the "Create Weighted Distance Map" button. The ratio weight analysis requires more user input. To run this analysis, the user must enter a ratio of less than 100 for each layer listed below the first layer, where the ratio assigned by the user indicates the user's preference of the first layer compared to the layer being weighted. Once a ratio has been entered, the form automatically calculates a normalized weight. After all layers have been normalized, the user can select the "Create Weighted Distance Map" button to complete the analysis.

Figure 7. Weighted distance analysis user interface

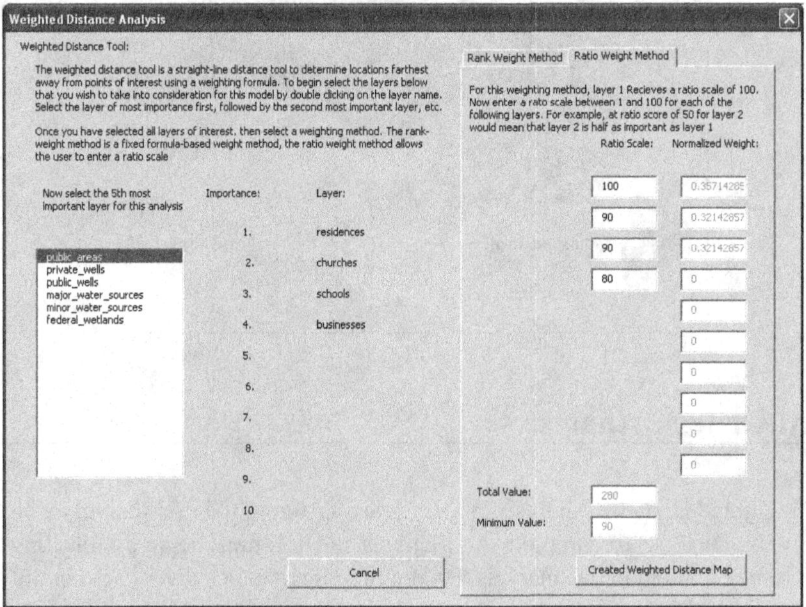

Figure 8. Ratio-weight analysis — Grundy County (right) Black Hawk County (left)

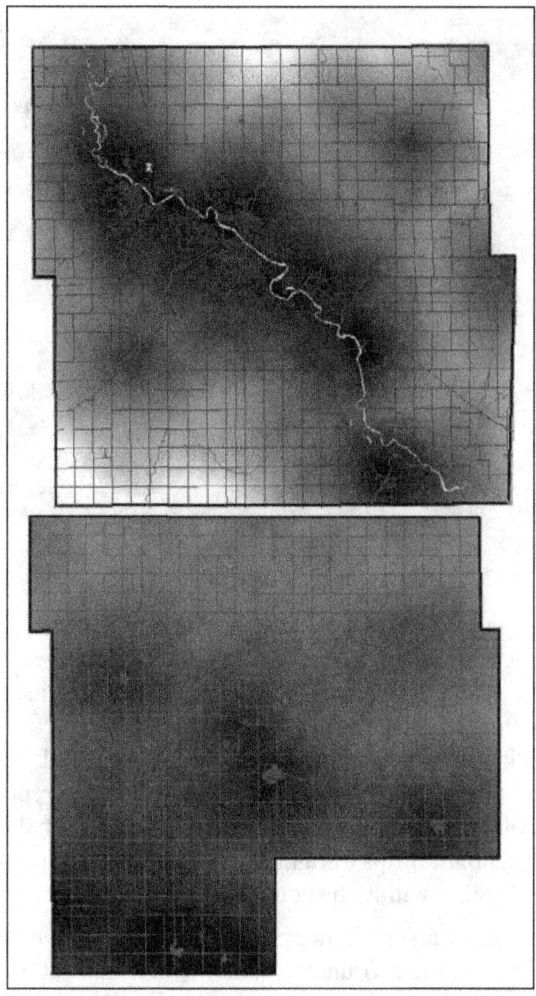

A multi-criteria evaluation analysis was also run for both Black Hawk and Grundy County. For this evaluation, all state-mandated setback objects are created equally with no preference to one over another. Using the ratio estimation procedure, each feature was given an identical ratio-weight, and the model was run. This type of analysis might be performed to simply determine overall suitability of a county for CAFO development. An official might use results from this type of analysis to encourage a producer to build in one part of a county over another. Figure 8 shows

Figure 9. Aerial photograph of Porkhaven CAFO and neighboring residences (Source: Iowa Geographic Map Server, 2004)

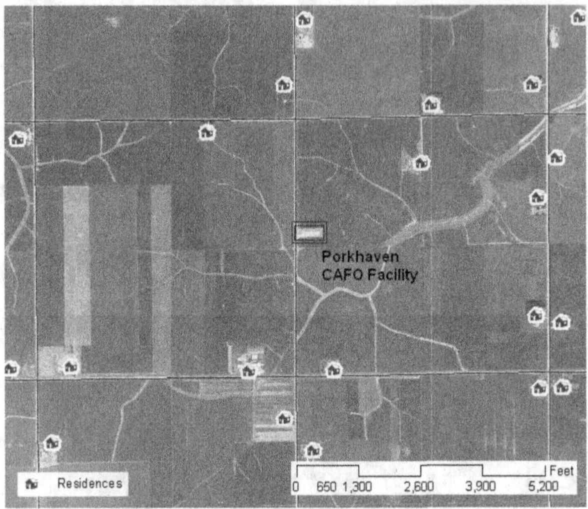

the results of that type of multi-criteria analysis for both Black Hawk and Grundy County, respectively. In the result map, areas of lighter colors are more suitable and areas of darker colors are less suitable for animal confinements. In Black Hawk County, the best locations for CAFOs, determined by the weighted distance analysis, are found primarily in the southeastern and north central parts of the county (Figure 8). The streets of urban communities stand out on top of areas represented by dark color. The darker colors indicate the lack of suitability for animal confinements in and around the urban areas. Strips of lighter tones between the urban communities indicate areas of suitability within the counties.

Similarly, Grundy County results indicate areas of greater and lesser suitability to animal confinements. Northern Grundy County, with its lack of urban areas seems to be most suited for CAFO development, as well as a corridor through east central Grundy County. The especially dark tones in southern Grundy County seem to indicate higher densities of residences in the Beaman/Conrad region of southern Grundy County.

Location-Specific Application Example

One location in Black Hawk County was chosen as a case study to show how the CAFO tools could be used in choosing a site for an animal feeding operation at farm level. The analysis completed in the case study would be similar to the type of

Figure 10. Results of a setback distance analysis

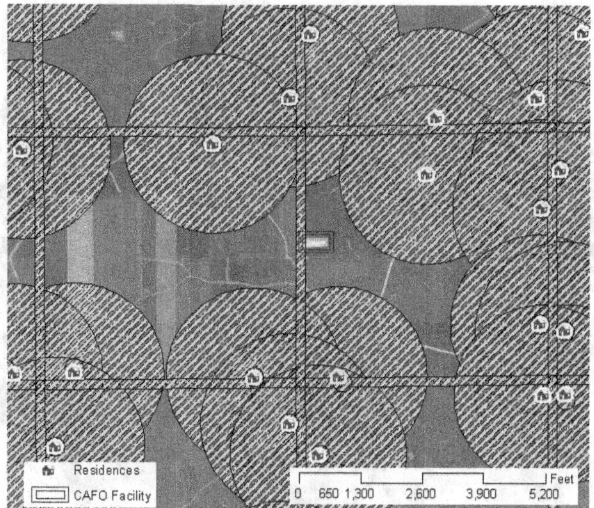

analysis a farm services center might complete to help a producer choose the best location for a new CAFO. The chosen location for this case study has an existing animal confinement in the region. This analysis has been able to show how the location of the confinement compares with what the CAFO tools would recommend as a best location. In Black Hawk County, a facility registered as Porkhaven Farm, LLP-Beck Site was chosen for the analysis. It is registered for 1,600 animal units, and is considered a Swine Grow to Finish Facility. It is located approximately 5 miles south-southeast of Hudson, Iowa, in Eagle Township, section 7, in southern Black Hawk County. The Porkhaven facility (Figure 9) is located over a half mile from its nearest neighboring residence, and over one and a half miles from all other objects requiring setback distances. The nearest water resource is a small stream over one and a half miles to the northeast. The facility lies approximately 800 feet beyond the nearest setback buffer (Figure 10).

When the ratio estimation procedure is run using equal weighting for all objects, the results clearly indicate that the facility has been placed in an ideal location (Figure 11). The darker colors indicate areas that are less suitable for animal confinements. Results from a combined setback analysis and multi-criteria analysis also indicate that the planner involved in identifying this CAFO facility did an excellent job in locating the facility in a place which was not only legal, but was truly the best location in the overall area.

Figure 11. Results of a ratio estimation analysis of area surrounding Porkhaven CAFO facility

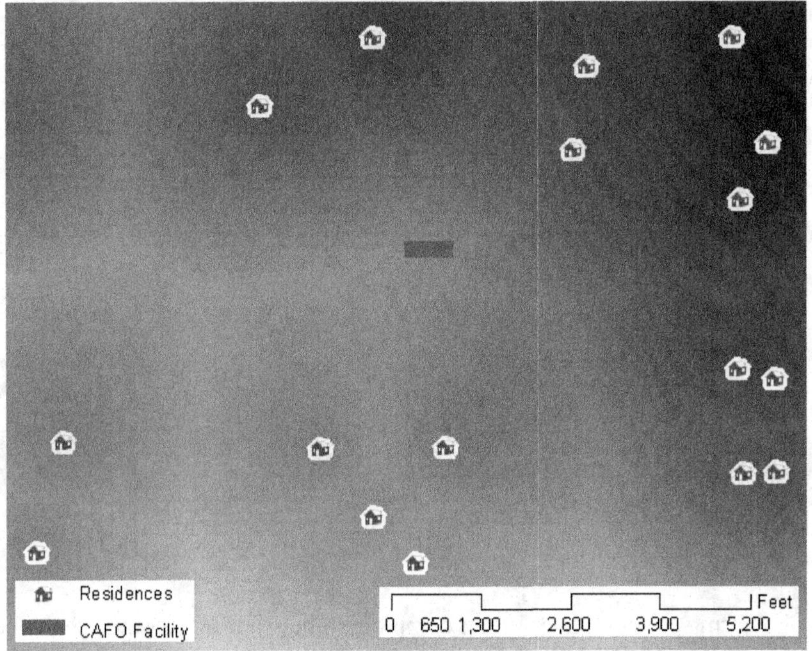

Conclusion and Future Directions

The main goal of this research was to develop a customized GIS-based suitability tool to aid in CAFO site selection, while also aiding in the understanding of how CAFO sites impact neighborhoods and are impacted by state regulations. This project has used the ArcGIS software and customization through VBA to complete the research objectives. The primary analysis tools created for this application include a setback analysis, and a multi-criteria analysis. The setback analysis tool aids in determining legal locations for CAFO facilities. It uses current setback distance requirements mandated by the state of Iowa. The multi-criteria analysis tool aids a producer in determining the best possible location for an animal confinement. It allows a user to develop different scenarios by assigning weights to multiple criteria to determine an optimal location. Each analysis tool has been tested using real data from the county governments. Results from the tests show how the tools developed can be used in determining suitable locations for animal confinements. The results show how setback distances limit the amount of land available for animal confinements, and also indicate that the amount of land available for a confinement facility is more limited in urban counties as compared to rural counties. The research clearly showed the usefulness of GIS-based decision support systems in planning CAFO locations.

Future direction would be the migration of this type of system into a Web-based environment to allow for broader access to the decision support tools. This application has shown how desktop GIS packages can be used to implement sophisticated models for site suitability studies relating to animal confinements. While this application has great potential for use in farm service organizations, most livestock producers do not have regular access to desktop GIS packages; therefore, an Internet-GIS based environment would lend itself well for the development of a decision support system for finding locations for animal confinements. Furthermore, none of the existing systems attempt to incorporate plume modeling to understand how odors emanate from a proposed facility. The future study will integrate an odor model in GIS-based suitability DSS in identifying CAFO ideal location.

Acknowledgment

The work was funded by the STORM Project at the University of Northern Iowa.

References

Abeles-Allison, M. (1990). *An analysis of local benefits and costs associated with hog operations in Michigan*. Unpublished thesis, Department of Agricultural Economics. Michigan State University.

Covington, E., Kloot, R. W., & Taduri, H. K. R. (2000). *GIS decision support system for animal feeding operations planning*. Paper presented at the 2000 ESRI User Conference Proceedings. Retrieved April 20, 2005, from http://gis.esri.com/library/userconf/proc01/professional/papers/pap570/p570.htm

Frey, M., Hopper, R., & Fredregill, A. (2000). *Spills and kills: Manure pollution and America's livestock feedlots*. Retrieved January 18, 2004, from http://www.cwn.org/docs/publications/spillkillmain.htm

Hallberg, M. C. (2001). *Economic trends in U.S. agricultural and food systems since World War II*. Ames, IA: Iowa State Press.

House File 519. (1995). *Iowa General Assembly. 76th General Assembly*. Retrieved February 10, 2004, from http://www.legis.state.ia.us/Legislation.html

Hurricane floyd floods farms, challenges regulators. (2000). *AWARE NEWS, 5*(1), 9. Retrieved January 19, 2004, from http://www.engr.uga.edu/service/extension/aware/vol5no_1.htm#_1_11

Iowa Geographic Map Server. (2004). *The USDA national agriculture imagery program (NAIP)*. Retrieved April 10, 2005, from http://cairo.gis.iastate.edu/map.html

Jain, D. K., Tim, U. S., & Jolly, R. (1995). Spatial decision support system for planning sustainable livestock production. *Computer Environment and Urban Systems*, *19*(1), 57-75.

Kim, J., Goldsmith, P. D., & Thomas, M. H. (2005, May). *Economic impact and social cost of confined animal feeding operations: A comparison and compensation analysis at the parcel level* (Working paper). Champaign, IL: University of Illinois at Urbana-Champaign. Retrieved August 15, 2006, from https://netfiles.uiuc.edu/pgoldsmi/www/working_papers/jungik4%20.pdf

Krapac, I. G., Dey, W. S., Roy, W. R., Smyth, C. A., Storment, E., Sargent, S. L., et al. (2002). Impact of swine manure pits on groundwater quality. *Environmental Pollution, 120*(2), 475-492.

Malczewski, J. (1999). *GIS and multicriteria decision analysis.* New York: Wiley

Otto, D., Orazam, P., & Huffman, W. (1998). Community and economic impacts of the Iowa hog industry. In Hays, D. (Ed.), *Iowa's pork industry — dollars and scents* (Chap. 6). Retrieved January 23, 2004, from http://www.econ.iastate.edu/outreach/agriculture/livestock/pork_dollars_and_scents/chapter6/introduction.html

Schiffman, S., Miller, E. A. S., Suggs, M. S., & Graham, B. G. (1994). The effect of environmental odors emanating from commerical swine operations on the mood of nearby residents. *Brain Research Bulletin, 37*(4), 369-375.

Taff, S. J., Tiffany, D. G., & Weisberg, W. (1996). *Measured effects of feedlots on residential property values in Minnesota: A report to the legislature* (Staff Paper Series, P96-12, 27). Minneapolis, MN: University of Minnesota Department of Applied Economics.

Warren County, Ohio. (2005). *What is GIS?* Retrieved April 20, 2005, from http://www.co.warren.oh.us/warrengis/definitions.htm

Wing, S., & Wolf, S. (1999). *Intensive livestock operations, health, and quality of lifeamong eastern North Carolina residents* (Report prepared for the North Carolina Department of Health and Human Services). Chapel Hill, NC: University of North Carolina at Chapel Hill.

Worley, J. W., Rupert, C., & Risse, L. M. (2001). Use of GIS to determine the effect of property line and water buffers on land availability. *Applied Engineering in Agriculture, 17*(1), 49-54.

Wyatt, P., & Ralphs, M. (2003). *GIS land and property management.* New York: Spon.

Section IV

Future Trends and Technologies

Chapter XI

Geo-Communication, Web-Services, and Spatial Data Infrastructure: An Approach Through Conceptual Models

Lars Brodersen, Aalborg University, Denmark
Anders Nielsen, National Survey and Cadastre, Denmark

Abstract

The introduction of Web services as index-portals based on geo-information has changed the conditions for both content and form of geo-communication. A high number of players and interactions as well as a very high number of all kinds of information and combinations of these characterise Web services, where maps are only a part of the whole. This chapter discusses the relations between the different components of SDI and geo-communication as well as the impact thereof. Discussed is also a model for the organization of the passive components of the infrastructure; that is, legislation, collaboration, standards, models, specifications, Web services, and finally the information. Awareness of the complexity is necessary, and structure is needed to make it possible for the geo-information community to pull together in the same direction. Modern Web-based geo-communication and its infrastructure looks very complex, and it will get even more complex. Therefore, there is a strong need for theories and models that can describe this complex Web in the SDI and geo-communication consisting of active components, passive components, users, and information in order to make it possible to handle the complexity and to give the necessary framework.

The Chapter's Delimination

The major concern of this chapter is *the requirements driven or user driven development* of SDI and geo-communication. Most GIS-, cartography- and SDI-literature lacks theories, models, and methodology for the systematic user requirement assessment, which comprises user awareness, situation awareness (task, time and place), and capability awareness.

This chapter describes *conceptual models,* that is, relations on a general level. This chapter is not a description of technical implementation methodology, that is, actual action or prototyping. The ideas presented in the chapter are of speculative nature. They are mainly based on the author's joint experience and empery from twenty-five respectively thirty-seven years in the business. The theoretical aspects in the chapter, particularly those regarding the geo-communication, are mainly based on C. S. Peirce's theories on semiotics and phenomenology.

Introduction

The role of geo-information and the distribution of geo-information have changed dramatically since the introduction of Web services on the Internet. In the framework of Web services, maps should be seen as a part of an index to further geo-information. Maps are no longer an aim in themselves. In this context, Web services perform the function as *index-portals* to further information. This index-function is based on geo-information, for example, maps.

The introduction of Web services as index-portals based on geo-information has changed the conditions for both content and form of geo-communication. A high number of players and interactions (as well as a very high number of all kinds of information and combinations of these) characterise Web services, where maps are only a part of the whole. These new conditions demand new ways of modelling the processes leading to geo-communication.

See Figure 1. A high number of players and interactions (as well as a very high number of all kinds of information and combinations of these) characterise modern geo-communication, where maps are only a part of the whole; these new conditions demand new ways of modelling the processes leading to geo-communication.

Figure 1. Web services, a new geocommunication

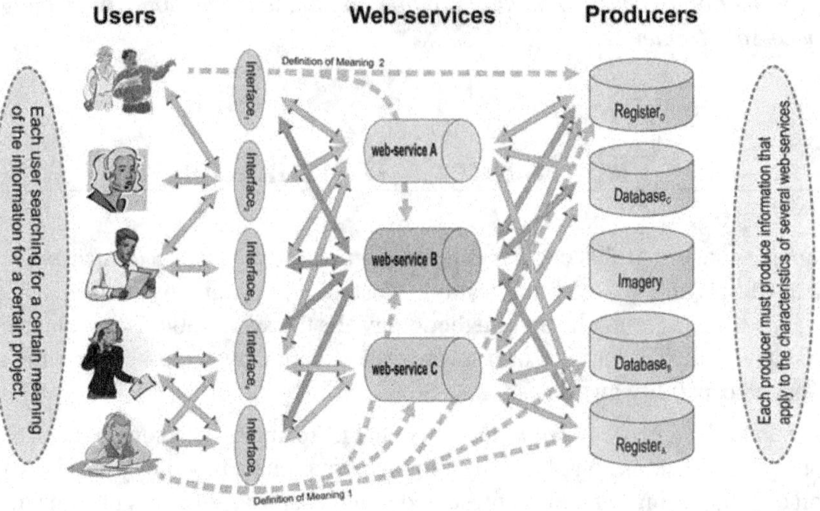

What is Geo-Communication

The purpose of any communication is to conduct the behaviour of the user. This is done by submitting detailed and precise information, on the basis of which the user may act. Decision and action is conditioned by this supply of information, and the following mental connection and integration with previous experience in the user's mind. In order that the producer may communicate the necessary information to the user, the producer must be able to analyse the phenomenon of which the communication consists and be able to describe the result of this analysis in detail. The purpose of the analysis is to select that kind of information that forms a reasonable basis for decision and the according action (Brodersen, 2005). Transmission of this kind of information, in writing or in graphical form, is part of geo-communication. All together geo-communication describes a *value-chain* from reality to decision and the according action.

The user may want a basis for making decisions on a possible trip, that is, a suggestion of an itinerary. For this purpose, the user starts a Web service intended for this use. The user types the start point and the end point of the trip, date and time, and after a short time, he will receive a number of proposals for the itinerary. On this basis, he will be able to make the decision, "Yes" or "No," to travel.

Figure 2 illustrates the above example of travel planning. The figure consist of the passive elements of geo-communication (plus a user), that is, geo-information and *spatial data infrastructure (SDI)*. All processes shown in the illustration can be iterative. The illustration can be seen as a longitudinal section of the overall process. Compare also Figure 5 showing the cross section of the geo-communication.

Figure 2. Longitudinal geoinformation

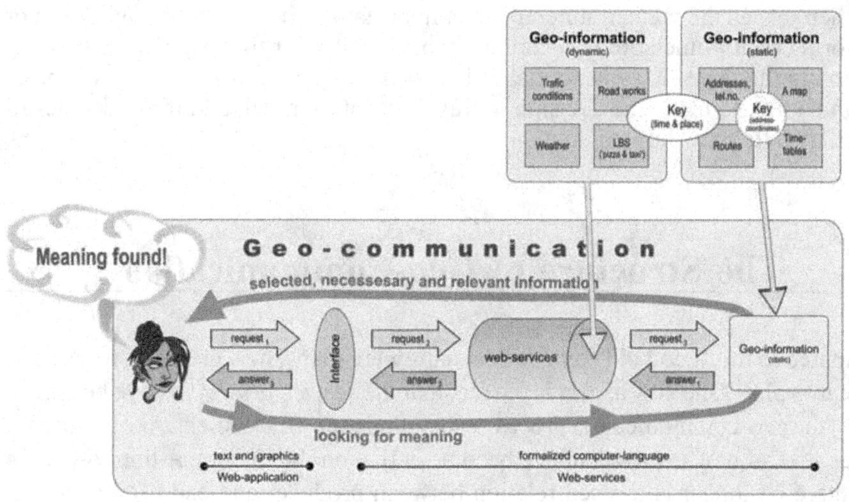

See Figure 2. The elements of a geo-communication illustrating the example of planning a trip; the user is looking for information enabling her to decide whether to take the trip or not. The primary problem for the producer is to catch this problem and to deliver the exact information having this meaning. The secondary problem for the producer is to master the complex network of processes and their mutual dependencies. All processes may be iterative. The illustration can be seen as a longitudinal section of the overall process. Compare also Figure 5 showing the cross section of the geo-communication.

A Web service application in many ways can be considered like a "black box": Users don't have to care about what happen behind the interface. Based on the business logic of the service a number of requests are sent to certain service-to-service database interfaces demanding certain geo-information, such as timetables, maps, road work, and so forth. This geo-information can be dynamic as well as static. The dynamic geo-information could be, for example, traffic conditions, weather conditions, road works, and so forth. Depending on the value of the dynamic geo-information, the need for certain static geo-information may vary. Static geo-information is, for example, maps, routes, addresses, timetables, and so forth.

The information retrieval is triggered by the initial user action. Another set of business rules is then used by the service to produce the desired output in the form of tables, text, and graphics, which together express the itinerary to be presented via the web application. It is important to note that the user does not ask for a certain timetable or a certain map, but only for the meaning of these in relation to the trip she wants to make. The meaning for the user is to have a basis on which first to make the decision to travel or not to travel, and if she decides to travel, then to know how to do it.

By means of other algorithms, these different types of geo-information are controlled against one another, resulting in a number of tables, text, and graphics, which together acts as the wanted itinerary. It is important to note that the user does not ask for a certain timetable or a certain map, but only for the *meaning* of these in relation to the trip she wants to make. The *meaning* for the user is to have a basis on which first to make the decision to travel or not to travel, and if she decides to travel, then to know how to do it.

The Structure of Geo-Communication

Compared to the "good old days" when maps were maps, new crucial aspects have come into play. One new aspect is the fact that the *service providers* have become a part of the geo-communication process with influence on the content. Another aspect is that several new producers have become active on the market. A third aspect is that there no longer is a given relation between producer and end user, as it was the case in the "good old days." A fourth aspect of the new way of modelling is the distinction between active and passive components in the spatial data infrastructure. All four aspects will be discussed in the following.

Example: Up until approximately 1990, there was in Denmark *one* producer of geo-information. The Geodetic Institute's production was linked strongly to the demands of the military, that is, the military's definition of meaning of the geo-information was the basis for all production. More or less everybody else in the Danish society had to be satisfied with those military-oriented maps and other products. This situation was due to the fact that the Geodetic Institute had a monopoly-like position in map-production, partly supported by legislation, and partly because of the extremely expensive means of production.

Figure 3. Up to approximately 1990 in Denmark: One producer, one definition of meaning, and several users

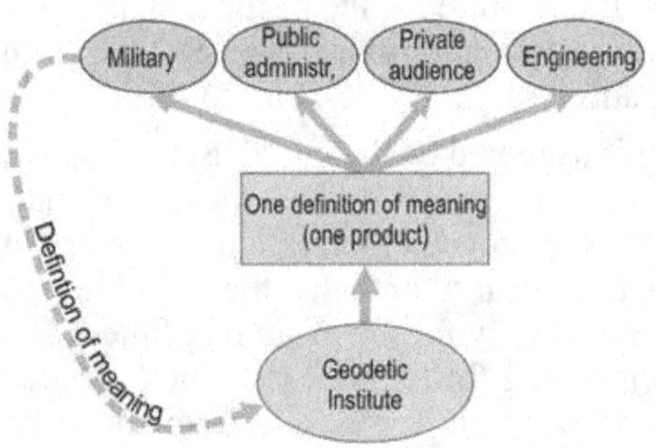

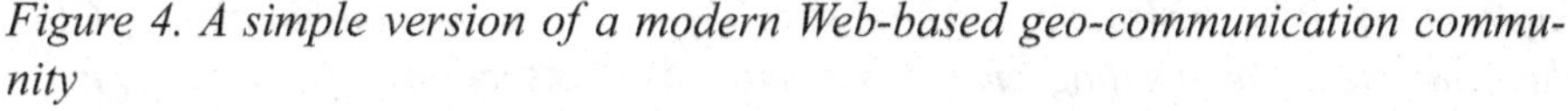
Figure 4. A simple version of a modern Web-based geo-communication community

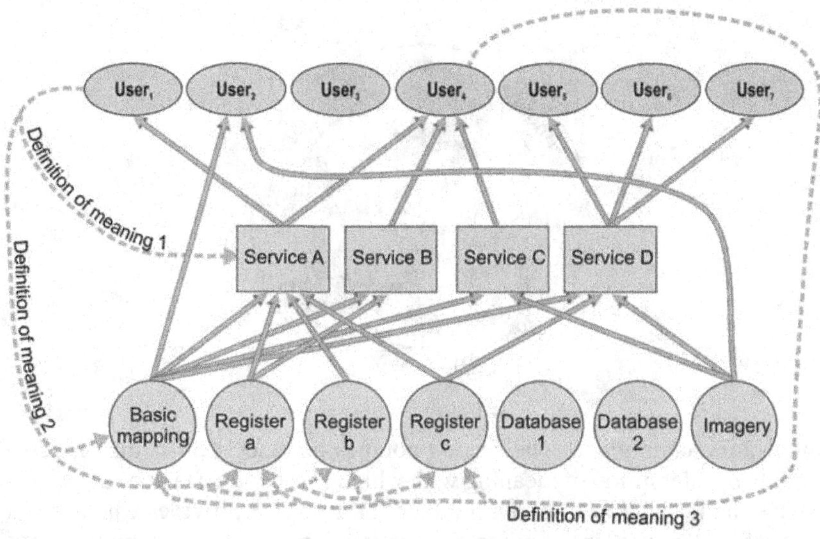

Since 1990, things have changed dramatically. The monopoly has been removed. The law concerned was cancelled, and the costs of the means of production were reduced dramatically. Several producers are now active in producing geo-information, and several Web service providers are carrying out the transmission of this geo-information to a huge number of users. Not only have a lot of producers and service providers become active. The most important aspect of the new era is that there are thousands of new users.

In the "good old days," the production of maps was extremely expensive, and therefore it was kept for the few. Today the Web-based infrastructure eases the admission to information so that nearly everybody can take part. This higher number of producers, service providers and users can be put into a diagram similar to the diagram in Figure 3 showing a part of the complexity of the new situation; see Figure 4.

The Web in Figure 4 illustrates a simple version of a modern Web-based geo-communication community; today there are several producers of geo-information and several Web service providers carrying out geo-communication. On top of the SDI a huge number of users are all trying to find that particular meaning of the geo-information that satisfy their particular needs. Therefore the producers have to cope with several, different types of definitions of meaning.

The first point to be made here is that the world of geo-communication has become extremely complex because of the higher number of producers, service providers, and users. The Web in the Figure 4 illustrates a *simple* version of a Web-based geo-

Figure 5. Modern geo-communication should be seen as the combination of GIS plus other elements; the diagram can be seen as a cross section of geo-communication, compare also Figure 2 with the longitudinal section of the overall process of geo-communication.

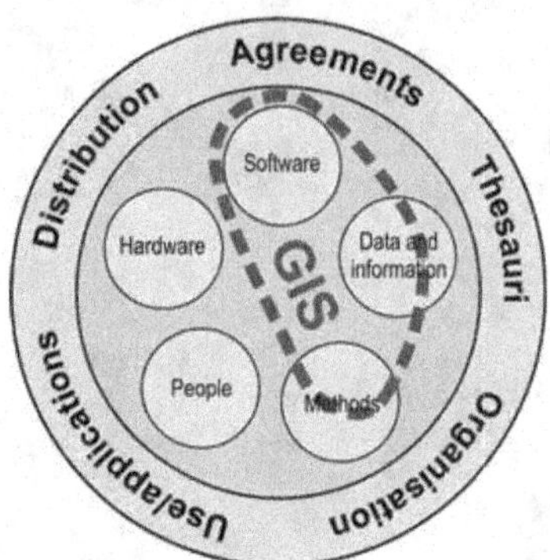

communication community. The second point to be made here is that there is no longer only *one* definition of meaning with which everybody has to be satisfied. All users have the possibility to find a producer or a service provider who accepts to take care of *that* particular definition of meaning demanded by that particular user. The producers have lost control of the users' behaviour.

Now, the good question is what to do about this increasing complexity? It reflects a complete new way of dealing with geo-communication and geo-information, and therefore new theories and models are needed. The way forward is to create models and theories that describe the new structure in geo-communication and SDI. The old theories and models are no longer sufficient.

Geographic information systems (GIS) is often understood as the combination of *software, data, and methods*, as the red dotted line in Figure 5 shows. This might well be so. But maybe this is no longer sufficient to be able to understand the complex era of modern geo-communication based on SDI. Figure 2 can be seen as a longitudinal section of the geo-communication process. The accompanying cross-section of the geo-communication looks like the diagram in Figure 5. Geo-communication should be seen and understood as consisting of GIS plus other elements, as Figure 5 illustrates.

Spatial Data Infrastructure (SDI)

Spatial data infrastructure (SDI) is the framework for geo-communication. Where geo-communication is the actual transmission of geo-information in writing or in

Figure 6. The combination of public services and the responsible organisations can be seen as the infrastructure of a society; SDI is concerned with geo-communication and the respective responsible organisations

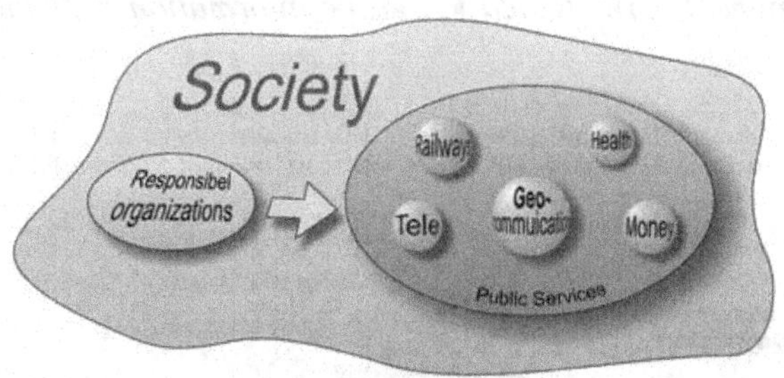

graphical form, SDI is the framework that makes it possible to carry out geo-communication. Therefore some kind of overlapping can be identified. The geo-communication view-point is concerned with the transmission of the meaning of the geo-information. The SDI view-point is concerned with the organisation and the services, systems, and so forth, that make the transmission of geo-information possible.

From an *organisational* view-point SDI can be seen as the combination of *organisations* and *public services*. Infrastructure consists of:

- *The basic organisation*, the system according to which a company, organisation, or other body is organised at the most basic level.
- *Public services or systems*, the large-scale public systems, services, and facilities of a country or region that are necessary for economic activity, including power and water supplies, public transport, telecommunications, geo-communication, roads, and schools.

From an *activity* view-point SDI can be defined as a combination of *active components* and *passive components:*

- *The active components* in SDI are those organisations that get things running. The active components have the *responsibility*, and they must be *active*. Otherwise nothing will happen.

The *active* components in SDI are:

Figure 7. The active components in SDI are those organisations that get things running, the active components have the responsibility, and they must be active; the passive components in SDI are those documents made by the active components, the passive components are created to get the information distributed about the active components activities

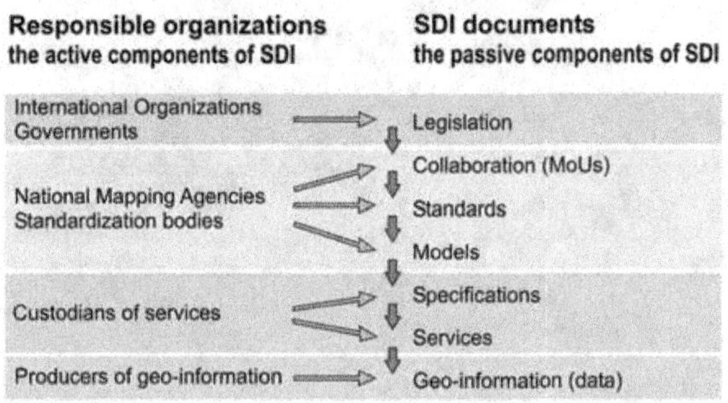

- International organisations like UN, NATO, and so forth
- Governments
- National mapping agencies
- Standardisation bodies
- Custodians for various services
- Producers of geo-information

The passive components in SDI are those documents that the active components have to produce to get the information about their activities distributed. These documents, the passive components, are the following, here presented in their mutual dependency. The mutual dependency is of *iterative* nature. The dependencies of the passive components go from *general* to *concrete*; that is, from legislation to geo-information.

The *passive* components in SDI are (here presented in their mutual dependency):

1.	Legislation	*Ideas, feelings*
2.	Collaboration (MoUs)	*Ideas, feelings*
3.	Standards	*Principles, rules, relations*
4.	Models	*Principles, rules, relations*
5.	Specifications	*Principles, rules, relations*
6.	Services	*Action, concrete*
7.	Geo-information (data)	*Action, concrete*

The active components and the passive components can be combined in one illustration as shown in Figure 7.

The Passive Components in SDI

The passive components are those documents containing and presenting the results of the activities of the active components. The passive components are dependent upon the activities in the organisations. There-fore they are called passive. These passive components are not active in themselves.

1. The **legislation** is made by the organisations, the active components. The legislation must act on a general level taking care of:
   - Enacting the framework for the deeper structures of SDI
   - Setting the areas of *responsibilities*
2. **Collaboration** (Memorandum of Understanding, MoU) are policy statements (position papers). Collaboration is based on the framework given by the legislation. Without this framework it is basically not possible to establish partnerships. Collaboration must act on a general level taking care of:
   - Setting the area(s) of *interest*

Figure 8. A few examples of standards; standardization is a necessary basis for activity within an SDI. Standards are general and often conceptually roomy, thus applicable to a wide range of projects and their specifications.

Principals of standards within the domain of SDI and geo-communication as well as some of their attributes

	Syntactics		Semantics	
	Realizations	Concepts	Concepts	Realizations
Formal, De jure	*As an example:* Implementation stand. spec. no. 19139 ? DIGEST part 1-3 DSFL (DK)	ISO 19100 series XML - GML		*As an example:* Spec. no. 19126 profile of 19110 DIGEST part 4 (FACC) DFDD FOT (DK)
Informal, De facto	ESRI Shape, coverage MapInfo mif, mid	Knowledge Implicit view of concepts		TOP10DK (DK)

- Establishing operational *partnerships* (within the framework of legislation)
- Inclusion of services as a full palette of joint government and commercial theatres
- Agreements upon the intention of sharing meta-information on services and registries

3. **Standards** are the necessary basis for activity within an SDI. Standards are the logic and practical conclusions of the agreements made in (2) collaboration. Collaboration is a declaration of intent. It expresses a convergence of will between the parties, indicating an intended common line of action. Standards define in greater detail, what to work on. Standards answer questions like "Which are the components or entities of the universe of discourse that we are going to work on?"; "How do we define our activities?" and so forth. Standards are general and can therefore be used for several concrete projects, where a specification is concrete and valid for one project. A few examples of standards (of which a few are Danish standards) can be seen in Figure 8.
4. **Models** describe how to use certain standards for a given project. Models bridge the gap between standards and specifications. Models describe:
   - Value model:
     - Identification of content
   - Business process engineering:
     - Information and resource flow

Figure 9. Web services bridge the gap between producer's databases and the users; Web services are the technology making the use of geo-information possible

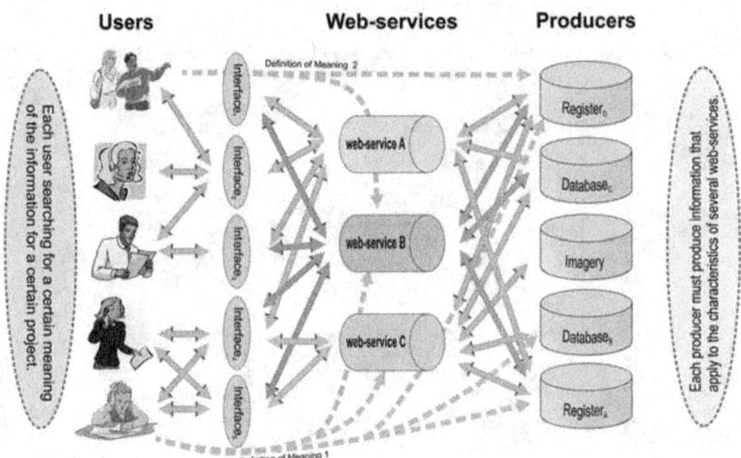

- Requirements-driven service development
- System use case:
  - Application schemas
  - General feature models
- The need for specifications:
  - Implementation process

5. **Specifications** are descriptions of what has to be done in a certain project. A specification can, for example, specify that things have to be done in accordance with certain standards. A specification is concrete and valid for one given project; standards are general and valid for several projects. Specifications describe *rules* and *contents* for one given project:
   - Categorisations and classifications of real-world phenomena (features) within a standardised universe of discourse
   - Definitions and descriptions of attributes on the level of the classified features
   - Definitions of the information flow; sources, update strategy; components value assessment, and so forth
   - Storage and security strategies

Figure 10. Geo-information and metadata in services in a global Web; user, producer, and service provider are all parts of the service Web, each of them carrying out their specific task (Idea: Dave McKellar, Canada)

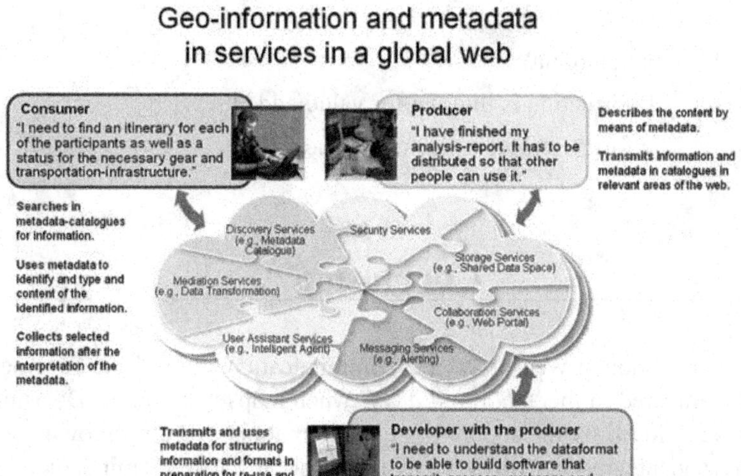

- Filtering and retrieval methodologies
- Strategies for multistage representation (incl. semantically and geometrical granularity and generalisation)
- Symbolisation strategy, design manuals, and legend drafting

The passive components numbered 1 through 5 can all be carried out on a piece of paper; nothing practical or actual has happened until here.

6. **Services** are the concrete, practical set-up of the passive components numbered 1 through 5. Services establish the technology; that is, the software, the hardware, the user-interfaces, and so forth. Compare also Figure 2, the longitudinal section of the geo-communication, as well as Figure 5, the cross section of the geo-communication.
7. **Metadata and information** is the "fuel" to put into the machinery (the services) once the services have been created. Metadata and Information is *not* the technology. Metadata and information are the actual, practical, concrete result of a certain production carried out in accordance with the characteristics of the services, with the specification, with the model, with the standard, with the MoU, and with the legislation.
   - Metadata:
     - Where to find the information (the data)
     - Enables an analysis of the information's fitness for use, the chacteristics of the information
     - Never create information (data) without metadata, and never separate the two
   - Information (data):
     - Information is the fuel for value-added service
     - Information (data) is not products

Conclusion

With the introduction of Web-based geo-communication, things have become most complex, compared to the "good old days" when maps were maps. Decision and action is conditioned by the supply of geo-information, and the following mental connection and integration with previous experience in the user's mind. In order that the producer may communicate the necessary information to the user, the producer must be able to analyse the phenomenon of which the communication consists and be able to describe the result of this analysis in detail. Transmission of this kind of information, in writing or in graphical form, is part of geo-communication. Altogether, geo-communication describes a *value-chain* from reality to decision and the according action.

The basis for Web-based geo-communication is the *spatial data infrastructure (SDI)*. SDI consists of both active components and passive components. The active components get things happening. The passive components are the documents describing the results of the activities with the active components. The passive components are the legislation, the agreements, the standards, the technology, the specifications, and the information, which are the crucial elements of the infrastructure and with it, the necessary basis for Web-based geo-communication. As there is a mutual dependency between all the components, none of them can be left out. If just one component is missing, the impact is that the geo-communication is based on a non-systematic and non-conscious foundation.

Modern Web-based geo-communication and its infrastructure looks very complex. That is surely true. We think that it will get even more complex. Therefore, there is a strong need for theories and models that can describe the "Web" in order to make it possible to handle the complexity and to give the necessary framework. There is also a strong need for political consciousness about these things because it is from there that the legislation comes.

References

Bernhardsen, T. (2002). *Geographic information systems: An introduction.* New York: John Wiley & Sons.

Brodersen, L. (2005). Semiotik i geokommunikation — fra virkelighed til handling. Frederikshavn, Denmark: Tankegang a·s.

Bødker, K., Kensing, F. & Simonsen, J. (2004). *Participatory IT design: Designing for business and workplace realities.* Cambridge, MA: MIT Press.

Caquard, S. (2003). Internet, maps and public participation: Contemporary limits and possibilities. In *Maps and the Internet* (345-358). Oxford, UK: Elsevier Science Ltd.

Hjelmager, J., Delgado, T, Moellering, H, Cooper, A, Danko, D, Huet, M, Aalders, H, & Martynenko, A. (2005). Developing a modelling for the spatial data infrastructure. *ICA Proceedings ICC2005.*

ISO/TC211 Standardisation on Geoinformation and Geomatics. ISO-19100 series. (n.d.). Retrieved from http://www.isotc211.org/

Jepsen, R., Nordestgaard, A., Peterson, J. E., & Lassen, M. (2003). *IT udvikling*. Frederikshavn, Denmark: Dafolo Forlag A/S.

Jiang, B. (2003). Beyond serving maps: Serving GIS functionality over the Internet. In *Maps and the Internet* (147-158). Oxford, UK: Elsevier Science Ltd.

Koláčný, A. (1969). Cartographic information: A fundamental concept and term in modern cartography. *The Cartographic Journal, 6*(1), 47-49.

Longley, P.A., Goodchild, M.F., Maguire, D.J., & Rhind D.W. (2005). *Geographical informations systems and science*. Chichester, UK: John Wiley & Sons Ltd.

Nebert, D. D. (Ed.). (2004). *Spatial data infrastructure cookbook.* Global Spatial Data Infrastructure (GSDI). Retrieved from http://www.gsdi.org/docs2004/Cookbook/cookbookV2.0.pdf.

Peirce, C. S. (1992). *The essential Peirce. Selected philosophical writings* (Vol. 1). IN, Indiana University Press.

Peirce, C. S. (1998). *The essential Peirce. Selected philosophical writings* (Vol. 2). IN, Indiana University Press.

Percivall, G. (Ed.). (n.d.). *OGC reference model* (Ref. No. OGC 03-040 Version: 0.1.3),Open Geospatial Consortium, Inc.

Peterson, M. P. (2003). Maps and the Internet: An introduction. In *Maps and the Internet* (1-16). Oxford, UK: Elsevier Science Ltd.

Peterson, M. P. (2003). Foundations of research in Internet cartography. In *Maps and the Internet* (437-446). Oxford, UK: Elsevier Science Ltd.

Østergaard, M., & Olesen, J.D. (2004). *Digital forkalkning*. Frederikshavn, Denmark: Dafolo Forlag A/S.

Further Reading

Brodersen (2005) is an attempt to develop a theory and models for a systematic user requirements assessment. It is based on Charles Sanders Peirce's theories on semiotics and phenomenology (Peirce, 1992; Peirce, 1998).

Chapter XII

A Data Visualization and Interpretation System for Sensor Networks

Fengxian Fan, Kunming University, People's Republic of China

Abstract

With the increase in applications for sensor networks, data manipulation and representation have become a crucial component of sensor networks. This chapter explores an implementation to process and interpret the data gathered by sensor networks. In a project supported by SensIT program at DARPA, we have built wireless sensor networks deployed to monitor rare plants or other endangered species. The environmental data, such as temperature, rainfall, and sunlight, around the plants are sent by the wireless sensor networks to a base station. The system presented in this chapter combines database management technology, geographic information system, and Web development technology to visualize the data gathered by the wireless sensor networks. The integration of our data visualization tools and the online collaborative discussion environment makes the system useful to different communities of potential users.

Introduction

Of all the global problems in the biosphere we confront today, few would argue that the extinction of species and destruction of ecosystems have the most serious consequences, and they are irreversible. Worldwide, the preservation of rare species presents a major challenge. In Hawaii, there are numerous species of plants and animals. Many of them are found only in Hawaii and are currently threatened or endangered.

In order to monitor the ecological environment and events around rare plants, the Pods project at the University of Hawaii has started to build wireless ad-hoc sensor networks (Biagioni & Bridges, 2002). A *sensor network* is a computer network made up of many spatially-distributed sensors which are used to monitor conditions, such as temperature, sound, vibration, pressure, motion, or pollutants. These sensors are usually small and inexpensive, so they can be deployed in large numbers. In a wireless ad hoc sensor network, the sensor nodes are self-contained units consisting of a battery, radio, sensors, and other accessories. The nodes self-organize their networks, rather than having a pre-programmed network topology. Every node in this system can transmit data of its own and also forward data from other nodes (Bose, Morin, Stojmenovic, & Urrutia, 2001; Nagar & Biagioni, 2002). In our project, we call these network nodes pods. Each pod contains a micro-computer which is needed for

Figure 1. A Silene Hawaiiensis plant in flower

collecting and transferring the weather data, micro-sensors, and other accessories. Currently the pod is designed to measure sunlight, temperature, wind, and rainfall. Some pods are also equipped to take high-resolution images of the plants periodically. In addition, the pod is designed and constructed to be inexpensive and easily camouflaged to avoid damage by curious visitors. The pods are deployed every few hundred feet, thus form a wireless ad hoc sensor network. A new wireless routing protocol (named multi-path on-demand routing protocol [MOR] has been designed for the network to provide energy conservation and routing efficiency. This network constitutes a monitoring system for scientists to observe the rare plants. On the Big Island of Hawaii, we have already made preliminary deployments of pods to monitor a rare plant species, Silene Hawaiiensis. Figure 1 is the picture of this rare plant which was taken automatically by a pod sensor, and is believed to be the first ever picture of a Silene Hawaiiensis in flower in the wild.

In this wireless ad hoc sensor network system, the collected data and images are transferred from one pod to another. They eventually reach a special pod — the base station. At the base station, the data are stored for further manipulation and accessible via the Internet.

It needs to be pointed out that field sites where the rare plants live are sometimes in harsh environmental condition or in remote areas. With the help of the data sent back by the wireless sensor network, the ecologists and botanists can observe the plants and their environmental conditions from the Internet, without disturbing the site or unnecessarily attracting attention to the endangered species. Then they can analyze and understand the reasons why the rare plants survive or disappear. In addition, the data transmission is near real-time, so the observers can decide whether the situation needs a site visit to the rare plants.

The gathered data which are sent back by our wireless sensor networks are stored in a database. Because the environmental weather data are recorded every few minutes, manipulating and translating the vast amount of data is crucial to the end users. Hence, we are developing an information interpretation system for the sensor networks.

The objective of this information interpretation system is to convert raw climate and weather data into visual formats that can be easily understood by people. The system also provides an environment on the Internet for people to access the data and to observe the area in which the sensor networks are deployed. In this system, users can get current (near real-time) or historical views of environmental data and thus derive conclusions based on substantial understanding of the available data. We also expect that people can form online communities to exchange their conclusions about their observations and to discuss their points of view interactively in this system. By means of these features, we can fulfill our ultimate goal: not only to gather the data from the area in which sensor networks are deployed, but also to convey and translate them for scientists to analyze, interpret, and discuss.

In the development of this information interpretation system, we adopted and combined several technologies: database management systems, geographic information systems, dynamic Web programming, and human-computer interactive design technology. One challenge we encountered is how to display the distribution of the data attributes in a real-world map in ways that would be intuitive and meaningful. After several trials and failures, we selected a *geographic information system* (GIS) as the main platform to visualize the data. Another challenge was how to handle the human- computer interaction when people are accessing the data display page on the Internet. To address this challenge we have cooperated with a human-computer interactive learning project and focused on developing a collaborative online discussion environment for the end users, scientists, students, or other people who are interested in environmental monitoring and conservation.

This chapter discusses the above technologies in more detail below, as follows. First, we focus on how we generate maps displaying the distribution of data attributes by means of information visualization techniques. Then we discuss how to apply the technology of usability engineering to develop an asynchronous interactive discussion system. Because of space limitations, we focus our description on the key ideas and technologies we successfully applied in our project.

Data Visualization

In order to pursue the goal of providing the information for people to review and examine, we applied to our information interpretation process the technology of *data visualization*, in which visual features such as shapes and colors can be used to code different attributes of the data. We need a software platform to execute this function, so we selected the geographic resources analysis support system (GRASS) geographic information system. We have used the global positioning system (GPS) to collect the geographic position coordinates — longitude and latitude — for each pod. This makes the application of GIS technology in our information interpretation system possible, and thus becomes an innovative feature for this aspect of usage in which we have combined GIS with sensor networks.

Figure 2 and Figure 3 are an example of the resulting weather data distribution map accompanied with the appropriate legend.

This map is generated based on the data for one day which are sent back by the Pods sensor networks in the area of the University of Hawaii at Manoa. The map of Manoa is the background (the background map in Figure 3 comes from the Tiger mapping service of the U.S. Census Bureau). In this map we use different colors to represent the different levels of temperature and sunlight in the areas being monitored. The rainfall is represented by rain drops with different densities of drops presenting

Figure 2. Legend for the weather data distribution map

		LIGHT		
		Low	Medium	High
TEMPERATURE	Low	1	2	3
	Medium	4	5	6
	High	7	8	9

the levels of rainfall. The map is intuitive and easy to understand. The temperature increases from SW to NE. The central area is the sunniest, but also has some rain. Most of the rainfall is measured in the SE corner.

Figure 3. One example map displaying the weather data spatial distribution which is generated from our information interpretation system

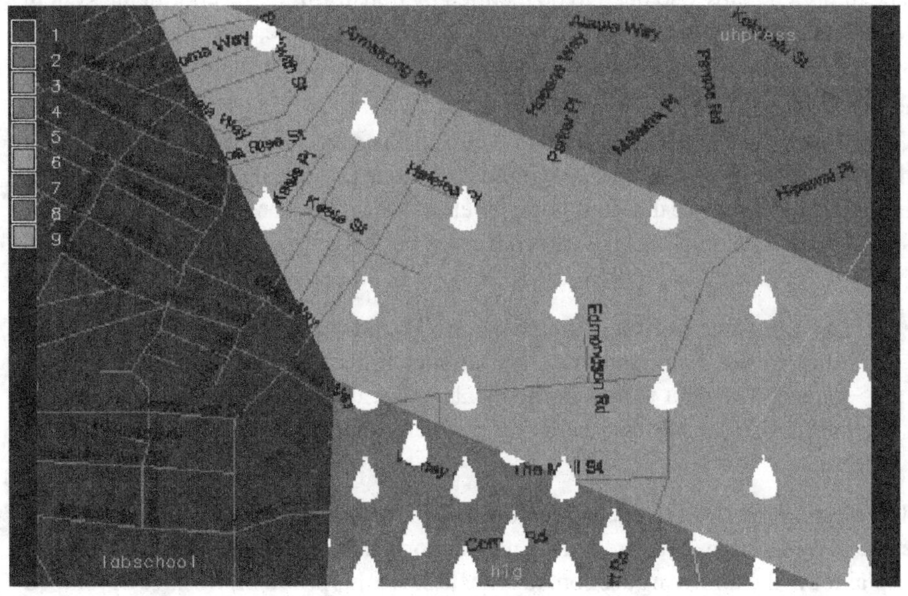

The level of the data is determined by comparing the data value at a specific pod with the average value over the entire area under observation. Standard deviation has been used as the threshold while comparing the different levels of the weather data.

The maps can also be generated based on monthly and yearly statistical data. In addition, if the observer wants to view the data for a specific time, the system can provide the near real-time monitoring maps to the user without an obvious delay. These features satisfy the diverse requirements from the observers or viewers.

The Application of GRASS GIS Technology in the Information Interpretation System

To develop the data visualization map using GRASS, we have used some particular techniques, stated as follows:

- **Background map importation and rectification:** While adopting GIS technology for our project, we need to import real-world maps containing the locations of the deployed pods as the background of the resulting weather distribution maps. We also need to do image processing on these maps to convert the maps to the GRASS GIS data format — raster file.

The imported maps also need to be rectified by transforming the coordinate system to a standard geographical coordinate system, for example, the UTM coordinate system. This is accomplished by adopting appropriate data manipulation models provided by GRASS.

Once the rectified map is imported into GRASS, we can place the different pods at the appropriate locations. The geographic positions of pods are obtained from GPS. In Figure 3, we can see that four pods, labeled with yellow location names (uhpress, stjohn, labschool, and hig) have been located on this map.

- **The interface between the PostgreSQL database and the GRASS GIS:** Since we are dealing with a large amount of data, we use a database for data storage. The data stored in the database includes rainfall, temperature, and light level which are gathered from the areas under observation.

The existing interface between the PostgreSQL database and GRASS is not applicable to our system, because it does not support our color coding scheme which is explained in the following section. In order to solve this problem, we have developed an interface to meet our requirements on the system. This interface is used to transfer the data from the PostgreSQL database into the GRASS GIS for processing, and to convert the data from the database format into category values that are suitable for GRASS data manipulation. In addition, because only snapshots in time are available, the aggregated data, such as average readings, should be calculated in some way.

Therefore, this interface has some special functions. It can access the database table to retrieve the desired weather data collected by pods. It can also implement the color coding scheme to convert the raw data to category values according to the levels (low, medium, and high) when compared with the average value of the data gathered by all pods in the entire area.

The Color Coding Scheme and Voronoi Diagrams

In this system, we have designed a color coding scheme for the weather data display map. The map is partitioned into areas, with each area holding a unique color to represent the level of the weather data. The algorithm for generating *Voronoi diagram* is used to divide the map into different portions.

- **The color coding scheme:** The purpose of the color coding scheme is to use different colors to represent the levels of attribute data such as temperature, light, and rainfall. However, the data collected by the sensors are independent of each other. This means we need to find a way to combine them in one diagram and make it meaningful and intuitive to viewers.

The goal of information design is to help users perceive, interpret, and make sense of what is happening (Rosson & John, 2002). In order to pursue this goal, we designed a data representation scheme with intuition and perception as the main concerns. For example, we use bright color to represent areas where the sun shines more brightly, and we use colors such as blue for cold and red for warm temperatures. This is strongly related to people's perception and expectations, and it gives a good context to interpret the displayed information. Over several iterations, we carefully designed the color coding scheme according to people's intuition. It is easy for viewers to understand what is going on in that area with the colored display.

The color coding scheme is implemented by the interface between the PostgreSQL database and the GRASS GIS. In the scheme, we use two bits to represent the levels of temperature and sunlight. Therefore, binary integer 00 means the value is medium. Integers 01 and 10 represent the value low and high respectively. The combination of temperature and sunlight is imported to GRASS as category values which are used to render the map with different colors. Table 1 shows the scheme in details. This table is the foundation of Figure 2 displaying the legend of the rendered resulting map.

Some parameters are more easily represented using shapes and symbols than using colors. In this case, as much as possible we use familiar shapes; for example, we use rain drops to indicate the area where it is raining. Hence, by color coding and shape representation we can efficiently convey detailed information to people who wish to observe or examine the environmental conditions on the site of their areas of interest.

We also apply two bits to represent the rainfall. But this two bit integer does not change the color scheme; rather we use shape symbols resembling rain drops to represent rainfall. If the area has different levels of rainfall, we can present the rain drops in different densities within different portions of the area, as is shown in Figure 3. This two bit binary integer is also converted into a category value by the interface between database and GIS.

The standard deviation is applied to determine the levels of the weather data value. For instance, if the temperature gathered by one pod is more than a standard devia-

Table 1. Color coding scheme

Temperature		**Sunlight**		**Category Value**	**Color**
00	Medium	00	Medium	0000 (0)	Green
00	Medium	01	Low	0001 (1)	Dark green
00	Medium	10	High	0010 (2)	Bright green
01	Low	00	Medium	0100 (4)	Blue
01	Low	01	Low	0101 (5)	Dark Blue
01	Low	10	High	0110 (6)	Bright Blue
10	High	00	Medium	1000 (8)	Red
10	High	01	Low	1001 (9)	Dark Red
10	High	10	High	1010 (10)	Bright Red

tion higher than the average of temperature over the entire area, it can be categorized as high temperature. So, when our system shows an area on the map that has higher brightness than the average for the whole map, an observer knows that the brighter area is at least one standard deviation brighter than what is reported by the other points on the map. The one standard deviation threshold is the default when the user initially accesses the map display page. The standard deviation serves as an initial value to distinguish the pods with higher or lower values from those with approximately the average value. Such diagrams reliably identify extremes of hot and cold. However, users with specific goals may want to use other threshold values rather than the standard deviation (as suggested to us by an anonymous reviewer). In the future, we would like to modify the system so the initial presentation uses the standard deviation for the threshold and users are able to dynamically modify these thresholds to produce different maps. In the section "Data Accessibility" we present an asynchronous online environment for users to input the data interactively.

- **Voronoi diagram generation and rendering:** After the data have been categorized based on our color coding scheme and transferred from the PostgreSQL database into GRASS, we need to divide the whole region in which we deployed monitoring pods into different areas. Then we could render the areas with different colors specified in our color coding scheme.

One of the main algorithms we adopted in GRASS is for generating Voronoi diagrams, in which each polygon covers one pod. As an important geometric data structure in geographic analysis, Voronoi diagrams are pervasive in GIS. The Voronoi diagram partitions a given space into distinct polygons (called Thiessen polygons [Preparata & Shamos, 1985]), and each polygon covers the area that is nearest to one pod. Thus, this method is called nearest neighbor interpolation. In GRASS we use the sweepline algorithm developed by Steve J. Fortune (Fortune, 1987) for generating Voronoi Diagrams. His algorithm avoids the difficult merge step of the divide and conquer technique and runs with complexity $O(nlogn)$. This property is important for relatively complicated data processing because we are sometimes dealing with large amounts of information.

Figure 4 illustrates an example of Voronoi diagrams generated by GRASS according to the locations of the pods. Within a Voronoi diagram, the area where monitoring pods are deployed is divided into tiled polygons. In the GRASS GIS, we render this diagram based on our color coding scheme. For example, the polygon holding the pod with high temperature and medium sunlight is rendered with red color, as is shown in the upper right corner of Figure 3.

The main purpose of our information visualization is to display the weather data on a real-world map. As mentioned before, we have imported into GRASS an existing real-world map which covers the area in which we deployed some observing

Figure 4. One example Voronoi diagram generated by GRASS

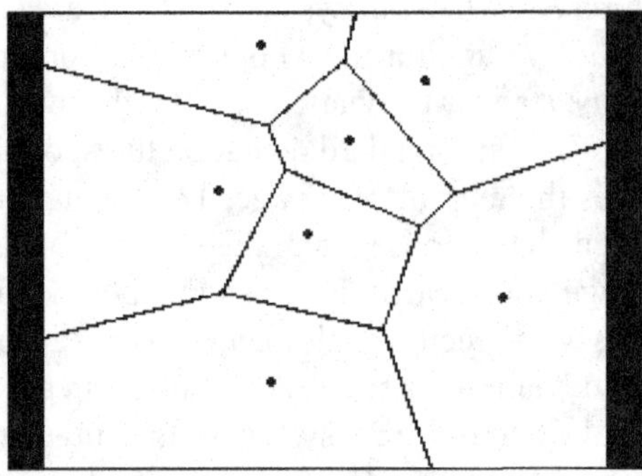

pods. This map is used as the background on the resulting display. So, we merge the real-world map with the rendered Voronoi diagram. Thus, we can display the distribution of weather attribute data in a two-dimensional space, that is, a map. This becomes a feasible way for people to view and examine the data in an acceptable visualization format.

Data Accessibility

Availability of the Visualized Data

We have provided two means for users to view the map on the Internet. One is dynamic map generation via a CGI program. This function satisfies the usage of viewing a map for a specific date and time. The other way is to create maps automatically at a particular time by using a program launching system (Linux cron). With this system and our especially designed programs, the daily, monthly, and yearly maps can be created and added to Web pages automatically.

- **Dynamic generation of maps:** As a widely-used technology for building dynamic Web documents, the common gateway interface (CGI) is applied to generate maps dynamically and display them on the Internet. The user can fill out a form online specifying the date and time for which the user intends to observe the data, then submit the form to the Web server. The CGI program runs through the entire data visualization process. It begins with the interface implementation to query the database and create the site file. It also runs the GRASS GIS to manipulate the site file, generate the Voronoi diagram, then convert and output the resulting map to an image file which is available from the Internet. Although CGI is a traditional technology for Web development, making the CGI program perform the entire task is rather challenging. First, the CGI program must be able to run GRASS and execute the required manipulation to the site file imported by the interface. Second, the CGI program needs a long time to query the database because the database table holds a large amount of data collected by pods. This situation has been improved by moving some of the calculations (for example, average, maximum, and minimum values) from the database management system, where they are relatively slow, to the CGI program. Therefore, the CGI program can generate a map within an acceptable time — around thirty seconds.

- **Automatic generation of maps:** The ecologists and botanists are often more interested in the statistical data representation, such as daily, monthly, and yearly environmental data. In order to meet this requirement we developed a series of programs to generate those three kinds of map using the statistical results based on the data gathered by the wireless sensor networks. We also applied a program launching system, cron, to start the program at a specific time. For example, for the daily maps, we can start the map generation program at 00:00am everyday. For monthly maps, the program can be launched at 00:00am on the first day of every month. The program can also add the generated maps to the corresponding daily, monthly, or yearly html files.

Interactive Data Access Environment

One major advantage of user interface design technology based on usability engineering over traditional displays is the possibility for dynamic redisplay. Computer-based displays can be dynamically restructured, changed in size, filtered, and animated (Rosson & John, 2002). This indicates the feasibility of constructing an interactive system to provide an online environment for viewers to query the data from the database, observe the events on different sites, and interactively discuss their points of view. We need various technologies of Web development and usability engineering to design and implement this functionality, and to do this we have cooperated with a research team led by Dan Suthers of the University of Hawaii.

- **Combination of visualization tools — an online asynchronous collaborative discussion environment:** We have developed various visualization tools. One of them emphasizes the spatial distribution using maps that we described above. Another one shows the chronological charting of the data. In addition, we have collected a lot of images which are taken by the cameras embedded in pods for observing the growth of the plants. These pictures are organized in Web pages with dynamic accessibility. All of these tools are developed for the Web, so they are available from the Internet. But they exist independently and reflect the different aspects of the plants' condition and environment. In order for end users to make use of these tools to view the collected data, we need to combine these data visualization tools. Therefore, we need to design an online asynchronous *collaborative discussion* system to provide artifact-centered discourse which can support *online communities* among the participants who are viewing the data. In this system, the users can choose the data visualization tools, send requests to the database, and get the visualized data display through the Internet. In addition, they can make online discussions in the system with the data visualization results, data distribution map, data charting, or other visualized data formats, as the artifacts to support their arguments.

As has been indicated to us by Kim Bridges, a botanist at the University of Hawaii and a Principal Investigator of the Pods project, the interpretation and analysis of the data gathered so far in our observations of the rare plant *Silene Hawaiiensis* has never been done in the field of ecology. As in all scientific studies, hypotheses about the observing targets need to be proposed, tested against the available data, and refined appropriately. In order to work with these hypotheses and reach the proper conclusions, the users need an online asynchronous collaborative working environment to exchange their ideas derived from their substantial observations. Within the online community formed among the viewers in the system, users can build discussion threads, such as the effect of temperature on the flowering of the plant, the influence of rainfall on the plant, and so on. The professionals or students can build their individual hypotheses and arguments based on the observations, by accessing the data visualization tools to view the current or historical data stored in the database. Users can then discuss their hypotheses asynchronously and interactively in various threads of conversation, which may lead them to draw reliable conclusions and to refine their theories.

The concept of knowledge representation has also been emphasized in this design because the conversations about the data will be as multifaceted as the data itself. One of the main goals of the information interpretation system is to provide an efficient platform for users to present their observation results. With relevant lines of discussion topic being distributed across multiple conversational threads and associated with different artifacts, the asynchronous collaborative discussion environment can achieve the ultimate goal of the information interpretation system. With substantial observations and discussions, scientists can eventually obtain the adequate information about the plant under observation. The development of this system can help scientists analyze the ecological environment of the plants, or even other species if we apply our system to observe them in the future.

- **Human-computer interaction design:** While designing the human-computer interface for the asynchronous collaborative discussion system described above,

> we applied the technology of scenario-based *usability engineering* (Rosson & John, 2002). We emphasize collaborative interactions among the discussion communities or groups with usability as the main concern in the design process. In our scenario-based usability engineering, we included requirement analysis, information and interaction design, prototyping, and usability evaluation. Connecting the different design stages is a series of user interaction scenarios. The scenario is actually a description of people activities. Representing the use of a system or application with a set of user interaction scenarios makes the system's use explicit (Rosson & John, 2002).

We started our usability engineering design from the interview with the potential users. The purpose of the interview is to understand the current work activities while observing the plant and their expectations on the system. Based on the interviews, we create the problem scenarios, which are descriptions of the current observation activities in the problem domain. We also guide the following design stages, activity design, information design and interaction design, with appropriate scenarios. Those scenarios are elaborated at the stage of prototyping. Web pages are selected as the tool for prototyping. Figure 5 is an example of the interfaces for discussion

Figure 5. One example of the interface for discussion with a charting of the temperature over time as the discussion artifact

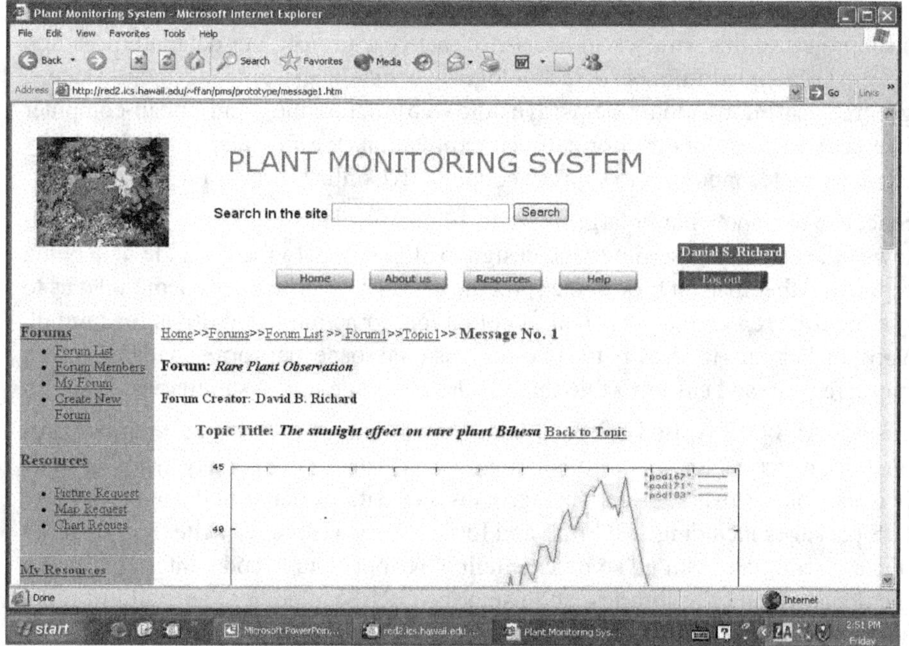

of the effect of rainfall on the plant. Below the chart on this figure (not shown in Figure 5, but available in the actual interface) is a discussion area where the community members can post messages. The resulting system allows users to choose a visualization tool from the function list as is shown in Figure 5. Then the system switches to perform the selected visualization function. When the visualized data form is presented, the user can add it to the discussion environment as an artifact to support his or her arguments.The usability evaluation is conducted based on these sketched prototypes. After several circles of evaluation and redesign, the prototypes have become closer to usability objectives. In addition, we also adopted other usability engineering methods, for example, usage centered design (Constantine & Lockwood, 1999), in our design process. We have created a series of essential use cases and navigation maps which give guidance to the entire design process.

In brief, the goal of the design for the online asynchronous collaborative discussion environment is to apply the technology of usability engineering to our information interpretation system. Therefore, end users will be able to reach reasonable and accurate conclusions based on the data collected by the pods.

Related Work

This chapter provides a relatively detailed description and rationale of the data interpretation system designed for the wireless sensor network project which is undertaken at the University of Hawaii. An article by Biagioni and Bridges (2002), co-authored by two Principal Investigators, summarizes the goals of the project. As a subproject of this wireless ad hoc sensor network project, our data interpretation system has adopted a number of technologies, such as database management systems, geographical information systems, dynamic Web programming, and human-computer interactive design, for the information interpretation. We have also applied usability engineering technologies to support collaborative online discussion.

Since we have potentially large amounts of data to display, we have carefully followed the tenets for user interface design to allow users to focus on the data being reported rather than on how to interpret the data. These principles encouraged us to use intuitive representations such as colors for temperature and drops for rainfall, Voronoi diagrams to identify the two-dimensional space that corresponds to a given measurement, and customizable thresholds to provide useful summaries.

The GRASS GIS is used for data management, image processing, graphics production, raster/vector spatial modeling, and visualization of many types of data. It is capable of reading and writing maps and data to many popular proprietary GIS packages including ARC/Info and Idrisi. Users wishing to write their own application programs can do so by examining existing source code, interfacing with the documented GIS libraries, and using the GRASS modules. This allows more sophisticated functionality to be integrated in GRASS. The application of GRASS

GIS in our information interpretation system enables the combination of geographic information system with sensor networks, thus becoming a unique technique for visualizing weather data collected by sensor networks.

Interpolation based on Voronoi diagrams (Preparata & Shamos, 1985) is a well-known technique in cartography. They tend to be involved in situations where a space should be partitioned into "spheres of influence." This makes applying Voronoi diagrams for climatology feasible, and it has become a widely-used method in this field (Thiessen & Alter, 1911). This interpolation method becomes an important feature of our information interpretation system for sensor networks.

Usability engineering (Constantine & Lockwood, 1999; Rosson & John, 2002) requires that a focus on user needs and capabilities pervade the entire design process. While adopting usability engineering technologies in the design of our information interpretation system, we need to consider both what information is significant to the user and what information can easily be communicated to the user. A reviewer has suggested generating the environmental data distribution map according to the user's setting rather than using the standard deviation to determine thresholds. This emphasizes the user's role and will make the system more interactive. In addition, a distribution chart of the gathered data will help to set the threshold. We look forward to implementing and evaluating this in future versions of the system.

Conclusion

While we are developing this information interpretation system specifically for the Pods wireless sensor network project, we also expect that it can be applied to more generic sensor networks, including wired networks. The end result should be to make the sensor networks friendlier to users and more flexible to meet the requirements of different applications. It successfully conveys the information gathered by the wireless sensor networks to ecologists, botanists, or other researchers. It also provides a system for them to view the environmental condition around the target of their observations. Based on the substantial understanding of the collected data, they can also discuss and exchange their viewpoints through the collaborative discussion environment provided by this information interpretation system.

References

Biagioni, E. S., & Bridges, K. (2002). The application of remote sensor technology to assist the recovery of rare and endangered species. *International Journal of High Performance Computing Applications*, *16*(3), 315-324.

Bose, P., Morin, P., Stojmenovic, I., & Urrutia, J. (2001). Routing with guaranteed delivery in ad hoc wireless networks. *Wireless Networks*, *7*(6), 609–616.

Constantine, L. L., & Lockwood, L. A. D. (1999). *Software for use: A practical guide to the essential models and methods of usage-centered design*. Reading, MA: Addison-Wesley.

Fortune, S. J. (1987). A sweepline algorithm for Voronoi diagrams. *Algorithmica*, *2*, 153-174.

Nagar, N., & Biagioni, E. S. (2002). Open issues in routing techniques in ad hoc wireless sensor networks. In *Proceedings of the International Conference on Parallel and Distributed Processing Techniques and Applications (PDPTA)*, Las Vegas, NV (Vol. 4, pp. 1867-1873). CSREA Press.

Preparata, F. P., & Shamos, M. I. (1985). *Computational geometry: An introduction*. New York: Springer-Verlag.

Rosson, M. B., & John, M. C. (2002). *Usability engineering: Scenario-based development of human-computer interaction*. UK: Academic Press.

Thiessen, A. H., & Alter, J. C. (1911). Climatological data for July, 1911: District no. 10, Great Basin. *Monthly Weather Review*, 1082-1089.

Chapter XIII

Towards a Global Real-Time Enterprise

Peter Ibach, Humboldt University Berlin, Germany
Miroslaw Malek, Humbolt University Berlin, Germany
Gerrit Tamm, University of Applied Sciences Erfurt, Germany

Abstract

Frictionless interoperation of business processes even across enterprise boundaries, complete up-to-date view of the overall status, and full remote control over the business parameters for individuals in charge — this is the holy grail of a "global real-time enterprise". Yet a vision, a number of enabling technologies brought us closer to accomplishing the challenges: sensing the position of mobile objects and processes status, distributing the status information with "zero latency," discovering it according to specific demands across organization boundaries, providing and securing uniform service-oriented access to all kinds of entities ranging from smart items to business processes, and aggregating the overwhelming variety of elementary services to form high-value composite services. In this chapter, we overview the enabling technologies that drive the development and further discuss market factors, security and privacy concerns, and standardization processes that have to be considered. Then we propose our SEMALON approach, the SEMAntic

LOcation Network, intended as a basic infrastructure for discovery and composition of location-based services. Finally we describe our experiences from a case study implementation, the NOMADS Campus, which is a distributed spatial information system for our campus at Humboldt University, Berlin.

Introduction

The "Internet of things" (Gershenfeld, Krikorian, & Cohen, 2004) with billions and soon trillions of seamlessly interconnected devices is about to take over, and we expect for the next years a literally exploding number of services that not only provide information about physical objects, originating from Web pages, database entries, or sensors, but also allow to trigger activities and control the objects by some actuators. To support processes in the physical world by information technology, a location-based mapping that connects physical objects and their correlated information is required. Spatial interrelationship is what will put mobile users in the position to navigate through the growing complexity and dynamics of physical and informational spaces. Through the spatial organization of physical and informational objects, virtual and real spaces will tightly interconnect.

The Vision: A Global Real-Time Enterprise

In such a ubiquitous computing scenario, a "global real-time enterprise" envisions that positions and other status information of all objects and corresponding processes can be monitored and controlled in real-time — both, internally as well as across enterprise boundaries. Clearly, a number of prerequisites have to be satisfied, including enabling technologies as well as economic regulations and open standards. Actual market trends, global competition, integration requirements, and standardization in information technology are driving more and more enterprises to adopt their coordination model. The organizational structures should be extremely flexible and enable the integration of suppliers and customers processes. Real-time enterprises supply information just in time to customers, suppliers, employees, and partners, and integrate processes, systems, and media over organisational boundaries. Emerging technologies, network economics, and global standards are the main accelerators for the proliferation of real-time enterprises. Information systems of real-time enterprises have to support permanent change of processes, data formats, and interface specifications.

The vision of a global real-time enterprise with end-to-end dynamic value Webs becomes a reality. All processes and information flow within the enterprise as well as external processes involving customers, suppliers, and partners will be instantaneously synchronized at all enterprise systems. Each service is transparent and can be managed with an IT-service-catalog. When a new Web-based service is available in the catalog, billing services and customer service are automatically added, and the service can be used right from the moment that it was added to the catalog. Collaboration within real-time enterprises based on RFID and the electronic product code will extremely reduce the transaction costs. Outdoor and indoor positioning systems based on Internet-driven standardization (initiatives around XML and Web services) make innovative business models possible.

Enabling technologies, first to mention among them are XML, RFID, and the EPC Network, seamless positioning technologies, and open service oriented architectures, develop at exponential pace and changing current information and business situation dramatically.

Current Applications/Architectures and their Limitations

Although there are numerous proprietary applications that deal very well with location information, interoperability of location information across application boundaries in a standardized open format over the Internet is still to be completed. Considering location semantics and mobility, the situation is even worse.

Present location-based services (LBS) are mostly bound to a specific technology reflecting the preferences of the service provider. Figure 1 shows two exemplary applications popular in the German LBS market: (1) The Jamba Finder allows cell phone users to look for objects nearby, for example, public buildings, fuel stations, cinemas, or restaurants. (2) Navigation systems as deployed in cars or independently usable via GPS equipped PDAs enjoy rapidly growing popularity.

Typically, proprietary protocols and interfaces are employed in these LBS applications to aggregate the different system components for positioning, networking, content, or payment services. In many cases, these components are glued together to form a monolithic and inflexible system. If such a system has to be adapted to new conditions, it very likely requires entire reengineering.

Let us consider a position-sensing service, for example, a satellite-based GPS. If a mobile device moves from outdoor to indoor environments, the signal will likely become unavailable and position sensing will fail. Without the location information expected from this subservice, composite services depending on it will become unavailable as well. To arrive at seamless operation, on-the-fly switchover to an alternative position-sensing service using a different technology is required. To choose from multiple possible position-sensing services, the decision has to consider service availability, quality of service properties, and costs.

Figure 1. Examples of current LBS value chains with participating service providers; multiple barriers hamper flexible service composition

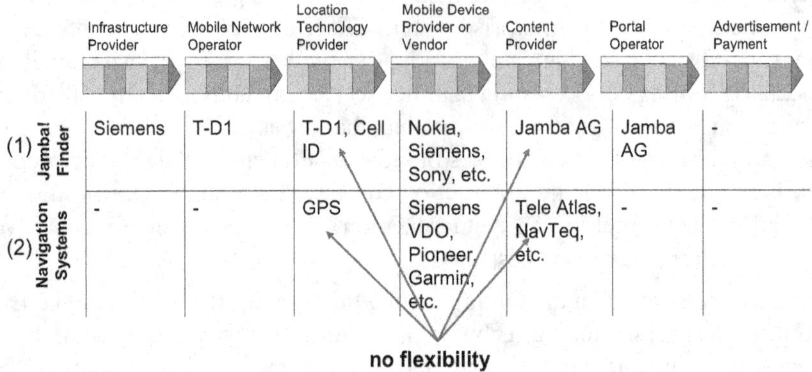

In the near future, most mobile and wearable devices are expected to have multiple available position-sensing technologies such as GPS, GSM, WLAN, and Bluetooth. Nevertheless, new technologies, like at present WiMax or RFID, are emerging. Thus, hardware devices and software components, their interfaces and architecture, have to be able to deal with changing conditions. Thus, adaptivity, the ability to cope with continuously-changing conditions, is crucial to make mobile location-based services highly available and overall successful.

Lots of research has focused on location-based services combining the concept of location-aware computing with distributed geographic information services based on Internet standards (Hazas, Scott, & Krumm, 2004; Hodes, 2003; Peng & Tsou, 2004; Rao & Minakakis, 2003; Reichenbacher, 2004). Unfortunately, a number of specific interoperability barriers exist in current LBS value chains, resulting in the "Multi-X Problem":

- Multiple connection technologies (GSM, UMTS, WLAN, Bluetooth, …)
- Multiple location technologies (GPS, Cell-ID, WLAN, Bluetooth, RFID, …)
- Multiple hardware, software, and service providers
- Multiple operating systems, programming languages, and system architectures
- Multiple application-specific ontologies describing location semantics
- Multiple content depending on specific location and granularity demands

Flexible service composition requires interoperability despite increasing multiplicity. Web Service standards seem promising to solve this challenging problem.

Enabling Technologies

Location-based services have been hyped as the "killer application" during the Internet bubble, whereas true market developments could not accomplish the exaggerated expectations. But with the advances of mobile devices, position sensing, and wireless connectivity, the market for Location-based Services is rapidly developing, particularly in the field of geographic, telematic, touristic, and logistic information systems.

Seamless Outdoor and Indoor Positioning Based on Commodity Communication Standards

Wireless emergency services require the ability to pinpoint the location of a cell phone placing an emergency call, for example, for firebrigade, ambulance, or police. E911 Phase II legislation in the U.S. requires cell phone companies to be able to locate handsets within 150 meters by 2006. E112 initiatives in Europe are similar.

Positioning techniques now are maturing to provide accurate positioning in outdoor and indoor environments at affordable cost, small size, and low power consumption. Hamerhead, for example, is a single chip assisted GPS solution at €6.50 and sufficiently sensitive that it works in most indoor environments. Infineon expects a market of more than 700 million mobile phones to be sold in 2008 where 25% of those will be equipped with A-GPS functionality.

Commodity mobile devices, such as laptops, PDAs, and cell phones can sense their position even without extra GPS receivers. Intel's PlaceLab project therefore has mapped the positions of millions of existing GSM, WLAN, or Bluetooth base stations all over the world. Their experiments in the greater Seattle area indicate 20 to 40 meter median accuracy and close to 100% coverage exploiting "radio beacons in the wild" (LaMarca et al., 2003).

At Humboldt University, Berlin we developed a WLAN positioning system called MagicMap that can perform software-only positioning within a few meters average deviation both outdoors as well as indoors (Ibach, Hübner, & Schweigert, 2004a; Ibach et al., 2005a). Related wireless positioning systems (WPS) have recently been released by companies such as Skyhook, Newbury Networks, or Cisco.[1] These new positioning techniques improve traditional satellite-based or telco-centered localization in many practical scenarios and are capable to bootstrap the broad adoption of location-aware computing.

Open Service-Oriented Computing and Web services

Enterprise applications were initially developed on closed, homogeneous mainframe architectures. In the explosively growing heterogeneous landscape of IT systems in the 1980s and '90s, integration of intra- and inter-company business processes became one of the most important and most cost-intensive tasks of the IT economy. Due to missing or non-transparent standards, many enterprises pursued integration by extremely expensive ad hoc solutions. With the spreading of the Internet and the increasing importance of electronic business, open Internet-oriented solutions have emerged. Enterprise-internal monolithic software was broken into smaller, autonomous, and flexible components. This enabled the access to services not only enterprise-internally, but along the whole value chain to suppliers, distributors, and customers. We characterize this observation as a shift from rigid systems to flexible service-oriented architectures.

In service-oriented computing, resources are accessed via services. Services expose well specified interfaces and are the basic building blocks for flexible and efficient composition of more complex applications. The fundamental concept is the composition of systems by extensive reuse of commodity software/hardware components. Many approaches share this very general concept of compositionality (see Figure 2).

However, a number of differences, for example, in wording, perception, implementation, and practical use, are indicating advantages of the service-oriented paradigm

Figure 2. Compositional architectures play an increasingly important role in value chains due to improved possibilities of interoperability, integration, composability, flexibility, reusability and thus increased efficiency at reduced total cost of operation

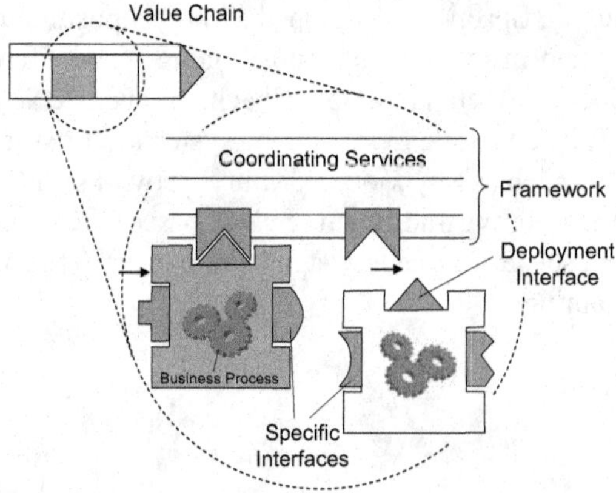

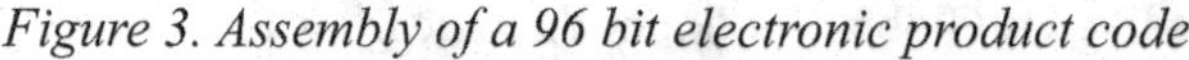

Figure 3. Assembly of a 96 bit electronic product code

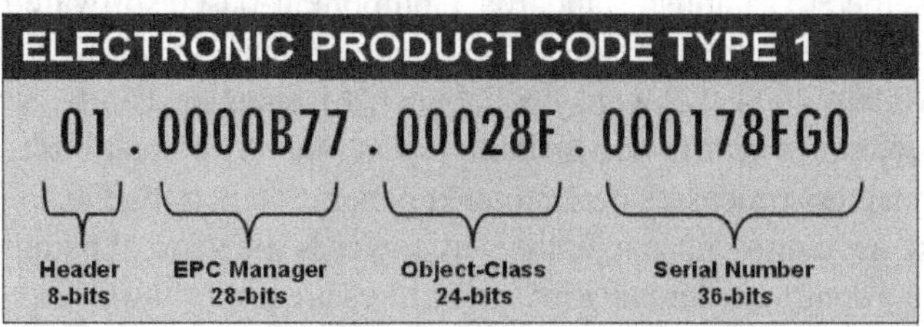

over previous approaches that were focusing on components, objects, modules, or other compositional entities. At the forefront, Web services and grid technologies are attracting a lot of attention accompanied by mixed opinions whether the expectations in reusability, composability, flexibility, maintainability, and return on investment that previous approaches have struggled with can finally be accomplished. See, for example, Erl (2004) and Linthicum (2003) for the growing importance of Web Services in enterprise application integration, and Bloomberg and Schmelzer (2002) and Gershenfeld et al. (2004) for a detailed discussion of pros and cons comparing Web Services to preceding concepts like CORBA. Commonly, the following advantages are attributed to Web Services (still waiting for further empirical inspection):

- Improved degree of interoperability and flexibility (barrier-free computing), across protocols, interfaces, programming languages, devices, connection lines, operation systems, platforms, enterprise boundaries, vendors, and service providers, through loose coupling based on the eXtensible Markup Language (XML)
- Service aggregation using choreography languages supports "two-stage programming" including flow control, exception handling, and transactional processing
- Integrated directory services such as UDDI or WS-Discovery
- Enhanced protocols for propagation, discovery, and invocation of "lightweight" services for embedded devices with limited processing and communication capacity in ad hoc networks
- Asynchronous dependable messaging and security and privacy support for identification, authorization, access control, and secure data transmissions

Web services are intended to facilitate the application-to-application interaction extending established Internet technologies. Thereby Web services and grid concepts are converging, guided by the open grid services architecture (OGSA). Its goal is to overcome the two predominant challenges at the same time: uniform access to services *and* processing resources.

Web services and grid toolkits like the Globus Toolkit or the Emerging Technology Toolkit have helped to establish standards. Component-based software for embedded systems (Müller, Stich, & Zeidler, 2001) and lightweight services (Milanovic, Richling, & Malek, 2004; Schwan, Poellabauer, Eisenhauer, Pande, & Pu, 2002) expanded the domain to span from distributed client-server applications and globally networked e-business processes down to next generation heterogeneous embedded systems. These developments paved the way towards the general paradigm of service-oriented computing where all kinds of entities are providing, using, searching, or mediating services while efficiently exploiting available resources. Driving the widespread acceptance of the service-oriented paradigm, Location-based Services might reveal the enormous economic potential of dynamic value Webs in mobile business (Ibach, Tamm, & Horbank, 2005b).

RFID and the EPC Network

Automatic object identification is a fundamental requirement for efficient supply chain management and usually solved by labeling objects with a bar code. However, bar code labels are using line-of-sight technology, that is, a scanner has to see the bar code to read it. Using radio frequency identification (RFID), in contrast, labels can be read via radio communication as long as they are within the range of a reader.

With passive labels that derive their energy from the reader's RF signal, a distance of 5 cm up to 10 m is achievable, depending on physical characteristics comprising used antennas and wavelength. RFID labels supporting collision-free communication protocols provide further significant advantage over conventional labels: They allow for bulk readouts and enable trolley or container scanning in a single pass. Current anti-collision RFID chips are approaching prices below $0.05 in mass production, making it affordable to label almost any commercial item electronically. Although RFID tags probably will never replace bar code labels completely, apparently, the broad use of RFID technology in supply chain management is forthcoming.

The Electronic Product Code

As they can be read out through optical barriers, RFID chips enable the automatic collection of huge amounts of data at various locations in a supply chain. Coming along with the RFID technology, a new numbering scheme to label items was developed.

The identification number follows the electronic product code (EPC) standard (Harrison, 2003). It is designed to uniquely identify commercial goods. Each EPC consists of three parts: (1) a number identifying the manufacturer, (2) a number for the product type, plus (3) a serial number for each individual item (see Figure 3).

While the EPC manager and the object class represent the same information as stored in traditional European article numbers (EAN), the serial number adds item-level granularity to product numbering. This allows for identifying each object individually, and is ideal for using it as a primary key and for integrating data about objects from various databases.

The EPC Network

The standardized Electronic Product Code that uniquely identifies each object is stored on the object's RFID tag. Some applications would certainly benefit from additional information directly stored on the object's tag, for example, prize, size, weight, place of origin, or date of expiration. However, capacity for additional information is very limited. Current chips in the range of $0.05 comprise a storage capacity of typical 128 bits. Of course there are further reasons, for example, availability and security issues, why certain pieces of information should not be stored on the object's tag. Just imagine, for example, information about transport damage or about the object's actual location. Therefore, the EPC network provides the infrastructure to maintain such additional product-related information. Thus, considerable information about each individual item can be stored, retrieved, and secured by appropriate access control facilities.

Data Discovery within the EPC Network

Since each EPC is globally unique, it can be used as a key for database lookup. For discovery of EPC-related data, the EPC Network provides a number of services that seamlessly integrate into Internet discovery standards: At first, the object naming service (ONS) is employed to retrieve data resources related to a specific EPC. The ONS returns the different data resources containing information about the specific object, whereby each resource is denoted by a uniform recourse name (URN). For each URN, the universal naming service (UNS) resolves the URLs, describing the physical locations of the data. Multiple locations are feasible, since the same data can be stored at different places. Finally, a URL is translated into an IP address by the DNS to arrive at an EPC information service (EPCIS) endpoint that manages the access to the designated data. The architecture is fully distributed, that is, requests to ONS, UNS, or DNS are delegated to nearby servers while appropriate caching and synchronization protocols reduce network traffic and response times.

Using this discovery mechanism, data related to an EPC can be located. Usually, the URL of at least the EPC information service of the product manufacturer is expected to be returned when retrieving information via an object's EPC. However, to improve supply chain efficiency, it is intended that various suppliers, distributors, retailers, contractors taking care of logistics, and other partners within a supply chain gather information and make it available by providing additional EPC information services. Companies may maintain their EPC information services on their own or delegate them to outsourcing partners.

The Physical Markup Language (PML) has been specified to standardize those pieces of information and to make them machine understandable and interchangeable. PML is XML-based whereby special conventions to express spatio-temporal annotations or containment information have been predefined by the Auto-ID Center. However, PML is designed to be expandable.

As a tagged item moves, usually because of some logistics processes, it passes several instances within the supply chain. Each instance might gather additional information about the item. For example, a retailer may want to store the time at which a certain product has arrived at his storehouse.

Due to this, more than one EPC information service will provide information about an object as it moves through the supply chain. In order to locate these diverse EPC information services, a dynamic approach is needed.

In "EPC Information Service — Data Model and Queries" by the Auto-ID Center (Harrison, 2003) two possible ways of handling that issue have been suggested. One solution is to organize EPCIS, holding information about a certain EPC, in a double-linked list. Each EPCIS points to its predecessor as well as to its successor

Figure 4. Players in the supply chain offer product information via individual information services (EPCIS); the ONS and the EPC discovery service help to locate services providing information related to a specific object

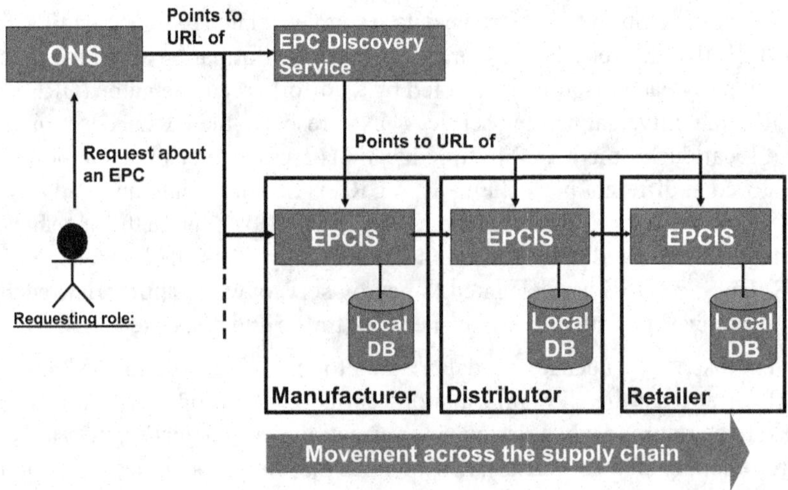

in the supply chain. To retrieve the most recent information about an object, each instance in the list has to be consulted for the successor until the list's end is reached. However, this approach only works as long as all of the participating EPCIS are available. Moreover, due to the expected inefficiency, alternatively a central service has been investigated. This central service holds a list of all EPCIS that are referring to an EPC. Once an EPCIS provides information related to an EPC, it has to register at this central service. VeriSign has announced an initiative to establish such a kind of service, called EPC discovery service. An overview of the mentioned services and how they are organized in the EPC Network is given in Figure 4.

Information Economy

Dynamic Value Webs

Web services appear promising to facilitate interoperability and enable dynamic value Webs, the on-demand aggregation of services even across enterprise boundaries. This is a prerequisite when striving for a global real-time enterprise. A lot of work on service-oriented computing refers to a vision that enables users to formulate abstract requirements, which are then performed by adaptive, self-configuring services (Milanovic & Malek, 2005). This in particular implies services that are able to find and to call other services automatically. Approaching this vision, software development based on Web service standards is expected to exhibit advantages over classical software development. However, experiences have shown that this vision of future Web services is still difficult to realize. As yet, the volume of transactions in the Web service market has by far not reached the expected level. Information asymmetries and uncertainties among suppliers, aggregators, and potential customers are the predominant causes for the modest development and enforcement of Web services (Tamm & Wuensche, 2003).

This chapter investigates the economic impact of service-oriented architectures for building dynamic value Webs in mobile environments using adaptive location-based services. It addresses the following three predominant difficulties: (1) service adaptivity to changing conditions in mobile environments, (2) interoperability including higher levels of semantics, and (3) assuring trustworthiness to all affected parties. Web services are modular self-describing software components (Alonso, Casati, Kuno, & Machiraju, 2004). Due to their standardization they may be used individually or may be aggregated to software bundles. Web services standards facilitate enterprise application integration (EAI), offer new ways of interconnecting both consumer and business partners, and provide a comprehensive framework to enable the evolution of dynamic value Webs.

Web services are digital goods which can be aggregated to dynamic value Webs on the basis of a service-oriented architecture. Compared to physical products, Web services are thus very flexible. A fast growing market for Web services was forecast. Unfortunately, the market for Web service has so far not lived up to the predicted expectations. Possible reasons for this relatively slow adoption may originate from the different perceived risks of suppliers and customers, which often rise from a lack of experience and knowledge about Web services. Suppliers' problems arise regarding configuration, display, and communication of Web services, contract, and escalation management (Tamm et al., 2003). Also, pricing, billing, and liability issues remain to be a problem. However, a major problem is that potential customers do not know where their data is saved, what is done with it, how stable the service is, and which of the promised privacy properties it keeps.

The following section uses information economics as a methodical approach for the scientific analysis of the information problems described above and for the development of strategies to overcome these problems. The theory of information economics is part of the new institutional economics. It is based on the idea of classifying the detectability of the quality of a product on the basis of the different consequences of information asymmetries. According to that, several strategies will be developed, aiming at a reduction of the classified types of uncertainties in the context of quality evaluation. The characteristics of the mobile service bundle are attributed to different information economics-based types. Then, the strategies recommended shall be deployed in order to facilitate the quality evaluation and the perception of the characteristics of the mobile service bundle. The following section describes the fatal consequences likely to occur if the actors on the mobile service market do not succeed in reducing information asymmetries.

Potential users equipped with only little experience and knowledge about the mobile service model lack methods to assess the quality of mobile services supplied. The lack of transparency perceived with regard to the quality of the performance characteristics of the mobile services bundle and the providers of a mobile services, as well as according to partners of the providers, leads to an information asymmetry on the demand side, and thus to the small number of contracts placed.

The information asymmetries prevailing between the supply and the demand side do not only cause high transaction costs, but can ultimately even result in a complete market failure.

Figure 5 relates and summarizes the main causes to the emergence of information asymmetries on the Web service market (Tamm et al., 2003).

Markets vs. Hierarchies

Web services use the infrastructure of electronic networks like the Internet, which introduces new combinations of business characteristics described as Internet economy

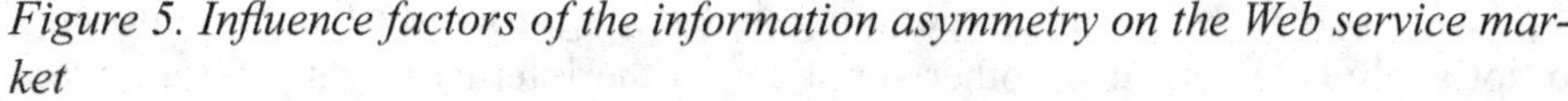

Figure 5. Influence factors of the information asymmetry on the Web service market

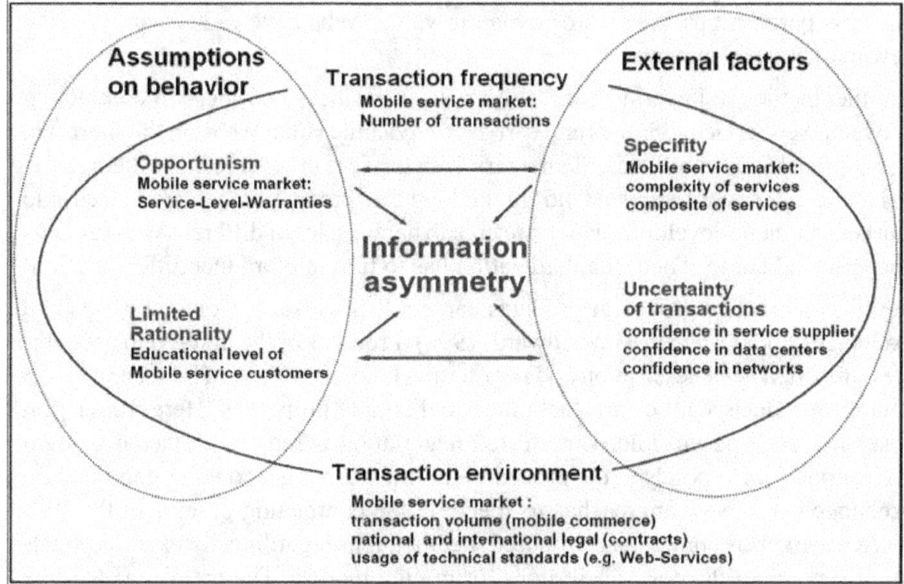

(Picot, 2004). Most differences compared to the "old economy" are advantages in the reduction of transaction costs. Malone, Yates, and Benjamin characterize the results of using new technologies in economic processes: "By reducing the costs of coordination, information technology will lead to an overall shift toward proportionately more use of markets — rather than hierarchies — to coordinate economic activity" (Malone, Yates, & Benjamin, 1997, p. 484).

Most companies on the Internet concentrate on their core competencies for specified services. That leads to a strong division of labor which creates learning-curve effects and increasing economies of scale and scope. Compared with physical markets, a Web service aggregator for dynamic value Webs faces relatively low search expenses, a better market transparency on the Internet, and moderate purchasing costs of elementary Web services. It will therefore outsource a lot and set its boundaries very tight.

Transaction costs in electronic markets like the Internet are lower than in physical markets. Nevertheless, providers of digital goods, especially suppliers of value Webs, must cope with the low willingness to pay for their products. Therefore, the Web service supplier has to consider strategies to decrease the transaction costs on the supply side. An important aspect of lowering transaction costs is the presence of trust between business partners. Trust develops in partnerships over a long period of time in which the partners are content with the quality of supplied products as well as prices. Costs for searching, negotiating, integrating, and especially monitoring do not apply here. However, other suppliers on the Internet might offer a better quality or a better price for the same elementary Web service. Hence, even in long business partnerships, carriers of dynamic value Webs have to constantly watch new market developments.

Another method of lowering transaction costs is the increased speed of contracting between Web service suppliers and carriers of dynamic value Webs. In the short run, one approach is to standardize elementary Web services in order to make them easier to handle and easier to understand. In the long run, complex automated electronic markets might be developed which are able to handle a lot of different Web services very fast and cheap. Then, standardization has to turn into product differentiation.

In this context, two groups of products can be distinguished: Contract goods and exchange goods (Alchian & Woodward, 1998). Products of the first group are complex and often need description and negotiation before purchase. The second group contains products with clearly delimited and simple properties. Here transaction costs are lower because no complicated negotiation is required. Standardizing a Web service corresponds to the procedure of transforming a contract good into an exchange good. New approaches to speed up the contracting process in the Web service market are contractually assured specifications regarding, for example, quality of service levels, policy assertions, or pricing models. The premise is that the properties of services are described, fixed, and understood by all interacting parties to build up dynamic value Webs. Following, we describe the principle advantages that Web service standards provide for service coordination and composition and investigate the applicability to set up adaptive location-based services.

The Need for Standards

Standardization of IT services and harmonization of the IT landscape are the main challenges in IT business today. From the economic perspective, IT services have to be described in a transparent and comparable way. Customers of IT suppliers expect increasing productivity, return on investment, and additional benefit by using information technology. IT services which support governmental and commercial business processes, have to be monitored including key performance indicators (efficiency) and key goal indicators (effectiveness). From the technological perspective, standards (e.g., XML, Web services) have to be developed and widely accepted in specific branches. Based on such standard software modules, interoperable IT architectures can be established. Most of the available spatial information is locked in non-standard systems, useless for interoperable architectures and real-time business process integration.

The Open Geospatial Consortium (OGC) develops, discusses, and releases technological standards for geospatial information systems. The OGC is a global industry consortium that envisions a world in which everyone benefits from geographic information and services made available across any network, application, or platform (Reed, 2005). Inherent in this vision is the requirement for standardization in geospatial technology and services. In this chapter we describe the current OGC standards based on Web service technology.

Geography Markup Language

The Geography Markup Language is one of the most important standards for geospatial information systems. Geography Markup Language is an XML grammar written in XML schema for modeling, transport, and storage of geographic information. GML provides a variety of objects for describing geography including features, coordinate reference systems, geometry, topology, time, units of measure, and generalized values.

The main characteristics of GML are features. A geographic feature is "an abstraction of a real world phenomenon; it is a geographic feature if it is associated with a location relative to the Earth" (Cox, Daisey, Lake, Portele, & Whiteside, 2005, p. xviii). Features are geographical characteristics of objects (e.g., landscapes, cities). Each feature includes geometrical (e.g., point, circle, polygon) and non-geometrical characteristics. Both types can be used optionally. A digital representation of the real world can be thought of as a set of features. The state of a feature is defined by a set of properties, where each property can be thought of as a triple (name, type, value). The number of properties a feature may have, together with their names and types, are determined by its type definition.

Geographic features in GML include coverages and observations as subtypes. Coverage is a sub-type of feature that has a coverage function with a spatial domain and a value set range of homogeneous two to *n*-dimensional tuples. A coverage can represent one feature or a collection of features. An observation models the act of observing, often with a camera, a person, or some form of instrument. An observation is considered to be a GML feature with a time at which the observation took place, and with a value for the observation. A reference system provides a scale of measurement for assigning values to a location, time, or other descriptive quantity or quality. A coordinate reference system consists of a set of coordinate system axes that is related to the earth through a date that defines the size and shape of the earth. Geometries in GML indicate the coordinate reference system in which their measurements have been made. The parent geometry element of a geometric complex or geometric aggregate makes this indication for its constituent geometries. A temporal reference system provides standard units for measuring time and describing temporal length or duration. A measure dictionary provides definitions of physical quantities, such as length, temperature, and pressure, and of conversions between different dictionary systems.

Figure 6 illustrates the advantages of GML. Existing services (e.g., map services) and additional data (e.g., length of road or number of lanes) can be integrated. By the usage of XML schema, existing data can be proofed and evaluated.

Open Geospatial Services

OGC Web Services Common Specification

The OGC Web services common specification (OWS) (Whiteside, 2005) specifies many of the aspects that are, or should be, common to all or multiple OWS interface implementation specifications. Those specifications currently include the Web map service (WMS), Web feature service (WFS), Web coverage service (WCS), and catalog service (CAT). These common aspects include: operation request and response contents; parameters included in operation requests and responses; and encoding of operation requests and responses. The OWS specification is a normative reference for all subsets of OWS. OWS describes common specifications for the following topics:

- Normative references
- Terms and definitions

Figure 6. GML example describing "Highway between Berlin and Hamburg"

```
<Road id="R456">
    <description> Highway between Berlin and Hamburg</description>
    <name>A 24</name>
    <nLanes>4</nLanes>
    <surfaceTreatment>bitumen</surfaceTreatment>
    <destination xlink:href="http://some.big.org/places/G6421,, />
    <pavement>
    <Polygon> ... </Polygon>
    </pavement>
    <centreLine>  <Curve> ... </Curve> </centreLine>
</Road>
```

- Conventions
- GetCapabilities operation
- Exception reports
- All operations except GetCapabilities, minimum abilities
- operation parameters
- Operation request and response encoding
- Guidance for OWS implementation specifications
- XML schemas

In the following sections we will give an insight into WMS and WFS.

OGC Web Map Service

OGC Web map service (WMS) (Sonnet, 2005) specifies how individual map servers describe and provide their map content. Since December, 2005, WMS is available as ISO 19128 standard.

WMS provides the operations GetCapabilities, GetMap, and GetFeatureInfo. WMS supports the just-in-time creation and presentation of maps based on personal requirements. With WMS it is possible to combine several different map information sources, which are remote and heterogeneous, to a specific and individual map information service. The present context specification states how a specific grouping of one or more maps from one or more map servers can be described in a portable, platform-independent format for storage in a repository or for transmission between clients. The WMS standard addresses basic Web computing, image access, display, and manipulation capabilities. It specifies the request and response protocols for Web-based client/mapserver interactions. Web mapping refers, at a minimum, to the following actions (McKee & Kottman, 2003):

- A client makes requests to one or more catalog servers to discover URIs containing desired information
- Catalog servers return URLs and also information about methods by which the discovered information at each URL can be accessed
- The client locates one or more servers containing the desired information, using OGC's catalog server technology, and invokes them simultaneously
- As directed by the client, each map server accesses the information requested from it, and renders it suitable for displaying one or more layers in a map composed of many layers. Map servers provide the display-ready information to the client, which then display it.

The description of WMS can be realized with Web map context documents. A context document includes information about the server providing layer in the overall map, the bounding box, and map projection shared by all the maps, sufficient operational metadata for client software to reproduce the map, and ancillary metadata used to annotate or describe the maps and their provenance for the benefit of human viewers. A context document is structured using eXtensible Markup Language (XML). XML schema is used for the validation of WMS context documents.

OGC Web Feature Service

In addition to the WMS, the OGC Web feature service (Vretanos, 2005) allows users to define and model personalized views on geospatial data and to save these views as features. By using Geography Markup Language (GML) for OGC Web feature service geospatial data can be recovered and updated. The requirements for a Web feature service are:

1. The interfaces must be defined in XML.
2. GML must be used to express features within the interface.
3. At a minimum a WFS must be able to present features using GML.
4. The predicate or filter language will be defined in XML and be derived from CQL as defined in the OpenGIS catalogue interface implementation specification.
5. The datastore used to store geographic features should be opaque to client applications and their only view of the data should be through the WFS interface. The use of a subset of XPath expressions for referencing properties.

OGC Web feature service (WFS) defines interfaces for data access and manipulation operations on geographic features using HTTP as the distributed computing platform and XML for data description. Via these interfaces, a Web user or service can combine, use, and manage geographical data by invoking the following WFS operations on geographic features and elements:

- Create a new feature instance
- Delete a feature instance
- Update a feature instance
- Lock a feature instance

Get or query features based on spatial and non-spatial constraints Web feature service allows a client to request spatial data, not a map, from a service. The spatial data is encoded in the GML. The WFS specifies interfaces that unambiguously model the behavior of feature identifiers. When a map layer (or "feature collection") contains multiple identical features, when features move, and/or when it is possible to access many different maps, it is sometimes necessary to have "feature identifiers" that help identify a particular feature in different maps as being the same feature. Different software systems with different feature identification approaches need a way to communicate such information, and that is what this specification will provide. WFS also specify common interfaces for communication about relationships between features. WFS include functions for the exchange of features and data of features. The specification of WFS describes in detail the following functions:

1. **GetCapabilities:** describes the characteristics (functions, services) of a WFS. Respond and request data are based on XML
2. **DescribeFeatureType:** describes meta data of WFS structure
3. **GetFeature:** requests feature data from the WFS
4. **Transaction:** adds, changes, and deletes data
5. **LockFeature:** locks feature data to ensure consistency if used concurrent to other requests

OGC Web Coverage Service

The Web coverage service (WCS) (Evans, 2003) provides access to detailed information about the geospatial data. With WCS, users of the geospatial data can get detailed information about requirements for client-site rendering, coverage of multi-geospatial data sources and obligatory transformation rules.

The Web coverage service describes the geospatial data and supports users with detailed descriptions of the geospatial data source. With this additional information, users of the geospatial data are able to create complex queries against the geospatial data sources. Instead of requesting graphical maps, users of the WCS can request the original geospatial data source with original semantics. Based on the original geospatial data, users of the WCS are very flexible to use the data for transformation, based on time and space criteria.

The Web coverage service provides the operations GetCapabilities, GetCoverage and DescribeCoverage. With the GetCapabilities operation, users get a XML-document, which includes a main description of the service. The XML-document also describes the data source from which the user can request coverage. It is possible to run the GetCapabilities operation once and store the XML-document for future reuse in single or multiple sessions. When the GetCapabilities operation is not able to respond with the XML-description document, an alternative source (e.g. image database) can be offered. With the DescribeCoverage operation, users can request a complete description of one or more coverages served by a selected WCS server.

With the GetCoverage operation, users request a single coverage layer of the geospatial data (e.g., sliced in time, elevation, or range components).

SEMALON — the SEMAntic LOcation Network

As part of *NOMADS*, *N*etworks *o*f *M*obile *A*daptive *D*ependable *S*ystems (Malek, 2003; Malek, 2004), which is a project for building a comprehensive service-oriented framework for ubiquitous computing, we are developing the *Sema*ntic *Lo*cation *N*etwork (*SEMALON*) based on open Web Services standards. In SEMALON, all resources are uniformly accessed via services. Services expose interfaces that can be semantically interpreted using ontologies. Multiple layers contain objects, their locations, and associated services (see Figure 7). Physical resources might be stationary, such as streets and buildings, or mobile, such as mobile devices or RFID-tagged items. Informational resources comprise Internet pages, objects in databases, and services.

Spatial Semantics

For semantic location determination, we distinguish the following LBS classes:

- Location-based services can be provided by some immobile unit, for example, a museum or a botanical garden. Typically, such immobile units provide **stationary LBS** which are fixed to a certain location. A common problem is to semantically detect the location, and find or filter stationary services related to that location. For example, a user's movement in a museum can tell that he might be interested in information about a specific exhibition object (e.g., he moves to that object and then, while looking at it stops moving for some seconds). A location-aware device could then request the appropriate service.
- Likewise, some immobile units may provide **general LBS** that are location-independently accessible but require a location parameter. Examples are a regional weather forecasting service or a service that processes queries like "where is the next subway station?"
- Regarding **mobile LBS**, the location is a parameter describing the context of a mobile device. Imagine a user traveling with his laptop: If the laptop recognized the availability of a specific LAN connection, it could figure out where

Figure 7. SEMALON — a globally scalable semantic network of location-based services

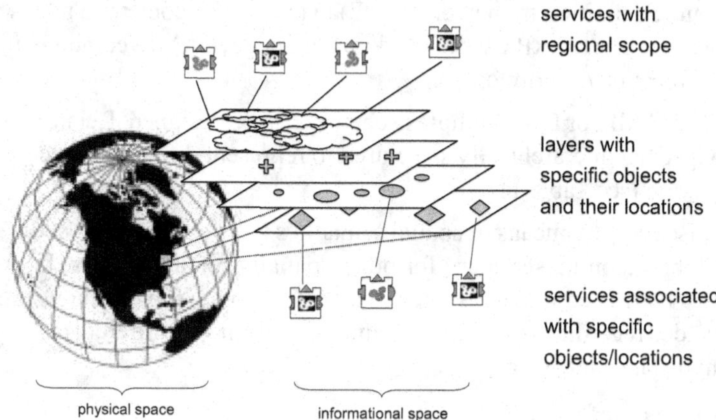

it is located (e.g., in the user's office) and adapt its behavior (e.g., synchronize certain files).

- Finally, **interdependent LBS** require multiple related location parameters, for example, a people-finding service that guides mobile users to meet at some specific place.

All these cases demand appropriate semantic interpretation of location. To accomplish semantic interoperability, one has to agree on suitable ontologies which define objects and relations for each specific application area.

Spatial Ontologies

Typically, locations are represented by geographic coordinates. In common use is the projection according to the World Geographic System, 1984 (WGS84); other projections comprise Universal Transverse Mercator, Swissgrid, Gauss-Krüger-grid, or the military grid reference system, which can be interchangeably converted by software algorithms.

Going beyond bare geo-coordinates or free-form textual descriptions, spatial ontologies can be used to define objects and relations by means of spatial semantics. A widely-accepted ontology that models physical objects and their location is the Geography Markup Language (GML), standardized by the OpenGIS Consortium and used in the geographic information system (GIS). The Physical Markup Language (PML) of the EPC network, standardized by the Auto-ID Center, is intended for product classification, but also allows for spatio-temporal annotations for object tracking and supply chain management. The World Wide Web Consortium is extending the resource definition framework (RDF) to relate Web content to its associated physical location. The DARPA Agent Markup Language (DAML) combines multiple schemes for location description.

Using GML, DAML, or RDF, complex schemes can be designed. Related elements can be grouped and hierarchically structured to represent different aspects of location information (see Table 1).

Typically, discovery by means of spatial semantics is done describing some known objects and, based on those, query for other spatially-related objects. In previous examples we have used radial distance to a central point. Table 2 shows how this can be expanded regarding two- or three-dimensional objects, different prepositions, and custom distance measures.

Ontology Translation

In our approach, ontology translation is handled by dedicated ontology translation service (OTS) instances. Inputs are: source ontology instances, including a reference to the source ontology, and references to one or multiple target ontologies. It outputs the information translated into the requested target ontologies. Typically, ontology translation is pursued in three steps:

1. **Discovery:** manually, automatically, or semi-automatically defining the relations between ontologies
2. **Representation:** A language to represent the relations between the ontologies

Table 1. GML example describing the Sony Tower at Potsdamer Platz in Berlin, comprising address, surface area, and geo-coordinates

```
<exp:Building fid = "Sony Tower">                              ← name of the building
 <exp:noFloors>26</exp:noFloors>                               ← number of floors
 <exp:use>Commercial</exp:use>                                 ← commercial type of use
 <exp:surfaceArea>216700</exp:surfaceArea>                     ← surface area in m2
 <exp:frontsOn>Neue Potsdamer Straße </exp:frontsOn>           ← street
<gml:locationOf>
          ...                                                  ← geo-coordinates, in WGS84 standard
</gml:locationOf>
</exp:Building>
```

Table 2. Describing spatial relations between objects

Object	Preposition	Distance	Use Case Example: look up …
point	undirected	meters	… WLAN hot spots *within a radius of 50 meters*
	south	flying time	… holiday destinations *south* of your location
	undirected	walking time	… restaurants *within 5 minutes of walk*
polygon	undirected	driving time	… SOS-telephones *along* a highway
	west	driving time	… customs facilities *west* of the country's border
polyhedrons	undirected	boolean	… people *inside* a specific room
	undirected	boolean	… *adjacent* offices in a tower block
	below	walking time	… parking levels *below* the first floor

3. **Execution:** Changing instances of the source ontology to instances of target ontology

One approach for ontology translation is to provide an explicit *m*-*n* mapping for any given pair of *m* source to *n* target ontologies. This potentially achieves maximum translation quality, but the required number of mappings grows quadratically, that is, at $O(m \cdot n)$. At the other extreme, the *m*-1-*n* translation introduces an intermediate ontology into which all source ontologies are translated and from which all target ontologies are derived (see Figure 8). This minimizes the number of required mappings to linear size, $O(m+n)$, but for many cases, it results in unacceptable loss of information. Therefore, we pursue a hybrid approach, where the best path over a manageable number of intermediate ontologies is chosen.

If a suitable translation path can be found, the source information can be exploited, for example, to trigger certain activities. Imagine, for example, a user who wants his mobile phone to automatically activate the hands-free speaking system inside a car or mute when inside a theater. Usually, a cellular phone cannot tell from geo-coordinates, determined, for example, by a GPS signal or by its cell ID, that it is inside a theater. But if the location description contains information that allows deriving from given geo-coordinates that the location is a theater, belonging to the category <silent space>, the "mute feature" could be automated (see Figure 9).

Accordingly, the location <Prater>, a theater in Berlin, would need to indicate that it is a <theater> in the <places> scheme, which defines that a <theater> is a <silent space> (see Table 3). Nested ontology translations of such kind are a major challenge of the Semantic Web.

Figure 8. Ontology translation as a hybrid of m-n and m-1-n mapping

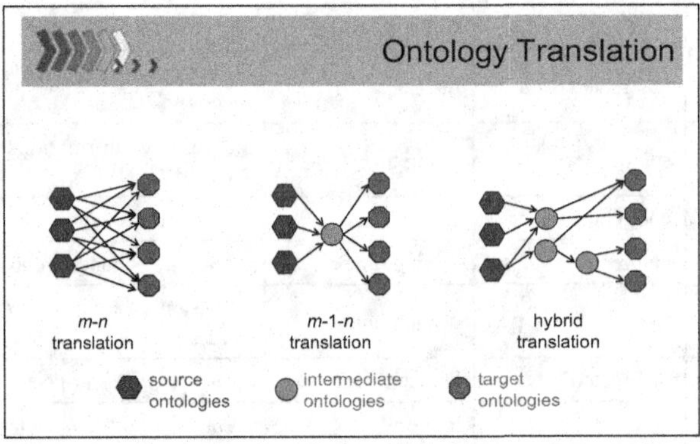

Adaptive Location-Based Services (ALBS)

From the perspective of a mobile user, the environment is ever-changing as he moves from one location to another. Adaptivity to location characteristics is essential for mobile service availability. In our approach, adaptivity of a composite location-based service — we call these services adaptive location-based services (ALBS) — is accomplished by choosing the appropriate chain of subservices for composition (see Figure 10). Prerequisites are general discoverability, interoperability, and composability of subservices through standardized communication protocols and directory services.

Lots of research has focused on location-based services combining the concept of location-aware computing with distributed geographic information services based on Internet standards (Hazas, Scott, & Krumm, 2004; Hodes, 2003; Peng & Tsou, 2003; Pinto, Boas, & José, 2003; Rao & Minakakis, 2003; Schiller & Voisard, 2004). In particular, the Open Geospatial Consortium (www.opengeospatial.org) is focusing on Web service standards for publishing, finding, and binding geospatial services.

In the Web services standard, interoperable communication is accomplished by exchanging XML data over HTTP. But Web services are not restricted to the WWW or a specific protocol. Rather, it is a promising solution for adaptive application synthesis in distributed, dynamically-changing environments. The notion of Web Services goes beyond prescribed client-server communication. Emerging standards for directory services such as UDDI (UDDI, 2005) or Web services choreography (BPEL4WS, 2005) allow for dynamic discovery of services and composition of multiple Web services to fully-fledged distributed applications.

Figure 9. Nested ontology translation from WGS84 geo-coordinates into the value <mute> in the <CellPhoneProfiles> ontology

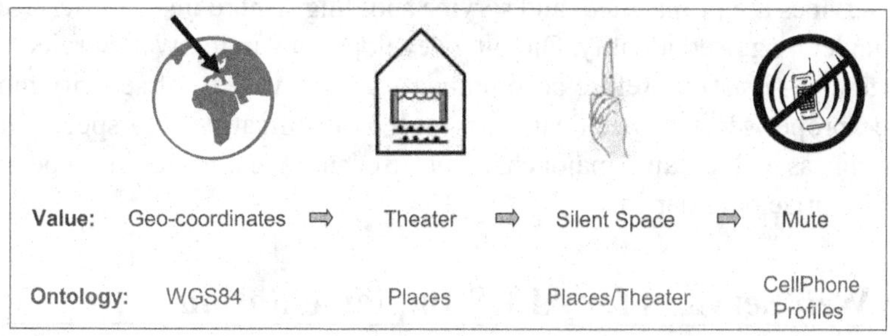

Table 3. Example RDF description of location <Prater>, a theater in Berlin, indication location semantics

```
<rdf:RDF xmlns:rdf="..."    xmlns:plc="..."     ← XML namespaces
  xmlns:geo="..." xmlns:scp="...">
  <plc:Places rdfID="...">                      ← place attributes
  <plc:category>theater</plc:category>          ← it is a theater
  </plc:Places>
  <scp:Scope rdfID="...">                       ← object's extent:
      <scp:type>undirected</scp:type>           ← radial distance of 20
      <scp:distance>20</scp:distance>           ← meters to
      <scp:metric>m</scp:metric>
  </scp:Scope>                                  ← the point with geo-coordinates:
  <geo:Point rdfID="...">                       ← Latitude: N52° 32.39'
      <geo:lat>52.539833</geo:lat>              ← Longitude: E13° 24.64'
      <geo:long>13.410666</geo:long>            ← Altitude: 91 meters above sea level (WGS84 standard)
      <geo:alt>91.000</geo:alt>
  </geo:Point>
</rdf:RDF>
```

Consider a location-based service that requires some input, for example, accurate position information or the user's choice of payment. The user might present these data to the LBS manually. Likewise, this information might be the result of a preceding Web service which, for example, reads the geographic position from an attached GPS device. In case of payment, information about user's choice of payment could be sent to an accounting service which, for example, uses a direct debit authorization. For service composition it is not necessary to know how the accounting is actually performed or how the access to the GPS device is implemented, as long as one can trust the responsible Web services. Authorization and trust will be fundamental for the success of location-based services and Web services composition.

Moreover, protecting privacy regarding the user's trace of information is a severe issue. Further dangers of intrusion to take care of are service spamming, where undesired services are propagated, and service spoofing, where insecure services are offered under disguised identity. Ongoing developments in the Web Services Trust Language (WS-Trust) therefore accommodate a wide variety of security models. However, proper service specification as well as justification of a specification's trustworthiness will remain a major challenge to ensure Web service interoperability across enterprise boundaries.

Using Web Services for ALBS Implementation

We use Web services standards to implement the appropriate selection of subservices and to process their composition. These comprise the service interface description in the Web Services Description Language (WSDL). In an interface description the port type specifies the service's request/response behavior. A service instance is accessed through a port. Each port has to bind to a port type and has to support additional binding information, for example, the used protocol.

For each application to be composed of subservices, a flow through required port types and optional port types guides the composition process. This flow can be specified using choreography languages (e.g., WSCL or BPEL4WS). Ongoing developments in Web services choreography incorporate far-reaching flow control where, for example, a group of services can be processed transactional or the flow may branch with respect to optional services availability or in case exception occurs. The composition process can be graphically expressed by a path through a network of accessible ports.

The composition process is triggered at service invocation. Whenever an ALBS is invoked, it is dynamically composed of suitable ports. Among the ports of each port type, the best match will be taken with respect to the specific context that determines availability and suitability of each port. Therefore, the Web services policy framework defines general purpose mechanism for associating policy expressions with subjects. Thus, specific property assertions can easily be attached to ports and registered in the repository.

For successful composition, at least one port of each required port type has to be accessible. In the example presented in Figure 10, there are five port types:

- **Connection:** Services of this type allow for access to available networks. This could be WLAN, LAN, Bluetooth, GSM, GPRS, or UMTS connections. Properties attached to these ports comprise information about bandwidth, costs, power consumption, encryption, or latency time.

Figure 10. Building dynamic value Webs by on-demand composition of adaptive location-based services

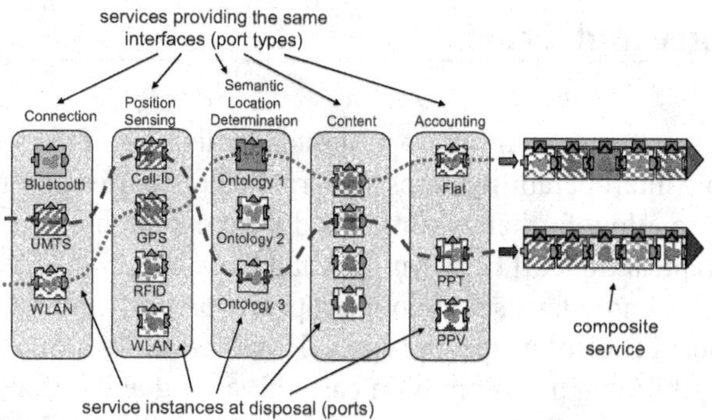

- **Position sensing:** This port type provides location information. Ports can be GPS-receivers, services based on stationary RFID-tags, or Bluetooth transmitters. Other services, for example, based on WLAN-positioning or Cell-ID in cellular networks, are possible candidates as well. The properties should contain information about the accuracy of the location information. Extensions of position sensing services might be able to recognize direction, speed, and variance of movement. (WLAN and Bluetooth positioning base on signal strengths of different access points. For each position, these signal strengths exhibit a certain characteristics that can be translated into location information by a signal characteristics map. Since the signal strengths vary, the map needs periodic update. Nevertheless, coverage and accuracy of the positioning may be insufficient for some LBS. However, this way PDAs, laptops, or other mobile devices can locate themselves independently of GPS availability.)
- **Semantic location determination:** Information about location semantics is offered by this port type. Input is the context-specific sensor data (containing geographic location, RFID numbers, available services, or other specific characteristics that could be utilized to reason about the position). The response includes the semantic position according to a given ontology.
- **Content:** This port type offers content for a given geographic or semantic location. It receives a message with the location information which then is processed. The returned message contains information (text, pictures, audio, or video if requested) about the given location. To process the location information semantically, some common ontology is required.

- **Accounting:** Accounting port type allows on-demand billing of services used.

Interoperability and Trust

Obviously, a major challenge is the appropriate standardization of the above service interfaces to enable interoperability across enterprise boundaries on one hand and to keep flexibility to allow further evolution and differentiation of the services on the other hand. a typical tradeoff between tight and loose coupling. Tight coupling, with all participating end points set up to interoperate properly, might be easier to implement and more efficient in specific cases. However, this approach will likely result in poor reusability and adaptivity in case of varying and unforeseeable deployment conditions. Here, Web services with their potential flexibility based on XML are expected to be advantageous.

In the earlier sections we have sketched how this might be approached in a restricted context, here, in the case of location-based services. However, to generally succeed in dynamic value Webs it requires getting over serious hurdles:

- To increase reusability and adaptivity, service specification on higher levels of semantics is required. Not only is the interpretation of such specifications challenging by itself. It additionally gives rise to multiple ways of interpretation, probably resulting in unintended behavior.
- In case of independent actors, opportunistic or even malicious behavior comes into play. Means (e.g., reputation systems) for coordination and cooperation become essential to prevent the market of dynamic value Webs from failing.

Higher levels of semantics need to consider support for contracts, contract negotiation, and assessment of fulfillment or violation in case of discord. Possible solutions range from peer-to-peer feedback systems to decentralized authorities that may impose reliable reputations or sanctions on participants. One of the most severe issues might be the support for reputation systems that aim at establishing trust. Supporting prerequisites are: security, identifiability, authenticity, timeliness, correctness, and other issues of dependability.

Plug and play in a global scale of interacting software components and hardware devices is not only a problem of connectivity, but moreover of making interacting units flexible and interoperable at a semantic level. Interacting entities need to "understand" interfaces and specifications and adapt such that they are able to utilize each other's abilities appropriately. Managing communication at higher levels of semantics is the key towards integration of information pieces, software components, business processes, and global distribution. Ultimately, the information infrastructure should carry the whole spectrum of human information exchange beyond people's limited physical reach in space and time.

The issues to be solved spread manifold up from the physical layer, where the raw data is transferred, to the higher levels of semantics, where data is associated with meaning. This extends from the communication infrastructure and end-user devices (comprising, e.g, increased communication reach, coverage, bandwidth, and usability of devices) to high interoperability and seamless operation in dynamic and mobile scenarios. Finding desired services as well as assessing and assembling them to comprehensive problem solutions is highly demanding. Additionally, to cope with the information asymmetry arising from uncertainty, ambiguity, and complexity inherent to dynamic value Webs, creates further challenges.

Case Study: NOMADS Campus — a Distributed Spatial Information System for Berlin Adlershof

We developed an adaptive location-based service prototype. It provides the basic functionality of a mobile information system for the "WISTA Adlershof Science and Technology Park" in Berlin, where natural science departments of the Humboldt University are located. A widely available WLAN-infrastructure gives mobile devices access to remote services and allows the setup of WLAN-based position-sensing services. We have defined some basic port types allowing all companies from the WISTA area to independently provide their location-based information and services. In our current demonstration setup, three institutes provide a WLAN position-sensing service and a map service as depicted in Figure 11.

Use Case Scenario

A user may use our NOMADS Campus system outdoors or indoors by a mobile device that visualizes the actual position in a map. Using the system at some specific position, the mobile device first discovers all services available for that specific position. In the example path shown in Figure 11, the user at the outdoor position <1> has no network connection and thus can only utilize local services. It discovers two local services: a position-sensing service that calculates the position by an attached GPS receiver and a map service where the map content is stored in the local memory (see Figure 12). However, the map cannot comprise detailed information since the necessary amount of data will quickly exceed the local storage capacity.

Figure 11. Example path of a mobile user visiting the WISTA science and technology park in Berlin, the path comprises three situations denoted by <1>, <2>, and <3> that require adaptive re-compostition of services and differ in availability of network connection (WLAN), type of position sensing, and source of the map

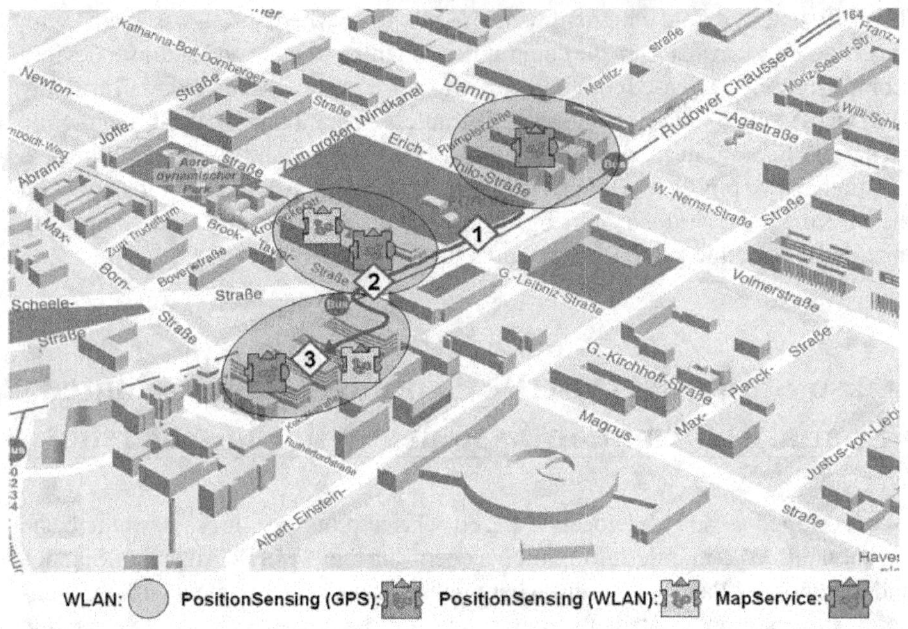

Figure 12. In the first case the user has no network connection and utilizes local services only

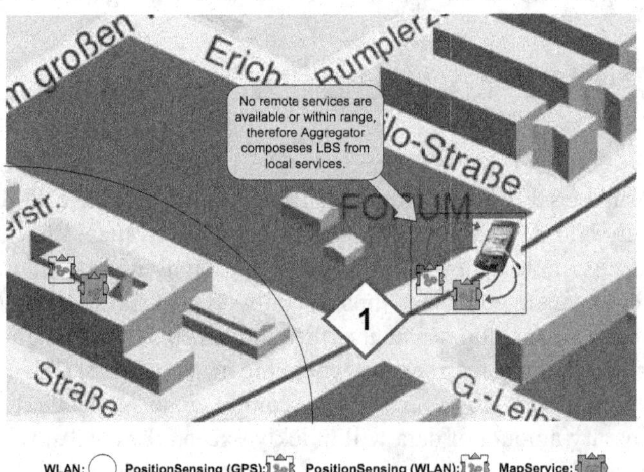

Figure 13. Mixed utilization of local and remote services in the reach of a WLAN network

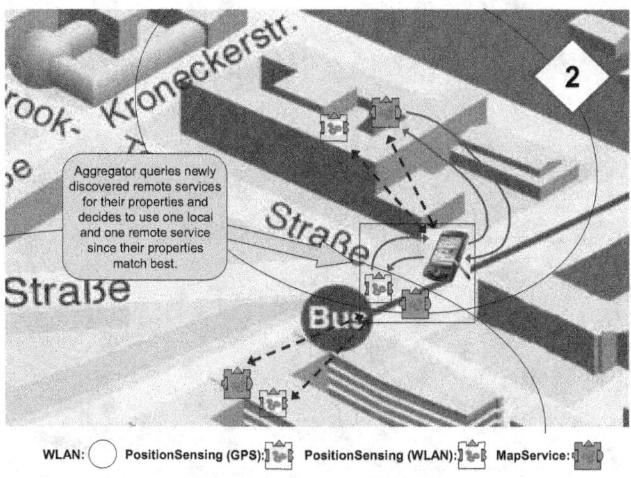

Obviously, the locally provided map also cannot reflect dynamics, for example, if building occupations have changed.

At position <2> the mobile user has WLAN network access (see Figure 13). Thus, he can utilize remote services in addition to the local services. In our example, he discovers a remote map service and a remote position-sensing service using WLAN signal trilateration which we provide by our tool MagicMap (Ibach et al., 2004a; Ibach et al., 2005a). Adaptive service composition decides for utilizing the GPS position sensing service which is, at this outdoor position, more accurate than the WLAN position sensing service. In addition, the remote map service is chosen since it offers detailed and up-to-date area information. To keep pace with dynamics in the area map, we are working on a Web crawler that scans the regional Websites for location information and, if location can be determined, assigns an icon to the location with a link to the Website.

If the user enters a building (see Figure 14), the GPS signal becomes unavailable and the adaptive service composition decides to utilize the remote WLAN position-sensing service instead. Note that the remote services at this position are provided be the responsible institution, in this example, the computer science institute. Therefore, the map service can provide an accurate indoor map containing individually-compiled information and services, for example, room occupations.

Location-based services will also be available for "virtual travelers." They explore the WISTA map on the Internet that visualizes location-specific information and stationary services. By point-and-click, it is possible to directly access these station-

Figure 14. In this example indoor situation, the mobile device utilizes remote services only

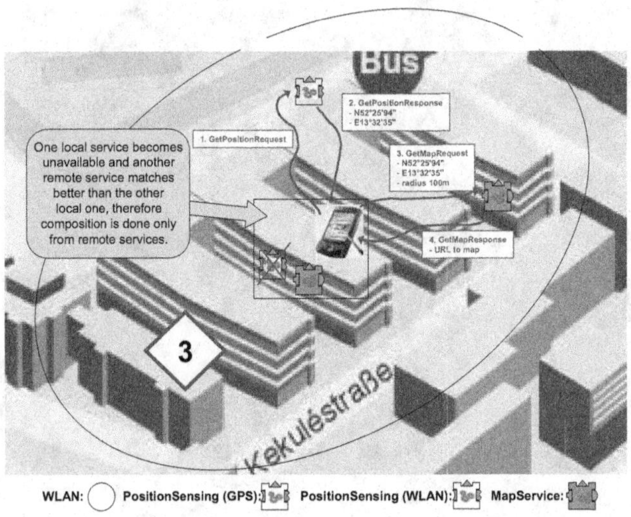

ary LBS or to forward the specific position to some general LBS. That way LBS link virtual to physical spaces. For example, if a user is visiting the Internet site of a company, the company's physical location will be determined and can serve as input for subsequent LBS. Vice versa there are LBS that link from physical to virtual spaces, for example, one that processes instructions such as "show me the Website of the restaurants located within 5 minutes' walk". In future, a position-sensing service will be able to determine the semantic position within the virtual space as well. For example, if position sensing detects that the user is visiting some product information site, it can take him to product-related offers, for example, test reports or best price comparisons.

Run-Time Adaptation

The sequence chart (see Figure 15) shows the message sequence of service interaction. The setup in this example consists of a service instance supervising the application control flow, the registry, for example, an UDDI-implementation, two ports connecting to position-sensing services (a GPS service and a WLAN positioning service), and two content ports. The example indicates how the composite service remains viable if some of its ports (here, the GPS positioning service) become temporarily unavailable, and how on-the-fly switchover to a replacement service (here, a WLAN positioning service[2]) takes place.

Figure 15. Sequence chart of service interaction

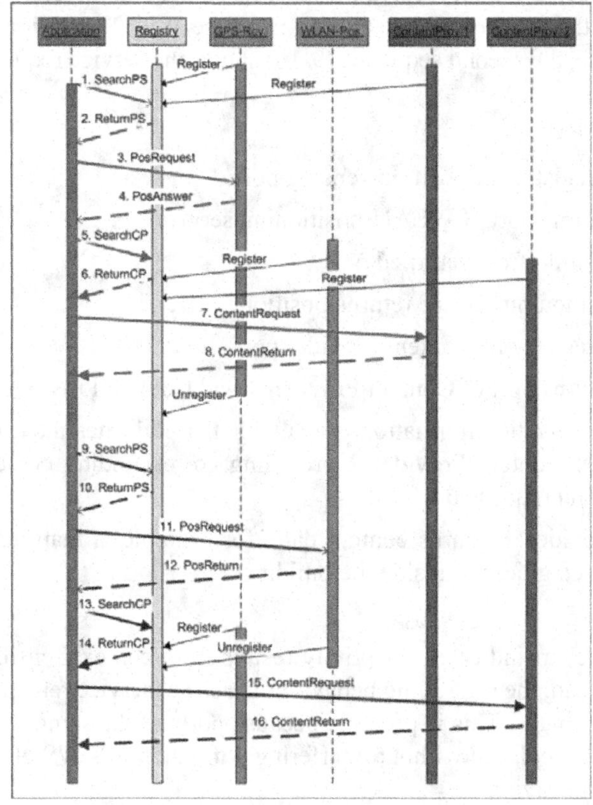

The first sequence (messages 1-8) shows a service request using the available GPS service:

1. Search the registry for position-sensing ports
2. Registry returns a GPS-receiver service port
3. Request position from returned port
4. GPS-receiver returns position
5. Search the registry for content port
6. Registry returns port of Content Provider 1
7. Request content from returned port
8. Content Provider 1 returns content data, for example, a city map in which the building is located

Before Message 9 is being sent, possibly the mobile user is entering a building, where the GPS device cannot receive the satellite signal and therefore unregisters its service from the registry. Supposing an in-house WLAN positioning service becomes available, the second sequence (9-16) shows the service request after this context change:

9. Search the registry for position-sensing port
10. Registry returns port of WLAN-positioning service
11. Request position from returned port
12. WLAN-positioning service returns position
13. Search the registry for content provider port
14. Registry returns port of Content Provider 1 and Content Provider 2
15. Supposing semantic information is available that indicates the user is inside the building, Content Provider 2 providing corresponding content will be prioritized and requested
16. Content Provider 2 returns content data, for example, a map that provides location-based guidance inside the building

As the sequence chart indicates, adaptivity results from context-sensitive service composition. Instead, the messaging behavior of each subservice remains independent of context changes. This is possible because ports of the same port type can be interchangeably replaced without interfering with the port's WSDL-prescribed request/response behavior.

Traditional monolithic LBS typically do not provide this degree of context adaptivity (here, to switch to WLAN positioning in case the GPS becomes unavailable) without being explicitly designed for every possible change of interoperation. Furthermore, they hardly adapt to emerging technologies that were not foreseeable at design time. In contrast, provided that messaging behavior of new services remains compatible with the given type definition, ALBS can adapt to changing or newly-emerging conditions without extra programming effort.

System Architecture

The fundamental concept of the service-oriented paradigm is to enable uniform access to all resources via services, including mobile or embedded devices, and hardware resources, for example, GPS receivers or WLAN adapters. In dynamic environments, where network topology, connections, and bandwidth are unstable and connected devices may have limited resource power, this requires specific methods for service propagation, discovery, invocation, and processing:

- **WS-Discovery**: The Web services dynamic discovery (WS-Discovery) standard defines a multicast protocol to propagate and locate services on ad hoc networks in peer-to-peer manner. It supports announcement of both service offers *and* service requests. Efficient algorithms (caching, multicast listening, discovery proxies, message forwarding, filtering, scope adjustment, and multicast suppression) keep network traffic for announcing and probing manageable. Thus, the protocol scales to a large number of endpoints.
- **Lightweight services**: For efficient invocation and processing of Web services on embedded devices with limited processing and communication power, "lightweight" services utilize specific real-time protocols, programming languages, scheduling algorithms, message queuing policies, or XML coding and parsing schemes.

In our example, the mobile device broadcasts its request to the resources within local reach and collects the service announcements. The GPS receiver announces a service for position sensing and the WLAN adapter announces two services, one for position sensing and one for connection (see Figure 10). These ports are stored in the local registry cache. Retrieved entries from the global registry are cached as well. To locate a service, the discovery service is instructed to retrieve the corresponding port type. Additionally, the discovery service can look for certain assertions to be satisfied. Furthermore, the ALBS application communicates with local services the same way it does with remote services. All services are propagated, discovered, and invoked by standard Web services protocols.

Outlook and Conclusion

We have presented a vision and a roadmap leading to creation of a "global real-time enterprise." We reviewed potential enabling technologies and examined them to assess how well they fit in a global enterprise environment. We specifically investigated the applicability of Web Services standards in the domain of mobile computing, in particular in the field of location-based services. We described how to flexibly compose elementary services along typical value chains using Web services technology and achieve high adaptivity at the composite service level. Furthermore, we outlined how location information can be processed semantically by using ontologies. As a case study, we have developed a distributed spatial information system, NOMADS Campus, which allows composition of services available on our campus and surrounding area according to the actual position.

We anticipate that the methodology will be applicable to future context-aware computing in distributed, heterogeneous, and dynamic environments at a great degree

Figure 16. The 0 allows for location-aware computing based on universal service-oriented communication

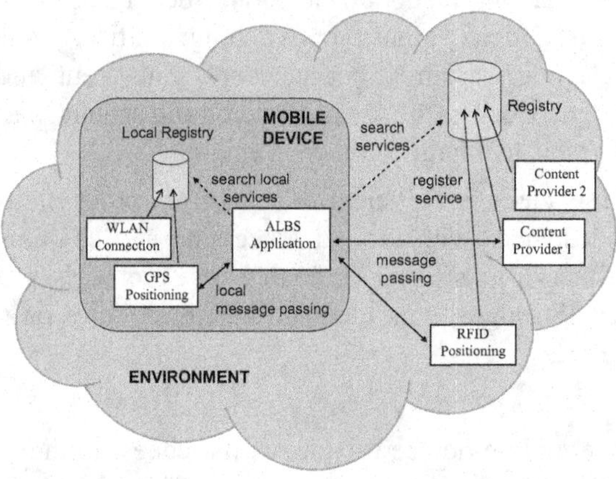

of interoperability. We are convinced that barrierless interoperability on location semantics will tightly interconnect physical and virtual spaces and have a catalytic impact on the markets of location-based services and mobile commerce.

The use of open Web services standards for location-based services has its appealing strengths. And, as it turns out, Web services standards are quite suitable to overcome a number of interoperability hurdles and to enable the evolution of dynamic value Webs. However, a number of desirable mobility characteristics were not originally provisioned in these standards and the integral Web services support for mobility and ad hoc adaptivity to changing conditions is still under development. Additional problems remain for future research to make dynamic value Webs flourish, finally forming a global real-time enterprise. Among the most demanding, we see widely-accepted ontologies for semantic interoperability, contracts for dependable service specification and composition, and reputation system for justification of specification trustworthiness.

References

Alchian, A. A., & Woodward, S. (1998). The firm is dead; Long live the firm: A review of Oliver E. Williamsons' The economic institutions of capitalism. *Journal of Economic Literature, 26*, 65-79.

Alonso, G., Casati, F., Kuno, H., & Machiraju, V. (2004). *Web services: Concepts, architectures, and applications*. Springer-Verlag.

Bloomberg, J., & Schmelzer, R. (2002). The pros and cons of Web services. *ZapThink Report*. Retrieved from www.zapthink.com

BPEL4WS. (2005). *Business Process Execution Language for Web Services, Version 1.1*. Retrieved from www-106.ibm.com/developerworks/library/ws-bpel

Cox, S., Daisey, P., Lake, R., Portele, C., & Whiteside, A. (2004). *OpenGIS® Geography Markup Language (GML) Implementation Specification, Version 3.0* (OpenGIS Project Doc. No. OGC 02-023r4).

Erl, T. (2004). *Service-oriented architecture: A field guide to integrating XML and Web services*. Prentice Hall.

Evans, J. D. (2003). *OGC Web Coverage Service (WCS) Specification, Version 1.0* (OpenGIS Project Doc. No. OGC 03-065r6).

Gershenfeld, N., Krikorian, R., & Cohen, D. (2004). The Internet of things. *Scientific American, 291*(4), 76-81.

Gokhale, A., Kumar, B., & Sahuguet, A. (2002). *Reinventing the wheel? CORBA vs. Web services*. Presented at the Eleventh International World Wide Web Conference, Honolulu, HI.

Harrison, M. (2003). EPC information service — data model and queries, Auto ID center. *White Paper*. Retrieved from http://www.autoidlabs.org.

Hazas, M., Scott, J., & Krumm, J. (2004, February). Location-aware computing comes of age. *IEEE Computer, 37*(2), 95-97.

Hodes, T. D. (2003). *Discovery and adaptation for location-based services*. PhD dissertation, University of California at Berkeley, Computer Science Department.

Ibach, P., & Horbank, M. (2004). Highly-location-based services in mobile environments. In *Proceedings of the International Service Ability Symposium 2004*, Munich, Germany.

Ibach, P., Hübner, T., & Schweigert, M. (2004a). MagicMap — Kooperative Positionsbestimmung über WLAN. In *Chaos Communication Congress*, Berlin, Germany.

Ibach, P., Stantchev, V., Lederer, F., Weiß, A., Herbst, T., & Kunze, T. (2005a). WLAN-based asset tracking for warehouse management. In *Proceedings of the IADIS International Conference E-Commerce*, Porto, Portugal.

Ibach, P., Tamm, G., & Horbank, M. (2005b). Dynamic value Webs in mobile environments using adaptive location-based services. In *Proceedings of the Hawaii International Conference on System Sciences (HICSS-38)*, HI.

LaMarca, A., Chawathe, Y., Consolvo, S., Hightower, J., Smith, I., Scott, J., et al. (2005). In *Place Lab: Device Positioning Using Radio Beacons in the Wild, Proceedings of the International Conferene on Pervasive Computing*, Munich, Germany.

Linthicum, D. S. (2003). *Next generation application integration: From simple information to Web services*. Addison-Wesley.

Malek, M. (2003). The NOMADS republic. In *Proceedings of International Conferences on Advances in Infrastructure for Electronic Business, Education, Science, Medicine and Mobile Technologies on the Internet, Scuola Superiore G. Reiss Romoli (SSGRR), Telecom Italia*, L'Aquila, Italy.

Malek, M. (2004). Introduction to NOMADS. *Computing Frontiers, 2004,* Ischia, Italy.

Malone, T. W., Yates, J., & Benjamin R. I. (1997). Electronic markets and electronic hierarchies. *Communications of the ACM, 30*(6), 484-497.

McKee, L., & Kottman, C. (2003). *OGC inside the OpenGIS specification*. OpenGIS.

Milanovic, N., & Malek, M. (2005). Architectural support for automatic service composition. In *Proceedings of the IEEE International Conference on Services Computing (SCC 2005)*, Orlando, FL.

Milanovic, N., Richling, J., & Malek, M. (2004). *Lightweight services for embedded systems.* Presented at the IEEE Workshop on Software Technologies for Embedded and Ubiquitous Computing Systems (WSTFEUS), Vienna, Austria.

Müller, P., Stich, C., & Zeidler, C. (2001). Components @ work: Component technology for embedded systems. In *Proceedings of the 27th Euromicro Conference*, Warsaw, Poland.

Peng, Z.-R., & Tsou, M.-H. (2003). *Internet GIS — distributed geographic information services for the Internet and wireless networks*. John Wiley & Sons.

Picot, A. (2004). *Zehn Eigenschaften der Internet-Ökonomie*. Retrieved from http://www.competence-site.de

Pinto, H., Boas, N. V., & José, R. (2003). Using a private UDDI for publishing location-based information to mobile users. In *Proceedings of the ICCC/IFIP 7th International Conference on Electronic Publishing (ElPub 2003),* Guimarães, Portugal.

Rao, B., & Minakakis, L. (2003). Evolution of mobile location-based services. *Communications of the ACM, 46*(12), 61-65.

Reed, C. (2005). Integrating geospatial standards and standards strategies into business process. *Open GIS Consortium (OGC) White Paper*. Retrieved from http://www.opengis.org

Reichenbacher, T. (2004). *Mobile cartography — adaptive visualisation of geographic information on mobile devices*. Dissertation submitted at the Institute of Photogrammetry und Cartography, Technical University, Munich, Germany.

Schiller, J., & Voisard, A. (2004). *Location based services*. Morgan Kaufmann

Schwan, K., Poellabauer, C., Eisenhauer, G., Pande, S., & Pu, C. (2002). Infofabric: Adaptive services in distributed embedded systems. In *Proceedings of the IEEE Workshop on Large Scale Real-Time and Embedded Systems (in conjunction with RTSS 2002)*, Austin, TX.

Sonnet, R. (2005). *OGC Web Map Context Documents, Version 1.1* (OpenGIS Project Doc. No. OGC 05-005).

Tamm, G., & Wuensche, M. (2003). Strategies to reduce information asymmetry in Web service market. In *Proceedings of the 11th European Conference on Information Systems (ECIS)*, Napoli, Italy.

UDDI. (2005). *Universal description, discovery, and integration of Web services*. Retrieved from www.uddi.org

Vretanos, P. A. (2005). *OGC Web Feature Service Implementation Specification, Version 1.1* (OpenGIS Project Doc. No. OGC 04-094).

Vogels, W. (2002). Technology challenges for the global real-time enterprise. In *Proceedings of the International Workshop on Future Directions in Distributed Computing*, Bertinoro, Italy. Retrieved from http://www.cs.cornell.edu/vogels/papers/fudicobook.pdf

Whiteside, A. (2005). *OGC Web Services Common Specification, Version 1.0* (OpenGIS Project Doc. No. OGC 05-008).

Endnotes

1 Wi-Fi Positioning System, www.skyhookwiereless.com; Wireless Location Appliance 2700, www.cisco.com; Wi-Fi Workplace, www.newburynetworks.com

2 Here, a connection switchover, for example, from UMTS to WLAN connection, will probably occur. However, this is processed analogously and is not addressed in the Figure.

Chapter XIV

Mining Critical Infrastructure Information from Municipality Data Sets: A Knowledge-Driven Approach and Its Applications

William J. Tolone, University of North Carolina at Charlotte, USA
Wei-Ning Xiang, University of North Carolina at Charlotte, USA
Anita Raja, University of North Carolina at Charlotte, USA
David Wilson, University of North Carolina at Charlotte, USA
Qianhong Tang, University of North Carolina at Charlotte, USA
Ken McWilliams, University of North Carolina at Charlotte, USA
Robert K. McNally, University of North Carolina at Charlotte, USA

Abstract

An essential task in critical infrastructure protection is the assessment of critical infrastructure vulnerabilities. The use of scenario sets is widely regarded as the best form for such assessments. Unfortunately, the construction of scenario sets is hindered by a lack in the public domain of critical infrastructure information as such information is commonly confidential, proprietary, or business sensitive. At the same time, there is a wealth of municipal data in the public domain that is pertinent to critical infrastructures. However, to date, there are no reported studies on how to extract only the most relevant CI information from these municipal sources, nor does a methodology exist that guides the practice of CI information mining on municipal data sets. This problem is particularly challenging as these data sets are typically voluminous, heterogeneous, and even entrapping. In this chapter, we propose a knowledge-driven methodology that facilitates the extraction of CI information from public domain, that is, open source, municipal data sets. Under this methodology, pieces of deep, though usually tacit, knowledge acquired from CI domain experts are employed as keys to decipher the massive sets of municipal data and extract the relevant CI information. The proposed methodology was tested successfully on a municipality in the Southeastern United States. The methodology is considered a viable choice for CIP professionals in their efforts to gather CI information for scenario composition and vulnerability assessment.

Introduction

A critical infrastructure (CI) is an array of assets and systems that, if disrupted, would threaten national security, economy, public health and safety, and way of life. These include, but are not limited to, utilities, medical facilities, public transportation, telecommunication networks, landmarks, buildings, and public spaces. In recent years, unfortunately, critical infrastructures have become symbolic targets as well as the mass casualty opportunities for terrorist attacks (Bolz, Dudonis, & Schulz, 2002). For instance, the World Trade Center is a symbol of America's capitalism and economic influence, the Pentagon is a symbol of America's military strength, and the railway station in Madrid represents a node in a geo-political network. Many critical infrastructures promote the congregation of people, which increases their attractiveness to terrorist acts. Because of the dual identity of critical infrastructures and the high level of vulnerability they bear, critical infrastructure protection (CIP) has topped the list of priorities in the practice of homeland security planning in the United States (Terner, Sutton, Hebert, Bailey, Gilbert, & Jacqz, 2004; Thieman, 2004). Since the tragic events of September 11, 2001, CIP drills have become an integral part of every counter-terrorism exercise across the country (Thieman, 2004).

An essential task in critical infrastructure protection (CIP) planning is the assessment of CI vulnerability with respect to the threat of potential terrorist attacks. For such a task, a set of *scenarios* is widely regarded in both academic and professional communities to be the best form for such assessments (Garrick, 2002). Unlike predictions which project critical infrastructure (CI) vulnerability with probability, a scenario set bounds the range of vulnerabilities by connecting initiating event, or initial conditions, to undesired end states (different levels of damage) with the sequence of events linking the two (Garrick, 2002). Functionally, a scenario set is both a bridge that connects the process of CIP analysis and modeling with that of CIP planning, and a cognitive apparatus that stretches people's thinking and broadens their views in the practice of CIP. This dual function entitles a scenario set to be a favored member of a family of instruments for CI vulnerability assessment and CIP planning. It also explains the popularity of scenario sets in CIP drills and counter-terrorism exercises; they serve as a foundation for emergency response maneuvers (Thiemann, 2004).

Despite its recognized advantages, however, the use of scenarios in CIP and homeland security planning is hindered by the difficulties in meeting its informational needs. To compose scenarios, a scenarist requires certain categories of information, each corresponding to one of the five components of a scenario (Xiang & Clarke, 2003). These five components are: (1) alternatives — the range of potential actions, or the spectrum of incidents/events; (2) consequences — the immediate and cumulative effects (physical, ecological, economical, and social) that each alternative would have on an area's security, economy, public health and safety, and way of life; (3) causations — the causal bonds between alternatives and consequences; (4) timeframes — the periods of time between occurrence of the alternatives and the sequence of the consequences; (5) geographical footprints — the place-oriented blueprints of alternatives, and the anticipated marks of their ramifications on an area's geography. The last component — hardly unique — is so pivotal to CIP scenario composition and utilization that it distinguishes CIP scenarios from their counterparts in business, industry, and at times, the military.

Satisfying these informational requirements for composing CIP scenarios is a difficult task. A major difficulty comes from the fact that an estimated 85 percent of all CI in the United States is owned and managed by the private sector. Consequently, much of the information related to the security of critical infrastructures and essential to homeland security planning and/or emergency management is not within the public domain, as such information is commonly confidential, proprietary, or business sensitive (Terner et al., 2004). The Protected Critical Infrastructure Information (PCII) Program, launched by the U.S. Department of Homeland Security (DHS) in February, 2004, under provisions of the Critical Infrastructure Information Act of 2002 (CII Act), enables the private sector to submit infrastructure data voluntarily to the federal government. The federal government assures that competitive data will be protected from public disclosure until and unless a PCII determination is made that the information does not meet PCII requirements.[1] Because of this voluntary nature, the success of this milestone development depends on collaborations from the private sector. Its efficacy remains to be seen.

On the other hand, there is a great wealth of open-source data at the municipal level that is pertinent to critical infrastructures. These data are commonly geographic and both collected and maintained by various municipal departments to serve the general civil needs of a community. Examples include, but are not limited to, digital orthophotos, [2] planimetric data sets, [3] tax parcel data, [4] and street centerline data. Because of their implicit connections to critical infrastructures, and owing to some of the important qualities they possess, high definition or precision (at a geographic scale of 1:2,400), refinement or completeness, and general availability, these data sets appear to be an attractive source of knowledge that await the practice of CI information mining. [5] However, to date, there are no reported studies on how to extract only the most relevant CI information from these municipal sources, nor does a methodology exist that guides the practice of CI information mining on municipal data sets. This problem is particularly challenging as these data sets are typically voluminous, heterogeneous, and even entrapping.

In this chapter, we propose a knowledge-driven methodology that facilitates the extraction of CI information from public domain, that is, open source, municipal data sets. Under this methodology, pieces of deep, though usually tacit, knowledge are first acquired from a group of CI domain experts. These pieces of knowledge are then employed as keys to decipher the massive sets of municipal data and extract relevant CI information. The benefits to extracting CI information for a municipality extend beyond the facilitation of vulnerability assessments for homeland security. Such information is also particularly relevant to emergency management activities including disaster preparedness, response, and recovery activities. Geographic information systems (GIS) are key enablers to this methodology.

The proposed methodology was tested successfully on a municipality in the Southeastern United States, and can potentially be applied to other municipalities and regions. It is considered a viable choice for CIP professionals in their efforts to gather CI information for scenario composition in support of vulnerability assessment and emergency management for several reasons. First, the methodology produces credible and useful results. Second, the methodology is generic and may be applied to most, if not all, municipalities across the United States as the required resources (data, computation, and knowledge acquisition, including domain experts) are generally, publicly available. Third, tested on four CI domains in our study, the methodology is flexible and thus may be adapted to any CI domains in any municipalities or regions within the United States. Last, the methodology generates results that can be readily refined and updated.

The remainder of the chapter is organized as follows. First, the methodology is outlined. Next, details of the methodology are illustrated through a case study. Case study outcomes are then described. Finally, the merits of the methodology are discussed, and future research directions are identified.

A Knowledge Driven Methodology for CI Information Mining

The methodology proposed here gathers CI information through an intertwined process of knowledge acquisition, rendering, and validation (Figure 1). After an initial search, a knowledge worker, the person who solicits, interprets, and renders a domain expert's knowledge, prepares a questionnaire and sends it to a domain expert or, in some cases, a group of domain experts, for answers. In addition, the knowledge worker may schedule both structured and unstructured interviews with these experts. The knowledge worker then geographically renders the elicited knowledge on the generally available open-source information. The renderings are typically in the form of digital maps, attribute tables, and rule bases. The renderings are then reviewed by the expert(s) to assure that the knowledge worker's interpretations are accurate, or at least do not "violently contradict any strong held feelings" of the expert(s) (Keeney & Raiffa, 1976, p. 271). Using the expert's feedback, the maps, attribute tables, and rule bases are refined. The corrected renderings are presented to the domain expert(s) for another round of validation. This interactive process continues until the domain expert(s) are satisfied with the results.

The remainder of the section provides a detailed account of this methodology. In some instances the initial search may generate sufficient knowledge such that a first rendering may occur prior to contacting domain experts. This initial rendering then serves as input to domain expert discussions.

Initial Search

The process of CI information mining begins with an initial search. This search involves a set of three tasks: (1) a survey of all the publicly-available information

Figure 1. A methodology for critical infrastructure information mining

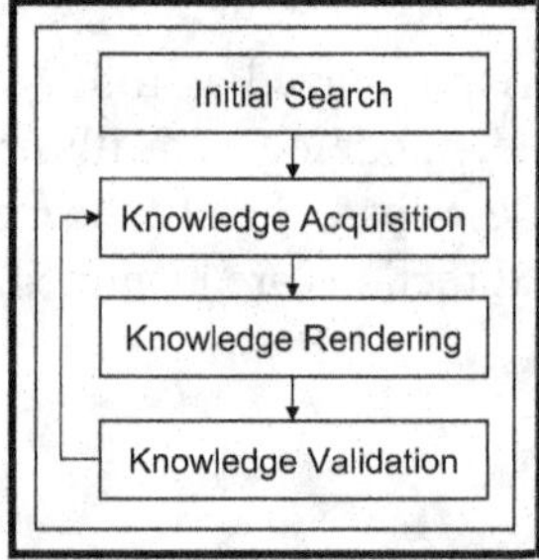

related to the domain; (2) the identification of individual domain experts for each CI component; and (3) the development of a list of questions for the interviews of the domain experts.

Publicly-available information usually resides in open source locations such as generally-accessible databases, journals, books, newspapers, the Internet, and even word-of-mouth. Much of the information from these sources is non-confidential, insensitive to business interests, and bearing little insights into the key issues related to CIP planning and management. However, both the information and the search process are necessary and valuable for CI information mining. They help knowledge workers become familiar with the problem domain; and they enable knowledge workers to identify individual domain experts and develop questionnaires in order to proceed to the next stage of the information mining process.

It should be noted that the thoroughness of the initial search contributes significantly to the success of the subsequent stage of knowledge acquisition. First of all, it makes the interviews, structured and unstructured, more productive while reducing the time commitment of domain experts, who usually have limited resources and in many cases must justify the hours spent with the knowledge workers. Secondly, domain experts are more likely to be forthcoming when knowledge workers are well prepared; although, this forthcoming nature of domain experts is independent of whether the knowledge worker utilizes a questionnaire during the interview.

Knowledge Acquisition

The task of knowledge acquisition deals with two levels of CI knowledge, surface and procedural. Surface knowledge is the most common information offered when seeking information on a subject. Surface knowledge is also referred to as declarative knowledge (Turban & Aronson, 2001). Such knowledge includes facts and figures that can usually be found easily at the beginning of knowledge acquisition, and in some cases, during the stage of initial search. Examples include, but are not limited to, schematic diagrams of a CI system hierarchy, iconographical representations of CI roles, and functional relationships among objects within a CI layer. The CI proprietors usually are willing to give this generalized information to interested parties as it satisfies most inquiries and raises little corporate security concerns.

Procedural knowledge (Turban & Aronson, 2001), on the other hand, is not easily accessible and typically not disseminated to outside seekers for security concerns. Procedural knowledge includes information such as safety protocols, problem diagnostic procedures, and emergency response plans. Furthermore, the spatial element of both surface and procedural knowledge, that is, information about the geographic footprints of CIs, either as individual layers or as components of a public utility system (e.g., a traffic control system), is usually regarded as highly sensitive. Consequently, information about locations, the geographic networks of CI objects, knowledge about proximity, and the spatial interactions among CI objects are not readily available.

Various methods have been suggested for knowledge acquisition. These include, but are not limited to, the method of "familiar tasks" (Duda & Shortliffe, 1983; Mittal & Dym, 1985; Stefik et al.,1982), structured and unstructured interviews (Hoffman, 1987; Weiss & Kulikowski, 1984), limited information tasks (Hoffman, 1987), constrained processing tasks (Hoffman, 1984, 1987; Klein, 1987), and the method of "tough cases" (Doyle, 1984; Hoffman, 1987). The method of "familiar tasks" is an observational method involving domain experts performing typical tasks. Structured and unstructured interviews are examples of question/answer methods for knowledge elicitation. The method of limited information tasks is similar to the method of "familiar tasks" except that the information presented to a domain expert is restricted in some way in an attempt to expose how an expert derives a solution. The method of constrained processing tasks is an observational method where the time a domain expert is allowed to reach a conclusion is limited. Finally, the method of "tough cases" involves presenting a domain expert with an unfamiliar case and requiring the expert to describe the protocol that he/she is using while deriving a solution.

Among these methods, interviews (both structured and unstructured) are the most common and widely accepted approach to knowledge elicitation (Hoffman, 1987; Millet & Harker, 1990; Xiang & Whitley, 1994). Although interviews are usually more time-consuming and less efficient than other methods (such as limited information tasks and constrained processing tasks), domain experts generally feel more comfortable with interviews and, therefore, are less hesitant to offer opinions (Ibid.). For example, during an interview conducted through our case study, a domain expert offered a detailed physical description of a critical node within the telecommunication network, providing details on square footage, parking area, number of stories, and surrounding land use. This invaluable tacit knowledge would have remained undiscovered without such an interview.

At this stage of CI information mining, a combination of structured and unstructured interviews is used to acquire deep procedural knowledge, following an approach developed by Xiang and Whitley (1994). The unstructured interview consists of an informal discussion with domain experts, where the knowledge worker conducts an unscripted conversation and slowly builds his/her understanding of the infrastructure. Interviews with these individuals usually last about an hour and consist of an informal question and answer session. The structured, more formal interview is usually conducted afterwards, where the knowledge worker submits a list of detailed questions to solicit domain experts' explicit inputs. A structured interview often further refines the knowledge acquisition process, providing greater clarification to the knowledge extracted during the unstructured interviews.

Ideally, a group of experts from each domain should be interviewed to minimize individual biases. Under this multi-expert approach, the knowledge acquisition process is conducted either in an interactive group setting or through individual interviews with domain experts. A group setting is considerably more time efficient because a knowledge worker can solicit input from multiple domain experts in a single session. However, there are several drawbacks associated with this method, including domination by one individual, lack of focus, and limited participation by all members (Moore, 1987). With individual interviews, on the other hand, the knowledge worker will need to consolidate all of the information obtained from the domain experts. This process can be cumbersome, and time-consuming, especially when the information is contradictory (Roth & Wood, 1990). In practice, therefore, the ideal multi-expert approach may yield to a sub-optimal single-expert approach for pragmatic reasons.

Another way to de-bias elicited knowledge is to use a shared information approach that encourages communications among the knowledge workers. During the interview process, each knowledge worker is assigned to a specific domain, working individually with domain experts. Under this shared information approach, the knowledge workers share with one another the knowledge they solicited from various domain experts through informal discussions at regular intervals. These "cross-domain" discussions can provoke questions that could prove useful in follow-up interviews with the respective domain experts. In our case study, for instance, a final, formal presentation of knowledge acquisition results proved to be a useful communication session for both knowledge workers and domain experts. The knowledge workers benefited from the additional informal knowledge validation provided by domain experts as well as from the information obtained from co-worker presentations. It also provided an excellent opportunity for domain experts of the various utility sectors to discuss their interdependencies.

Knowledge Rendering

Knowledge rendering is a process in which knowledge workers interpret the knowledge elicited from domain experts and express this understanding using an appropriate representation. More specifically, in the case of CI information mining, knowledge rendering refers to the exercise through which knowledge workers develop a *spatial representation* of the infrastructure layer based on the knowledge acquired from the domain expert(s). Geographic information systems (GIS) are a key enabler to this step of the proposed methodology. In our case study, for instance, a domain expert supplied the knowledge worker with a detailed description of the physical characteristics of a critical node in a telecommunication network (for example, parking lot size, building height, etc.). To render this piece of knowledge spatially, the knowledge worker first selected all the service provider's properties from a publicly available tax parcel data file. The worker then superimposed these selected land parcels onto digital orthophotos of the study area, and removed all the parcels that did not match the physical characteristics. The worker finalized the rendering by saving all the remaining parcels on a new map. The map is referred to as a *proxy* or *surrogate* data layer in that it is not a map of the real data *per se*. Instead, it is a geographic rendering of the domain expert's knowledge on the open-source municipal data (tax parcels and digital orthophotos, in this case) as interpreted by the knowledge worker. In addition to maps, the rendering of domain expert's knowledge can take other forms, such as iconographic representations, flowcharts, and tables.

Knowledge Validation

During the final phase of the CI information mining process, the knowledge worker submits the newly-rendered proxy data layer to the domain expert for validation. A series of structured or unstructured interviews are scheduled, where the domain expert is asked to verify that the spatial renderings are consistent with the knowledge that he/she provided in the previous interview(s). The proxy data layers submitted to the domain experts are usually presented as digital maps. These layers are continuously updated and refined during the process based on feedback from the domain experts. This phase is complete when the domain experts are satisfied with the knowledge rendering as presented and have verified that the knowledge worker did not misrepresent any of the knowledge.

Implementation of the Methodology: A Case Study

The above-described methodology was initially developed to mine information from four critical infrastructures in a municipality in the Southeastern United States. These infrastructures include the electric power grid, telecommunication, natural gas distribution, and transportation networks. As an illustration of the application of the methodology, this section provides a detailed description of mining exercise for information about the natural gas supply system.

A pipeline network supplies natural gas to residential and commercial customers throughout the metropolitan area. Commercial pipelines transmit large volumes of natural gas at a high capacity of 420 PSI (pounds per square inch, 1 PSI = 6895 Pascals).[6] Residential pipelines distribute small volumes at a capacity of 70 PSI or lower. While this case study involves only one gas distribution domain expert, the techniques were successfully applied to groups of domain experts, as described in the previous section, during an extended case study that also included electric power, telecommunications, and transportation infrastructures. Discussion in the following section, however, is limited to the focused case study.

Initial Search

Because of the security concerns with gas pipeline data, it is not surprising that the initial search for publicly-available data yielded only modest results. Among the most relevant are the pipeline system's general structure and a digital map of the major transmission pipelines from Texas to New Jersey. In addition, the knowledge worker collected information about the domain experts who are affiliated with the natural gas provider in the region, and the information on the land parcels designated as easement for natural gas providers.

Knowledge Acquisition

Through a series of structured and unstructured interviews with a gas distribution domain expert, the knowledge worker obtained two important pieces of knowledge about the locations of the local pipeline network and the physical characteristics of the regulator stations, the nodes on the network. During a visit to the company, the knowledge worker was also given an image file, a screen shot from a GIS data file, of the local pipeline network. From the image file, it was clear that the easement areas on the property parcel data set are major pipelines in the municipality area.

Knowledge Rendering

The process of knowledge rendering consisted of three steps: construction of the regional pipelines (higher than 70 PSI); identification of the regulator stations, and creation of a local pipeline network (70 PSI and lower). This process proceeded under the guidance of the knowledge acquired from the domain expert.

In constructing the regional pipelines, the knowledge worker first superimposed a map layer of the easement areas on top of the digital orthophotos, and found some interesting physical characteristics of these easement areas: flat, open, linear, around 15 feet in width, either a little higher or lower than the surrounding ground surface. With the image file of the local pipeline network provided by the natural gas company as a reference, the knowledge worker then created a proxy of the regional pipelines by connecting those easement areas.

To identify the locations of the regulator stations, the knowledge worker first selected from a tax parcel database all the land parcels that are owned by the gas company and put them on a new map. The knowledge worker then superimposed the map on the digital orthophotos to examine, within each land parcel owned by the natural gas company, whether the physical characteristics of the regulator stations described by the domain expert were found. Typically, a regulator appears to be a small structure on a digital orthophoto with an electrical generator in the back. Another characteristic is that regulators are usually located at regular intervals along the pipeline. The knowledge worker then placed a node on the identified regulator to represent its location. Finally, all the nodes were saved on a new map layer.

The creation of local distribution pipeline network (70 PSI and lower) was guided by rules acquired from the domain expert. These rules are (1) 90% of the pipes follow the collector and neighborhood streets, and roughly 10% of the streets in a municipal street centerline file do not coincide with pipelines; (2) pipelines do not follow major highways — interstates and arterials; and (3) newly-developed neighborhoods that do not have natural gas supplies are shown on the image file that the company provided as empty areas. Applying these rules to the street centerline files of the study area, the knowledge worker produced a map of the proxy distribution pipeline network.

Knowledge Validation

The completed renderings of the gas pipeline network and regulator stations proxy data layers were submitted to the domain expert for validation. Again, because of security concerns, the domain expert did not explicitly confirm whether the renderings were "right" or "wrong." He instead directed the knowledge worker's attention to places where erroneous assumptions in the pipeline placement had occurred. Based on this feedback, the knowledge worker made adjustments on the pipeline alignments on the digital maps, and checked on the tax parcel database to assure that the updates were thorough and complete.

It should be noted that during the process of knowledge acquisition, rendering, and validation, spatial techniques equipped in GIS and open-source data sets, especially digital orthophotos, played a significant role. By showing the geographic objects in their actual forms, rather than cartographic symbols (points, lines, areas, or pixels) (Lillesand & Kiefer, 2000), digital orthophotos provide an advanced tool that was far more effective and efficient than the traditional maps and aerial photos for knowledge rendering and validation. The use of GIS enables the knowledge workers to manage the complex task of rendering an entire utility network. It helps track various features such as transmission poles, transmission stations, and gas pipelines all within a same spatial domain. In this fully integrated system, all of the features are related by location, and multiple data layers can be dynamically linked for visual analysis and for map production (Harder, 1999).

Products of the Information Mining Process

The surface and procedural information gathered through the application of the described methodology can be categorized into two interrelated groups: information about the functionality of a CI system, and information about the geography of CI system structures. This section presents a description of some case study

Figure 2. A functional hierarchy of the natural gas distribution system

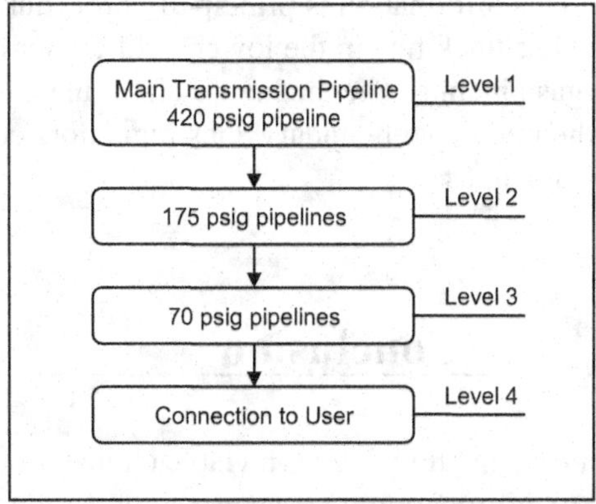

Figure 3. A geographic rendering of the natural gas distribution system

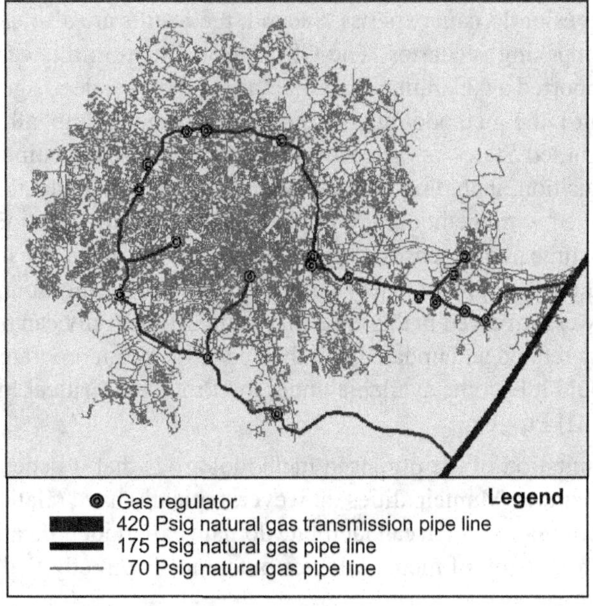

outcomes as related to the natural gas distribution system for the case study region. The presentation of these outcomes is limited due to the sensitive nature of the information gathered.

Figure 2 shows the hierarchy of the natural gas pipeline network. This information is principally surface information about natural gas distribution. Level 1 represents the main national gas pipeline (e.g., the West/East pipeline running from Texas to New Jersey). The 175 PSI lines at Level 2 transmit natural gas to the municipal area. The Level 3 network (70 PSI or lower) distributes natural gas to the local service areas.

A geographic representation of the natural gas distribution network in the study area is provided in Figure 3. This information is principally procedural as it is specific to the region of interest. The thick line in the lower right corner of the map represents the main national gas pipeline. The medium weight line models the regional pipeline that encircles the municipal boundary. Gas regulators connect the region pipeline to local service pipelines.

Conclusion

We contend that the proposed methodology is a viable choice for CIP professionals in their efforts to gather CI information for scenario composition and vulnerability assessment for several reasons. First, the methodology produces credible and useful results, as demonstrated through the case study (the CI information gathered was credible in the eyes of domain experts). Second, the results are also useful for CIP scenarists in composing scenarios. The CI information from this case study has successfully supported a CI simulation project funded by a federal agency (Tolone et al., 2004). Third, the methodology is executable for most, if not all, municipalities across the United States as the required resources for data, computation, and knowledge acquisition, including domain experts, are generally available. Fourth, the costs associated with methodology implementation are modest, most of which are related to the time and expenses of knowledge workers. Fifth, the methodology is adaptable and can be applied to any CI domain, although only four domains of CI information were involved in this case study. Finally, not only can methodology results be readily refined and updated, but they can also be incorporated into a real CI database should it become available under the Protected Critical Infrastructure Information (PCII) Program.

The principal limitation of the proposed methodology is that it depends upon access to domain experts. Municipalities, however, typically have relationships with location utility providers, which can facilitate domain expert identification and ease access issues. The fidelity of methodologies outcomes is directly tied to the level of access to domain experts and the willingness of such experts to be forthcoming in their participation.

The case study application of the proposed methodology highlighted two important lessons learned. As previously noted, the geospatial renderings of gathered information were critical to effective participation by the domain experts in the knowledge validation step. Without such renderings, the knowledge validation step would be significantly hampered. Geographic information systems are a key technology to generating such renderings. In addition, knowledge validation using domain experts must be conducted systematically to be effective. Improved techniques and methodologies for verification and validation of infrastructure models constitute the primary direction for future research.

Acknowledgments

The authors are grateful to the following individuals at the University of North Carolina at Charlotte for their contributions to the project: Bei-Tseng Chu, Mirsad Hadzikadic, Vikram Sharma, Deepak Yavagal, Robin Gandhi, Katie Templeton, Gustavo Borel Menezes, Stuart Phelps, Jocelyn Young, Paul Smith, and Huili Hao.

References

Benbasat, I., & Dhaliwal, J. S. (1989). A framework for the validation of knowledge acquisition. *Knowledge Acquisition, 1*, 215-233.

Bolz, F., Dudonis, K., & Schulz, D. (2002). *The counterterrorism handbook: Tactics, procedures, and techniques* (2nd ed.). Boca Raton, FL: CRC Press.

Casazza, J., & Delea, F. (2003). *Understanding electrical power systems.* New York: John Wiley & Sons.

Doyle, J. (1984). Expert systems without computers or theory and trust in artificial intelligence. *AI Magazine, 5*(2), 59-63.

Duda, R. O., & Shortliffe, E. H. (1983). *Expert Systems Research. Science, 220*, 261-276.

Frawley, W., Piatetsky-Shapiro, G., & Matheus, C. (1992). Knowledge discovery in databases: An overview. *AI Magazine, 13*(3), 57-70.

Garrick, J. (2002). Perspectives on the use of risk assessment to address terrorism. *Risk Analysis, 22*(3), 421-423.

Harder, C. (1999). *Enterprise GIS for energy companies*. Redlands, CA: ESRI Press, Inc.

Hoffman, R. R. (1984). *Methodological preliminaries to the development of an expert system for aerial photo interpretation* (Tech. Rep. No. TRETL-0342). Fort Belvoir, VA: Engineer Topographic Laboratories.

Hoffman, R. R. (1987). The problem of extracting the knowledge of experts from the perspective of experimental psychology. *AI Applications in Natural Resources Management, 1*(2), 35-48.

Keeney, R. L., & Raiffa, H. (1976). *Decision with multiple objectives: Preferences and value tradeoffs*. New York: John Wiley & Sons.

Klein, G. A. (1987). Applications of analogic reasoning. *Metaphor and Symbolic Activity, 2*, 201-218.

Lillesand, T., & Kiefer, R. (2000). *Remote sensing and image interpretation*. New York: John Wiley and Sons, Inc.

Millet, J., & Harker, P. T. (1990). Globally effective questioning in the analytic hierarchy process. *European Journal of Operational Research, 48*, 88-97.

Mittal, S., & Dym, C. L. (1985). Knowledge acquisition from multiple experts. *AI Magazine, 6*(2), 32-36.

Moore, C. M. (1987). *Group techniques for idea building*. Newbury Park, CA: Sage Publications, Inc.

Roth, M., & Wood, C. (1990, October 31-November 2). A Delphi approach to knowledge acquisition from single and multiple experts. In *Proceedings of the 1990 ACM SIGBDP Conference on Trends and Directions in Expert Systems*, Orlando, FL (pp. 301-324).

Stefik, M., Aikins, A., Balzer, R., Benoit, J., Birnbaum, L., Hayes-Roth, F., & Sacerdoti, E. (1982). The organization of expert systems: A tutorial. *Artificial Intelligence, 18*, 135-173.

Terner, M., Sutton, R., Hebert, B., Bailey, J., Gilbert, H., & Jacqz, C. (2004, March 1). Protecting critical infrastructure. *GeoIntelligence*. Retrieved from http://www.geointelmag.com/geointelligence/article/articleDetail.jsp?id=90043, 1-2.

Thieman, K. J. (2004). *The use of scenarios and geographic information systems and technology (GIS &T) in counter-terrorism exercises and planning*. Master's thesis, Department of Geography and Earth Sciences, University of North Carolina at Charlotte.

Tolone, W. J., Wilson, D., Raja, A., Xiang, W. N., Hao, H., Phelps, S., & Johnson, E. W. (2004). Critical infrastructure integration modeling and simulation. In *Proceedings of the 2nd Symposium on Intelligence and Security Informatics (ISI 2004)* (LNCS 3073). Berlin: Springer-Verlag.

Turban, E., & Aronson, J. E. (2001). *Decision support systems and intelligent systems.* Upper Saddle River, NJ: Prentice Hall.

Weiss, S., & Kulikowski, C. (1984). *A practical guide to designing expert systems.* Totowa, NJ: Rowman and Allanheld.

Xiang, W. -N., & Clarke, K. C. (2003). The use of scenarios in land use planning. *Environment and Planning B: Planning and Design, 30*, 885-909.

Xiang, W. -N., & Whitley, D. L. (1994). Weighting land suitability factors by the PLUS method. *Environment and Planning B: Planning and Design, 21*, 273-304.

Endnotes

1 http://www.dhs.gov/dhspublic/interapp/editorial/editorial_0404.xml

2 Digital orthophotos are digital versions of aerial photographs that are constructed to rectify image displacement due to changes in aircraft tilt and topographic relief.

3 Planimetric data sets are the digital version of planimetric maps that present only the horizontal positions for features represented. They are distinguished from topographic maps by the omission of relief in measurable form. A planimetric map intended for special use may present only those features essential to the purpose to be served. Features that are usually shown on a municipal planimetric map include streets, utility lines, building footprints, tree lines, water bodies, and contour lines.

4 Tax parcel data delineate land parcel boundaries and identify those people or institutions that bear the tax burden for each parcel.

5 Data mining (also known as knowledge discovery in databases—KDD) is defined as "The nontrivial extraction of implicit, previously unknown, and potentially useful information from data" (Frawley et al., 1992, p. 58).

6 In figures and maps, PSI is referred to as "psig" — "pounds per square inch pipe."

Chapter XV

Cognitive Mapping and GIS for Community-Based Resource Identification

Lyn Kathlene, Colorado State University, USA

Abstract

This chapter describes and analyzes the effectiveness of two methodological techniques, cognitive mapping and geographical information systems (GIS), for identifying social service resources. It also examines the processes used to integrate hand-drawn map information into geocoded data points and provides recommendations for improving efficiency and precision. As a first step to integrate Jefferson County social service delivery into community-based child welfare "systems of care" (SOC), both formal and informal services had to be identified. Cognitive mapping, a process by which participants draw visual representations of geographical areas, was conducted with 247 participants in Jefferson County, Colorado. Over 3,500 resources were identified and entered into a GIS to analyze the availability, capacity, and distribution of social services in the county and within communities. Identification of community resources via cognitive mapping and GIS analysis provide: (1) a comprehensive database of existing services; (2) a basis to build communication networks and cooperation among government and community providers; (3) the ability to create an efficient system that avoids duplication of efforts; (4) an understanding of the geographical distribution of resources; (5) the identification of resources lacking in the county and specific communities; and (6) knowledge differences among diverse participant groups.

Introduction

In December, 2003, the Colorado Institute of Public Policy (CIPP) at Colorado State University was contracted by Jefferson County, Colorado, Division of Human Services, to conduct a resource identification analysis. The project was one component in the first year of a five-year Health and Human Services — Children's Bureau grant to create a "systems of care" (SOC) in child welfare social service delivery.[1] Jefferson County, Colorado, was one of eight pilot sites awarded an SOC grant. The CIPP component was to identify services available at the community-level and discover services that were lacking.

SOC is a major paradigm shift in social service delivery. It removes the locus of authority away from one individual, the social service worker, and replaces it with a group of service providers, family, and community members to develop *collectively* a comprehensive plan to move the child and family out of crisis. The provision of services are to be coordinated, *community-based*, culturally competent and individualized (Stroul, 1986).

To integrate Jefferson County social service delivery into community-based comprehensive child welfare SOC, both *formal* and *informal* services had to be identified. Informal services are of particular interest since these are likely the least well-known (there was no official directory) and serve populations at a community SOC level (rather than county-wide). For definition purposes, informal services were identified for participants as private or not-for-profit programs, including services such as church soup kitchens, non-profit agencies providing transportation services for the elderly, and in-home daycare providers not registered with the county. Formal services are public programs at the state, county, and local level, such as Jefferson County Mental Health Services, Title XX daycare providers, public schools, public transportation, and park and recreation programs.

To identify existing resources at the community level, cognitive mapping, a process by which participants draw visual representations of geographical areas, was conducted with 247 participants in Jefferson County, Colorado. Participant groups in the mapping included social service, non-profit, and faith-based providers, social service clients (Temporary Assistance for Needy Families (TANF) recipients, youths, foster care providers, and adoptive parents), residents and ethnic/racial enclaves (Latino, Eastern European, Native American, and African American). In addition, all resources listed in the Jefferson County resource guides were included in the resource database. Over 3,800 unique resources were identified and entered into a GIS — ArcMap, a component of ArcView — to analyze the availability, capacity, and distribution of social services in the county and within communities. Census data was overlaid to identify high-need areas and ethnic enclaves.

Here, a novel application of GIS for designing improved social service delivery systems is described. The chapter also discusses complications involved in working with human service agencies, and reconsiders the processes developed to merge cognitive mapping information into ArcMap.

Cognitive Mapping: Origin and Uses

Cognitive mapping has not been comprehensively integrated with GIS to the degree discussed in this project, although elementary integration has been done in some previous projects (Fulton, Horan, & Serrano, 1997; Kathlene, 1997; Kathlene & Horan, 1998; Horan, Serrano, & McMurran, 2001).[2] The potential usefulness to the human services sectors through projects that use the combined methodologies is substantial. To better understand this "fit," a brief review of cognitive mapping follows.

Cognitive mapping did not originate from research on humans. Rather, the term "cognitive map" was originally used to describe the mental representations that rats develop as they navigate the same maze multiple times (Tolman, 1948). Quickly, researchers became interested in using the information from cognitive maps in the human context, and the resulting collection of methods became known as cognitive mapping. Later, the term expanded to include mental depictions of more abstract entities, like ideas or chains of events. Since its inception, cognitive mapping has been used as an approach to a number of real-world issues.

Cognitive mapping's first practical application was in the field of urban planning when Kevin Lynch (1960) found that certain places or elements in a city generated a positive emotional reaction among its residents. This type of research, he felt, could be used to better design cities so as to make them more memorable. Jack Nasar (1988) extended Lynch's study by including a model of how city attributes influenced the affective responses of residents and visitors.

Cognitive mapping is also used to evaluate mental representations of smaller areas. Mapping of specific neighborhoods (Quaiser-Pohl, Lehmann, & Eid, 2004; Uzzell, Pol, & Badenas, 2002), college campuses (Hardwick, Wooldridge, & Rinalducci, 1983; Holahan & Dobrowolny, 1978; Sholl, 1987), and buildings (Moeser, 1988; O'Laughlin & Brubaker, 1998; O'Neill, 1991) adds to knowledge about how spatial abilities develop and are utilized, the skills related to map creation, and the mapping abilities of various groups. Numerous overlying maps of these smaller areas have been used to program autonomous mobile robots (Yoshino, 1991).

Almost anyone can successfully complete a mapping exercise. Studies have found the quality of female and male's maps are similar (Evans, 1980; Magana & Norman, 1980; O'Laughlin & Brubaker, 1998); nearly all ages can successfully participate (Quaiser-Pohl, Lehmann, & Eid, 2004); and map quality is not influenced by drawing skill (Evans, 1980; Hardwick, Wooldridge, & Rinalducci, 1983). The only criteria that affects map quality is familiarity with the target area, where quality increases with familiarity (Evans, 1980; Fridgen, 1987; Unger & Wandersman, 1985). Familiarity, however, can distort maps. For example, locations of importance to the participant are often drawn larger or more centrally than other map elements (Holahan & Dobrowolny, 1978; Kathlene, 1997). Finally, at the coding stage, the use of multiple coders without knowledge of the study hypothesis is commonly used (Daniels & Johnson, 2002); yet, studies have found nearly perfect agreement among multiple coders (Quaiser-Pohl, Lehmann, & Eid, 2004).

For this project, the above issues did not present problems. Each of the participants was directed to draw the area they self-identified as their most recognizable; therefore, they had high levels of familiarity. The maps required particularly little drawing skill as participants were only asked to draw boundaries (for which they are provided a ruler), mark their home with an "X," and identify landmarks with squares. Since the objective in the study was to identify resources of importance to the participant; having the maps drawn to scale was irrelevant because the exact geographic coordinates for each location are determined during the coding process. Coding the maps involved recording objective location information, thereby removing the problem of coder subjectivity. In short, information gleaned from the maps was not dependent upon the drawing skills of the participants.

Adaptation of Mapping Methods for Resource Identification

Each use of mapping described above required a unique adaptation of the method. Participants in these studies were asked to sketch maps, arrange pictures of pieces of paper according to their location or importance, locate points on a map, circle areas on a map, recognize features on an aerial photograph, or label features on a blank map. The literature effectively suggests that as many methods of mapping exist as purposes for using it.

In this project, participants attending a mapping workshop were first provided background on the overall goals of the SOC project as well as their role as a mapper in

Figure 1. Example of hand drawn cognitive map

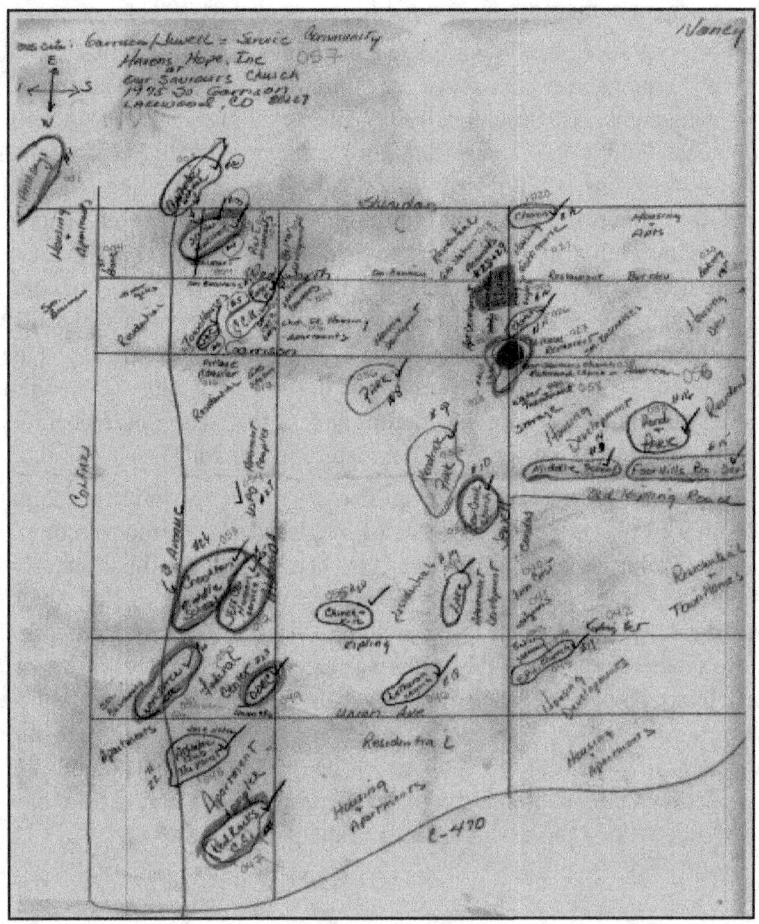

achieving those goals. The hope was that understanding the importance of the project would encourage conscientious participation. Then, participants were provided with a large blank sheet of paper and asked to indicate the street or physical boundaries within which they most commonly travel. Street maps of the area were available to help them in this and later tasks. Workshops consisted of three to sixteen people, and at each session they were encouraged to work cooperatively with their fellow workshop participants. Following a visualization exercise to assist them in accessing non-verbal memories, they were asked to fill in details such as streets, natural features, and resources they commonly use. It was explained that these maps were not meant to be artistic works; simple boxes and lines drawn with their rulers would suffice to represent objects and locations. Once the maps were complete, participants were asked to label various types of resources with colors corresponding to commercial businesses, community resources, government agencies, community strengths, and community weaknesses. They also completed a survey asking for detailed description of the important resources and features on their maps and to provide any additional information regarding resources lacking in their area. Each map was then entered into a GIS database. Figure 1 is an example of a cognitive map drawn for the Jefferson County Project.

GIS Analysis Technique

The GIS for this cognitive mapping project provides aggregated spatial analysis of the maps. GIS combines the thousands of data points collected from the participant-drawn maps, which greatly enhances the value of cognitive mapping information. In addition, each distinct physical address has dozens of descriptors that identify not only who provided the information but also secondary data such as the participants' perceptions of a particular resource or service (Longley, Goodchild, Maguire, & Rhind, 2001). The data is accessible in Excel-type tables that can be easily queried and displayed on a digital street map (Longley, Goodchild, Maguire, & Rhind, 2001). This analysis allows for preliminary interpretation of the data set, such as the dispersion or clustering of resources in geographic areas (Heagerty & Lele, 1998; Reich & Davis, 2003). GIS can incorporate external data sources, such as census data, which can be layered with the cognitive mapping data. Integrating the cognitive mapping data with GIS software creates nearly limitless ways to analyze the data and allows for easily-interpreted visual results.

Technical Capacity for the Project

For this project the particular GIS capabilities were:

- Visual representation of addresses and areas via data points, data lines, and data shapes
- The ability to layer data points for sorting, categorizing, and selection purposes

- Accompanying tables of descriptive variables for each data layer with the ability to search and sort individual data points based on particular variable(s)
- The ability to export the data to conduct advanced spatial analysis

The cognitive mapping process was greatly enhanced, especially for analysis purposes, by using GIS to create unique, specialized parameters (for a theoretical model, see Jordan, Raubal, Gartrell, & Egenhofer, 1998). The potential outcomes of such a union include:

- The capability to export a large quantity of data in an Excel-type format that can be searched and sorted based on any given number of criteria
- The ability to organize and sort data in a spatial manner (i.e. in the form of maps)
- The opportunity to create an easily-updated database for organizing additional data gathered by the cognitive mapping process and through other resource identification processes

Structure of the GIS for the Project

The structure of the GIS system for this project was based on three principles:

1. The structure needed to be flexible and allow for the maximum amount of data to be stored and easily accessed
2. The structure needed to be relatively simple such that an inexperienced GIS user can understand the sorting, searching, and selecting potential of the system
3. The GIS system needed to be able to organize data from a variety of sources and be easily updated over time

The first step to organizing the data was to create basic social service or resource categories (in GIS terms these categories are referred to as layers). Each layer needed to be broad enough to encompass a variety of unique data points (identified resources) but narrow enough to create a good classification system for a beginning search and find procedure. These basic layers were the essential framework of the GIS system and the search capabilities of the system that providers could use; therefore, they had to match either the basic social service field breakdown of resource types and/or be intuitively organized.

Ultimately, 24 layers were created for the project including Housing, Mental Health Services, Transportation, Health Care, Emergency Services, Domestic Violence, and Victim Services. Within each layer were key fields with similar categories across all the layers. For example, the data field "Resource Type" exists in each of the 24 layers and contains only one of five values: Governmental, Community Non-Profit, Faith-Based, Private, or Unknown. This allowed queries and linkages to be made across layers. As an illustration, a user could search for all the community non-profit sponsored resources or services in two or more of the layers and combine these results on one map.

Search or selection functions work on a layer by layer level in ArcMap. Within the Housing layer there were attributes such as Resource Name, Resource Address, and Resource Hours of Availability. These attributes are easily sorted. For example, there should only be one Lakewood Housing Authority (LHA), but if there are two locations for LHA, they can be distinguished from one another in the data table due to the different values entered in the Resource Address cell. However, not all searches are done based on a known name or location; therefore, a more extensive list of attributes must exist to properly describe each resource. Some examples of other attribute identifiers were Resource Type (government-sponsored, private, faith-based, or community non-profit) or Funding Source. Another type of attribute is a binary descriptor such as Used by Respondent Yes/No. This would apply to data points identified by clients and useful in various types of qualitative analysis. Below is a simplified example of a layer table structure and associated attributes.

It is easy to see in Table 1 the large number of possible searches based on only seven attributes. For example, a provider might want to find all government-sponsored housing resources. The search would use "*Resource Type*=Government." The first two rows would be selected from the search. If housing resources provided by community non-profits is of interest, the search would be written as "*Respondent Category*=Client and *Resource Type*=Community Non-Profit and *Used by Respondent*=Yes." In the table above, this would select only the last row.

Table 1. Housing layer attribute table

Survey ID	Respondent Category	Resource Name	Resource Type	Hours of Availability	Funding Type	Used by Respondent
0105	Client	LHA	Government	9am-5pm	Government	No
0431	Provider	LHA	Government	9am-5pm	Government	N/A
0302	Community Member	Lakeside Apartments	Private	N/A	N/A	Yes
0746	Client	Allison Care Center	Community Non-Profit	N/A	Private	Yes

Each row represents one unique data point on the GIS map and therefore represents one unique resource. Resources can be identified and placed on the map multiple times, as in the above example, with the first and second row both being the Resource Type "LHA." What distinguishes the two data points, however, is not the location on the map but the multiple attributes in the table listed above. Here, LHA was identified once by a provider and once by a client, information that indicates common knowledge. Alternatively, if only clients identify the Allison Care Center, a knowledge gap in Jefferson County Human Services providers and resource manuals is revealed, which can be easily remedied. Creating a comprehensive database with separate rows of multiple criteria allows for flexibility in the analysis of resources ranging from a simple resource search engine to a complex spatial analysis tool to numerically describe the layout of resources and services in Jefferson County.

GIS Analysis of Community Resources

To do the GIS analysis, the resources identified by the mapping and focus group participants were verified using the 2004 Denver Metro phone book (www.dexonline.com) and/or MapQuest (www.mapquest.com). The addresses were entered into an Excel spreadsheet, the type of resource and service was coded into one or more of the 24 types of resources, and the participant group and demographics were entered.[3] The spreadsheet was imported into ArcMap and geo-coded to place the identified resources with known addresses on a common geographical coordinate system.

The 24 layers of resource and service types were created by: (1) working with participants in four pilot sessions to understand how they conceptualized services; (2) presenting the pilot workshop information to Jefferson County Human Service employees to add categories that aligned with their current resource guides and experiences; and (3) aligning with the Aires taxonomy used by Colorado 2-1-1 system.[4] The resulting twenty-four layers allowed for some resources/services to be coded into more than one layer, thereby increasing the ability of information seekers to find the desired resources. For example, a service dedicated to providing transportation to elderly individuals would be included in Aging and Adult/Senior Services as well as Transportation Services. The dual coding in this project and used by the 2-1-1 system produces a comprehensive searchable database that can reach a specific resource through multiple avenues.

At the onset of the project, the research team decided that a method for determining when the mapping process had reached a saturation level of redundant information was needed. A novel method, a "repeat rate," was created. The repeat rate was set at 80% based on the time and cost involved in identifying additional resources. The repeat rate estimates the projected number of new points to be expected from each additional map. So, for example, on the first map every identified resource is unique and a new point in the database, the repeat rate is zero. By the 100th map, if 50% of the points collected were previously identified on any of the previous 99 maps, the non-repeated points for that map would be 50%. At some point, theoretically, no new information will be gleaned from additional maps, resulting in a 100% repeat rate. In practical terms, full saturation cannot be reached; but more importantly, a trade-off must be made between additional information and cost to acquire the information. In this project, there was an average of 20 resource points per map. Each map took approximately four hours to process (from address coding the points to data entry into ArcMap). An 80% threshold repeat rate was chosen as a break-even level. At this rate, only one additional new resource would be identified per one hour of coding time. Less than one additional new resource per hour of work was deemed an inefficient use of resources.

Selected Results

While the cognitive mapping process identified formal and informal resources, without the ability to do aggregated and stratified analyses the collected data would only have provided a list of resources known by the mappers. To create a comprehensive SOC child welfare system requires detailed knowledge about the geographical distribution of the density of community resources and the types available in the community. Additionally, to understand and correct the community-level information gaps among providers, community members and clients, a geographical analysis stratified by resource categories and information sources (e.g., county resource guides, social service workers, community providers, faith-based providers, and clients) was needed. GIS is able to provide such geographical analysis. Importantly, data presented in visual form facilitated information dissemination among a wide variety of stakeholders.

Seven Jefferson County cities were the focus of the mapping project. Clients and community resident groups were drawn from Lakewood, Arvada, Wheat Ridge, Golden, Littleton, and the mountain communities of Conifer and Evergreen. A total of 42 workshops were held at locations in each of these communities. Special sessions were held with members of the dominant ethnic groups, identified using census data imported into ArcMap. The groups included Native American, Russian, and Latino community residents,[5] with Latinos being the largest ethnic population in Jefferson County. To determine the areas in Jefferson County with the highest growth rate of Latinos, 1990 and 2000 census data was imported into ArcMap and the percent change was calculated. The highest concentrations of the Latino population were found in the central eastern area of Jefferson County (Lakewood and Arvada) on the border of Denver County. Figure 2 shows the Latino growth

Figure 2. Latino population growth in Jefferson County, 1990-2000

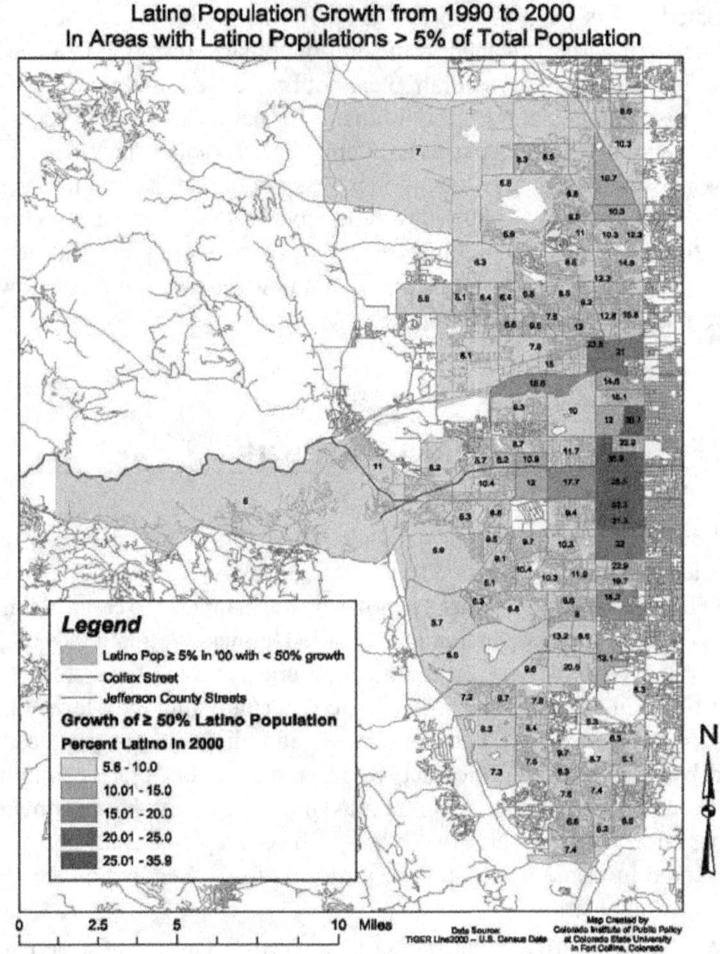

patterns from 1990 to 2000. Numbers on the map are the percentage of the area's Latino population in the 2000 Census.

Current and past users of Jefferson County social services were identified by Jefferson County. Since the database was confidential, Jefferson County would not allow CIPP to pull a stratified sample. In addition, over half the client records were miss-

Figure 3. Client home locations and range boundaries

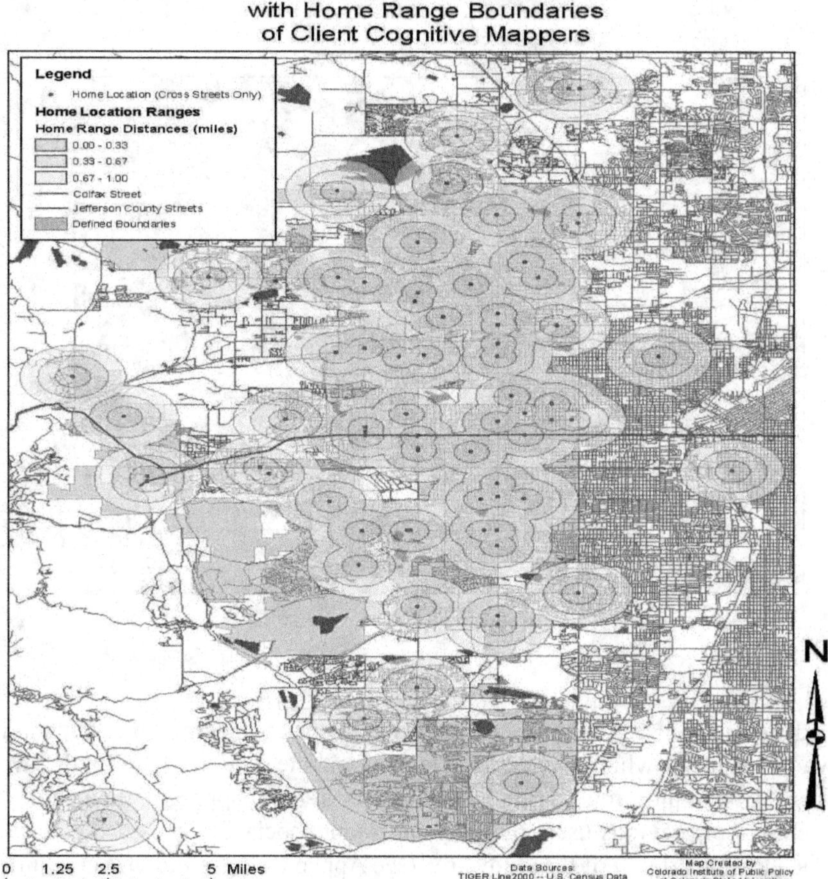

ing complete address information. Because of these difficulties, all complete client files with zip codes in the study area were mailed invitations by Jefferson County to participate in the study. Fortunately, the clients, foster, and adoptive parents who participated were distributed throughout the study area. The following map shows the home location cross-streets of the participants and the extrapolated hypothetical boundaries of their identified communities, ranging from one-third mile to one mile

Figure 4. All Jefferson County, Colorado, resources identified by participants and resource guides

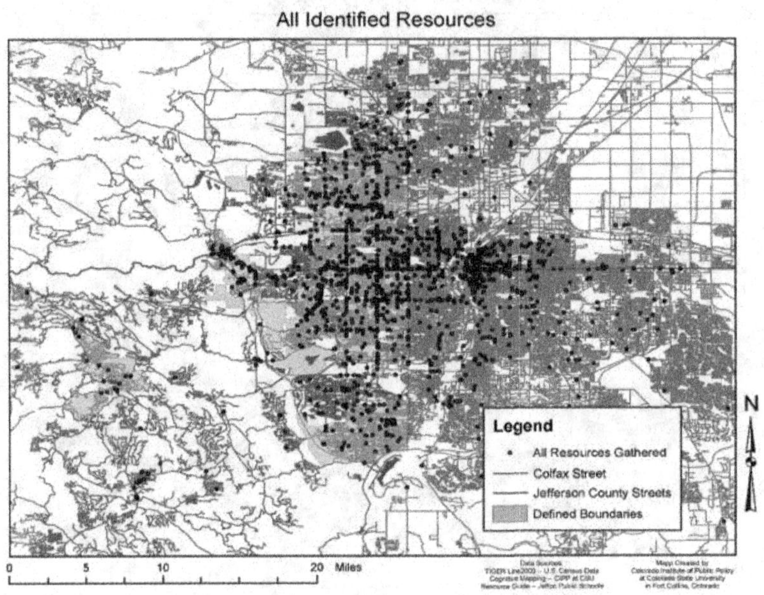

around their residence. The buffer area was based on actual community boundaries drawn on the maps, which ranged from larger than one mile to a handful that were smaller than one-third mile. Figure 3 indicates that the mapping participants who were current or previous users of Jefferson County social services had collective knowledge of nearly all of the study area (see Appendix A for demographic information of the participants).

Figure 4 shows the 3,845 resources identified and mapped. The number of unique points is 1,819 after removing the repeated information. Identified resources are distributed across all the Jefferson County study areas with a scattering throughout Denver County and a dense clustering along the main arterial east-west street, Colfax.

Next are selected categories of resources to illustrate how GIS was used to inform SOC planning efforts.

- **Childcare:** One hundred and eleven different childcare providers were identified. As Figure 5 shows, there is very little overlap in knowledge between

Figure 5. Childcare resources identified by participants vs. Jefferson County resource guides

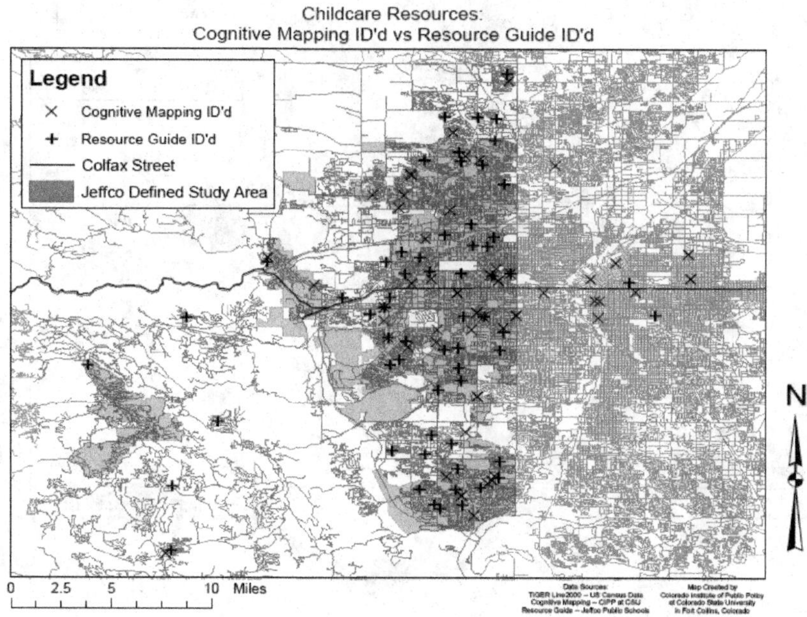

the Jefferson County resource guides and the participants in the mapping workshops. This could indicate: (1) clients and providers are not familiar with the childcare resources which Jefferson County has identified; and (2) Jefferson County is not effectively disseminating this information. Many of the childcare resources identified in the Jefferson County resource guides are before-school and after-school care programs. In contrast, the cognitive mapping participants identified pre-school childcare facilities rather than before and after-school programs. Based on this analysis, the current guides are lacking in pre-school childcare resources. It is likely this information is housed with a specific organization rather than listed within Jeffco's resource guides; however, *a consolidated database will facilitate resource integration, information referral, and client access.*

- **Education:** There were 366 education resources identified. This is the category in the Jefferson County guides with the most resources. As would be expected, the Jefferson County Public Schools Resource Guide has all the primary and secondary public schools, as well as a few private schools in the county. Figure 6 shows there is very little additional information provided by

Figure 6. Education resources: Cognitive mapping vs. resource guides

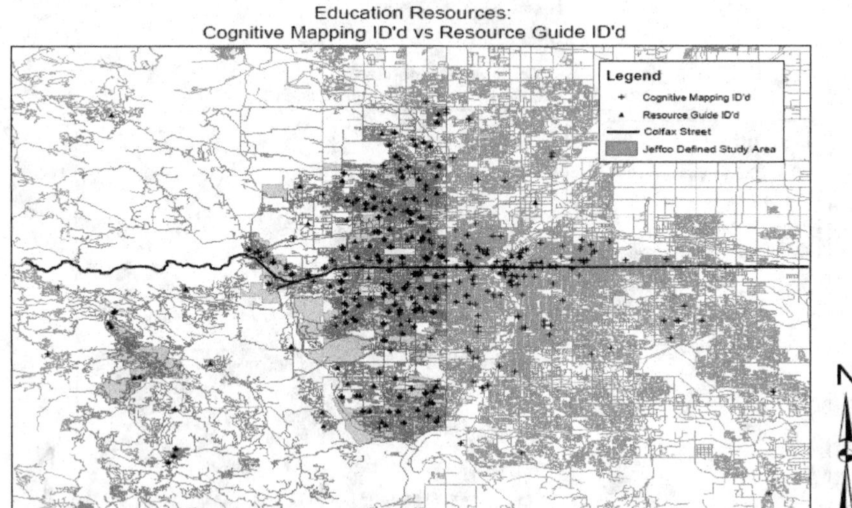

the mapping sessions with regard to education resources in Jefferson County; however, the mapping identified a significant number of resources in Denver that are known and used by Jefferson County residents. The Jefferson County education resources not identified in the resource guides were typically services such as breast-feeding classes located at hospitals, ESL classes available at community centers and/or libraries, and other educational services available at libraries, these important educational services are missing in Jefferson County's guides.

- **Health care resources:** Of the 190 health care resources, 140 were identified by the cognitive mapping process with only one-third of the services identified by both participants and the Jefferson County resource guides. As seen in the Figure 7, however, the Jefferson County resource guides also have information about several health care services in Denver. Most of the Denver and Jefferson County services were also identified by the cognitive mapping process. *Information from the cognitive mapping process increases the resource base by two-thirds, adding significantly to health care knowledge of Jefferson County.*

Three of the 24 resource categories have been provided above for sake of brevity. However, there were several trends that appeared in almost all of the resource

Figure 7. Health care resources: Cognitive mapping vs. resource guides

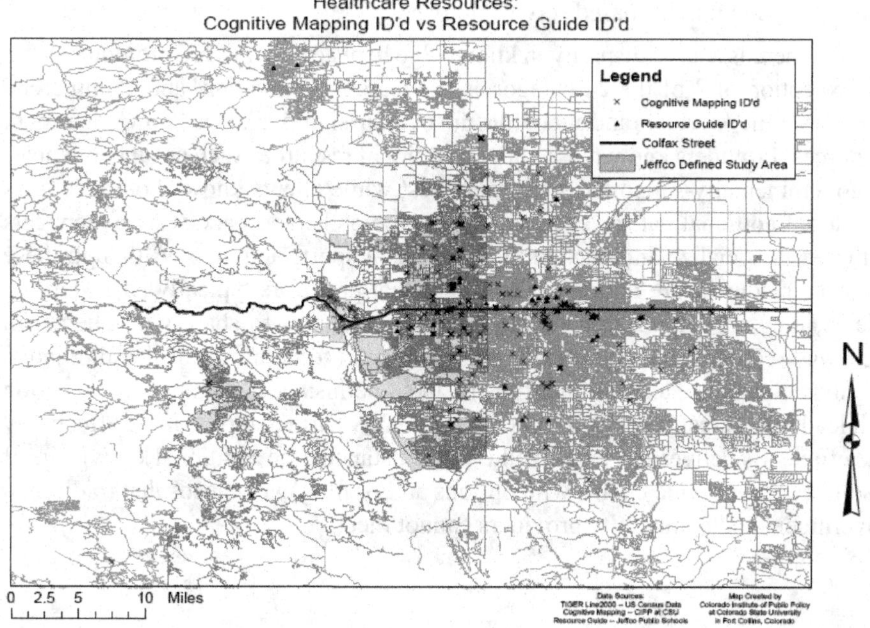

categories. First, the Jefferson County resource guides failed to provide adequate information. Except in education and childcare, the resource guides fell far short of the number of resources identified by the mapping participants. While there are many childcare resources in the Jefferson County information guides, there is little overlap between the childcare listed in the Jefferson County guides and the childcare identified by the cognitive mapping. The GIS maps effectively demonstrate such knowledge gaps.

Second, there are a significant number of resources in Denver County (east of Jefferson County) that providers and clients identify. Reasonable accessibility to Denver County, as well as lack of availability of the resources in Jefferson County, likely accounts for this trend. Building a community-based SOC will require Jefferson County to find ways to offer some of these services locally, a challenge that will require developing community partnerships to overcome the financial constraints which the County faces.

Third, opposite of the previous trend, Jefferson County resource guides provide mainly Denver locations for some types of resources, even though the same resources exist in numerous places in Jefferson County. Available resources closer to Jefferson County residents are a fundamental component of SOC and, in this trend, require only disseminating the information effectively, which is a low-cost method to improve community-based service delivery.

Finally, there is a large disparity in knowledge between clients and providers. With the exception of 3 of the 24 categories, Education, Recreation, and Commercial Resources, the providers and clients did not overlap significantly in knowledge about resources. Providers know more about traditional resources such as other agencies or governmentally-supported social services, while clients know about resources of a less traditional nature, such as churches, motels, and parks where teenagers gathered to socialize and engage in recreational sports activities. Although these informal resources are not referral services that providers typically pass along to clients, they are important community-based resources to share with clients. In creating a community-based SOC, providers need to be aware of the alternative methods clients use to meet their needs. In some instances, this new information will lead to the creation of government/community partnerships to more effectively and efficiently deliver services. In other circumstances, the additional knowledge of resources will provide clients with options and/or fill gaps in needs that traditional government and community providers cannot meet.

Lessons Learned

Several problems directly and indirectly related to the GIS component of the project became apparent and required adjustments to the procedures or accommodations to the expected output. These include research procedures that are incompatible with social service agencies' capacity, issues of client confidentiality, repeat rates, incomplete and/or inaccurate databases for coding resource locations, coding protocols, and mapping accuracy.

First, as has been found before, many county and local agencies lack leadership that understands the value of GIS in policy decision-making (Greene, 2000; Nedovic-Budic, 1996; Ventura, 1995; Worrall & Bond, 1997). Hence, many agencies lack the technical ability to employ GIS and, consequently, also lack the understanding to work effectively and efficiently with the researchers. Furthermore, because social service agencies typically do not have a GIS analyst on staff, data and map files have limited usefulness beyond the initial analysis as presented in the final report. Finally, human service agencies have organizational procedures that create significant barriers in implementing research projects, barriers that need to be addressed in the project planning stages (Ventura, 1995). Jefferson County Human Services suffered from all three impediments and was exacerbated by the high turnover of the staff. In the first year, two-thirds of the project staff left. By the middle of the second year, only one person out of nine key project staff remained. Those who left included the project manager and the principal investigator, both of who had been replaced twice. Within 18 months, none of the people who conceptualized and wrote the HHS grant were involved in the project. Institutional memory was wiped clean and new staff was unfamiliar and wary of many components laid out in the grant proposal, including the untraditional resource identification method. Higher administrative support for the innovative project waned, and "business as usual" reasserted itself as the dominant paradigm. It became clear that the resource database developed through the mapping process would not be updated on a regular basis and, perhaps, not disseminated throughout the organization if left to Jefferson County. The CIPP sought out a more stable organization to house the resource data, Colorado 2-1-1, with the permission of the first project manager.

Second, human service agencies as well as educational institutions cannot share client/student data. This presents a significant research barrier when the project requires participation of these populations. Ideally, individuals within the organizations would have both the access to the data and sophistication to manipulate the data in accordance with standard research protocols. This is unlikely to be the case in institutions which are financially strapped and lack the vision or political will to invest in trained personnel and needed research tools. To ameliorate these conditions, project planning must include agreed-upon protocols for effectively and efficiently handling confidential data.

Third, unique to this project was the creation of a "repeat rate" to set a standard for data density. The 80% repeat rate was selected for efficiency of resources, based on an extrapolation of the average number of points per map and time needed to code and enter the data for each map. Unknown was how many participants/maps were needed to reach the 80% repeat rate in each of the 24 categories. Initially, the CIPP recommended target was 450 participants. This number was revised downward by Jefferson County Human Services to a maximum of 250 participants. From the 247 actual participants, the 80% repeat rate was reached in only two of the 24 resource categories. The average repeat rate was 55% across all categories, indicating that more than 250 participants were needed to reach 80%. Whether 450 participants were ultimately required is unknown. More importantly, did the lower repeat rate significantly affect the quality of the project? Certainly, fewer resources were identified at the 55% rate; but 1,480 resources not in Jefferson County resource guides were identified; not an insignificant contribution to building a more comprehensive social services.

Fourth, in the process of coding the maps and sorting the data to find repeated addresses or groupings by type of provider, and so forth, it was discovered that precise alphanumeric coding was critical. With the large number of data fields (attributes) assigned to each participant, there were inconsistencies in some of the categories. The data cleaning was more extensive than anticipated. Future projects should utilize numeric coding in attributes to the fullest extent possible and develop strict alphanumeric standards for addresses, organizational names, and other alpha fields.

Finally, to find resource addresses, MapQuest and the Denver metro area phone book were used. MapQuest was the most efficient method but had the most errors, as discovered when the address was imported into ArcMap. A cross-check with the phone books corrected most of these errors.

Nine percent of the mapping points were unidentifiable due to a combination of missing information in MapQuest and the phone book, and poor location information on the hand drawn maps. The latter accounted for a greater proportion of the unidentified points, especially resources such as neighborhood parks and unnamed resources such as "soup kitchen." Rather than rely solely on participants naming the nearest cross streets to such resources, the closest known commercial entity should be identified. This redundancy will reduce missing data due to participant error in naming streets.

Future Trends

While this project was limited to identifying resources, spatial patterns of resource locations, and knowledge gaps, the collected data can be mined further. More specific uses can be created, such as a searchable Web-based provider resource database and the identification of physical and/or service areas with inadequate resources in relation to socio-economic deprivation areas. The latter allows providers to demonstrate specific needs, important for several reasons, including the pursuit of future programmatic funding. These specific uses are described in greater detail as follows:

- **Provider resource database:** In the future, the Web-based database can be converted into a tool for social service providers to identify available resources and the most accessible locations for clients (Worrall & Bond, 1997). The end user (a case-worker) would be able to search for particular resources based on any number of criteria or a combination of criteria. For example, one might enter necessary criteria such as Rental Assistance Housing Resource located within three miles of a given location that also caters to Spanish-speaking clientele. After these attributes or criteria are entered into the appropriate locations on the Webpage, a list of all the resources or providers that fit the criteria could be retrieved, similar to the business name search feature available through a site such as MapQuest. Finally, digital maps could be generated with driving directions for the case-worker to print out for the client. It is also possible to map the public transportation routes to services.

- **Needs assessments:** The database can be used to conduct comprehensive, quantifiable, and defensible needs assessments. A social service provider administrator or grant writer could search the data described above in conjunction with Census data and the County's client locations to reveal areas of need or areas of excess (Bond & Devine, 1991; Worrall & Bond, 1997).[6] A strategic plan could be developed to determine where a new office or access point for a particular resource should be located to serve the greatest number of clients. This type of spatial analysis based on quantifiable numbers and distances can be used to justify a particular course of action either for internal/external accountability or to acquire funding for various projects aimed at community resource and social service distribution.

Acknowledgments

The author would like to thank April Smith, Department of Psychology, Colorado State University, and Mary Tye, Department of Psychology, Colorado State University, for running the workshops and coding the data; David Wallick, Colorado Institute of Public Policy, Colorado State University, for conducting the GIS analysis; and Juliana Hissrich for providing administrative support to the project.

Conclusion

Cognitive mapping combined with GIS analysis is a powerful method for identifying community resources by providing: (1) a comprehensive database of existing services; (2) a basis to build communication networks and cooperation among government and community providers; (3) the ability to create an efficient system that avoids duplication of efforts; (4) an understanding of the geographical distribution of resources; (5) the identification of resources lacking in the county and specific communities; and (6) knowledge differences among diverse participant groups. The addition of 1,480 resource locations within the seven study areas (only a portion of Jefferson County) nearly tripled the number of resources and services listed in the Jefferson County guides.

Ultimately, service delivery in SOC is about building partnerships across the multiple services *and* bringing in new, even sometimes untraditional, community partners. Family involvement is the key in this collaborative arrangement. Similar to untraditional community partners and resources, families as partners do not fit easily within current social service delivery structures, values, and beliefs. Recognizing, valuing, and partnering with resource providers identified by clients and community members is one important step toward shifting practices. Cognitive mapping with GIS provides a tool for taking the first critical steps.

References

Bond, D., & Devine, P. (1991). The role of geographic information systems in survey analysis. *The Statistician, 40*, 209-215.

Daniels, K., & Johnson, G. (2002). On trees and triviality traps: Locating the debate on the contribution of cognitive mapping to organizational research. *Organization Studies, 23*(1), 73-81.

Evans, G. W. (1980). Environmental cognition. *Psychological Bulletin, 88*(2), 259-287.

Fridgen, J. D. (1987). Use of cognitive maps to determine perceived tourism regions. *Leisure Sciences, 9*(2), 101-117.

Fulton, W., Horan, T., & Serrano, K. (1997). *Putting it all together: Using the ISTEA framework to synthesize transportation and broader community goals*. Claremont Graduate University, University Research Institute, Claremont, CA.

Greene, R. W. (2000). *GIS in public policy: Using geographical information for more effective government*. Redlands, CA: ESRI Press.

Hardwick, D. A., Wooldridge, S. C., & Rinalducci, E. J. (1983). Selection of landmarks as a correlate of cognitive map organization. *Psychological Reports, 53*(3), 807-813.

Heagerty, P. J., & Lele, S. R. (1998). A composite likelihood approach to binary spatial data. *Journal of the American Statistical Association, 93*(443), 1099-1111.

Hjortso, C. N., Christensen, S. M., & Tarp, P. (2005). Rapid stakeholder and conflict assessment for natural resource management using cognitive mapping: The case of Damdoi Forest Enterprise, Vietnam. *Agriculture and Human Values, 22*, 149-167.

Hobbs, B. F., Ludsin, S. A., Knight, R. L., Ryan, P. A., Biberhofer, J., & Ciborowski, J. J. H. (2002). Fuzzy cognitive mapping as a tool to define management objectives for complex ecosystems. *Ecological Applications, 12*, 1548-1565.

Holahan, C. J., & Dobrowolny, M. B. (1978). Cognitive and behavioral correlates of the spatial environment: An interactional analysis. *Environment and Behavior, 10*(3), 317-333.

Jordan, T., Raubal, M., Gartrell, B., & Egenhofer, M. J. (1998, July). An affordance-based model of place in GIS. In *Eighth International Symposium on*

Spatial Data Handling '98 Conference Proceedings, Vancouver, BC, Canada (pp. 98-109).

Kathlene, L. (1997). *29th street greenway corridor citizen survey panel: Results of mapping exercise, phase 3*. Minneapolis, MN: University of Minneapolis, Humphrey Institute of Public Affairs.

Kathlene, L., & Horan, T. (1998). *GIS survey of 29th street corridor, Minneapolis, MN*. Minneapolis, MN: University of Minneapolis, Humphrey Institute of Public Affairs.

Longley, P. A., Goodchild, M. F., Maguire, D. J., & Rhind, D. W. (2001). *Geographic information systems and science*. New York: John Wiley and Sons, LTD.

Lynch, K. (1960). *The image of the city*. Cambridge, MA: MIT Press.

Magana, J. R., & Norman, D. K. (1980). Methodological inquiry into elicitation procedures: Cognitive mapping and free listing. *Perceptual and Motor Skills, 51*(3), 931-934.

Horan, T., Serrano, K., & McMurran, G. (2001). *GIS for livable communities: Examiniation of community perceptions of assets, liabilities and transportation improvements.* San Jose, CA: San Jose University, Mineta Transportation Institute, College of Business.

Moeser, S. D. (1988). Cognitive mapping in a complex building. *Environment and Behavior, 20*(1), 21-49.

Nasar, J. L. (1988). *The evaluative image of the city*. Thousand Oaks, CA: Sage Publications.

Nedovic-Budic, Z., & Godschalk, D. R. (1996). Human factors in adoption of geographical information systems: A local government case study. *Public Administration Review, 56*, 554-567.

O'Laughlin, E. M., & Brubaker, B. S. (1998). Use of landmarks in cognitive mapping: Gender differences in self report versus performance. *Personality and Individual Differences, 24*(5), 595-601.

O'Neill, M. J. (1991). Evaluation of a conceptual model of architectural legibility. *Environment and Behavior, 23*(3), 259-284.

Quaiser-Pohl, C., Lehmann, W., & Eid, M. (2004). The relationship between spatial abilities and representations of large-scale space in children — a structural equation modeling analysis. *Personality and Individual Differences, 36*(1), 95-107.

Reich, R. M., & Davis, R. (2003). Spatial statistical analysis of natural resources (Tech. Rep. No. NR512). Fort Collins, CO: Colorado State University.

Sholl, M. J. (1987). Cognitive maps as orienting schemata. *Journal of Experimental Psychology: Learning, Memory, & Cognition, 13*(4), 615-628.

Stroul, B. (1996). Profiles of local systems of care. In B. A. Stroul and R. M. Friedman (Eds.), *Systems of care for children's mental health* (pp. 149-176). Baltimore: Paul H. Brookes Publishing Co.

Tolman, E. C. (1948). Cognitive maps in rats and men. *Psychological Review, 55*(4), 189-208.

Unger, D. G., & Wandersman, A. (1985). The importance of neighbors: The social, cognitive, and affective components of neighboring. *American Journal of Community Psychology, 13*(2), 139-169.

Uzzell, D., Pol, E., & Badenas, D. (2002). Place identification, social cohesion, and environmental sustainability. *Environment and Behavior, 34*(1), 26-53.

Ventura, S. J. (1995). The use of geographical information systems in local government. *Public Administration Review, 55*, 461-467.

Worrall, L., & Bond, D. (1997). Geographical information systems, spatial analysis, and public policy: The British experience. *International Statistical Review, 65*, 365-379.

Yoshino, R. (1991). A note on cognitive maps: An optimal spatial knowledge representation. *Journal of Mathematical Psychology, 35*, 371-393.

Endnotes

1 The project was supported by grant #90CA1715/01, CFDA #93.570 from the Federal Department of Health and Human Services through Jefferson County, Colorado.

2 The term cognitive mapping is used for a variety of techniques, including "fuzzy cognitive mapping," a technique that builds mental maps of perceptions from focus-group and interviews (Hjortso, Christensen, & Tarp, 2005; Hobbs et al., 2002). In this project, cognitive mapping means hand-drawn maps of tangible community resources and locations, a geographical data collection technique new to GIS.

3 Nine percent of the mapping points could not be accurately located and were dropped from the analysis. Of the remaining 89%, two possible location errors could occur in transferring the cognitive map information into a database for ArcMap. First, multiple coders could use different alphanumeric codes, thereby making the same resource appear as a different resource. To correct this error, the data was cleaned by conducting sorts on multiple columns in the excel spreadsheet to reveal unknown duplicates. For example, a search

on "Research Name" might find the same resource with inconsistent address codes. If the address did not match exactly (e.g., one was coded with "St." and another coded with "Street," the coding was corrected to be consistent. Similar searches were done on other categories such as street address, street name, and zip code. The data was cleaned accordingly. The second error was from incorrect addresses in the MapQuest and/or Dex directory. The Dex directory is the official metropolitan phone and address directory and should have a high level of reliability; however, the actual reliability rate is unknown. To correct for possible errors, all identified social services not in the Jefferson County resource guides (e.g., soup kitchens, English as a Second Language courses, support groups, etc.) were called to verify the address. It was assumed that the Jefferson County resource guides had accurate information.

4 All identified resources were provided to Colorado's 2-1-1 system, which is the national abbreviated dialing code for free access to health and human services information and referral (I&R). 2-1-1 is an easy-to-remember and universally-recognizable number that makes a critical connection between individuals and families in need and the appropriate community-based organizations and government agencies. Housing the data with 2-1-1 allows statewide access to resources and bi-annual updating to keep the information current. Colorado 2-1-1 system is the depository for the resources collected in this project. Web searchable database of resources can be found at http://211colorado.org/

5 CIPP provided Jefferson County with the ethnic enclave areas based on the 2000 Census. The Asian communities fell outside the project boundaries set by Jefferson County (see Figure 1) and, unlike Russians, Latinos, and Native Americans, Jefferson County did not request mapping with the Asian community.

6 For example, it might be found that 65% of all users of a certain type of resource (this data would be collected by cognitive mapping alone) live "x" number of miles away (analysis performed by the GIS system) from a particular needed or frequently-accessed resource (gathered through cognitive mapping and other sources).

Appendix

Only forty percent of the participants provided demographic information, which limits the ability to determine the gender, age, and ethnicity/race of the participants. However, there is no way to determine the representativeness of the sample on these traditional demographics since the population characteristics are unknown. Even among the clients, the demographics are not available because most of the client records were incomplete. Unlike many social research projects, demographic representation is less of a concern. For the identification of resources, a cross-section of the types of people who use or provide services and the geographical distribution of their knowledge was most important, of which both criteria were met.

Table 2. Demographics of participants (n=100)

Demographic characteristic	All participants (n=100)	Providers (n=19)	Clients (n=72)	Community Residents (n=9)
Number and percent female	85%	90%	82%	100%
Average age	34.39	39.75	31.86	44.83
Number and percent Caucasian	62%	68%	64%	33%
Number and percent Latino	19%	5%	24%	11%
Number and percent African American	6%	0%	4%	33%
Number and percent Native American	9%	21%	4%	22%
Number and percent Other	4%	5%	3%	0%

Chapter XVI

Spatial Reasoning for Human-Robot Teams

David J. Bruemmer, Idaho National Laboratory, USA
Douglas A. Few, Idaho National Laboratory, USA
Curtis W. Nielsen, Idaho National Laboratory, USA

Abstract

This chapter presents research designed to study and improve an operator's ability to navigate or teleoperate a robot that is distant from the operator through the use of a robot intelligence architecture and a virtual 3D interface. To validate the use of the robot intelligence architecture and the 3D interface, four user-studies are presented that compare intelligence modes and interface designs in navigation and exploration tasks. Results from the user studies suggest that performance is improved when the robot assumes some of the navigational responsibilities or the interface presents spatial information as it relates to the pose of the robot in the remote environment. The authors hope that understanding the roles of intelligence and interface design when operating a remote robot will lead to improved human-robot teams that are useful in a variety of tasks.

Introduction

Robots have been used in a variety of settings where human access is difficult, impractical, or dangerous. These settings include search and rescue, space exploration, toxic site cleanup, reconnaissance, patrols, and many others (Murphy, 2004). Often, when a robot is used in one of these conditions, the robot is distant from the operator; this is referred to as *teleoperation*. Ideally, robots could be a useful member of a team because they could be used to accomplish tasks that might be too difficult or impractical for a human to perform.

The potential, however, for humans and robots to work as an effective team is limited by the lack of an appropriate means for the operator to visualize the remote environment and how the robot fits within the environment. As an example, several recent research efforts have investigated the human-robot interaction challenges associated with real-world operations including search and rescue and remote characterization of high-radiation environments (Burke, Murphy, Coovert, & Riddle, 2004; Casper & Murphy, 2003; Murphy, 2004; Yanco, Drury, & Scholtz, 2004a). Across these disparate domains, researchers have noted that it is difficult for operators to navigate a remote robot due to difficulty and error in operator understanding of the robot's position and/or perspective within the remote environment.

A primary reason for the difficulty in remote robot teleoperation is that for the overwhelming majority of robotic operations, video remains the primary means of providing information from the remote environment to the operator (Burke, Murphy, Rogers, Lumelsky, & Scholtz, 2004a). Woods, Tittle, Feil, and Roesler (2004) describe the process of using video to navigate a robot as attempting to drive while looking through a "soda straw" because of the limited angular view associated with the camera (Woods et al., 2004). The limited angular view of the camera presents problems for robot teleoperation because obstacles outside of the field of view of the camera still pose navigational threats to the robot even though they are not visible to the operator.

To alleviate navigational threats to the robot, current research at the Idaho National Laboratory (INL) is aimed at providing tools that support mixed-initiative control where humans and robots are able to make decisions and take initiative to accomplish a task. The goal is to create a set of capabilities that permit robots to be viewed as trusted teammates rather than passive tools. If this is to happen, the robot as well as the human must be enabled to reason spatially about the task and environment. Furthermore, true teamwork requires a shared understanding of the environment and task between team members in order to understand each others' intentions (Dennett, 1981). The lack of an effective shared understanding has been a significant impediment to having humans and intelligent robots work together.

In response to this challenge, the INL has developed a mixed-initiative robot control architecture that provides a framework for robot intelligence, environment modeling, and information sharing. In order to support a shared understanding of the environment and task between robotic and human team members, a virtual three dimensional 3D interface was developed through collaboration with researchers at Brigham Young University (BYU). The combination of the virtual 3D interface and intelligence on the robot can be used to improve the human's and robot's ability to reason spatially about the environment by presenting a shared understanding of the environment. The technology used to achieve the shared understanding of the environment is presented next.

System Design

Through the Office of the Secretary of Defense (OSD) Joint Robotics Program (JRP), the Space and Naval Warfare Systems Center (SPAWAR) at San Diego and the INL have worked together to develop, mature, and integrate promising robotics technologies from throughout the robotics community including components for perception, communication, behavior, and world modeling. One of the results of this collaboration is the development of the INL Robot Intelligence Kernel, which is currently used to unite selected components into a behavior-based architecture that can be transferred to a variety of fieldable, unmanned ground vehicle systems.

The robot intelligence architecture is the product of an iterative development cycle where behaviors have been evaluated in the hands of users, modified, and tested again. In fact, many of the strategies and interface components that originally seemed elegant from a conceptual standpoint, proved to be frustrating for users. For example, during a preliminary experiment that evaluated robot intelligence, but provided minimal spatial reasoning tools to the operator, it was noted that although most participants felt a high level of control, some participants indicated that they were confused by the robot behaviors (Marble, Bruemmer, & Few, 2003). In particular, the automatic initiation of robot behaviors to get the robot out of a narrow hallway led to operator confusion and a fight for control between the robot and human, because operators thought the robot could go through the hallway but the robot sensors indicated that it would not fit. The lack of adequate spatial representation tools prevented the operator from realizing this fact and, consequently, the human and robot engaged in a fight for control of the robot's movements. Findings such as these serve to motivate improvements to the robot intelligence architecture and the development of interface components that could support spatial reasoning.

Currently the robot intelligence kernel is divided into four modes of control (Tele, Safe, Shared, and Autonomous) affording the robot different types of behavior and levels of autonomy (Marble, Bruemmer, & Few, 2003; Marble, Bruemmer, Few, & Dudenhoeffer, 2004). The modes of autonomy in the robot intelligence architecture include:

1. **Tele mode** is a fully-manual mode of operation, in which the operator must manually control all robot movement.
2. **Safe mode** is similar to tele mode, in that robot movement is dependent on manual control. However, in safe mode, the robot is equipped with a level of initiative that prevents the operator from colliding with obstacles.
3. In **shared mode**, the robot can relieve the operator from the burden of direct control, using reactive navigation to find a path based on perception of the environment. Shared mode provides for a dynamic allocation of roles and responsibilities. The robot accepts varying levels of operator intervention and supports dialogue through the use of a finite number of scripted suggestions (e.g., "Path blocked! Continue left or right?") and other text messages that appear in a text box within the graphical interface.
4. **Autonomous mode** consists of a series of high-level tasks such as patrol, search a region, follow a path, or go to a place. In autonomous mode, the only user intervention occurs on the tasking level; the robot itself manages all navigational decision-making.

To investigate the challenges of sharing control of the robot between the robot and the operator, the experiments reported in this research focus on the middle ground that falls between teleoperation and full robotic autonomy (i.e., safe mode and shared mode). Although the experiments restricted each participant to only one level of control, normal operation would permit the user to switch between all four modes of autonomy as the task constraints, human needs, and robot capabilities change. As an example, tele mode could be useful to push open a door or shift a chair out of the way, whereas autonomous mode could be used to reduce human workload or in an area where communications to and from the robot are sporadic.

In order to protect the robot from collisions with obstacles in robot control modes that have some robot autonomy (safe, shared, autonomous), a *guarded motion* behavior based on a technique described by Pacis, Everett, Farrington, and Bruemmer (2004) is implemented. In response to laser and sonar range sensing of nearby obstacles, the guarded motion behavior scales down the robot's velocity using an event horizon calculation, which measures the maximum speed at which the robot can safely travel in order to come to a stop approximately two inches from an obstacle. By scaling down the speed in small increments, it is possible to insure that regardless of the commanded translational or rotational velocity, guarded motion will stop the robot at a consistent distance from an obstacle. This approach provides predictability and ensures minimal interference with the operator's control of the vehicle. If the robot is being driven near an obstacle rather than directly towards it, guarded motion will not stop the robot, but may slow its speed according to the event horizon calculation.

In order for the robot to be navigated successfully, spatial information of the environment must be available. The robot intelligence kernel gathers spatial information from the environment with a laser range finder. Information from laser scans is combined into a map of the environment using a technique developed at the Stanford Research Institute (SRI) called consistent pose estimation (CPE) (Gutman & Konolige. 1999; Konolige, 2004). This map-building algorithm is designed to build an occupancy-grid based map of the robot's environment as the robot explores the environment (Elfes, 1987; Moravec, 1988). The mapping algorithm is particularly useful because it provides an accurate spatial representation of complex environments that are previously unknown to the robot or the operator.

Since no single robot platform is appropriate for all tasks, the INL robot intelligence architecture can port to a variety of robot geometries and sensor suites and is currently in use as a standard by several research teams throughout the human-robot interaction (HRI) community. Experiments presented later in this paper were performed with an iRobot "ATRV mini" or an iRobot "ATRV Jr" shown in Figure 1. On each robot, the intelligence architecture utilizes a variety of sensor information including inertial sensors, compass, wheel encoders, laser, computer vision, thermal camera, infrared break beams, tilt sensors, bump sensors, sonar, and ultrasonic sensors.

The default configuration of the interface used to interact with the robot consists of a single touch screen display containing five re-sizeable windows as shown in Figure 2 (Bruemmer et al., 2005). The upper left-hand window on the screen contains a video feed from the robot as well as controls for panning, tilting, and zooming the camera. Frame size, frame rate, and compression settings can be accessed from a sub-window, but are held constant throughout the experiments reported here.

The upper right-hand window contains sensor status indicators and controls that allow the operator to monitor and configure the robot's sensor suite as needed. The

Figure 1. The robots used for Experiments 1 – 4

Figure 2. The standard interface

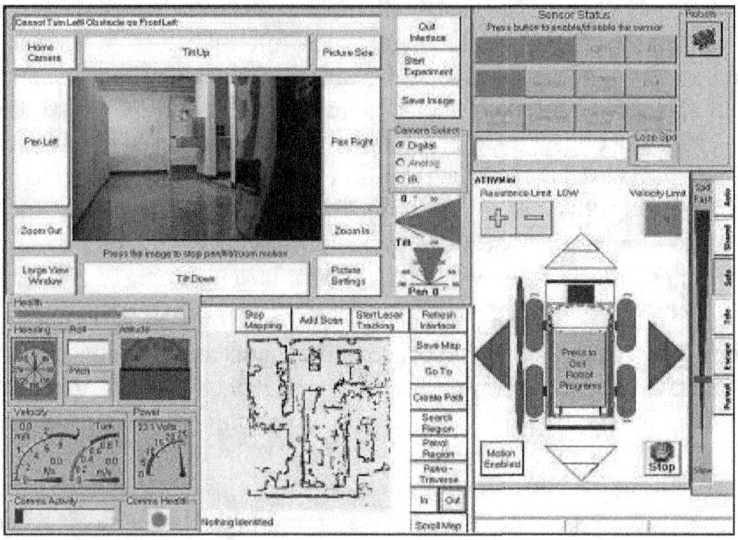

lower right-hand window pertains to movement within the local environment and provides indications of robot velocity, obstructions, resistance to motion, and feedback from contact sensors. The interface indicates blockages that impede motion in a given direction as red ovals next to the iconographic representation of the robot wheels (lower right of Figure 2). The current snapshot of the interface indicates that movement right and left is not possible because of an object close to the wheels on the left side of the robot. These indicators are designed to inform the operator as to why the robot has overridden a movement command. Since the visual indications can sometimes be overlooked, a force feedback joystick is also implemented to resist movement in the blocked direction. The joystick vibrates if the user continues to command movement in a direction already indicated as blocked. At the far right of the window the user can select between different levels of robot autonomy.

The lower central window displays the map of the environment as it is discovered by the robot and allows the user to initiate a number of waypoint-based autonomous behaviors such as *search region, patrol region*, *create a path*, or *go to a place*. Additionally, the map can be moved and zoomed in and out to provide a desired perspective. The lower left-hand window contains information about the robot's operational status such as communication activity, power, and the robot's pitch and roll.

A virtual three-dimensional (3D) display (Figure 3) was designed to support the operator's awareness of the spatial information in the robot's environment and show the information related to the robot's current pose within the environment. The virtual 3D component has been developed by melding technologies from the INL (Bruemmer et al., 2005), Brigham Young University (BYU) (Nielsen et al., 2004),

Figure 3. The virtual 3D interface

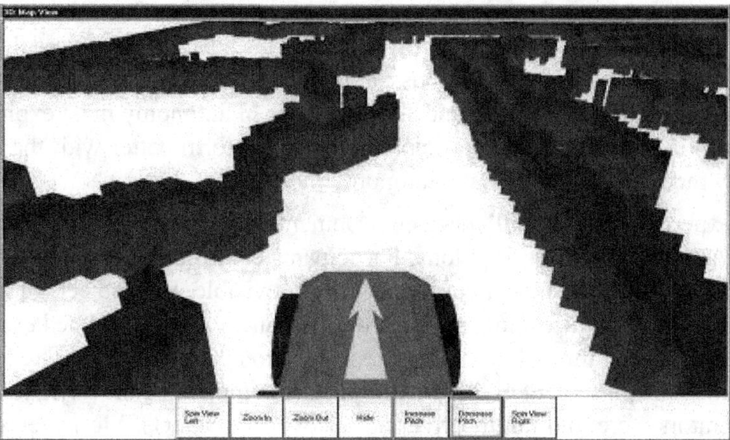

and the Stanford Research Institute (SRI) (Gutman & Konolige, 1999; Konolige, 2004). The 3D display is not based on true 3D range sensing, but rather by extruding the 2D map built by the robot into a 3D perspective. The map information in the 3D interface and the standard interface both originate from the map-building algorithm on the robot. The only difference is the manner in which the information is presented to the operator.

The map information produces the basis for the 3D representation that includes obstacles and other semantic entities that are of significance to the operator such as start location, labels, and waypoints. These items can be inserted by the robot to indicate percepts and intentions or by the human to identify and classify targets in the environment. Also, the user is able to add, verify, remove, or annotate semantic entities displayed within the map. Collaborative construction of the map enhances each individual team member's understanding of the environment and provides a basis for the human-robot team to "communicate" naturally about the environment through the visualization of relevant spatial information.

In the 3D interface, the operator may also insert translucent still images excerpted from the robot video, which are overlaid onto the corresponding area of the 3D map display, providing a means to fuse real video information with the virtual representation of the environment (Nielsen et al., 2004). By changing the virtual display's zoom, pitch, and yaw, it is possible to move the virtual perspective of the robot and environment from an egocentric perspective (i.e., looking out from the robot), to a fully exocentric view where the entire environment (map) can be seen at once.

The experiments presented next utilize the robot intelligence kernel as described in this section to compare the safe and shared modes of robot control along with the use of the standard interface and the 3D interface in navigation and exploration tasks.

Experiment 1

The first experiment was intended to: (a) show that the behaviors on board the robot (e.g. guarded motion and autonomous navigation) were useful in an exploration task, and (b) to compare the safe and shared modes of autonomy in an exploration task. It was hypothesized that participants would perform better with the shared autonomy mode than with the safe autonomy mode.

For this experiment a 20' × 30' maze environment was created using conventional office dividers and cylindrical pylons. Participants controlled the robot from a remote station where the robot environment was not visible. Five objects of interest (two mannequins, a stuffed dog, a disabled robot, and a small simulated explosive device) were placed throughout the arena in locations that remained fixed for all participants. The placement of these items further complicated the navigation task since operators were told not to drive into or over the objects. Moreover, certain objects remained hidden except from certain vantage points so the operator was required to maneuver the robot in order to see all the objects of interest.

Each participant was given 60 seconds to locate as many of the five items in the search area as possible using the standard interface and either the *safe* or the *shared* autonomy mode. Prior to the experiment, participants were instructed on the use of the joystick for controlling the robot and the camera on the robot (e.g., pan, tilt, and zoom), but were given no opportunity to practice controlling the robot until the experiment began. Operators with the *safe* autonomy mode were reminded that the robot would take initiative to avoid collisions but that they (the operators) should seek to avoid collisions as well. Operators with the *shared* autonomy mode were reminded to let the robot do most of the driving, but that if they wanted to redirect the robot, it would temporarily yield control to their joystick commands.

There were 107 participants drawn as volunteers from attendees of the 2003 INL annual science and engineering exposition at the Museum of Idaho in Idaho Falls. The participants consisted of 46 females and 61 males, ranging in age from 3 to 78 years old, with a mean age of 14. Participants were asked demographic questions including their age and gender, and whether they had experience in remote systems operation. It was determined by self-report that none of the participants had experience remotely controlling robots, or had knowledge of or access to the remote environment. Furthermore, none had prior experience with or knowledge of the interface or robot control system; therefore, it was determined that all of the participants could be regarded as novice users. Participants were assigned to either the *shared* or *safe* autonomy modes alternately based on their sequence in participation.

On average, participants who used the robot's *shared* autonomy mode found an average of 2.87 objects while those who used the *safe* autonomy mode found an average of 2.35 objects (Bruemmer et al., 2005). Comparisons between different age groups and gender were analyzed, but a significant difference in the number of items found did not exist based on age or gender. Although this experiment was not intended to support a careful comparison of age and gender groupings, it does support the claim that the interface allowed a wide variety of participants to find objects successfully. Participants were able to find objects successfully in both safe mode and shared mode, indicating that both the guarded motion used in safe mode and the autonomous navigation behaviors used in shared mode were usable by participants. Across all age and gender groupings, performance was better in shared mode than in safe mode, providing evidence that the robot's ability to navigate the environment can actually exceed the ability of a human operator. The performance benefit experienced by allowing the robot to navigate suggests the potential to use robot initiative and autonomy not only as a last resort (i.e., when communication fails or operator workload increases), but as a basis for collaborative interaction between a human and a robot.

Taken on its own, this first study demonstrates the utility of robot autonomy, but leaves many questions to be answered by further experiments. The first experiment did not look beyond overall performance (as measured by items found) to discern the reasons for the observed difference in performance between safe mode and shared mode. In response to this limitation, it was determined that the next experiments should empirically measure differences in operator workload, operator error, and operator confusion in order to provide deeper insight. Additionally, this experiment utilized a relatively small search environment. Areas of the environment required careful maneuvering, but the task was not designed to reward path planning or strategy. Future experiments address this question by using larger environments that require some path-planning and strategy to explore the environment efficiently.

Experiment 1 also raised the question of how useful the streaming video provided by the interface actually was to users when navigating the robot. In tight spaces where spatial information is important to prevent collisions, participants often found the entire visual field filled by an immediate obstacle, thereby diminishing the usefulness of the video for navigation. Furthermore, video information fails to illustrate obstacles outside of the current visual field, which makes it difficult for the operator to remember the location of obstacles on the sides of the robot. One hypothesis was that in such instances video promoted a false sense of spatial awareness and led to operator confusion. As an example, consider the common scenario of a robot approaching an open doorway in safe mode. The door frame disappears from the video feed before the robot has reached the doorway. However, the operator, already viewing video information from the next room, may believe that the robot is already through the door. To prevent a collision with the doorframe, the robot may stop and refuse to move forward. Although the robot communicates that it is blocked in front, the user may be confused by the lack of obstacles in the visual feed. Put simply, the default interface used in Experiment 1 did not provide the operator with an adequate representation of the spatial information around the robot. Experiment 2 was designed to explore the use of a new interface component intended to better support an operator's understanding of the spatial information around the robot.

Experiment 2

Observations from Experiment 1 suggest that video may not provide an adequate perspective of the remote environment, nor means for the operator to predict robot behavior or understand the robot's intentions. However, humans are visual and prefer pictures and diagrams when attempting to understand or communicate (Pashler, 1990). In order to address the *human-robot-interaction* (HRI) limitations observed in Experiment 1, some means were required to support collaborative understanding and yet take advantage of the functional utility associated with visual representation. In addition to these human factors, there were also significant engineering reasons for assessing alternatives to video presentation of the remote environment. In particular, video demands high-bandwidth, continuous communication, and is therefore ill-suited for many of the very environments where robots could be most useful. Except for short ranges, transmission of high-bandwidth video is only possible when line of sight can be maintained either with a satellite or another radio antenna. For instance, high-bandwidth video cannot be transmitted through layers of concrete and rebar, making it inappropriate for urban terrain or urban search and rescue. Likewise, forest and jungle canopy precludes reliable transmission of video.

In response to these human and engineering factors, collaboration between the INL and Brigham Young University (BYU) was used to develop a new 3D interface component that could provide a better perspective of the spatial structure of the environment around the robot. The improved presentation of the spatial information may help the operator gain insight into the reason for robot initiative and diminish the likelihood of operator confusion. The purpose of this experiment is to assess the effectiveness of the 3D interface in a spatial exploration task where the operators were to use the robot to construct a map of an environment. The hypothesis was that the 3D interface without video would support the operator in the spatial exploration task better than the standard interface with video.

The experiment was performed over a seven-day period within the St. Louis Science Center in 2004 and utilized 64 visitors who volunteered to take part in the experiment. The majority of participants were high school students from schools in the St. Louis area. These students were not pre-selected, but rather volunteered to take part in the study while visiting the Science Center. As before, the experiment was set up as a remote deployment such that the operator control station was located several stories above the robot arena so that the operator could not see the robot or the robot's environment. The arena was built by the production staff of the Science

Figure 4. A partial view of the arena built at the St. Louis Science Center

Center and contained artificial rocks, artificial trees, mannequins, and plywood dividers to create a maze environment (Figure 4).

Due to the distance and physical occlusions separating the control station from the actual robot environment, analog video was not possible. Instead, state-of-the-art video compression was used to digitize the analog video into a motion JPEG (MJPEG) format and wirelessly transmit from the robot to a nearby access point connected to the building's network. The building's wired network was then used to transfer the video data two stories up to the operator. Exploiting the wired infrastructure in place throughout the building made it possible to provide continuous, reliable video at a high frame rate. The presentation speed and resolution of this video exceeded that possible through an entirely wireless data link. This configuration ensured that the comparison between video and the 3D map display was not merely a function of current communication bandwidth constraints, but rather an investigation of the fundamental differences between an interface based primarily on viewing raw video and one which presented the environment and obstacles as they relate to the robot's pose.

Before the experiment, each participant was given basic instructions on how to use the interface, and no participant was permitted to drive the robot until the start of the trial run. Participants only used the safe mode autonomy level in order to simplify the comparison of performance between the two interfaces. Participants were assigned to alternating display conditions (standard interface with video, standard interface with the 3D window in place of the video) in order to ensure equal numbers of participants in each condition and no participant was allowed to operate the robot in more than one trial. A time limit of three minutes was set in place to help

Figure 5. A near-complete map built up by one of the participants

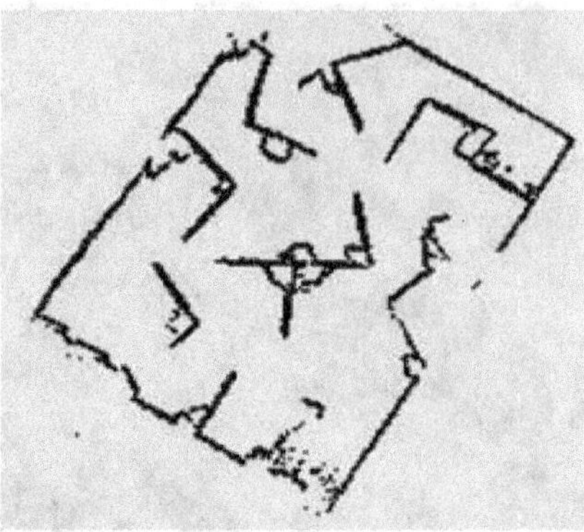

insure that the measured performance was a function of the interface presentation rather than a function of operator interest or time spent on the task.

At the beginning of each experiment, the map built by the previous participant was erased by restarting the map-building algorithm on the robot. Each participant was then instructed to drive the robot around the environment in order to build as large a map as possible as quickly as possible. All participants were given access to the same 2D map component (Figure 5) within which the robot presents the map that it builds as it explores new territory. Exactly half of the participants used the standard interface and were able to see both the 2D map and the video module. The other half of participants used the same interface except that the 3D interface module entirely occluded the video module.

During each trial, the interface stored a variety of useful information about the participant's interactions with the robot. Joystick bandwidth was recorded as the number of messages sent from the joystick indicating a change of more than 10% in the position of the stick. This information is used as an indirect measure of workload (Clarke, Yen, Kondraske, Khoury, & Maxwell, 1991; Khoury & Kondraske, 1991). The interface also recorded the number of joystick vibrations caused by human navigational error. The map produced by the robot for each experiment was also saved in order to assess performance based on coverage of the environment. This approach provided a reasonable assessment of the operator's ability to explore the environment in the time available. Immediately after completing a trial, each participant was asked to rank on a scale of 1 to 10 how "in control" they felt during the operation, where 1 signified "The robot did nothing that I wanted it to do" and 10 signified, "The robot did everything I wanted it to do."

In the three minutes provided, 80% of the participants explored over half of the total environment. One person, a 3D display participant, was able to build the entire map in the allotted 3 minutes. As described above, task performance was calculated by comparing the map generated during the exploration task with the complete map of the task environment. This comparison showed no significant difference between the use of the video module and the 3D module. Using joystick bandwidth as an indication of human workload and joystick vibration as a metric for human navigational error, analysis shows that operators using the virtual 3D display worked less and demonstrated fewer instances of navigational error. On average, the joystick bandwidth for participants using the 3D module was 1,057 messages from the interface to the robot, compared to 1,229 average messages for operators using the video module. Further, there were, on average, 11.00 instances of navigational error with the 3D module and 14.29 instances with the video module as measured by joystick vibrations (Bruemmer et al., 2005).

In addition to reduced workload and fewer navigational errors, use of the virtual 3D display slightly increased the operator's subjective "feeling of control" while operating the robot. The average feeling of control for the 3D display was 7.219 compared with an average of 7.059 for the video.

The second experiment provided initial evidence that the virtual 3D perspective of the robot's environment supported an operator's ability to reason spatially about the task and environment better than streaming video information. Results suggest that although there was no significant change in performance (as measured by the percentage of the map discovered), there was reduced operator workload, less navigational error, and a slightly improved sense of control.

One motivation for the development of the virtual 3D display had been to promote a shared understanding between the robot and the operator of the task and the robot's environment. To assess the effectiveness of the virtual 3D display in this regard, it is useful to consider that a decrease in joystick vibrations not only represents a reduction in operator navigational error, but also a reduction in the instances where the operator failed to understand the reason the robot took initiative to protect itself. Recall that the joystick vibrates only if the operator commands movement in a direction in which the robot has already recognized an obstacle and taken initiative to prevent a collision. These results indicate progress towards the goal of providing a representation that supports spatial reasoning and a shared understanding of the environment. More broadly, these results provide evidence that it may be possible to support navigational needs of human operators without using video. This finding provides an important counterpoint to opinion within the field of human-robot interaction that reliable, continuous video is essential for remote navigation (Baker, Casey, Keyes, & Yanco, 2004).

From an engineering perspective, this experiment shows that it is possible to have a robot build a map of the robot's environment as the environment is explored and communicate the map back to a remote user fast enough to support real-time robot navigation by the operator. The significance of this result to the area of remote systems can be seen most clearly when one considers the reduction in communication bandwidth made possible by using the 3D map display. Whereas the video alone requires 3,000,000 bits per second (bps), the total interface bandwidth with the virtual 3D interface was only 64,000 bps. This bandwidth savings allows control to extend into new domains using data transmission methods that can be used in underground bunkers, caves, nuclear reactors, and urban search and rescue sites where it is often impossible to maintain a video feed.

Despite the fact that the human-robot team can function effectively without video, there is no reason to disregard the potential benefits of video in those instances when video is available. Experience with operators and subject area experts from energy, defense, and emergency management contexts indicate that operators expect and can exploit video in remarkable ways (Casper & Murphy, 2003; Marble, Bruemmer, & Few, 2003; Yanco & Drury, 2004;). Many applications require the human to play a role in visual search and detection. Although this experiment suggests that video could be replaced with the 3D representation, the optimal interface will likely provide a dynamic balance between the video and virtual displays.

Experiment 3

The second experiment showed that the virtual 3D display could support the operator's comprehension of the spatial information regarding the task and environment. The question still remains, however, as to whether the use of the virtual 3D display could be improved with shared control where the human and robot engage in a dynamic sharing of roles and responsibilities. A previous usability study by Marble et al. (2003) showed that shared mode offered the greatest potential for operator confusion and frustration. Consequently, it was hypothesized that shared mode might provide the greatest potential for the virtual 3D display to reduce navigational error and operator workload.

One goal of this experiment is to compare the safe and shared autonomy modes when the 3D interface is used. Another goal is to show that the benefits of sharing control between the human and operator observed in the first experiment are not merely due to the high cognitive workload placed on the operator when using the standard interface, but are related to the robot's ability to navigate itself through the environment. The typical assumption found in the literature is that robot autonomy trails behind human performance, but may be useful when the human's ability to spatially reason about the task and environment is encumbered (i.e., operator workload increases, communications fail, or map and position accuracy begins to degrade) (Goodrich, Olsen Jr., Crandall, & Plamer, 2001; Nielsen et al., 2004; Trouvain, Wolf, & Schneider, 2003). It was hoped that this experiment could provide evidence that the robot's ability to reason about the environment can improve performance even when the operator's ability to reason spatially is unhindered (i.e., data link connectivity is maintained, human workload is minimal, and mapping and localization is reliable).

The task for this experiment is similar to that of Experiment 1 where the participants were asked to find as many items of interest as possible. For this experiment, however, in order to minimize individual human workload, the control task was separated into specific operator functions, namely navigation, driving, and operation of a pan, tilt, and zoom camera. Instead of using only individuals, groups of participants were assigned roles where members had responsibility over one aspect of the robot control. In addition to minimizing individual human workload, an added benefit of assigning different roles was that it afforded an opportunity to observe the exchange of information between team members in different roles. In fact, it became very clear that operators in different roles require different perspectives. For example, the navigation or planning role requires an exocentric display where the operator can see the entire environment while the driving role requires an egocentric perspective so the operator can visualize the robot's situation in the environment. As Scholtz (2002) points out, the roles of human operators do not remain static, and interfaces should be able to adapt accordingly.

This experiment included 120 volunteers grouped into teams of six members. The participating teams consisted of one team of teachers, three teams of eighth grade students, and the remainder of the teams being drawn from local high schools. Participants were recruited from a solicitation of local schools through the St. Louis Science Center's outreach program. Participants knew and selected the other people in their team prior to participation in the experiment. Age and gender were not recorded due to the fact that most participants were of similar age and the fact that gender was mixed for each team.

The experiment was run over seven days at the St. Louis Science Center in 2004. Teams of participants were assigned to alternating conditions so as to ensure equal numbers of teams in each condition. No participant was allowed to take part on more than one team. As in the previous experiment, the robot was located in the lower level of the Science Center, while the control center was located on the top level. This experiment used the same environment as was used in Experiment 2 with the same lighting and placement of obstacles. Three mannequins were placed in locations in the environment designed to force teams to coordinate their information in order to discover aspects regarding each particular mannequin's location. The mannequins remained in place throughout the entire experiment. An equal number of teams used the shared and safe modes of autonomy while controlling the robot. The interface components were divided across three separate stations, each with its own monitor and input devices. No interface component was visible at more than one control station. Two participants manned each station resulting in a total of six people dedicated to robotic system control. The stations were arranged in an arc such that the participants at each station could communicate easily with the others, but could not see the other displays.

The first control station was dedicated to the application payload, which in this case was a pan, tilt, and zoom camera. Using a joystick that allowed operation of the various camera controls, the application payload participants used the visual feedback from the robot to seek out the three mannequins and to provide navigational advice. The second control station was dedicated to driving the robot. Participants were permitted to see the virtual 3D interface along with the local environment window, the sensor status window, and the robot state window from the standard interface (Figure 2). Primarily, the operators at the driving station used the virtual 3D display, but were constrained to an egocentric perspective which precluded a global view of the environment. The final station was the navigation station where participants had access to the 2D map being built as the robot traveled through its environment. This gave them a bird's eye view of the environment and the robot's position in it. Additionally, participants at the navigation station were given a hard-copy of a map showing the locations of the three mannequins. Having two participants at each station was not necessary, but ensured that workload was minimal. Task completion required the three groups to self-organize in order to arrive at and gain a visual lock on all three of the mannequins as quickly as possible.

On average, less time was required to find the three mannequins for the teams using the shared robot autonomy mode. The average completion time for shared mode teams was 467 seconds compared to an average completion time of 641 seconds for the safe mode teams. Safe mode teams also demonstrated a greater workload, as measured by joystick movement, than that of their shared mode counterparts. Safe mode teams made, on average, 2,744 significant joystick movements compared to an average of 1,725 significant joystick movements for shared mode teams. Using joystick vibration as a metric for human navigational error shows that safe mode teams made 25.1 errors on average compared to 16.8 errors for the shared mode teams (Bruemmer et al., 2005).

As with the first experiment, participants using the shared mode experienced increased performance efficiency when compared to their safe mode counterparts. The results from Experiment 3 show that with a representation that supports the human and robot's ability to reason spatially, performance can be significantly improved by sharing control between humans and a robot. Moreover, it shows that reducing the workload placed on the human driver and increasing the importance of strategy and intelligence does not diminish the performance benefits of sharing control between human and robot team members.

Previous research has shown that effective teams utilize a shared mental model of the task and current situation (Cooke, Salas, Cannon-Bowers, & Stout, 2000; Yen et al., 2001). Similarly, the findings from Experiment 3 suggest that in order to fully realize the benefits of sharing control between human and robot team members, it is advantageous to provide a shared model of the environment. Unlike most interfaces for remotely controlling a mobile robot, the virtual 3D display presents information from the robot's environment from a perspective that helps the operator perceive and comprehend the spatial information around the robot. Improved comprehension of the robot's environment makes it easier for the operator to predict robot behavior and understand occasions of robot initiative (Endsley, 1988).

In many operational scenarios, it is not only possible, but probable that the roles of driving, navigating, and operating the application payload will be distributed among multiple human operators. Several researchers have pointed out the high cognitive burden associated with remote deployment of mobile robots and have argued that effective control requires multiple human operators (Burke et al., 2004; Casper & Murphy, 2003; Murphy, 2004). Although detailed analysis of these different roles (i.e., driver, navigator, payload operator) was beyond the scope of this experiment, anecdotal observations (recorded during and after the experiment) suggest interesting areas for further investigation. One observation was that just as performance can be degraded by a fight for control between the driver and robot; there is also the potential for similar conflicts between human operators primarily because they visualize the information differently. Their ability to reason spatially about the task and environment is dependent on the different perspectives associated with their roles. Further experimentation will be necessary to characterize the reasons for these choices and quantify their effect on team performance. One explanation found in the literature is that team success depends on the ability of each team member to understand the perspective of other members (Yen et al., 2001). If this is true, the most effective human-robot teams will be those that utilize a collaborative model of the environment and task. Such research questions provide a fertile ground for further experimentation into the challenges of providing shared representation, not only between human and robot, but also between humans.

Experiment 4

Experiments 1-3 showed that the INL control architecture, including the 3D interface and the robot intelligence kernel could reduce reliance on continuous video, increase overall task efficiency, and reduce operator error and workload. However, it is unclear what role the perspective of the virtual 3D environment had in bringing about these benefits. It is possible that the benefits due to the 3D perspective are largely due to the simplification brought through the abstraction process. However, it is also possible that the main benefit of the 3D display is that it provides a perspective that illustrates more of the spatial information near the robot and is, therefore, more useful for navigation and exploration tasks than the video display typically used in remote robot operation (teleoperation). The purpose of this study is to investigate the role of perspective in the 3D interface in terms of operator error, workload, and overall task efficiency.

This experiment included 216 participants drawn at random from attendees of the INL's 2004 annual community exposition. The participants consisted of 61 females and 155 males, ranging in age from 3 to 70 years old, with a mean age of 12. The robot used for this study was an ATRVmini designed by IRobot. Participants were assigned the task of discovering the physical structure of the environment using the safe autonomy mode on the robot and the 3D interface which was populated by the map as the robot was navigated through the environment.

To test the role of perspective in the 3D interface, each volunteer was assigned one of four different perspectives (first person, close, elevated, and far). The *first person* perspective places the camera inside the robot, so the view is what it would be if the participant was sitting in the robot. It is similar to the perspective provided by the video in the standard interface where the user sees the video from the perspective of the robot's camera. The *close* perspective is zoomed out slightly and uses a virtual camera position somewhat above and behind the robot such that the front half of the robot is also visible at the bottom of the screen. The *elevated* perspective zooms the map display out and places the camera behind and above the robot such that more of the map is visible in the interface. The *far* perspective zooms out further by placing the virtual camera position directly above the robot. It is far enough above the robot to allow the entire map to be visible on the screen. This is often referred to as a "bird's eye view." Figure 6 illustrates the different perspectives used for this experiment.

A maze environment was constructed on the first floor of the Museum of Idaho using cubicle wall dividers. On the second floor of the museum, a control station was set up that consisted of a laptop and monitor to display the interface and a joystick with which to control the robot. The participants could see the interface, but did not have

Figure 6. Perspectives of the virtual 3D environment used in Experiment 4; clockwise from top left: 1st person, close, far, and elevated

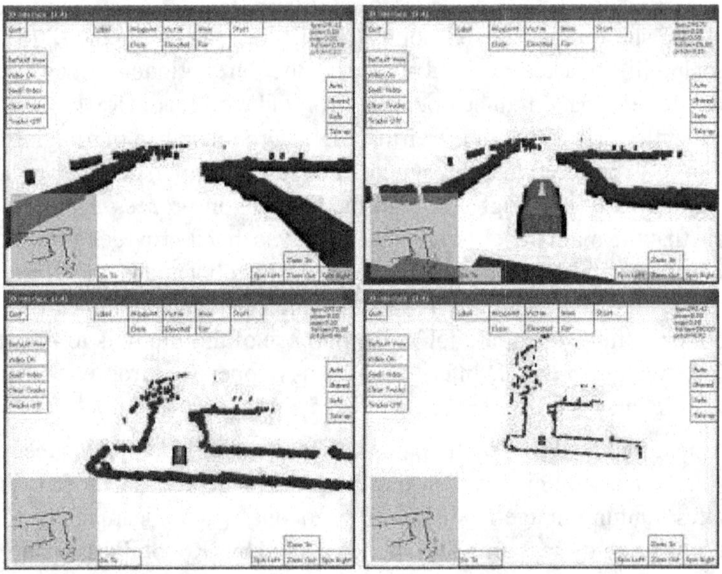

the ability to see the actual robot or the maze itself as they drove the robot.

Prior to the experiment, each participant was instructed on the use of the joystick for controlling the robot. They were then requested to build a complete map of the maze as quickly as possible without running the robot into obstacles. Participants were also informed that the robot would prevent collisions, but that they should drive the robot in order to prevent such instances. Each participant used one of the four perspectives, which were assigned to volunteers in successive, cyclical order. Information, including the time required to complete the task, the initiative exercised by the robot, and the total joystick bandwidth used to guide the robot, was measured and recorded automatically and stored in a data file on the interface computer. Also, information on age, gender, and a self-assessment of video game skill (on a scale of 1 to 10) was recorded for each participant.

The results suggest that the 1st person perspective was by far the most difficult to use, and the other three perspectives (close, elevated, and far) were similar to each other in their influence on the operator's ability to control the robot. In particular, participants using the 1st person perspective took, on average, 133 seconds to discover the environment, while the close, elevated, and far perspectives had averages of 95, 96, and 97 seconds respectively. Additionally, participants using the 1st person perspective had an average joystick bandwidth of 1,345, compared to 764, 724, and 693 for the close, elevated, and far perspectives respectively. There was not a significant difference in the number of times the robot took initiative to protect itself between any of the four different perspectives.

The results presented here suggest that the 1st person perspective within the 3D display is inferior to the exocentric perspectives that show the robot and how it fits in relation to its environment. Although perspective is a critical factor in terms of time and joystick usage, it does not, at least for this study, seem to play a critical role in terms of operator navigational error (i.e., instances which necessitated robot initiative to protect itself). It is perhaps not surprising that perspective plays an important role; but what is surprising is that once the perspective moves from the 1st person to include the robot, there seems to be little difference between the various exocentric perspectives used. The close, elevated, and far perspectives all seemed to be very similar in terms of time, joystick usage, and robot initiative. This suggests that in comparison to the video module on the standard interface, the operator only needs a little more spatial information concerning obstacles near the robot in order to improve navigation significantly.

Additional studies will be necessary to further understand the benefits and limitations associated with different perspectives. Most likely, there will not be one optimal perspective. Rather, perspective should change based on the task element (e.g., navigation, search, patrol), the level of robot autonomy (e.g., direct human control, shared control, autonomous tasking), and the number of robots employed (Scholtz, 2002).

Conclusion

In this chapter we presented tools that improve a human-robot team performance in navigation and exploration tasks. The tools include behavior-based intelligence on the robot and a virtual 3D interface through which the operator views the information from the robot. The role of intelligence on the robot is to reduce the operator's need to understand the spatial environment immediately near the robot by empowering the robot to move and avoid obstacles without any operator control. The role of the virtual 3D interface is to improve the operator's ability to perceive and comprehend the spatial information around the robot, which enables the operator to issue more informed commands to the robot.

The reason the virtual 3D interface helps so much in the navigation and exploration experiments presented is because information is presented as it spatially relates to the robot. In contrast, the standard interface displays information in a manner that requires the operator to cognitively interpret the information into a holistic understanding of the robot's environment. This extra cognitive effort may impair the human's ability to anticipate or predict how the robot will respond to instructions. With the 3D interface, since information from the robot is automatically integrated by the manner of the presentation, the operator has more cognitive resources to anticipate how the robot will respond to instructions.

In the experiments where the human-robot interaction used the shared control mode as opposed to the safe control mode, performance also improved because the operator was not concerned with the low-level navigational control of the robot. Since the operator plays more of a supervisor role when the robot has navigational intelligence, the operator has more cognitive resources to allocate towards anticipating and predicting how the robot will respond to the environment.

By allowing the operator to visualize the robot's environment more clearly and providing the robot with intelligence to handle elementary aspects of navigation tasks, we bring the robot and the operator into a more unified frame of reference. With a unified reference frame the human and the robot move towards a true teaming paradigm where responsibilities and roles can shift dynamically depending on the needs of the human, the robot, or the task at hand. Improving the ability of robots and humans to work together has the potential to increase the applications and situations where robots can be effectively utilized as a valuable team member.

Acknowledgments

The authors wish to thank the following individuals for their contributions to this work: From the INL: Miles C. Walton, Julie Marble, PhD, Ron Boring, PhD, and

Dan Henry; from Stanford Research Institute International: Kurt Konolige, PhD; from Brigham Young University: Mike Goodrich, PhD; and from Washington University in St. Louis: William D. Smart, PhD, and James Garner.

References

Baker, M., Casey, R., Keyes, B., & Yanco, H. A. (2004). Improved interfaces for human-robot interaction in urban search and rescue. In *Proceedings of the IEEE Conference on Systems, Man, and Cybernetics* (pp. 2960-2965). The Hague, The Netherlands: IEEE Press.

Bruemmer, D. J., Few, D. A., Boring, R., Walton, M., Marble, J. L., Nielsen, C., & Garner, J. (2005). Shared understanding for collaborative control. *IEEE Transactions on Systems, Man, and Cybernetics Part-A, 35*(4), 494-504.

Burke, J. L., Murphy, R R., Coovert, M. D., & Riddle, D. L. (2004). Moonlight in Miami: A field study of human-robot interaction in the context of an urban search and rescue disaster response training exercise. *Human-Computer Interaction, 19*, 85-116.

Burke, J. L., Murphy, R. R., Rogers E., Lumelsky, V. J., & Scholtz, J. (2004a). Final report for the DARPA/NSF interdisciplinary study on human-robot interaction. *IEEE Transactions on Systems, Man, and Cybernetics Part-C, 34*(2),103-112.

Casper, J., & Murphy, R. R. (2003). Human-robot interactions during the robot-assisted urban search and rescue response at the World Trade Center. *IEEE Transactions on Systems, Man, and Cybernetics-Part B, 33*(3), 367-385.

Clarke, D., Yen, S., Kondraske, G. V., Khoury, G. J., & Maxwell, K. J. (1991). *Telerobotic network workstation for system performance and operator workload monitoring* (Tech. Rep. No. 91-013R). National Aeronautical and Space Administration, Johnson Space Center.

Cooke, N. J., Salas, E., Cannon-Bowers, J. A., & Stout, R. (2000). Measuring team knowledge. *Human Factors, 42*, 151-173.

Dennett, D. (1981). True believers: The intentional strategy and why it works. In A. F. Heath (Ed.), *Scientific explanations: Papers based on Herbert Spencer lectures given in the University of Oxford*, Reprinted in Dennet (Ed.), *The International Stance, MIT, 1987, 13-35.*

Elfes, A. (1987). Sonar-based real-world mapping and navigation. *IEEE Journal of Robotics and Automation, 3*(3), 249-265.

Endsley, M. R. (1988). Design and evaluation for situation awareness enhancement. In *Proceedings of the Human Factors Society 32nd Annual Meeting, 1*, 97-101. Santa Monica, CA: HFES.

Goodrich, M. A., Olsen Jr, D. R., Crandall, J. W., & Plamer, T. J. (2001). Experiments in adjustable autonomy. In *Proceedings of the IJCAI Workshop on Autonomy, Delegation, and Control: Interaction with Autonomous Agents*. Seattle, WA: Morgan Kaufmann.

Gutman, J. S., & Konolige, K. (1999). Incremental mapping of large cyclic environments. In *Proceedings of the IEEE International Symposium on Computational Intelligence in Robotics and Automation (CIRA)*, 318-325. Monterey, CA: IEEE Press.

Khoury, G. J., & Kondraske, G. V. (1991). *Measurement and continuous monitoring of human workload associated with manual control devices* (Tech. Rep. No. 91-011R). National Aeronautical and Space Administration, Johnson Space Center.

Konolige, K. (2004). Large-scale map-making. In *Proceedings of the American Association for Artificial Intelligence, 19*, 457-463. San Jose, CA:, AAAI Press.

Marble, J. L., Bruemmer, D. J., & Few, D. A. (2003). Lessons learned from usability tests with a collaborative cognitive workspace for human-robot teams. In *Proceedings of the Institute of Electrical and Electronics Engineers (IEEE) Conference on Systems, Man, and Cybernetics, 1*, 448-453. Washington, DC: IEEE Press.

Marble, J. L., Bruemmer, D. J., Few, D. A., & Dudenhoeffer, D. D. (2004). Evaluation of supervisory vs. peer-peer interaction for human-robot teams. In *Proceedings of the 37th Annual Hawaii International Conference on Systems Sciences* (50130b). Waikoloa, HI: IEEE Press.

Moravec, H. P. (1988). Sensor fusion in certainty grids for mobile robots. *AI Magazine, 9*(2), 61-74.

Murphy, R. R. (2004). Human-robot interaction in rescue robotics. *Institute of Electrical and Electronics Engineers (IEEE) Transactions on Systems, Man, and Cybernetics-Part C, 34*(2), 138-153.

Nielsen, C. W., Ricks, B. W., Goodrich, M. A., & Crandall, J. Bruemmer, D.J. (2004). Enhancing functionality and autonomy in man-portable robots. In *Proceedings Ieee Conference on Systems, Man, and Cybernetics* (Vol. 3, pp. 2853-2858). The Hague, The Netherlands: IEEE Press.

Pacis, E. B., Everett, H. R., Farrington, N., & Bruemmer, D. J. (2004). Enhancing functionality and autonomy in man-portable robots. In *Proceedings of the SPIE Defense and Security Symposium* (Vol. 5422, pp. 355-366). Orlando, FL: SPIE.

Pashler, H. (1990). Coordinate frame for symmetry detection and object recognition. *Journal of Experimental Psychology: Human Perception and Performance, 16*, 150-163.

Ricks, B. W., Nielsen, C. W., & Goodrich, M. A. (2004). Ecological displays for robot interaction: A new perspective. In *Proceedings of the IEEE/RSJ International Conference on Intelligent Robots and Systems (IROS)* (Vol. 3, pp. 2855-2860). Sendai, Japan: IEEE Press.

Scholtz, J. (2002). Human-robot interactions: Creating synergistic cyber forces. In *Proceedings of the 2002 Workshop on Multi-Robot Systems*. In Alan C. Schultz & Lynn E. Parker (Eds.), *Multi-Robot Teams: From Swarms to Intelligent Automata. Proceedings of the 2002 NRL Workshop on Multi-Robot Systems* (Vol. 2, pp. 177-184). Dordrecht, The Netherlands: Kluwer Academic Publishers.

Trouvain, B., Wolf, H. L., & Schneider, F. E. (2003). Impact of autonomy in multi-robot systems on teleoperation performance. In *Proceedings of the 2003 Workshop on Multi-Robot Systems* (pp. 253-264).

Woods, D., Tittle, J., Feil, M., & Roesler, A. (2004). Envisioning human-robot coordination in future operations. *Institute of Electrical and Electronics Engineers (IEEE) Transactions on Systems, Man & Cybernetics: Part-C: Special Issue on Human-Robot Interaction, 34*(2), 210-218.

Yanco, H. A., & Drury, J. (2004). Where am I? Acquiring situation awareness using a remote robot platform. In *Proceedings of the Institute of Electrical and Electronics Engineers (IEEE) Conference on Systems, Man and Cybernetics,* (Vol. 3, pp. 2835-2840). The Hague, The Netherlands: IEEE Press.

Yanco, H. A., Drury, J. L., & Scholtz, J. (2004a). Beyond usability evaluation: Analysis of human-robot interaction at a major robotics competition. *Journal of Human-Computer Interaction, 19*, 117-149.

Yen, J., Yin, J., Ioerger, T., Miller, M., Xu, D., & Volz, R. (2001). CAST: Collaborative agents for simulating teamwork. In *Proceedings of the 17th International Joint Conference on Artificial Intelligence* (pp. 135-142). Seattle, WA: Morgan Kaufmann.

About the Authors

Brian N. Hilton received a PhD in management information systems from Claremont Graduate University, School of Information Science, USA, in May, 2004. His current research interests lie in spatial information system development, Internet-based geographical information systems, and the use of emerging technologies in information system development. He holds an MS in management information systems (Claremont Graduate University) and a BA in economics (Richard Stockton College of New Jersey). Dr. Hilton is a research associate at the Claremont Information and Technology Institute.

***

Tarun Abhichandani is a PhD student at the School of Information Systems and Technology, Claremont Graduate University (CGU), USA. His research interests include middleware for videoconferencing applications, transit-based e-government initiatives, and P2P technologies. In the past, he has held various positions while designing and administering organization-wide networking infrastructure, database applications, and ERP systems. He holds a master's degree in management of information systems (MIS) from CGU and a master's degree in banking and finance from Mumbai University, India.

Brian Bakker works as a geographical information systems specialist for Aerial Services, Inc., USA, a photogrammetry and mapping company based in Cedar Falls, Iowa. He is currently involved in developing several custom geographical information systems applications. Mr. Bakker holds a Bachelor of Arts in management information systems, and Master of Arts in geography from the University of Northern Iowa. During his graduate study, he has developed several Web-based applications using ArcIMS and ArcObjects.

Lars Brodersen was educated as chartered surveyor, and graduated with a degree of cand.geom. from Aalborg University, Denmark. He was employed as a map editor at the Schweizer Weltatlas at the Swiss Federal Institute of Technology Zürich (ETH Zürich) from 1981 to 1986. He obtained the title as Dr.sc.techn in cartography from ETH Zürich in 1986, followed by two years as head of the cartography department in a private company in Odense, Denmark. From 1987 to 1993, he was the head of section for surveying and registration at the Greenland Home Rule Agency. From 1993 to 2003, he was employed at the National Survey and Cadastre Denmark as head of section for product development and later as senior research scientist in geo-communication. In between two years in the Sultanate of Oman as production control manager at the National Survey Authority in Oman. Since 2003, he has been employed as associate professor in geo-communication and geo-information at Aalborg University, Denmark.

David J. Bruemmer graduated from Swarthmore College in 1998 with a BA in computer science and a BA in religion. He is currently a principal research scientist at the Idaho National Laboratory (INL), USA, where he serves as technical director for unmanned ground vehicle systems. As a consultant to the Defense Advanced Research Projects Agency, Mr. Bruemmer worked to coordinate development of autonomous robotics technologies through several offices and programs. Since arriving at the INL, he has led development of a robot intelligence architecture that has been ported to a variety of robots for applications including remote characterization, mine sweeping operations, military reconnaissance, and search and rescue operations. He has been a guest editor of the *Intelligent Systems Magazine* and is the program chair for the 2006 Conference on Human Robot Interaction. His interests include autonomous robot behavior, swarm robotics, mobile manipulation, and teaming between unmanned air and ground vehicles.

Richard J. Burkhard is an assistant professor of management information systems in the College of Business at San Jose State University, USA, and a doctoral candidate at the School of Information Systems and Technology at Claremont Graduate University. Rich's research focuses on virtual organizations, technology-mediated group work in business and medical environments, and design theory approaches to support these efforts.

Liping Di is a professor of geographic information science and director of Laboratory for Advanced Information Technology and Standards (LAITS), School of Computational Sciences, George Mason University, USA. Dr. Di received his PhD degree in remote sensing/geographical information systems in 1991. Before joining GMU in 2000, he was a chief scientist at Raytheon ITSS Company. Dr. Di has engaged in geospatial information science research for over 20 years. He has published more than 100 papers in the fields and led the development of several federal, national, and international standards on geospatial interoperability.

David E. Drew holds the Joseph B. Platt Chair in the management of technology at the Claremont Graduate University, USA. He recently completed a ten-year term as dean of the School of Educational Studies. His graduate seminars in both the education and the executive management PhD programs focus on multivariate statistical analysis and mathematical modeling. Previously he held senior research positions at the Rand Corporation, the National Academy of Sciences/National Research Council, and the American Council on Education. Earlier he held a research faculty position at Harvard University, from which he received his PhD For many years, the focus of Professor Drew's research and writing has been the evaluation of science reform efforts.

Fengxian Fan, faculty member of Kunming University, People's Republic of China, is teaching courses on computer sciences. She is also vice-director of the research institute on computer-control technology at KU and is responsible for research projects' technical issues. Prior to coming to Kunming University, she received her ,master's degree on mechanical engineering at the National University of Defense Technology in China. In 2001, she came to University of Hawaii (UH) as a visiting scholar and joined the research group of the "Pods" project supported by DARPA.

In 2004, she received her master's degree of science on information and computer sciences at UH.

Douglas A. Few graduated with a BS in computer science from Keene State College in 2003. Currently Mr. Few is a principal research scientist with the Robotic and Human Systems group at the Idaho National Laboratory (INL), USA. Mr. Douglas Few's interests include human-robot interactions, mixed autonomy robotic systems, generic robot control architectures, and system reliability algorithms. Prior to joining INL, Mr. Few supported robotic research efforts around the world in his position as software support engineer for iRobot Corporation's Research Robot Division. Additionally, he served as a project manager for CHI Engineering Services Portsmouth, NH, a small engineering firm catering to the needs of the natural gas industry.

Shan Gao completed her master's degree in the Department of Information Systems and Operations Management at the University of Auckland, New Zealand, in 2002. She is currently working as an information system specialist on a number of information systems projects. She also holds a BCom in information system and accountancy as well as a BEng in mechanical engineering. Her practical experience in information system includes system and database design and development, ERP system implementation, and enterprise systems integration. Her primary research interests are in decision support systems, geographical information systems, geographical information systems-enterprise applications integration, and spatial data mining. She is a co-author of four conference papers and one journal article.

June K. Hilton has taught all levels of secondary and postsecondary science and mathematics and has served as mathematics and science department chair in three secondary schools. She currently teaches physics and chemistry at Claremont High School, USA. Dr. Hilton holds teaching credentials in Rhode Island, New Jersey, and California, and also has national board certification in adolescent/young adult science and physics. She received her PhD in education from Claremont Graduate University in December, 2003. Her research centers on the use of technology to increase student achievement.

Peter Ibach received his master's degree in computer science from University of Dortmund (Germany) in 1994. Then, he worked as a system engineer at the IBM service center in Cologne, Germany. Since 1995, he has been a research associate at Computer Science Department of Humboldt University, Berlin, Germany, and since 2003, he has been a member of the Berlin Research Center on Internet Economics. His research interest focuses geospatial/location-based services and adaptive service composition.

Shriram Ilavajhala graduated from the University of Northern Iowa with a master's degree in computer science and geography. He is currently working as a faculty research assistant with the Department of Geography at University of Maryland, College Park, USA. His research interests include Web-based geographical information systems, open source geographical information systems, user interface design, information systems, and application software development. He can be reached at ishriram@gmail.com

Gunjan Kalra is a senior software scientist at Quantum Leap Innovations, USA. She is involved with research and development of novel approaches in the area of data retrieval, information integration and dissemination, data mining, and multi-agent systems including policy management. Gunjan has over five years of experience in designing and developing agent-based systems and in applying artificial intelligence techniques to real-world problems. Prior to joining Quantum Leap, Gunjan worked as a research programmer in the Laboratory of Information Technology at University of Maryland, Baltimore County (UMBC). She received her M.S. degree in computer science from UMBC and her B.E. in computer engineering from University of Mumbai (Bombay). Gunjan also spent part of her career with Mahindra British Telecom as a network programmer on their Sterling 5000 Billing Mediation System.

Lyn Kathlene is the director of the Colorado Institute of Public Policy (CIPP) at Colorado State University, USA, an interdisciplinary research institute that addresses major policy issues facing the Rocky Mountain West. In addition to the Institute's research projects, Dr. Kathlene has worked extensively with communities, facilitated research-based stakeholder dialogues, directed numerous community action projects, and published reports and articles on citizen participatory planning, research methods, and the impact of institutional culture on policymaking. Her research examines the policy formulation process with a focus on how people and groups that have typically lacked political power can be effectively heard; how participatory policymaking can change the process and outcomes of public policy; and how community features affect democratic engagement.

Wei-Shinn Ku received his bachelor's degree in computer science from National Taiwan Normal University, Taipei, Taiwan, in 1999. He also obtained an MS in computer science and an MS in electrical engineering from the University of Southern California, USA, in 2003 and 2006, respectively. He is currently a PhD student in the Computer Science Department at the University of Southern California. His research interests include spatial/temporal data management, geographical information systems, and peer-to-peer systems. He can be reached at wku@usc.edu.

Miroslaw Malek is professor and holder of chair in computer architecture and communication at the Department of Computer Science at Humboldt University in Berlin, Germany. His research interests focus on dependable distributed systems including service composition and ad hoc networks. He has authored and co-authored over 150 publications, and founded, organized, and co-organized numerous workshops and conferences. Malek received his PhD in computer science from the Technical University of Wroclaw in Poland, spent 17 years as professor at the University of Texas at Austin, and was also, among others, visiting professor at Stanford, and guest researcher at Bell Laboratories and IBM T. J. Watson Research Center.

Robert K. McNally is a master's student in geography at the University of North Carolina at Charlotte, USA.

Ken McWilliams is a master's student in geography at the University of North Carolina at Charlotte, USA.

Anders Nielsen is a senior cartographer with the National Survey and Cadastre, Denmark. He was born in Denmark in 1955. Education: Craftsmanship in cartography, topography, surveying, photogrammetry, and remote sensing at the National Mapping Agency in Copenhagen, The Geodetic Institute. Supplementary courses in these disciplines at the Technical University of Denmark. Occupation: A large part of his career has been devoted to the photogrammetric survey of Greenland. Since the late 1990's full time occupation with geospatial standardization, primarily in the defense mapping domain.

Curtis W. Nielsen graduated with a B.S, an M.S. in computer science in 1999 and 2003, respectively from Brigham Young University (BYU) where he is also currently pursuing a PhD in computer science (to be finished in January 2006). Currently, Mr. Nielsen is a principle research scientist with the Robotic and Human Systems group at the Idaho National Laboratory (INL), USA. Prior to joining INL, Mr. Nielsen was a research assistant at BYU, where he developed interface technologies and performed user studies to improve mobile robot teleoperation. Mr. Nielsen's interests include computer graphics, robotics, human-robot interaction, and search and rescue.

Todd G. Olson is a real estate and land use attorney, as well as a land development consultant who has specialized in new urbanist, transit-oriented, and conservation-oriented development. As part of his practice, he has spent over 16 years applying principals of conservation biology to actual habitat conservation projects at various scales, from a 750-acre private conservation bank to a 2-million-acre multiple-species conservation plan encompassing thousands of different landowners. Todd developed and documented the "Habitat Transaction Method" in 1992, establishing himself as a recognized expert in systems of conservation credits. Recently, he has led a team in developing the Conservation Studio suite of map-based conservation planning tools.

Anita Raja is an assistant professor of software and information systems at the University of North Carolina at Charlotte, USA. She received a B.S. Honors in computer science with a minor in mathematics summa cum laude from Temple University, Philadelphia, USA, in 1996, and a M.S. and PhD in computer science from the University of Massachusetts, Amherst, USA, in 1998 and 2003, respectively. Her research interests are in the field of artificial intelligence including design and control of multi-agent systems, meta-cognition, bounded-rationality, adaptive agent control, multi-agent learning, and organizational design.

Ramanathan Sugumaran is an associate professor of geography and GeoTREE director at the University of Northern Iowa, USA. Dr. Sugumaran has over 14 years of experience in remote sensing, geographical information systems, global positioning systems spatial decision support systems (SDSS) applications for natural resources and environmental planning and management. He is and has been working with federal, state, local, and tribal government agencies (FSLT) for the past 10 years and developed several SDSS tool and techniques. He has published/presented more than 70 articles in journals, conferences (national and international), and books.

Vijayan Sugumaran is an associate professor of management information systems in the Department of Decision and Information Sciences at Oakland University, Rochester, Michigan, USA. His research interests are in the areas of geographic information systems, decision support systems, ontologies and semantic Web, intelligent agent and multi-agent systems, and knowledge-based systems. Dr. Sugumaran has published over 90 articles in journals, conferences and books. Dr. Sugumaran is the editor-in-chief of the *International Journal of Intelligent Information Technologies.*

David Sundaram is a senior lecturer in the Department of Information Systems and Operations Management, University of Auckland, New Zealand. He has a varied academic (BE in electronics and communications, PG Dip in industrial engineering, and PhD in information systems) as well as work (systems analysis and design, consulting, teaching, and research) background. His primary research interests include the (1) design and implementation of flexible and evolvable information and decision systems; (2) process, information, and decision modeling; (3) triple bottom line modeling and reporting; and (4) enterprise application integration with a focus on ERP-DSS integration.

Gerrit Tamm studied industrial engineering and financial management at the Technical University, Berlin, and at the University of California, Berkeley. Dr. Tamm finalized his doctoral thesis "Web-Based Services: Supply, Demand, and Matching" at the Berlin-Brandenburg Graduate School of Distributed Information Systems. He was the director of the Berlin Research Center on Internet Economics in 2003, and the manager of the Competence Center "Integrated Information Management" at University St. Gallen. He was business development manager at Lycos Europe and Teamtoolz, Inc., San Francisco. Dr. Tamm is the founder of Asperado, Absolvent.de and Electronic Business Forum. Dr. Tamm is a member of the UDDI Advisory Board.

Qianhong Tang is a doctoral student in public policy at the University of North Carolina at Charlotte, USA.

William J. Tolone is an associate professor of software and information systems in the College of Information Technology at the University of North Carolina at Charlotte, USA. He received his doctoral degree from the University of Illinois at Urbana-Champaign, USA, in 1996. His areas of specialization are in modeling and simulation, computer-supported cooperative work, secure collaboration architectures, enterprise integration, information environments, agent-based systems, and meta-level architectures. Since 2003, Dr. Tolone has been lead researcher on several awards investigating techniques for multi-infrastructure modeling and simulation.

David C. Wilson is an assistant professor in the College of Information Technology at University of North Carolina (UNC) at Charlotte, USA. He received his doctoral degree from the University of Indiana, USA, in 2001. Dr. Wilson is an expert in intelligent software systems and a leading name in the field of case-based reasoning. Dr. Wilson's research emphasizes the development of intelligent software systems to bridge the gaps between human information needs and the computational resources available to meet them. It involves the coordination of artificial intelligence techniques with multimedia, database, Internet, and communications systems to elicit, enhance, apply, and present relevant task-based knowledge. Dr. Wilson's current research encompasses several projects focused on smart spatial systems.

Judith Woodhall is the managing director of COMCARE, USA, a non-profit organization dedicated to advancing emergency response. Currently she is focused on a number of initiatives to deploy data interoperability solutions for the geographic targeting and cooperative exchange of emergency incident information among emergency response entities. Prior to COMCARE, Judith served as president for a regional management consulting firm, as the chief operating officer and chief information officer for a financial services organization, as chief information officer for an executive search and Internet solutions company, and as the head of a global organization responsible for e-business initiatives. Judith earned a bachelor's degree from the University of Rochester and a master's degree in computer systems management from the Rochester Institute of Technology.

Wei-Ning Xiang is a professor of geographic information science at University of North Carolina at Charlotte, USA. He received his doctoral degree from the University of California at Berkeley, USA, in 1989. Since he joined the faculty at UNC Charlotte in 1990, Dr. Xiang has conducted teaching, research, and service activities in the areas of geographic information science, spatial modeling, spatial decision support systems, multi-attribute assessment and evaluation, and land use/environmental planning. He was PI or Co-PI of over 30 funded research projects. His scholarly publications appeared in *International Journal of Geographic Information Science*, *Environment and Planning B*, *Lecture Notes in Computer Science*, *Journal of Environmental Management*, and *Landscape and Urban Planning*. He served on the editorial board of *Environment and Planning B*. In 2002, he was a visiting professor and research fellow at National Center for Geographic Information and Analysis, University of California at Santa Barbara.

Genong (Eugene) Yu is a post-doctoral research associate at the Laboratory for Advanced Information Technology and Standards (LAITS), George Mason University, USA, and a non-degree graduate in computer science. He has been trained as a geographer through education led to degrees of Bachelor of Science (1985, Peking University, Beijing, China), Master of Science (1991, University of Aberdeen, Aberdeen, UK), and Doctorate (2004, Indiana State University, Terre Haute, USA) and practiced as a remote sensing and geographical information system specialist since 1985. His current research interest is in multi-agent systems, geospatial Web services, neural networks, and multi-scale mathematics for remotely-sensed data analysis.

Peisheng Zhao is a research assistant professor of geographic information science at the Laboratory for Advanced Information Technology and Standards (LAITS), School of Computational Sciences, George Mason University, USA. Dr. Zhao received his PhD degree in cartography/geographical information systems in 2000. His research has been focusing on intelligent geospatial Web services for integration and interoperation of distributed geospatial data. He has published more than 20 papers in journals and conference proceedings.

Roger Zimmermann is currently a research assistant professor with the Computer Science Department and a research area director with the Integrated Media Systems Center (IMSC) at the University of Southern California, USA. His research activities focus on streaming media architectures, peer-to-peer systems, Web services, and geospatial databases. He has made significant contributions in the areas of geotechnical information and database integration and mobile location-based services. Dr. Zimmermann has co-authored a book, a patent, and more than 70 conference publications, journal articles, and book chapters in the areas of multimedia and databases. He is on the editorial board of SIGMOD DiSC, the *ACM Computers in Entertainment* magazine and the *International Journal of Multimedia Tools and Applications*. He is a member of ACM and IEEE.

Index

Symbols

A

B

C

D

E

L

M

N

O

P

Q

R

S

T

U

V

W